DEVELOPING WITH FOREIGN INVESTMENT

EDITED BY
VINCENT CABLE AND
BISHNODAT PERSAUD

CROOM HELM
London • New York • Sydney
and the
Commonwealth Secretariat

Croom Helm Ltd, Provident House, Burrell Row,
Beckenham, Kent, BR3 1AT
Croom Helm Australia, 44-50 Waterloo Road,
North Ryde, 2113, New South Wales

British Library Cataloguing in Publication Data

Developing with foreign investment.
1. Investments. Foreign — Commonwealth of Nations 2. Investments, Foreign — Developing countries 3. Commonwealth of Nations — Economic conditions
4. Developing countries — Economic conditions
I. Cable, Vincent II. Persaud, Bishnodat
338.9′00917124 HC59.7

ISBN 0-7099-4825-5

Published in the USA by
Croom Helm
in association with Methuen, Inc.
29 West 35th Street
New York, NY 10001

Library of Congress Cataloging-in-Publication Data

Developing with foreign investment.

Includes index.
1. Investments, Foreign—Developing countries.
2. Investments, Foreign—Government policy—Developing countries. I. Cable, Vincent. II. Persaud, B. (Bishnodat)
HG5993.M62 1987 332.6′73′091724 87-3603
ISBN 0-7099-4825-5

Printed and bound in Great Britain by Mackays of Chatham Ltd, Kent

CONTENTS

FOREWORD BY THE COMMONWEALTH SECRETARY-GENERAL

The chapters contained in this volume represent a condensation of a large amount of work carried out by and for the Commonwealth Secretariat over the last few years on the subject of foreign investment in developing countries.

The Commonwealth has a great variety of states: rich and poor; large and small. But meetings of Heads of Government and Finance Ministers have none the less been able to build a consensus on controversial issues. Few subjects have been more controversial in the past than foreign investment, and the role of transnationals in development. Yet within recent years there has been a broadly-based recognition that foreign investors do have a positive role to play in development within the general context of a stronger private sector. Reflecting this, the Secretariat has assisted with policy development in Commonwealth countries; its project in foreign investment policy has been at the centre of this activity.

Over a number of years the Economic Affairs Division of the Secretariat has organised a series of regional seminars for policy makers in the foreign investment field. The papers and proceedings of the meetings which have been published separately have aroused sufficient interest for us to believe that at least an edited selection of the papers would merit commercial publication: hence this venture with Croom Helm.

A similar collaboration with Croom Helm in 1982 led to the book Problems and Policies in Small Economies , which proved to be a timely addition to the growing literature on the economics of small states.

The chapters in this volume range from conceptual issues, through a series of country strategies to project-specific experiences. They contain several important messages. One is that the whole context of policy discussion has shifted away from the confrontational approach to transnationals and direct foreign investment of the 1970s. There is now a greater recognition that where foreign investors can contribute to development on reasonable terms by foreign exchange earnings, by sharing large project risk and by transferring technology, they should be welcomed or, at the very least, treated pragmatically.

But while this situation creates opportunities, it also has dangers. One is of exaggerated expectations of what foreign investment can accomplish in a short time; the case studies make it clear that investor perceptions change slowly and in response to the fundamentals of economic performance. Another is that foreign investors may be tempted to disregard the sensitivities of host countries in relation to sovereignty - especially in small states which are highly vulnerable to the power of big corporations - and to the need for a fair distribution of the returns from investment between shareholders in rich countries and the host developing country. Now is the time to put investor-host country relations on a sustainable long-term footing. To this end, the Secretariat is assisting developing countries through its Technical Assistance Group to bargain more effectively with transnationals.

I should like to express my appreciation to the substantial number of Commonwealth governments and Secretariat staff who have contributed to our work on foreign investment; to the World Bank and International Finance Corporation, which have given financial and intellectual support; and to those who have helped prepare these papers for publication; and rather specially to Mrs. Margaret Cornell for the editing work.

Shridath S. Ramphal

NOTES ON CONTRIBUTORS

Bishnodat Persaud is Director and Head of the Economic Affairs Division, Commonwealth Secretariat and Vincent Cable is Special Adviser of the Economic Affairs Division, Commonwealth Secretariat.

Sheila Page is a Research Officer at the Overseas Development Institute, London.

Helen Hughes is Executive Director, National Centre for Development Studies, Australian National University and Graeme S. Dorrance taught at the London School of Economics.

G.K. Helleiner is Professor of Economics at the University of Toronto.

Pang Eng Fong is Associate Professor at the School of Management, National University of Singapore.

Mohammed Ariff is Professor of Analytical Economics and Dean of the Faculty of Economics and Administration, at the University of Malaya and Chee Peng Lim is currently at UN, ESCAP.

Delisle Worrell is Research Director at the Central Bank of Barbados; his collaborators are Harold Codrington, also at the Central Bank; Zorina Khan at the University of West Indies and University of California and Lawson Nurse at the Barbados Industrial Development Corporation.

R.C. Wanigatunga is a Senior Economics Officer at the Commonwealth Secretariat.

Bishakha Mukherjee is a Senior Economics Officer at the Commonwealth Secretariat.

Rod Sims was Special Adviser (Economic) in the Technical Assistance Group of the Commonwealth Secretariat and is now in the Department of the Prime Minister and Cabinet, Australia.

Christopher Goss was Special Adviser (Economic) in the Technical Assistance Group of the Commonwealth Secretariat and is now with the International Finance Corporation,

Washington, D.C. and Roger Nellist is a Chief Project Officer in the Technical Assistance Group of the Commonwealth Secretariat.

Philip Daniel is Special Adviser (Economic) in the Technical Assistance Group at the Commonwealth Secretariat and a Fellow of the Institute of Development Studies at the University of Sussex.

Trevor M.A. Farrell is at the Department of Economics, University of West Indies.

C.O. Khong is a Senior Economics Officer at the Commonwealth Secretariat.

N.A. Rweyemamu is a Chief Economics Officer at the Commonwealth Secretariat.

Roger C. Riddell is a Research Officer at the Overseas Development Institute, London.

John Samy is the Permanent Secretary for Economic Development Planning and Tourism, Fiji.

Chapter One

NEW TRENDS AND POLICY PROBLEMS IN FOREIGN INVESTMENT: THE EXPERIENCE OF COMMONWEALTH DEVELOPING COUNTRIES

Vincent Cable and Bishnodat Persaud

Introduction

There is a growing recognition of the importance of the private sector and of direct foreign investment (DFI) in the development process. A considerable number of developing countries have become more receptive to DFI, and are exploring ways of increasing inflows(1).

Several considerations lie behind these changing perceptions. The first is an increasing preference for investment in equity form over commercial bank borrowing, which has proved to be unpredictable, onerous and inflexible in its servicing obligations, and unobtainable for many countries. Foreign investment provides not only an initial capital inflow but the subsequent outflow of profits is determined by the performance of the investment. Second, direct foreign investment is a means of obtaining not only capital but also technology, scarce management and skills, and improved marketing 'know-how' and outlets for non-traditional exports of manufactures, processed commodities and traded services.

The serious anxiety among many developing countries over their external financing position and the serious deficiency in development finance has heightened awareness of both these factors. Foreign investment is seen as assisting the balance of payments both through the initial injection of capital in the short run and the generation of foreign-exchange earnings in the long run. There has also been a heightened awareness of project risk and of the role which foreign investment might play in spreading risk beyond the host country. These views are, however, still subject to considerable controversy. Some question the net benefits of foreign investment. There are particular anxieties over the long-term balance-of-payments impact and over the employment and technological implications. Some governments are reluctant to risk the loss of domestic sovereignty.

In this volume we review recent experience of foreign investment and foreign investment policy primarily in relation to Commonwealth developing countries, in order to seek out the lessons in policy terms. We recognise the dangers in seeking to generalise from among countries so different in population, resources, income level and political orientation but believe there are, none the less, useful insights to be drawn from comparative experience.

The Changing Character of DFI in Developing Countries

In the accompanying tables we have tried to give a flavour of the main trends over time, and the main differences between host countries, in relation to DFI. This analysis is based on statistics which, in relation to investment flows and (even more) stocks, are notoriously prone to error, inconsistency and misunderstanding(2).

The first point to note is that the revival of interest in DFI as a source of external finance occurs against a background of actual decline in its relative importance (Table 1.2). There was a pronounced fall in the share of DFI in the aggregate flow of external resources to developing countries from 24% in the 1967-73 period to 16% in 1974-80, while private commercial lending grew in relative importance from 11 to 28%. Even though net bank lending has since dropped sharply, so has foreign investment(3) and there is no evidence yet of any substitution effect at work, at least on a global scale (Table 1.3).

Even in countries where DFI has grown rapidly, its relative contribution to domestic investment has not necessarily risen. Thus, in Malaysia, the foreign share of corporate capital fell from 62% in 1971 to 34% in 1983 despite a quadrupling of its nominal value. Even in Singapore, where DFI increased over ten times between 1970 and 1981, local Singaporean investors maintained their share (about two-thirds) of total equity. The lesson is significant. It indicates the unlikelihood even of rapidly growing foreign investment acquiring a dominant position in a growing economy.

Secondly, DFI is increasingly concentrated in a small number of the relatively high-income developing countries. Five countries (four of them relatively high-income - Brazil, Mexico, Malaysia, Singapore - the fifth being Indonesia) now account for approximately 40% of the stock of DFI as against 25% in 1970. Table 1.4 shows that low-income developing countries account for a small share of both the stock and flow of foreign investment in relation to their combined GNP as well as their population, and almost half the stock and recent flow is accounted for by Indonesia. In 1984-5 there has been an increase in the importance of low-income developing countries in terms of the share of new flows, but this is largely attributable to China. It is important to note, however, that similar - possibly greater - concentration now exists in relation to commercial lending since only a few developing countries are now considered creditworthy by banks and capital markets.

It is not too difficult to hypothesise as to why these disproportions occur. For a given population, the domestic market of a low-income country is relatively small and thus has more limited attraction for foreign investors. In many low-income countries poverty is both a cause and an effect of poor infrastructure. And in sub-Saharan Africa there has been a multifaceted and prolonged economic crisis which explains the declining share of risk capital in capital flows to Africa and in Africa's share of foreign investment in developing countries. The IMF acknowledges: 'countries with small internal markets, few natural resources, a relatively underdeveloped infrastructure and limited possibilities for manufactured exports may not be able to attract substantial direct investment even with liberal regulations and generous incentives'(4). Cross-section analysis also suggests that per capita income is the most important single factor in explaining differences in the amount of (per capita) foreign investment as between countries(5). Least developed countries have a negligible share of foreign investment in developing countries and it accounts for a negligible share of their net resource inflows; by contrast upper middle income countries have the highest proportion on both measures (Table 1.5).

In general, foreign investment has a self-reinforcing character, being attracted to countries where development is already rapid and successful. But for country-level policy-makers such a general tendency is not a helpful indicator of national possibilities; we therefore look in detail at the experience of low-income countries which have been successful in attracting investors (Sri Lanka and Kenya) or which have been able to overcome infrastructure constraints (such as Papua New Guinea).

Thirdly, at a global level, there has been an increase in the importance, as a source of DFI in developing countries, of Japanese, German and Third World transnationals though the United States remains the predominant source with around 50% of the stock and flow. The different approaches of these transnationals to the organisation of production, to technology transfer, to joint ventures and to various forms of official intervention and support have proved significant in, for example, enabling Japanese companies to secure an important role in Indian industry following recent liberalisation. Third World transnationals from Hong Kong, India, Korea and Taiwan have been particularly important in

Singapore, Malaysia and Sri Lanka and are seen as conferring advantages in terms of 'appropriate' technology.

Nevertheless, a particular feature of the countries studied in this volume is the very high share of foreign investment from traditional sources: Britain and (in the case of Fiji and PNG) Australia and New Zealand (Table 1.6). Moreover, there is a marked distinction between those cases where such investment was in the most dynamic sectors of the host-country economy - in Singapore, for example, the UK share of foreign equity has increased from 10% in 1970 to over 30% in 1981 - and those where the UK's DFI stock is predominantly in investments dating from the colonial period, and declining in importance, as in Malaysia. By focussing on Commonwealth countries this volume gives emphasis to important but neglected areas of foreign investment policy discussion: how to maximise new investment, through reinvestment, and obtain the best value from traditional foreign investors; how to attract new flows from new investors while preventing a drain of capital from existing investors (this being a particular problem for countries with a stock of 'settler' capital, such as Zimbabwe and Kenya).

Fourthly, there is a widely observed tendency for DFI in developing countries to gravitate increasingly towards manufactures and related financial services, rather than the traditional sectors: plantation agriculture, mining, retailing and utilities. This reflects, in large part, the preference of governments in the host countries for local ownership in these fields. The trend is evident both for countries which have become significant exporters of manufactures or services (Malaysia, Singapore, Sri Lanka) and for others where foreign investment has been attracted into manufacturing of an import-substituting kind (Kenya). For many of the open small island economies (Trinidad and Tobago, Papua New Guinea and Fiji), however, the traditional sectoral pattern of foreign investment remains. In this volume we recognise the quite specific issues involved in negotiating with foreign investors in different fields and particular attention is given to mining (Sims and Goss and Nellist) and manufacturing for export (Helleiner).

Fifthly, in the majority of the case studies, there were indications of the growing importance of 'new forms' of overseas investment reflecting the preference either of host countries or of companies for reducing the direct equity component of foreign investment. The process by which traditional majority-owned investment has given way to 'new forms' - notably joint ventures and licensing agreements - is impossible to quantify but is widely documented, especially in petroleum, mining and import-substituting manufacturing(6).

To take examples, India has, as a matter of policy, sought technology collaboration arrangements while restricting the role of foreign equity. In Malaysia, the case study notes: 'licensing and franchising arrangements and management contracts, which represent the new forms of foreign investment, are growing in importance'. Joint ventures, turnkey arrangements, and management contracts have been of rapidly growing significance in Trinidad and Tobago. In Kenya, management and technical agreements have proliferated, especially in import-substituting industry and in joint ventures with the government as a partner. In these instances, a host government preference for reducing the role of traditional DFI has been the main influence. But in some cases the initiative has come from the transnationals themselves, presumably to reduce risks and because also of other evolutionary factors such as the involvement of smaller transnational corporations. In Fiji, for example, foreign investors - especially the Australians - have followed a strategy of withdrawal but coupled with this has been 'the harnessing of local enterprise through subcontracting', designed to retain control without ownership involvement.

There are, however, other cases where governments have pressed for a higher foreign equity stake. This is a central feature of recent minerals negotiations in Papua New Guinea. And in Singapore new forms of investment are 'not common, given the government's willingness to allow foreign firms to form wholly owned subsidiaries. Firms with little or no foreign equity but that have licensing or other arrangements with foreign technology supplies account for less than 10% of recently established firms'.

DFI As a Source of Development Finance

Increasing Capital Inflows. As we noted earlier, the importance currently attached to foreign investment in development derives from two considerations: the need developing countries have in general for additional external finance in order to raise their rate of growth, and the advantage of foreign investment over external commercial borrowing mainly arising from the closer link between financial return and project performance.

As regards the first, there is a large gap between the magnitude of developing country current-account deficits which can be predicted if growth in these countries is to achieve reasonable levels, and the likely availability of finance(7). In the 1986 World Bank World Development Report, the difference between the 'high' and 'low' growth scenarios for developing countries is mirrored in, respectively, a $9 bn and $64 bn deterioration in the current-account balance from 1985 to 1995. Foreign investment (net) has a modest but positive role to play in financing this gap, increasing from $11 bn in 1985 to $19.1 bn in 1995 (in 1985 prices) in the high growth and to $14.2 bn in the low growth scenario, these representing an annual real growth of respectively 5.7% and 2.6%. The difference between the 'high' and 'low' figures partly reflects the response of foreign investors to higher or lower growth in developing countries, and partly the policy orientation of host countries.

Substitutability. Foreign investment cannot be treated entirely as additional to other commercial flows. At the project level, there is a choice between different combinations of loan and equity finance. Part of the argument for emphasising foreign investment is that it can substitute for loan finance, especially where the latter is constrained, but even where it is not.

Some of the expansion in bank lending over the past decade was a substitute for private direct investment. This trend was encouraged by the relatively low interest rates throughout most of the 1970s and by the restrictions which host countries placed on direct investment. The question now arises as to how to reverse this process of substitution when the real cost of borrowing has risen and the benefits to host countries of equity capital as compared to commercial borrowing are more clearly perceived.

The papers in this volume highlight the need for caution about overstating the potential for substitution. Most obviously, the scope for substitution is largely limited to the private sector; direct investment cannot be used to finance more development infrastructure. But even in private sector projects, substitution may not be easy. Simply as a matter of fact, much of what is described as foreign investment is, in fact, lending. DFI conventionally defined (by the IMF) includes borrowing from parent companies and affiliates. Helleiner, in his paper, describes a survey of DFI projects in which half of the new capital led to debt obligations. And he points to a more general tendency for transnationals to act as intermediaries in international capital markets, thus generating external debt obligations (activities which may in fact be desirable in boosting overall capital inflows, even if not in equity form).

In several of the countries studied, there is evidence that what is described as foreign investment may have only limited equity characteristics. In Sri Lanka, 'a noteworthy feature was the substantial role played by long-term loans - chiefly long-term suppliers' credits in financing investment in fixed assets'. And in a separate study of export-oriented investment (in Africa) it is observed that 'there is a general shortage of equity capital and investors prefer to use loans (or retained profits) rather than new equity for investment'(8). In countries where DFI is centred on raw material extraction there have been strong corporate pressures to reduce equity risk.

However, in one or two cases of countries with a long record of attracting DFI - notably Barbados and Singapore - the predominantly 'equity' character of foreign investment is preserved, for two related reasons. First, there is a good expectation of high returns to equity (the average return to foreign investors in Singapore is around 18%); so assets are held predominantly in this form by choice. Second, where earnings are rapidly increasing this provides substantial capital expansion from firms' own profits. But for many other countries - with less well established investor confidence - it can prove difficult to attract DFI in equity form other than through the growth of retained profits in existing undertakings, and rather easier to raise loan finance. This suggests a need for looking at policies, and new instruments, which can introduce a greater foreign 'equity' element into projects.

Financial Terms. Equity financing through DFI now looks attractive to developing countries relative to loan financing because of high real interest rates (just as borrowing appeared attractive when real interest rates were negative). But, if it is to grow substantially, the expected return to investors will need to be high in relation to the return on lending. Some profits will be reinvested but some will be remitted. This will create a negative flow of investment income to set alongside capital inflows. As Table 1.7 shows, in overall terms, net transfers on foreign investment are currently negative for developing countries as a whole.

Among the countries studied, Singapore enjoys a large excess of new foreign investment inflows over net investment income payments. Since Sri Lankan policy changed in 1977, there has been a positive balance of DFI inflows over profit remittances. In Barbados, total private sector remitted profits and interest have almost exactly balanced private inflows over the past decade. On the other hand, despite generally rising inflows of foreign private capital to Kenya, there has been a consistently negative net flow overall. Zimbabwe since independence has experienced net disinvestment of private investment as well as a net outflow of investment income. These two cases illustrate the rather special problems of post-colonial economies in which a large part of the foreign-owned capital stock is held reluctantly by former residents with limited commitment to reinvestment. But in other cases too (Trinidad and Tobago for example) net flows are consistently negative. Where this occurs, the fear of outflow of existing capital and/or the repatriation of profits may be sufficiently high relative to the promise of new inflows to make DFI seem unattractive as a source of external finance, especially at times of balance-of-payments difficulty. This may in turn lead governments to introduce exchange restrictions which will make new inflows of DFI even more difficult to attract. But where a government has a politically favourable attitude to DFI a more positive approach would be to explore the possibility of policies which would increase inflows of direct investment rather than to set up a vicious circle by restricting the remittance of profits.

There are, in particular, two ways in which a simple calculation of net transfers seriously understates the benefits of DFI. Foreign investment should give greater stability than commercial lending: it is generally tied up in illiquid fixed assets while loan finance has been, by contrast, often short-term and requiring continual refinancing (though a major disinvestment could, of course, be highly disruptive for a small economy). Table 1.2 shows that both gross flows and net transfers from foreign investment are more stable overall than those from commercial borrowing.

Second, as discussed in detail in the Helleiner paper, there has been a recognition that foreign investors are well placed to generate foreign exchange from export-oriented projects. Transnationals enjoy an advantage over indigenous and public sector operations, deriving from their scale, specific market knowledge and distribution chains in creating markets, especially for non-standardised goods and services requiring marketing expertise. Furthermore, alternative arrangements - such as management contracts in mining and tourism, and subcontracting for manufacturing exports - have some disadvantages. They do little to reduce external control while removing risk from the private investor. And both theory and experience have combined to show that, other things being equal, countries pursuing export-oriented strategies, rather than import substitution, are likely to attract more DFI and in more economically valuable ways(9). Several of our case studies support the proposition that foreign investors can make a major contribution to exporting. In Singapore, wholly foreign-owned firms in manufacturing export 71% of their output, as against 32% for wholly local firms. In Barbados, foreign-owned firms are shown to be relatively highly export-oriented and fast growing. Much of the increase in foreign investment in Malaysia in the 1970s occurred in the two industries which are predominantly export-oriented (electronics and textiles). The export growth experienced in Sri Lanka since 1978 can be largely attributed to non-traditional products originating in DFI enterprises.

There is, however, some less positive evidence. In Fiji, foreign investors have, in recent years, contributed a lower share of their output in the form of exports (in manufacturing) than domestically owned firms. Foreign companies are described as having become 'peripheralised' as a result of mergers and take-overs: 'peripheralisation is associated with the adoption of narrow regional marketing strategies .... (and) may jeopardise export-led growth'. In Trinidad and Tobago, too, examples are cited of transnational companies apparently contributing little in terms of marketing (refined oil or fertiliser) which nationals could not do with equal facility.

The considerations which apply in marketing raw materials are somewhat different, but the potential of foreign investment for generating exports is recognised by most governments. The Papua New Guinea experience of export-oriented mining suggests that 'a company with major equity at risk, and thus a strong interest in project profitability is likely to perform more efficiently and to place greater value on the long-term stability of its relations with the host country than a minor shareholder, management contractor or mere supplier of technology'.

For a good many host countries - India and Zimbabwe for example - there is a wish to attract foreign investment on a selective basis, limiting its role to export-oriented enterprises, especially in manufacturing. This selectivity - expressed, for example, in 'performance criteria' - has begun to arouse some concern among companies because it suggests a direction of capital towards relatively high-risk and possibly low-profit activity. Thus a broad consensus on the desirability of more DFI has to be qualified to the extent that host countries and investors may have quite different, possibly conflicting, expectations of it.

Host Country Policies

Given that countries wish to attract more foreign investment - usually selectively - how is this to be done? How do host governments influence the climate for investments? What particular policy instruments are crucial? What are the realistic possibilities of using inducements to attract new flows to countries whose size, location, resources and history are not otherwise attractive from the standpoint of investors? We have tried in these studies to cast some light on the perceptions and expectations of both investors and official decision-makers.

<u>General Business Climate & Investor Confidence</u>. DFI decisions

are project-specific but one important ingredient is likely to be the assessment of a country's overall attractiveness. Several key factors influence this assessment. First, cross-country surveys suggest that the major influence on DFI in developing countries is the wish to gain access to a large host-country domestic market (or a regional market). By contrast, low labour costs and tax/financial incentive advantages are relatively unimportant. A survey made for the Malaysia study showed the largest number of foreign investors to be motivated by the lure of the Malaysia market and only 10% by labour-cost considerations. Second, there are successful examples of countries attracting foot-loose foreign investment which is clearly not pulled by the domestic market - Singapore and Barbados, for example - and, in these cases, factors repeatedly cited (ahead of low labour costs and specific incentives) are long-term social and economic stability and a climate conducive to business in general. Third, in terms of economic policy, as Hughes and Dorrance point out, the policies that have had the greatest impact both in attracting DFI and ensuring high social returns to the host country are not special incentives, but countries' principal economic policies. Financial, fiscal and trade policies are by far the most important. Together they set the price levels in relation to the rest of the world.

This, then, leaves the question of how countries can attract DFI when the 'fundamentals' are, for reasons largely beyond government control, unsatisfactory: the countries may be poor and small; have little resource endowment; have a legacy of political instability; and face a period of prolonged painful adjustment in order to rectify economic weaknesses. For this reason, we shall deal in more detail with the experience of incentive schemes and free trade zones which may - at the margin at least - have some effect in stimulating foreign investment flows.

We would, however, stress that direct investment is project-specific. Even in the most unpromising country situation it is possible to have good projects and negotiate mutually acceptable arrangements with investors. As the chapters by Sims and Goss and Nellist show, Ghana and Tanzania have been able, through patient and well conceived negotiations, to come to agreements with major mining and oil transnationals, despite the generally unattractive investment climate prevailing at the time.

Tax Incentive Schemes. Although many developing countries have introduced far-reaching fiscal incentives for inward investment - tax holidays, supported by accelerated depreciation allowances and investment allowances or subsidies

- surveys suggest they are of modest importance in influencing investment decisions in general(10). Businessmen appear to regard them as of limited significance for the post-tax profitability of new investments in relation to other influences; even with a carry-forward provision, tax holidays do not offset the lack of markets or the high costs of production. Furthermore, incentives are often regarded as volatile and the tax holidays illusory.

Why then do most developing countries pursue such policies? And what is rational behaviour for a small country caught up in competitive bidding for foreign investment? The country studies here suggest that the right kind of tax regimes and incentives may, indeed, be important, especially when pursuing export-oriented investment(11). Singapore recognises that its own generous but selective incentives are 'important, but not decisive' especially where there are double taxation agreements, 'but are more likely to matter more to export-oriented industries - the kind Singapore is wooing - than to import-substituting or resource processing industries which are location specific'. The Malaysian study also suggests that large-scale investments do require incentives. It appears that investment incentives are viewed as compensation for disincentives which are caused partly by over-regulation. In Barbados, there have been 'increasingly liberal incentive schemes' and econometric analysis gives some but not conclusive evidence of their positive impact. Incentives are seen by investors as 'secondary - but incentives are widely available and it would be unwise not to offer them'. And where governments do not try to compete investors are conscious of the absence of incentives: 'potential investors visiting Kenya have expressed surprise at the lack of a tax holiday incentive'. Potential investors have also criticised Zimbabwe's high corporate taxes and incentives which are less attractive than those offered by other SADCC countries. (But corporate tax, 'while a factor in investment decision-making, is not a dominant deterrent'.)

It is in the mining and petroleum sectors that the tax and incentive regime is particularly crucial since, for large projects, economic rents in tax revenue can be an important component of overall government revenue. There is a difficult exercise here of judging whether companies have sufficient reward for high-risk exploration and extraction, while ensuring that society maximises the long-term flow of revenue by capturing resource rents. The PNG experience suggests the best kind of tax regime avoids devices which increase the risk of loss, such as high flat rate royalties and export taxes and concentrates on measures which tax revealed profitability. Taxation over and above normal company income tax is levied only after the achievement of a specified rate of return on project outlays.

The conclusions which can be drawn are as follows. First, contrary to some conventional academic wisdom, fiscal incentives may be important but they need to be looked at in the context of corporate tax levels as a whole and the needs of particular types of investors. Second, relative tax and incentive levels are one criterion in investment decisions and if host countries are not to lose through competitive bidding, then greater exchange of information and co-ordination, at least on a regional basis, is called for.

Trade Policy and Special Zones. Many developing countries are seeking to attract export-oriented investment in a context where there is a high level of protection which raises domestic costs. This makes it difficult to export and to attract DFI into export activities. Where comprehensive liberalisation is not feasible, a 'second-best' solution is a free trade zone. Such zones can also serve as a focus for infrastructure development of a kind considered necessary for export-oriented activities. Among the countries studied here, and more than any other Asian developing country establishing export processing zones, Malaysia has succeeded in attracting large amounts of foreign investment into the FTZs. But there has also been growing criticism of the poor backward linkages to local development and of wasted resources. The rationale and consequences of Sri Lankan policy have been similar, but the scale of activity is much smaller. Established and committed projects have provided 50,000 jobs. As in Malaysia, there are criticisms of the low net foreign-exchange gain (20-35% of the gross figure). And the success of the zone, like other attempts to attract 'foot-loose' foreign investment, hinges on confidence, which is very vulnerable to changing perceptions of stability.

Experience elsewhere is much less encouraging. There is no successful, functioning, zone in sub-Saharan Africa. The Indian zones, as shown in the study, have failed to attract more than a small amount of overseas investment into export activity. Elsewhere some zones that had achieved considerable success, as in Mauritius, now face difficulties with protectionist barriers overseas and depressed world markets and there has been a sharp increase in firm closures. The government there has been obliged to extend its ten-year tax holiday incentive to keep them in production(12).

Recent experience raises serious question marks over the role of special zones as a focus for export-oriented investment. For small states, the distortions associated with a zone may be such that it is necessary to take the more radical step of giving the entire country the equivalent of effective free trade zone status - the Singapore 'model'(13).

For countries which have a large domestic market, the main incentive which can be offered is some degree of access to that market. This option is being considered in Malaysia and in India and illustrates a central point in this discussion, that purely export-oriented investment is, in itself, likely to be very elusive, and what is really at issue is the degree of market liberalisation as a whole.

Foreign-Exchange Controls. Freedom to remit profits and dividends and repatriate capital is clearly an essential ingredient in an attractive climate for foreign investment. Yet many developing countries are trying to attract DFI in order to escape from an initial situation of balance-of-payments crisis. The starting point may, therefore, be a history of exchange restriction and control. How do governments proceed from this position?

A not untypical situation is that existing in Kenya which wishes to attract foreign investment and recognises basic freedom to remit capital and dividends, but maintains various forms of exchange control which affect the importation of goods necessary for production, the ease and extent of repatriation of capital, and local currency borrowing. These restrictions form the basis of most negative business perceptions of an otherwise attractive location. In Zimbabwe, controls are even more far-reaching - covering external remittances and capital repatriation as well as import allocations - though post-1979 venture capital is allowed free remittance up to 50% of net after-tax profits. One way of escaping from some of these dilemmas is through projects which are self-sufficient in foreign exchange. But there will be little new foreign investment, or expansion of existing investments, unless there is substantial freedom for investors to enjoy the returns in foreign exchange. One way of reconciling these objectives is through export projects in which the foreign investors are allowed to retain a portion of foreign-exchange earnings abroad; Tanzania, Zimbabwe and Ghana all provide recent examples. Escrow accounts, to handle foreign-exchange transactions and under the control of project organisers, provide a mechanism for facilitating this type of arrangement as it is evolving through 'limited recourse financing'.

Restrictions and Procedures. Many countries impose limitations on the operations of foreign companies. Whatever restrictions exist, it emerges strongly from these studies and from wider surveys that the speed and simplicity of official clearance are of the essence in forming favourable business perceptions. Thus, Barbados was recently described as one of four (out of twenty-five) locations most characterised by 'exceptional ease, freedom and absence of red tape'. The Singapore study brought out the importance of 'an efficient investment promotion agency'. Even where there are substantial controls on DFI, as in Malaysia, importance is attached to a simple 'one-stop' agency. Applying this general concern to a context where major mining investments would be deterred by prolonged negotiations, the PNG Government has opted for a simple approach based on widely applicable rules: 'This approach is not, in theory, optimal .... but is favoured on practical grounds; negotiating capacity is limited and clearly stated terms are seen to function, in themselves, as an incentive to mineral exploration'. The necessity of streamlining controls is perhaps most acute in countries where there is a framework of planning and regulation, since delays in decision-making may become more of a deterrent than the regulations themselves.

New Forms of Foreign Participation

Restrictive policies towards DFI in the past have encouraged the 'unbundling' of the various components in investment projects. But, as Helleiner points out, these new arrangements involved 'an independent evolution of investment and international business practice relating to risk-sharing, management and financing, and the appearance of smaller internationally oriented firms; the product of business evolution and decision-making rather than government policies'. As we noted earlier, the transnational corporations themselves would have encouraged some of these changes since joint ventures and lack of equity participation were means of reducing risks.

The economic need which now exists for foreign equity participation both to increase capital inflows and spread risks emphasises the scope for a revival of traditional forms of DFI for many developing countries. It is important therefore that policies are not so restrictive as to stand in the way of increased inflows of DFI. On the whole policies are becoming more flexible and this trend should continue.

The experience from 'unbundling' provides valuable lessons for those governments where countries' economic circumstances lead to their adopting a more selective approach to foreign participation and which see traditional DFI as an obstacle to the development of local capacities in respect of one or more components of the investment package. Some countries, for instance, have benefitted from insistence on the establishment of local R & D facilities and from increasing the proportion of skilled and management positions held by nationals, over time. For such countries there may be more advantage in introducing a greater 'equity', risk-sharing, element into, say, management and turnkey contracts, or linking loan repayments to the capacity to pay, rather than seeking a return to traditional forms of foreign investment by transnationals.

There are, in other respects, new issues and new ways of approaching policy. First, there is a growing interest in portfolio investment which could potentially mobilise some of the vast resources of insurance companies and pension funds (the latter $1,500 bn in the US alone). For investors, developing country stock markets offer a high-risk, high-reward option; for developing countries, there is access to foreign equity capital in the form of a variety of (usually) minority shareholdings. Singapore has long experience of portfolio investment on a substantial scale but there has recently been a burst of interest elsewhere with financial intermediaries acting on behalf of overseas shareholders: the India Fund, the Bangkok Fund, the Emerging Markets Growth Fund and now an Asia Pacific Fund(14). All are examples of attempts to tap this source of finance in an orderly manner. And bodies such as the International Finance Corporation have an important role to play in facilitating it(15).

Second, the serious problem of indebtedness, especially in Africa, creates difficulties for new foreign investment since, in many cases, servicing of private debt and trade credit associated with foreign investment has been disrupted. At the same time, the debt problem creates opportunities for foreign investment inasmuch as an 'equitisation' of debt can be achieved. Debt-equity conversions are so far very few and largely confined to major debtors, but the creation of mutually acceptable 'rules of the game', drawn up under the auspices of international organisations, would be a useful step in widening their appeal.

Implications for Developed Countries

Host-country policies are obviously crucial to the creation of a satisfactory climate for foreign investment. But there are several respects in which industrial countries can also make a vital contribution. First, they can play a catalytic role multilaterally and bilaterally. The expanding operations of the IFC are welcome in this respect though, like private investors themselves, the IFC has only a modest share of its assets in low-income countries (around 15%) and has tended to overlook the particular problems of small states. Second, and more controversially, there is investment protection. There has been scepticism about the value of investment-protection agreements and concern over their asymmetrical obligations but none the less, several countries which have recently experienced a marked positive inflow of DFI have done so in the wake of policies to stimulate it, including bilateral agreements. Thus, PNG has agreements with the UK, West Germany and the USA (OPIC)and Sri Lanka with 14 countries including several other developing countries; Malaysia and Singapore have a substantial number too. And while the purely legal consequences of such agreements may be unimportant, they may influence investor perceptions. Thus, as the Zimbabwe paper notes, the absence of Zimbabwe's signature to the OPIC agreement could well have been perceived by US investors as increasing project risks. The growing importance of Japan as a capital exporter underlines the importance of official insurance; half of all Japanese overseas direct investment is officially insured (compared with 10% in most industrial countries). Implementation of the World Bank's Multilateral Investment Guarantee Agency is one important step in the creation of a comprehensive network of investor insurance.

On a more general level, one factor critical to the success of export-oriented investment is the assumption that markets will remain open to the goods produced for them. The success of Sri Lanka in attracting export-oriented manufacturing investment, and of better established producers such as Malaysia or Singapore, is dependent on access to industrial country markets and, thus, on the defeat of protectionist forces.

Finally, we have emphasised that DFI and loan finance are in many respects complementary. The necessity for developed country governments to do more to stimulate the flow of officially guaranteed export credits and other official loans is a major element in the Baker initiative for indebted countries, and is linked both to the adjustment efforts of the developing countries and their success in attracting foreign investment. The complementary character of different forms of capital flow is particularly evident in the case of aid and foreign investment. Aid flows can create the infrastructure within which DFI can operate and assist the indigenous private sector. Official development assistance can also alleviate the external financing constraints which often lead to policies inimical to DFI. The main relevance of increased DFI in developing countries is that it is largely additional and complementary to other, especially concessional, flows; not an alternative.

Conclusion

Many of the preoccupations of the 1960s and 1970s in relation to transnational corporations and development have changed. Direct foreign investment is no longer a major channel of resource flows to developing countries; the strengthening of the indigenous private and public sectors in most developing countries has provided powerful counterweights to transnationals; most companies have adapted to the changing political environment in developing countries and have learnt to operate where necessary through joint ventures or non-equity arrangements; developing country decision-makers, for their part, have become more pragmatic and willing to recognise the contribution which foreign investors can make to capital formation, export earnings and technology transfer. Thus, the atmosphere is now generally less confrontational and more businesslike.

This businesslike approach to foreign investment, combined with a more positive attitude to the private sector in general, is likely, in due course, to lead to increased foreign investment flows to developing countries. The danger, however, is that exaggerated expectations are being aroused, not least by industrial country governments which, rather irresponsibly, have encouraged the notion that large and rapid increases in foreign investment can be generated to act as a substitute for aid and for other official flows of finance. Experience shows - including that of cases in this volume - that foreign investor perceptions do not change quickly; that the process of generating large inflows of capital is gradual and cumulative; that foreign investment is usually complementary to other capital flows, private and official; and that special incentives and sudden declarations of support for foreign investment cut little ice. Provided expectations are modest and realistic, there is every prospect that foreign investment can play an increasingly influential role in development.

NOTES AND REFERENCES

In this volume we use the term 'free trade zones' to refer to the general category sometimes described as export processing zones. It is recognised, however, that these terms have different technical meanings - see, inter alia, UNIDO, Export Processing Zones in Developing Countries (1980).

1. UN Centre on Transnational Corporations (UNCTC), Trends and Issues in Foreign Direct Investment and Related Flows (New York, 1985). See also Sheila Page's chapter in the present volume.

2. Table 1.1 seeks to tabulate data from the most important developing countries and those covered in this study. The main problems arise from the fact that one main source of flow data (the IMF) uses a flexible concept of

foreign control in defining direct investment - which is taken by some countries to mean as little as 10% foreign ownership; in others much more. The IMF definition takes in indirect as well as direct capital contributions, such as net loans from companies to their subsidiaries and also reinvested profits, though country coverage is often inconsistent. There are often problems, too, in converting data from domestic to foreign currency when some transactions (reinvested profits) are conducted in the former and others in the latter. Other sources, DAC for example, use different measures - e.g. some major IMF listed flows are not recognised by DAC (China, Trinidad, Malaysia, Singapore, Botswana). The problems are greatly compounded when the stock of capital is measured because of discrepancies in the treatment of assets and liabilities as well as the inherent limitations of book value measures.

3. The average annual flow of foreign investment to developing countries in constant (1983) prices and exchange rates rose from $7.8 bn in the five years 1970-74 to $13.7 bn from 1975 to 1979 and then fell to $11.1 bn in 1980-84, with $7.8 bn and $7.5 bn in 1983 and 1984.

4. International Monetary Fund, Foreign Private Investment in Developing countries, Research Department Occasional Paper No. 33, (1985).

5. J. Dunning, 'Explaining the international direct investment position of countries; towards a dynamic or developmental approach', Weltwirtschaftliches Archiv, 1981. F. Schneider, and B. Frey, 'Economic, and Political Determinants of Foreign Direct Investment', World Development, (1985).

6. Charles Oman, New Forms of International Investment in Developing Countries, (OECD Development Centre, Paris, 1984).

7. UN Committee for Development Planning, Doubling Development Finance, (UN, New York, 1986).

8. J. Currie, Papers and Proceedings of a Seminar on Foreign Investment in Africa, (Commonwealth Secretariat, London, 1986).

9. V. Balasubramanyam, 'Incentives and Disincentives for FDI in Less Developed Countries', Weltwirtschaftliches Archiv, (1984).

10. David Lim, 'Fiscal Incentives and Direct Foreign Investment in LDCs', Journal of Development Studies, Vol. 19 (1983).

11. S. Guisinger, Investment Incentives and Performance Requirements: A Comparative Analysis of Country Foreign Investment Policies, (World Bank, 1983).

12. Currie, Papers and Proceedings.

13. A specified zone may none the less have advantages in terms of concentrated infrastructure.

14. P. Wellons, D. Germidis, B. Glavanis, Banks and Specialised Financial Intermediaries in Development, (OECD Development Centre, Paris, 1986).

15. For example, the proposed GRIP scheme (Guaranteed Recovery of Investment Principal) has an intermediary character whereby investors place their equity capital via the IFC.

Table 1.1. Direct investment in individual developing countries

		1979	1980	1981	1982	1983	1984	1978 Stock	Sum of Flows 1979-84	1984 External Debt	1984 GNP
Low Income		$m. current prices						$m.	$m.	$m.	$bn
China	IMF	0	0	0	386	543	1,124	-	2,053	n.a.	292.2
	DAC	0	24	26	42	-3	39		128		
India	IMF	0	0	0	0	0	0	2,500	0	30,678	165.3
	DAC	49	79	92	72	6	-37		260		
Sri Lanka	IMF	47	43	49	64	38	33	70	274	3,087	5.9
	DAC	7	11	10	11	12	61		112		
Bangladesh	IMF	0	0	0	0	0	-1	80	-1		12.2
	DAC	-8	9	5	7	1	0		14		
Pakistan	IMF	62	59	107	66	31	64	790	389	11,656	33.4
	DAC	9	22	23	6	-1	1		60		
Kenya	IMF	78	78	60	80	46	40	520	382	3,811	5.6
	DAC	56	24	38	13	-2	0		129		
Ghana	IMF	-3	16	16	16	2	3	280	50	1,800	4.3
	DAC	1	3	24	2	0	3		33		
Tanzania	IMF	6	0	0	0	0	0	170	0	3,232	3.9
	DAC	8	5	19	17	2	-4		47		
Malawi	IMF	-1	0	1	0	0	0	100	0	885	1.3
	DAC	11	12	24	6	-3	0		40		
Middle income											
Hong Kong	DAC	342	374	1,088	652	603	681	2,100	3,740	1,130	31.8
S. Korea	IMF	11	-7	60	-76	-57	73	1,500	4	43,058	81.1
	DAC	1	-208	261	107	-62	246		345		
Taiwan	IMF	123	119	91	71	130	130	n.a.	664		52.0
	DAC	67	162	119	57	120	208		633		
Singapore	IMF	941	1,669	1,917	1,803	1,445	1,458	1,700	9,233	2,120	16.1
	DAC	354	650	980	280	417	634		3,315		
Malaysia	IMF	573	934	1,265	1,397	1,261	912	2,880	6,342	12,100	30.5
	DAC	77	242	252	-429	234	90		466		
Indonesia	IMF	226	183	133	225	292	222	5,760	1,281	32,480	75.9
	DAC	-383	300	2,584	537	303	423		4,530		
Thailand	IMF	51	187	288	189	348	406	445	1,469	15,278	40.9
	DAC	38	218	219	128	200	322		1,125		
	IMF	7	-106	172	16	105	-6		188		

Philippines	DAC	330	128	115	126	-168	130	1,820	659	2,438	32.2
	IMF	128	109	89	21	25	47		419		
Botswana	DAC	2	0	0	2	1	1	570	6	281	0.9
	IMF	75	95	38	0	0	0		208		
Ivory Coast	DAC	9	12	22	58	71	0	530	172	7,406	6.6
	IMF	0	0	0	35	49	39		123		
Liberia	DAC	41	72	288	313	250	-23	1,230	941	1,007	1.0
	IMF	304	-734	543	430	345	200		1,088		
Nigeria	DAC	-49	206	451	631	71	-252	1,130	1,058	19,724	51.3
	IMF	35	62	-38	0	0	0		59		
Zambia	DAC	41	37	103	62	-3	-1	330	239	3,888	2.4
	IMF	0	2	4	-1	-2	-3		0		
Zimbabwe	DAC	53	86	107	46	-	1	400	293	2,134	5.3
	IMF	1,211	541	747	285	471	713		3,968		
Egypt	DAC	38	30	120	310	384	208	245	1,090	23,206	37.7
	IMF	265	788	944	257	183	268		2,705		
Argentina	DAC	667	936	530	379	105	94	3,340	2,760	45,839	62.0
	IMF	2,223	1,544	2,313	2,534	1,373	1,556		11,543		
Brazil	DAC	1,532	887	1,348	1,610	674	1,159	13,520	7,210	104,384	197.5
	IMF	1,332	2,186	2,537	1,655	459	391		8,560		
Mexico	DAC	1,047	2,017	1,226	-1,038	-326	538	6,000	3,464	97,307	165.4
	IMF	5	2	7	4	1	-2		17		
Barbados	DAC	12	4	5	3	0	0	100	24	368	1.0
	IMF	10	34	38	36	32	23		173		
Fiji	DAC	11	14	13	5	-2	-5	220	36	424	1.2
	IMF	-26	-28	-11	-16	-19	n.a.		-44		
Jamaica	DAC	-24	3	2	14	1	1	900	-3	3,107	3.0
	IMF	4	1	1	2	2	5		15		
Mauritius	DAC	9	13	0	7	1	2	24	32	560	1.0
	IMF	13	16	18	21	11	15		94		
Papua New Guinea	DAC	19	40	-40	85	12	40	860	156	1,976	2.4
	IMF	94	184	258	245	285	299		1,365		
Trinidad	DAC	4	54	-8	18	-45	-3	1,300	20	1,100	8.9

Sources: 1. 1978 Stock and DAC flows from OECD, Geographical Distribution of Financial Flows (Various).
2. IMF flows from International Financial Statistics.
3. External debt is gross external liabilities from World Bank Debt Tables.

Note: The major difference between IMF and DAC estimates is that the former uses a flexible definition relying heavily on the host country's own assessment of foreign investment flows. See note 2.

Table 1.2. Net flows of resources from industrial to developing countries(%)

	1960-66 (ave)	1967-73 (ave)	1974-80 (ave)	1981-85 (ave)
Concessional Aid	60.0	41.3	37.0	33.0
Other Official Flows	5.4	6.7	5.3	10.5
Private Direct Investment	19.6	24.0	16.3	11.2
Export Credit	7.5	11.7	13.7	9.5
Private Commercial Lending	7.5	16.3	27.7	35.8
	100.0	100.0	100.0	100.0

Source: Calculated from OECD/DAC tables.

Table 1.3. Current account financing by different groups of countries, 1970-84 ($ bn)

		1970	80	82	83	84
All developing countries						
Capital importers						
Financing:	Official transfers	2.43	11.64	11.16	11.77	11.96
	Official loans	3.65	21.57	21.79	20.81	25.61
	Private loans	4.60	36.84	41.79	27.97	24.56
	DFI	2.32	10.60	13.24	10.34	9.38
Total		15.00	80.65	87.78	70.89	71.51
C. Acct. Balance		-12.58	-67.84	-100.37	-56.66	-35.59
Low-income Africa						
Financing:	Official transfers	0.38	2.11	1.52	2.01	1.93
	Official loans	0.25	2.37	1.86	1.92	2.23
	Private loans	0.03	0.98	0.34	-0.01	-0.21
	DFI	0.17	0.24	0.22	0.21	0.09
Total		0.83	5.70	3.94	4.13	4.03
C. Acct. Balance		-0.68	-5.84	-5.43	-4.90	-4.59
Low-income Asia						
Financing:	Official transfers	0.37	1.95	1.89	2.01	1.95
	Official loans	0.97	3.41	3.88	3.54	4.22
	Private loans	0.02	1.47	0.07	0.66	2.32
	DFI	0.03	0.16	0.49	0.55	0.64
Total		1.39	6.99	6.33	6.76	9.13
C. Acct. Balance		-1.55	-9.69	-1.36	-1.00	-3.08
Middle-income oil importers						
	Official transfers	1.09	5.57	5.84	5.83	6.27
	Official loans	1.67	11.00	10.73	11.69	12.96
	Private loans	3.67	22.19	26.19	12.85	15.31
	DFI	1.23	6.01	7.24	5.87	5.73
Total		7.56	44.77	50.00	36.24	40.27
C. Acct. Balance		-7.45	-33.82	-57.89	-39.71	-24.37

Source: Based on IMF World Economic Outlook

Table 1.4. Major categories of developing countries and foreign investment, 1984

	Share of five-year (1980-84) flow of net investment	Share of 1981 stock of foreign investment	Share of GNP 1984	Share of population 1984
Low Income ldcs	20.8	17.1	32.0	75.4
of which lowest-income	0.7	n.a.	2.8	8.7
India & China	0.7	2.5	19.1	49.6
Indonesia	8.2	7.8	3.3	2.3
Others	11.2	n.a.	6.8	14.8
Lower-Middle income ldcs	6.0	n.a.	14.2	10.8
of which Nigeria	2.2	1.1	2.9	2.7
Egypt	2.1	0.5	1.4	1.3
Upper-Middle income ldcs	73.2	n.a.	53.8	13.8
of which Brazil	11.2	15.6	8.8	3.7
Mexico	4.8	9.4	7.4	2.1
Argentina	4.2	5.1	2.8	0.8
Malaysia	0.8	3.2	1.4	0.4
Singapore	5.9	3.5	0.7	0.1
Hong Kong	6.7	3.4	1.4	0.2
(off-shore Banking Centres)	(15.2)	(13.0)	(0.2)	(-)
(percent)	100.0	100.0	100.0	100.0
Total	$59.4bn	$110 bn	$224 bn	3,600 mn

Notes: Totals for net flows and stock of investment adjusted to exclude the main offshore banking centres plus Greece, Spain and Portugal.

Low-income ldcs have $500 or less per capita income in 1984. Middle-income ldcs have $500 to 1300 per capita.

Sources: OECD, Geographical Distribution of Financial Flows and stock data from UNCTC, Transnational Corporations in World Development, 1985.

Table 1.5. Net resource flows and foreign investment. Distribution of flows and financing patterns, by income group (%)

	Low-income countries	of which African ldcs	of which Asian ldcs	of which Others	and of which least developed	Lower middle-income countries	Upper middle-income countries	All ldcs	Total $ bn
Region as a % of foreign investment flow									
(ave) 1975-76	13	4	-	9	1	18	69	100	9.8
1980	14	4	-	10	3	3	83	100	11.2
1982	12	3	3	6	1	12	76	100	12.8
1984	25	2	12	11	1	12	63	100	10.4
1985	25	n.a.	n.a.	n.a.	1	12	63	100	8.0
DFI as % of total flow to groups of developing countries									
(ave) 1975-76	7	9	-	10	2	16	20	14	
1980	6	4	-	10	3	2	12	9	
1982	5	5	10	6	1	9	15	11	
1984	8	3	21	8	1	12	19	13	
1985	6	n.a.	n.a.	n.a.	1	9	16	10	

Source: OECD, Financing External Debt, 1986.

Table 1.6. Share of stock of foreign investment by home country in different developing countries (%) 1980

	Australia	Canada	N. Zealand	Germany	France	Italy	Japan	UK	US	Total (incl. others)
Latin American and Caribbean	0.3	3.2	-	5.9	3.1	2.0	3.5	10.1	62.1	100.0
Barbados	1.1	14.7	1.1	-	-	-	-	48.8	34.0	100.0
Trinidad	-	8.1	-	0.5	0.5	0.5	1.0	43.1	37.7	100.0
Jamaica	-	8.9	-	1.4	0.3	-	-	35.6	51.4	100.0
Brazil	0.2	3.0	-	11.9	4.9	2.4	8.4	9.4	47.8	100.0
Mexico	0.1	2.6	-	4.2	1.8	0.8	1.3	3.7	79.7	100.0
Africa	0.2	2.5	-	4.6	18.1	2.2	1.4	40.2	15.9	100.0
Botswana	-	-	-	-	-	-	-	76.9	7.9	100.0
Cameroon	-	-	-	5.0	65.0	1.0	-	7.0	4.0	100.0
Kenya	0.8	0.6	-	3.8	1.0	1.0	1.0	75.6	7.9	100.0
Malawi	-	-	-	4.3	0.8	-	-	78.0	5.2	100.0
Mauritius	-	0.3	-	3.1	9.3	-	3.1	68.7	6.2	100.0
Nigeria	0.1	1.1	-	7.0	6.5	1.6	3.0	53.6	16.6	100.0
Senegal	-	-	-	7.7	67.9	-	3.8	5.8	2.9	100.0
Swaziland	-	-	-	-	-	-	-	87.0	5.5	100.0
Tanzania	-	-	-	6.4	2.4	1.6	2.4	73.6	8.0	100.0
Zambia	0.7	0.3	-	3.4	0.3	1.1	0.3	73.0	15.2	100.0
Zimbabwe	0.2	2.5	-	-	0.4	0.2	-	86.8	7.1	100.0
Asia/Pacific Region	7.2	0.8	1.0	3.2	1.3	0.4	12.5	25.6	33.5	100.0
Bangladesh	1.5	-	-	3.0	1.5	-	1.5	36.3	42.4	100.0
Fiji	41.5	-	21.4	0.4	0.4	-	1.8	19.1	2.8	100.0
Hong Kong	7.3	1.2	0.5	1.7	1.0	0.1	14.8	31.5	30.6	100.0
India	0.6	1.1	-	6.7	1.5	0.8	2.1	39.1	39.5	100.0
Indonesia	5.2	0.7	-	3.7	1.4	0.4	20.9	12.6	38.3	100.0
Korea	-	-	-	1.9	1.2	-	49.1	2.1	43.5	100.0
Malaysia	6.3	0.7	0.6	1.4	0.7	0.3	7.2	40.1	15.0	100.0
PNG	66.9	-	2.8	0.7	-	-	1.4	19.4	3.2	100.0
Philippines	2.0	1.0	0.1	2.6	0.5	-	13.3	5.2	62.2	100.0
Singapore	6.4	0.3	0.6	3.0	0.8	0.2	7.7	29.4	34.4	100.0
Sri Lanka	-	-	-	2.0	-	-	1.0	75.5	16.3	100.0
Thailand	1.7	2.8	-	3.6	0.8	0.5	22.4	15.2	36.0	100.0
Vanuatu	33.5	1.5	3.0	-	9.0	-	1.5	12.1	7.5	100.0

Source: UNCTC based on 1980 Stock Estimates.

Table 1.7. Net transfer of resources to capital-importing developing countries, 1979-85 ($bn)

	1979	1980	1981	1982	1983	1984	1985
Net transfer mediated through all credits							
Net capital flow	47.9	54.2	62.5	50.8	39.7	32.0	13
Net interest paid	-17.2	-23.6	-34.8	-50.0	-48.3	-53.9	-54
Net transfer	30.7	30.6	27.7	0.8	-8.6	-22.0	-41
Net transfer mediated through direct investment							
Net flow of investment	10.1	9.8	14.2	12.0	8.9	8.5	9
Net direct investment income	-11.4	-13.7	-13.5	-13.1	-11.6	-11.3	-13
Net transfer	-1.3	-4.0	0.7	-1.1	-2.7	-2.8	-4
Net transfer mediated through official grants	12.0	12.7	13.1	10.7	11.0	12.3	14
Total net transfer	41.4	39.3	41.5	10.4	-0.3	-12.5	-31

Source: UN, World Economic Survey.

Chapter Two

DEVELOPING COUNTRY ATTITUDES TOWARDS FOREIGN INVESTMENT

Sheila Page

Starting in the late 1970s and accelerating sharply in 1983-4, there has been a widespread shift in developing country policies toward transnational companies, away from the restraints and regulation that characterised the early 1970s. The widely held view that it has been the current balance of payments or debt crises of some developing countries which have forced a relaxation or reversal of their controls on foreign investment(1) is only partially correct: there are other reasons which also seem to be powerful explanations of the policy changes. The impact of direct foreign investment on developing countries is being re-examined not because of new developments in the theory or methods of analysis, but because of changes in the external economic situation, in technology, in the nature of the companies, and in company-government relations in general. The potential range of costs and benefits has been well known for some years, but which are now most likely or most important, and their relative significance in terms of developing countries' present needs or objectives, has changed.

Recent Characteristics of Direct Investment

The United States remains the predominant source of developing countries' foreign investment, accounting for over 50% of the total. Major increases in recent years have come from Japan and also France and Germany. The United Kingdom share has declined sharply. The increases correspond roughly with the countries where demand for imports is likely to grow most. The investments of the different investing countries may differ in a variety of ways which have not yet been systematically explored. Surveys suggest that the Germans are the most unwilling to accept co-ownership of their subsidiaries. The Japanese, however, have used a variety of sub-licensing and other associate relationships. Although it has been suggested that direct ownership is a means of quality control, and among British firms desire for direct control appears to decrease with level of technology, the Japanese are known for their intervention in associated firms for quality control. The differences may therefore reflect differences in industrial organisation in the investing country, and be simply a fixed characteristic of each country's investment which developing countries must take into account. The tendency of investment to increase in the countries where it is already present rather than to seek new outlets would suggest that developing countries should seek to discover whether these country trends are likely to continue. Although both Japanese and US investment has been heavy in Asia and Latin America, Japan has had a sharper shift towards investment in Asia, which now accounts for about half its assets in developing countries. The UK distribution is very different, with Africa much more important in both the existing stock and new flows (not surprising, as unremitted profits are an even higher proportion of UK investment than for the other investing countries).

Among recipients, the share of Asia has risen, although with severe fluctuations, and overtook that of Latin America in 1983. Investment has been concentrated on the newly industrialising countries (NICs), and even among these there has been a clear increase in the concentration of foreign investment; Brazil and Mexico, and more recently Singapore and Malaysia, dominate the figures.

Investment by developing countries themselves in other developing countries appears to be increasing, although, as many only publish net flows, it is difficult to find good evidence. Within Asia, Hong Kong and Singapore may be important, but do not publish data. Korea outflows have increased and may be going to Africa as well, and outflows from the Philippines are growing. India may also be investing more in Africa. In Latin America, Brazil has the only recorded high outflows, some of which go to other Latin American countries, but it is also investing in Africa(2). Venezuela has also been an important source within Latin America, especially to Colombia(3).

If there has been a general change in investors' purpose, from import-substitution to investment for export, this could suggest very different criteria for the choice of country or industry. The export-oriented firm is more likely to be interested in low labour costs and labour-intensive processes; the import-oriented firm is more concerned with the effective size of the developing country's market, as determined by policy measures such as protection. The importance of market and operational familiarity, and the related role of reinvested profits, means that in practice much of the investment for one motive follows from investment for the other. Recent examples include the turning of car manufacturers (particularly Volkswagen) from investment to satisfy individual Latin American markets from behind trade barriers, to exporting from Brazil and Mexico. Low demand

and expectations in the intended markets can lead to an effort to find new markets, rather than withdrawal. The costs of production may be competitive after an initial period of high costs behind protection (the traditional infant industry argument, after all). A firm already present in a country may be among the first to be aware of new government incentives. Attitudes toward risk may also play a part: a country that has a sufficient domestic market to be a useful fall-back, if expected exports prove unsuccessful (or the reverse), may be better placed to attract either export-promoting or import-substituting investment than one which is more suitable for one, but much less so for the other. These arguments again suggest that developing countries may have few new opportunities and a relatively narrow range of choice.

Changes in automation which reduce the need for long runs to take advantage of economies of scale may reduce the cost of locating an import-substituting industry in a developing country with a small market or of the consequential loss of output in the investing country if its exports are significantly reduced, but they also lower the advantages of world-wide production and marketing which gave some of the incentive towards export-oriented investment. It is too soon to say which of these will be a more powerful influence on the total quantity. Advances in bio-technology on the one hand and more traditional considerations of the likely result of 10 years' very low investment in primary commodities on the other both suggest that the share of raw-material-based rather than manufacturing investment may be larger in the future than would be expected on the basis of projections of recent trends. The labour-training, technology and wage-share effects of foreign investment may therefore be less than previously indicated.

Recent changes in the form of foreign companies' participation in developing countries appear to include an increase in the share of local capital including the public sector, in many cases, particularly in oil and in Latin American countries(4), and some increase in 'new-form', non-equity linkages between companies. These include agreements to provide initial technical information or continuing advice and (independently or in association) various forms of marketing agreement. If the developed country firm only undertakes a long-term obligation to market the host country's output this seems some distance from foreign investment. But it is common for some of what is normally considered management, especially production decisions and quality control, to be done by a customer firm in such industries as clothing, and more generally among Japanese firms. If the foreign firm also supplies the inputs, and possibly the machinery for processing them, then the foreign involvement at every level except equity participation becomes very close to foreign investment, and most of the potential effects other than financing may be present. They represent efforts to isolate one (or a subset) of the potential benefits of foreign investment. They may be preferred either because they avoid the need to estimate the full net effect of a whole investment package (permitting a simpler decision and more limited or well-defined commitment on both sides) or, as they are frequently confined to the setting-up of a project or to a single product or process, because they require a shorter-term commitment, even if it is a renewable one. Both characteristics may reduce perceived risk.

The lack of data (and indeed of standard definitions) on these arrangements makes it difficult to measure their direct effect so far. An increase in local shares of equity has clearly occurred: a number of developing countries have required this, de facto or de jure, since the late 1960s and histories of individual large firms confirm it. Quantitatively, of course, it is the move to state ownership in the OPEC countries that dominates.

The evidence on other types of relationship is more difficult to obtain. Regulations and different company practices on such payments as royalties and technical fees mean that these are more likely to give information about the negotiating strength of the two companies or legal limits than about the role of foreign companies in providing technical assistance. To the extent that reduced foreign shares and non-equity participation have occurred, they diminish the capital-inflow benefits of foreign investment. In particular, they reduce the extent to which the foreign investor bears the risks attached to the investment, with this reinforced by any move towards fixed fees, particularly at the beginning of an investment. There may also be indirect effects on the behaviour of the investor. Theorists as opposed to practitioners in foreign investment have tended to argue that fears of trade-distorting export behaviour by transnationals were irrational because they would, as profit maximisers, be indifferent among different sources of supply among their subsidiaries or between them and the home company. If only a share of the subsidiaries' profits goes to them, however, this argument ceases to hold.

There may, however, be one extremely significant result of the existence of new arrangements and even of the exaggerated importance that may have been given to them. They have encouraged both sides to consider the range of potential costs and benefits of foreign investment more analytically, and the cases that have occurred, or at least been considered, have provided a body of evidence on the appropriate range of costs of the different elements of a foreign investment package. Combined with local participation, which except in its most superficial forms at least gives an outsider (which in some cases is the government) access to the accounts of the subsidiaries, this has greatly increased the knowledge actually available on the activities of foreign investors. Even where precise figures about a particular flow may not be available this has reduced the fear and lack of confidence in dealing with investors that came from ignorance. The existence of some cases of arms-length technology fees or sales of semi-processed parts, even if they are only a minority or in different markets, gives evidence of a 'reasonable' level for this component of a foreign investor's return. For example, it is simply no longer true that there can be no effective supervision of the possible transfer pricing malpractices of transnationals. The decrease in the feeling of helplessness that many developing countries expressed before the 1970s may make them more willing to consider foreign investment as a source of finance, and investing companies also can make better estimates of the effects of government restraints on parts of their activity.

Changes in the Behaviour of Transnationals

The last ten years have seen a variety of attempts to increase the legal control on transnationals, internationally and by both investing and host countries. As with the new forms of investment, the associated effects on attitudes may be more important than any substantive change. There are several reasons that suggested an international approach. One was the need for a consistent approach to activities which necessarily involve more than one country. This was first perceived by some developing country governments which feared evasion or lack of enforceability from national approaches. Trade unions have also seen advantages in restricting the ability of corporations to move production to avoid labour legislation or negotiated labour agreements. The companies, however, appear now to have seen advantages to themselves in standardising the constraints that they face and in restricting their level to the most that can be agreed by all governments. A related reason was the need to define limits on national jurisdiction in cases where both home and host country might claim to be the appropriate regulatory authority. A final reason was the belief, now perhaps less widely held than ten years ago, that because of their size, a small country government could not control transnationals, and even a larger country would have difficulty.

In 1977 the United Nations Centre on Transnational Corporations (UNCTC) began efforts to negotiate a legally recognised code, the object being to define the proper operations of transnational companies, the obligations between them and governments, and enforcement mechanisms. Issues still outstanding(5) include whether the code should be legally binding, the definition of a 'transnational corporation', whether tncs are entitled to equal, or even special, treatment by host governments, and the conditions for nationalisation. The fundamental nature of these disagreements suggests that they are unlikely to be agreed internationally.

Attempts have followed to develop 'guide-lines' covering a narrower range of countries, potentially with more common interests or political beliefs, on a narrower range of issues. In some cases they are only recommendations. The earliest was probably the regulation under the Andean Pact, discussed below. The ILO has made a declaration on social policy (1977). The EEC has attempted to negotiate a code for its members, including provisions on labour participation in decisions, and UNCTAD has made proposals on a Code of Conduct on the Transfer of Technology. In 1976 the OECD adopted voluntary guidelines for its transnationals, which move strongly in the direction of protecting them from government actions rather than the reverse.

Perhaps a more important consequence for the developing countries has been the opportunity for the exchange of information, and the build-up of information within organisations such as the UNCTC. As with the greater information on market prices, this has strengthened the bargaining position of individual countries(6). (The increase in contacts and hence policy co-ordination has, however, also taken place on the investing country side.) It includes the provision of advisers for particular negotiations and actual training programmes. This could increase if the negotiations are broken up into groups dealing with individual issues. This greater spread of information is also partly a simple result of longer experience of transnationals, and has been cited by companies as a risk even among their own associates or licensees: as initial agreements for technical or other associations come to an end, the developing country company has greater information about the company and its operations and about its relations with other associates. It is even possible that the extensive economic research on the subject in the early 1970s may have contributed.

There have been increases in the accounting requirements on companies, particularly in the United States and Japan, and in some cases in the information which must be provided to workers within a firm, particularly in the European countries. There have also been efforts to increase the international comparability of accounts, through a UN working group.

Companies have also been subject to a variety of social and political pressures which have resulted in a large number of increased national controls and some international codes. These include restrictions as disparate as controls on advertising powdered milk and some drugs, reporting requirements on labour conditions in South African branches, guidelines on data transmission and disclosure, and efforts to control pollution. The move toward shareholder responsibility pressure groups has also increased knowledge and comparisons among companies. The division between 'investing countries' and 'developing countries' is no longer as sharp as in the 1960s or early 1970s, and this increased range of experiences has altered countries' points of view. The growth of South-South investment described above means that some developing countries have experience as investors, or have dealt with investors which were also developing countries. On the other side, the industrial countries, and in particular the United States, have had greatly increased experience of being the recipients of direct foreign investment. The need which they have felt to regulate inflows has weakened their automatic support for their investing companies against other recipient governments. There had already, of course, been resistance in the European countries, particularly in France, to the spread of US investment in the 1960s but there was a large rise in investment by the European countries in the United States in the 1970s; by Japan in both the United States and Europe rather later; and, in some ways the most interesting, the presence of a group of foreign investors as alien and unpredictable to the industrial countries as these could seem to the developing, the OPEC countries. The United States had introduced, from 1965, regulation of new foreign investment and also attempted to control the overseas activities of its own firms(7). The controls by both the United States and the European countries became increasingly discriminatory as they faced first the problem of potential OPEC purchases of key firms and then the recessions and consequent concern over industrial strategies of the second half of the 1970s. Their worries about subjection to alien forces and working conditions are increasingly reminiscent of developing country literature(8).

These developments may well strengthen the bargaining position of the developing countries. Broad international codes are probably not sufficient, but these may no longer be seen as the most desirable approaches by developing countries that may prefer to make their own policies and now have the confidence to do so. Against this, however, there has been a more recent sharp change in US policy towards direct support of private investment in general and its own overseas investors in particular. Concern over discrimination against foreign investment has been extended (in particular in the Reagan statement on international investment of 1983) to emphasis on restricting government intervention to control investment and ensuring such general company interests as intellectual property rights. This has been accompanied, in the United States and the European investing countries, by increased pressure on developing countries to sign Bilateral Investment Treaties (BITs) guaranteeing no discrimination against foreign investors and specifying dispute settlement terms, thus extending the area within which the bargaining over foreign investment takes place, and thereby diluting the advantages gained from greater bargaining strength against investing companies. The Latin American countries have not in general signed. The Caribbean countries, however, have gone further than the BITs, accepting a Caribbean Basin Initiative which links investment to trade concessions.

Developing Country Attitudes Towards Foreign Investment

It is not possible to identify a separate developing country position on direct foreign investment, but it is an issue on which developing country economists, particularly in international agencies like ECLA, the UNCTC and UNCTAD, and in industrial countries have tended to raise new problems and arguments. The importance of French influence should not be underrated. France, as noted in the last section, was the location of some of the strongest debate on US investment in European countries in the 1960s, and the French universities have been important training grounds for Latin American, particularly South American, economists.

The organisation of academic and government employment and the simple fact of small numbers of economists have meant a close association between research and policy-making, which may have influenced the direction of research. Among developing countries, those in which foreign investment has been concentrated have been those with most economists, but even in some of the middle income Latin American countries, there was effectively no independent economic research until recently, and certainly no surplus of economists above those necessary for day-to-day government and private sector operations, as is still the position in the poorer Asian and many African countries.

The position of such organisations as ECLA can be traced in general terms back to the argument that the tendency of economic and political power is to move away from the 'periphery' to the industrial countries. Developing countries are made dependent on, and also remodelled on the pattern of, the capitalist industrial countries. The transnational companies were seen as promoters of either their own or their home country government interests against those of developing countries, or, combining the two, of the interests of capitalism. It was the power of capital, and the size of financial flows, within countries and across borders, on which attention was fixed. The theoretical analysis of transnational companies as basically providers of capital led to emphasis (and frequently to restrictive policies) on their role in the banking sector(9), and on the shares of foreign owners relative to local, in individual companies or in the developing country's total capital.

The theoretical arguments were reinforced by empirical work on the large profits made by transnationals, initially in some Latin American countries, particularly in the pharmaceutical industry, but later in other industries and areas, done in the late 1960s and early 1970s, some under UNCTAD. Arguments were developed that transnationals took more out of a country in the return on their investment than they contributed. Other possible benefits were assumed to be of negligible importance, or to be outweighed by other costs: inappropriate industrial structure or technology or income distribution effects. Transnationals' interests were seen as not merely different from those of developing countries, but in direct conflict with them: transnationals held the initiative in their operations; they looked for opportunities to expand (the growth-orientated view of company strategy, rather than profit maximising, that was not uncommon in economics in the 1960s)(10); and their operations were uncontrollable, either because of their economic power within the developing country or because they were supported by their own governments which were also in conflict with the host country's interests.

Many economists, not only in developing countries, still hold all these views. In particular, the view that transnationals' main advantage, and attribute, is possession of capital or access to it, still commands strong support. In August 1981, however, a set of articles in the CEPAL Review illustrated some modifications to this view. Transnationals can be regulated, as well as simply banned or left free; what is important is for the developing country government to have a clear view of its objectives, with the implication that it can then implement them; transnationals may accept regulation, rather than demanding assistance or walking out. A paper for a 1984 conference by the Andean Pact on foreign investment specifically denied that the transnational companies would make common cause against a government(11).

Some of the change in views can be attributed to the changes in the nature of investment noted in the last section. Any one investor, in particular the US, is less important to a developing country, so that it can take risks. Latin America is less important to US investors, so political intervention may be less likely(12). The increase in the proportion of manufacturing rather than mining investment has tended to mean smaller, and therefore weaker companies (although the evidence on this is not conclusive). The decline in the role of foreign investment as a source of finance and its slower absolute growth have reduced its power to threaten. There has also been increasing awareness that the Eastern European countries have apparently been able to negotiate satisfactory agreements with transnational companies without sacrificing their ability to plan their economies(13) and without transforming them to fit into international capitalism. One of the most important reasons for the change was the success of the OPEC countries against the oil companies in 1974: not merely the initial raising of the price, but taking control and ownership from the archetypal transnationals, and dealing in a product that the industrial country governments clearly considered essential to their national interests. The economic limitations on the power to behave in similar fashion to other investors have emerged since (oil was particularly suitable for 'new forms' because extraction does not, on land, require firm-specific technical expertise and oil is a homogeneous product), but the point about political power and sovereignty was learned.

The role of investment as a supplier of capital has clearly re-emerged in analysis(14) and policy since 1982, but the focus of the argument has been transformed: in the early 1970s the view was of the developing country as the passive beneficiary or equally passive victim of exploitation; now, it is in terms of the developing country taking the initiative, encouraging entry, setting the terms for operation and rates of return. This change in attitude, which is so complete that economists and policy-makers may not be fully conscious of its novelty, may be a lasting product of the role of commercial bank lending in the 1970s. In these negotiations, unlike those with either the aid-giving agencies or international companies, the developing country governments were in the position of clients, to be treated with respect, not ordered to follow conditions or to concede privileges to an investor under threat of losing the grant or the investment.

Changes in Developing Country Policies on Foreign Investment

The policies of individual countries will be discussed later in this volume in the country chapters. Two major general shifts appear to have occurred: towards increased regulation, around 1970; and away from it, starting about 1977, and intensifying in 1983-4. In the 1960s, there had been some stimulus from policy in some Asian countries (including Malaysia and Thailand around 1960). Some Latin American countries, notably Brazil, Mexico, and Argentina, the principal recipients, had regulated the entry, sectors, location, or share of foreign participation of foreign investment for many years, but the Andean Pact's Decision 24, adopted in 1970, was a joint attempt by the members (then Peru, Colombia, Bolivia, Venezuela, Ecuador and Chile), which were neither major recipients nor large markets, to provide detailed regulation not only of the conditions under which foreign investment could be established, but how it should operate and remit its profits and other income to the investing country. In particular, it limited foreign ownership and the permitted rate of return, as well as regulating imports by the foreign companies and attempting to avoid company restrictions on exports. It was unusual for developing countries in being collective: this may have reflected lack of confidence in the power of a single country against the powers of the transnationals. The major Latin American countries also introduced new legislation at this time, including Argentina and Mexico in 1973. The actions by the Asian countries have normally been individual. Among those which took action at about the same time were Malaysia (as part of the New Economic Policy); slightly later (1973) India, and, on a very minor scale, Thailand.

The relaxation began in 1976-7 with incentives in some sectors in Latin America(15) and Pakistan(16) and more general relaxation in other countries, sometimes as part of a more 'open' strategy: Argentina, Egypt, Thailand, later Korea. This was before the second oil price rise or the recession of 1980-82 and the financing crisis. There have also been smaller policy changes in the Philippines and Morocco. There was an important revision of Andean Pact regulations in 1976, and since 1982 its regulations, particularly on remittances, have been relaxed, but more significantly the individual countries have effectively taken back the power to conduct their own negotiations with transnationals. Colombia and Peru in particular have made it clear that this freedom will be used to promote foreign investment, with very flexible regulation of ownership shares and profit remittances. The members are, however, also interested in trying to revise the Pact provisions, suggesting that policy-makers see the change not as a temporary one to meet current financial needs but rather as a definite shift in strategy, in particular an increase in the emphasis on foreign investment as a source of technology rather than merely capital inflow.

Malaysia is actively promoting investment, particularly in primary goods. Some African countries are taking a more favourable attitude particularly towards investment from Latin America and Asia as noted earlier, but Zimbabwe is also finding it necessary to consider signing an agreement with the United States(17). The willingness of the Caribbean countries to enter the Caribbean Basin Initiative represents a change in attitude for several of them from the immediate post-independence period. Mexico, with one of the oldest traditions of restriction, has set up a Foreign Investment Commission to publish lists of priority industries and with the freedom to permit increases in foreign ownership above the previous limit of 49%(18). Some of the permitted majority ownership, however, will be to consolidate debts to the home country as equity; this has already been done for some companies and represents a straight substitution of foreign investment for debt commitments.

The precise nature of this policy change, and the timing of its acceleration, make it impossible to ignore the importance of simple need, rather than the longer-term explanations developed above, but because of the importance of investors' perceptions about the durability of a change, it is important to stress that the change had begun earlier. It must also be noted that not all the financially hardest-hit countries have changed their policies: Brazil has tightened its controls on entry to one sector, informatics, and Argentina has delayed remittances and restricted their form to bonds.

The changes in general policies have not been accompanied by reductions in attempts to regulate foreign investment in order to maximise its potential financial effects (for example, control or supervision of remittances) or to obtain other possible benefits, in technology or on the balance of payments. Investment may be restricted or forbidden in some sectors either for the same types of non-economic reasons that may restrict the scope of private relative to public investment, or to ensure that what may be viewed as a limited amount of potential inflows goes to areas where there is little or no possibility of local investment. Brazil, for example, restricts such industries as petroleum and shipping, and 'complementarity' rather than 'competition' with local investment is frequently mentioned by host countries. Any such criterion is an attempt to maximise the non-capital and non-trade attributes of foreign investment, frequently without identifying them more precisely. Similar concerns are behind restrictions or prohibition of foreign purchases of existing companies, or shares in them. It is perhaps reasonable to take the attitude that if foreign investment does have other advantages or if the capital and trade advantages are sufficiently large, then such restrictions will not deter it, and if it does not, it is not desirable.

On remittances, most countries exercise some control either permanently, with fixed limits, or through exchange controls. Such controls are intended to meet the criticism of excessive returns and sometimes to prevent exploitation of economic rents by foreign investors. If, however, they are effective, companies may shift to using inter-company loans instead of equity finance; this can reduce the flexibility of return that was cited as an advantage of foreign investment over debt. If the government attempts to regulate the total return to the foreign investor, in profits, interest, and other service payments, this may reduce the incentive to enter the country at all, or to go into the more risky investments. Governments taking such action implicitly take the view that the financial advantage to a foreign investor is sufficient to risk this. The Andean Pact had adopted such control since the adoption of Decision 24, although the limits have been effectively increased in 1983. Other countries, for example Brazil, discourage high outflows by an increasing tax rate.

Technology transfer or training, or other desirable internal effects, can also be encouraged by more specific regulation; training requirements, restrictions on the number of expatriate workers, refusal to permit one part of a company's operations, for example assembly and sales of a final good, without the more technically advanced parts of production.

There does not appear to have been any general alteration in such regulation recently. In one area, trying to exploit the trade effects of foreign investment, there may have been an increase in regulation by tying other privileges or concessions, typically on taxes or remittances, or even permission to make a new investment, to the share of output exported, or to increases in this. Such export requirements are sufficiently common to have become a major target for US policy-makers worried by the implications for US imports.

The continuation of all these policies suggests that developing countries are taking a more discriminating view of foreign investment than would be implied either by the old policies of restricting all forms, to avoid its dangers, or by suggestions that it must be welcomed without restriction to finance deficits. Clearly promotion of foreign investment and discriminating among different types can be achieved by offering subsidies or other concessions as well as by manipulation of restrictions, and this is also occurring, but again with emphasis on discrimination rather than general measures.

Implications For Future Policy

The account given here of how recent changes in attitudes may have altered the effects to be expected from foreign investment for a developing country, and the country's ability to regulate these, cannot lead to a general conclusion about the balance of benefits and costs. Following the line of the more recent developing country economic arguments, therefore, the first step is for countries to know what their own objectives are, including, in the context of direct investment, what their need for external finance is, and what their general policies ought to be towards controlling the scale and direction of activities of private sector (national or international) firms. Clearly they also need to know what alternatives are available, in particular alternative forms of finance and alternative local substitutes for the firms. The 'effect' of transnationals on output and the size and sometimes the sign of any balance-of-payments effect depend on what the realistic alternative is.

Another set of questions which is very inadequately understood is _what_ countries can do to attract foreign investment if they do decide they want it, and quantitatively _how much_ they need to do. There are two problems. First, the evidence of surveys and some econometric work is that the conventional tax exemptions, investment, export, or import subsidies etc, are not effective, provided a country offers roughly a conventional range of inducements. The convention can change, however, particularly when there is a general move, as appears to be taking place, to attract investment, so that countries can be 'left behind'. General economic and political conditions, which past studies and more general theories of the determination of investment both imply should be more important, are unlikely to be easy to change: internal or external wars and depressed local markets are obvious difficulties in many of the countries with new policies towards foreign investment. If it is export-oriented investment that is sought, the host country is competing with the investing country and with other potential host countries and needs to have or to create a particular advantage. But a 'created' one (eg. a subsidy) may not be accepted as a permanent change by an investor. Preparing lists of potential projects, and even full outlines, (a strategy being encouraged by UNIDO), does not take advantage of the management and project identification skills of the investors, and may take too sanguine a view of the real opportunities: the concentration of investment does not suggest that there are a large number of potential investors prepared to look at ready-made projects.

The second problem is that the lags, especially for completely new foreign investment, are almost certainly very long. One study(19) found five-year lags between investment decisions and start-up. For a country that is changing its policy, there are the additional lags of perception(20) and acceptance as permanent. There is little evidence, and much current controversy (in the context of possible debt default), over how rapidly investors' views change on individual countries and whether this is faster or slower if a group rather than a single country is concerned. Certainly a long period of effort and then of waiting must be expected, and any structural change in a country's relationship with the rest of the world is likely to be slow and uncertain.

It is noteworthy that a high proportion of the special measures to promote (or remove previous restrictions from) foreign investment are intended to attract new investors, not to increase existing investment. This is possibly a deliberate concentration of effort because re-investment and expansion are assumed to be easier to ensure, while new investment may produce a long stream of further investments once the investor is established. The importance of familiarity and existing commitments may make it less necessary to offer inducements, or avoid restrictions, for current investors. Countries may also wish to increase the number of companies and investing countries as a form of portfolio diversification. In view of the small number of potential investors and the urgent need for quick responses, however, it is not clear that this is the most efficient use of the scarce potential for financial attractions and the even scarcer supply of government policy-makers' efforts.

NOTES AND REFERENCES

1. See for example the UN Centre on Transnational Corporations (UNCTC), Transnational Corporations in World Development, Third Survey, ST/CTC/46 (United Nations, New York, 1983), p.10.

2. See Paul Collins, 'Brazil in Africa: Perspectives on Economic Cooperation Among Developing Countries, Development Policy Review, Vol.3, No.1 (May 1985).

3. Junta del Acuerdo de Cartagena, 'Evolución de la Inversión Extranjera en el Grupo Andino entre 1970 y 1982', paper prepared for conference, July 1984.

4. See UNCTC, Transnational Corporations, for an extended discussion of the available evidence.

5. Ibid, pp.108-20.

6. See F.I. Nixson, 'Controlling the Transnationals? Political Economy and the UN Code of Conduct', International Journal of the Sociology of Law (February 1983).

7. Michael Hudson, 'International Direct Investment: the End of Autonomy', Managing International Development, Vol.1, No.1 (January/February 1984).

8. By 1984 some of the most important international conflicts in regulating transnationals are between industrial countries.

9. See Clara Ogata Shimokawa, Politicás Explicitas de Tratamiento al Capital Extranjero en al Peru (DESCO, Lima, 1981), p.39.

10. c.f. Fernando Gonzales-Vigil, Capital Extranjero y Transnacionales en la Industria Peruana (Horizonte for Instituto para America Latina, Lima, 1983), pp.78-80.

11. Sergio Bitar, 'Corporaciones Transnacionales y las nuevas relaciones de America Latina con Estados Unidos' paper prepared for conference at Junta del Acuerdo de Cartagena, Lima, July 1984.

12. Ibid.

13. See, for example Alberto Jimenez de Lucio, 'The East, the South and the Transnational Corporations', CEPAL Review (August 1981).

14. Sergio Bitar 'La Inversión Extranjera de Estados Unidos eu America Latina; Tendencia Recientes' paper prepared

for conference at Junta del Acuerdo de Cartagena, Lima, July 1984.

15. See Bitar, 'Corporaciones Transnacionales'.

16. UNCTC, Transnational Corporations, pp. 57-8; UN, World Economic Survey 1981-2 (New York, 1982).

17. See Roger Riddell's chapter in this volume.

18. See Nacional Financiera SA, 'Promoción de Inversiónes Extranjeras', El Mercado de Valores, Vol.44, No.9 (February 1984).

19. John D. Daniels and Charles J. Quigley Jr, 'Pull Factors for Direct Investment', Foreign Trade Review, Vol.15, No.3 (October/December 1980).

20. A 1983 survey still found the view that Latin American controls were increasing, Group of Thirty, Foreign Direct Investment 1973-85 (New York, 1984), p.34.

Chapter Three

FOREIGN INVESTMENT IN EAST ASIA

Helen Hughes and Graeme S. Dorrance

Characteristics of Private Direct Foreign Investment Flows to East Asia

The $15 bn flowing annually to developing countries represents about a third of the $45-50 bn global direct investment flows, roughly in proportion to the developing countries' share in the world economy. Of this, about $5 bn goes annually to East Asia.(1)

Three approaches to direct foreign investment (DFI) have evolved in East Asia during the past 30 years. The first, open model, confined to Hong Kong, lays almost no restrictions on foreign investors, leaving market forces to balance socio-economic with private returns; it must be noted that Hong Kong has no natural resources with corresponding resource rents to complicate the application of this model. At the other extreme are the other countries of East Asia, which began to industrialise with import-substituting policies that created monopolistic rents, while several have rich natural resources with corresponding natural resource rents. The policy response was to attempt to limit transnational corporations' appropriation of such rents by restricting access, but this had to be offset by incentives to entry.

Model III evolved from model II. East Asian countries found that import substitution stifled growth, and they attempted to offset import-substitution incentives by export subsidies. In Korea and Taiwan this led to export growth because the administrative resources required for such a system were available, but it also led to the misallocation of resources and waste. Taiwan accordingly began to liberalise in the 1970s, and Korea is trying to follow this path. Malaysia and Thailand had relatively low protection and exports were thus relatively easy to undertake. In the Philippines protection was high so that inequitably administered import substitution plus export subsidies led to much greater inefficiency than in Korea and Taiwan. In Indonesia the main concern with foreign investment was in mineral exploitation; industrialisation has barely begun, and industrial exports are negligible. Singapore had relatively low protection in 1965 when, with independence from Malaysia, it changed to a strongly outward-oriented policy, and moved swiftly in the direction of a very open attitude to foreign investors.

The economic policy framework in East Asia that complemented trade policy was, with only a few exceptions, oriented toward world prices. Indonesia, Korea and the Philippines suffered from periodic breakdowns of monetary policies with consequent bouts of inflation and overvaluation of exchange rates, which were brought into line fairly rapidly. But prices in most of the East Asian countries have risen less than world prices since the 1960s when inflation became a problem, and earnings tended to lag behind prices, though real earnings rose in all countries but the Philippines. With the exception of the Philippines and to a lesser extent Indonesia, public revenues were used to improve the basic infrastructure for business directly and indirectly (through improved health, education and housing) throughout the region, the overall effect being to provide the best investment climate in developing countries. Foreign investment was not, however, simply correlated with growth and investment climate, but reflected the policies adopted toward transnational corporations.

Foreign investment data are very limited and must therefore be used with great caution. Reinvestment is generally underestimated, there is no clear line between equity and loans, and flows cannot be cumulated to give stocks because of price changes. Table 3.1 shows data compiled by two international agencies. There is considerable evidence, however, of a wide spectrum of DFI flows into the East Asian countries. Singapore and Hong Kong have employed DFI relatively intensively whether intensity is measured as a share of capital inflows or of total investment, or per capita. Korea and Taiwan, the other two rapidly growing countries, have used foreign investment the least intensively of the group.

In addition, World Bank figures show that East Asian countries have relied less heavily on borrowing from world capital markets through banks(2) and DFI is accordingly a higher proportion of total capital inflows than in most developing countries. Singapore and Malaysia have had a relatively high percentage of direct investment in capital flows. Because domestic investment to GDP ratios are higher in East Asian countries than in most other developing countries, DFI is a relatively low ratio of gross investment. The share of direct investment in total investment is not necessarily a guide to the impact of investment on productivity and exports. Quantitative indicators of such impact are not available, and nor are the qualitative ones that would suggest how entrepreneurship, attitudes to work, skill formation and technology adaptation are affected by DFI. However, it seems that the characteris-

Table 3.1. Net private DFI in selected East Asian countries, 1976-82 ($USm.)

	1969-76	1976	1977	1978	1979	1980	1981	1982[a]
Hong Kong								
IMF data [b]	n.a.	n.a.	n.a.	n.a.	n.a.	n.a.	n.a.	n.a.
OECD, etc. data	633	154	145	252	342	374	1,088	528
Indonesia								
IMF data (total)	1,247	344	235	279	226	184	133	225
OECD, etc. data	2,869	747	-67	418	-383	300	2,583	530
Korea								
IMF data	491	75	72	61	17	-5	59	-77
OECD, etc. data	633	83	28	184	1	-208	261	108
Malaysia								
IMF data	1,862	381	406	500	574	935	1,124	1,230
OECD, etc. data	526	133	134	-5	77	242	252	260
Philippines								
IMF data	231	126	209	164	74	39	404	253
OECD, etc. data	567	154	116	144	330	128	115	124
Singapore								
IMF data	2,686	651	335	739	941	1,669	1,916	2,093
OECD, etc. data	402	67	85	147	354	650	980	192
Taiwan	436*	69*						
IMF, etc. data	...	68	44	110	122	124	91	171
OECD, etc. data	867	18	19	28	67	162	119	59
Thailand								
IMF data	569	80	106	51	50	186	291	185
OECD, etc. data	159	18	42	38	38	218	219	128

a Preliminary.

b Hong Kong does not publish data on its capital transactions.

* Own figures.

Sources: For OECD, etc. data: OECD, Development Cooperation, passim for 1976-82, K. Billerbeck and Y. Yasugi, 'Private Direct Foreign Investment in Developing Countries', World Bank Staff Working Paper No. 348, July 1979 for 1969-76.
For IMF, etc. data: IMF, Balance of Payments, Vol. 34 (1983), Part I, and Statistical Yearbook of the Republic of China, 1984.

tics of foreign investment, and the conditions under which it operates in the fast growing countries, are such that the benefit to the economy for each dollar invested is greater in East Asia than it is in most other developing countries.

The Sectoral Structure of DFI. Before World War II the bulk of DFI in East Asia was in the resource-rich South East Asian countries, particularly in resource-intensive sectors such as plantations and mines, although Japan had also expanded into manufacturing in Korea (mainly in the north of the country) and to a lesser extent in Taiwan. After 1945 Japanese investment was liquidated. Most of the Netherlands investment in Indonesia was expropriated in the 1950s. The situation was different in the other East Asian countries where many firms returned in the late 1940s and 1950s. In the Philippines, the bulk of DFI was from the United States, and in Hong Kong, Malaysia and Singapore it was British. British, French, German and Scandinavian firms co-existed in Thailand. Some US firms had invested in public utilities in the Philippines but elsewhere public utilities were state-owned. This post-colonial situation had changed dramatically by the 1960s.

Some foreign interest remained in tin mining in Malaysia and Thailand. Transnationals invested heavily in petroleum and gas exploitation throughout the region, notably in Indonesia. Foreign firms were also welcomed back to the Indonesian mineral and timber industries after the political changes of 1965. Table 3.2 suggests that Indonesia was the only East Asian country with significant DFI in mining, but of all the dubious data available, this is the most dubious. The limited mineral resources of Korea and Taiwan have been developed by domestic entrepreneurs. Although Thailand has held back mineral development because it has been unable to reach a consensus on the role that foreign firms should play in its mineral sector, there has been DFI in minerals in the Philippines.

DFI began to flow into East Asian manufacturing and associated service sectors in the 1950s. There was limited foreign investment in the import-substituting protected industries in Korea and Taiwan, but Hong Kong was keen to attract transnationals to become a base for export-oriented manufacturing. However, in all three economies, local entrepreneurs retained a strong hold on the economy, for DFI remained a small proportion of gross private domestic investment. As the economic reforms took hold in Taiwan and Korea respectively in the late 1950s and early 1960s, manufacturing and associated service sectors began to expand rapidly. Taiwan and Korea joined Hong Kong as the world's most rapidly growing countries. But because they did not liberalise their trade regimes, but rather offset protection

Table 3.2. Sectoral distribution of stock of foreign investment in East Asian countries (%)

	Hong Kong		Indonesia		Korea		Malaysia		Philippines		Singapore		Thailand	
	1971	1978	1972	1977	1973	1978	1971	1977	1972	1978	1972	1977	1969	1977
Agriculture	-	-	20.5	13.7	1.2	1.4	-	-	-	-	-	-	-	-
Mining	-	-	23.2	10.7	0.1	0.3	-	-	5.7	11.2	-	-	-	-
Manufacturing	100.0	100.0	50.3	64.1	76.9	73.4	100.0	100.0	39.2	54.3	100.0	100.0	97.3	81.0
Services	-	-	1.5	6.4	21.8	24.9	-	-	52.5	30.1	-	-	2.5	19.5
Other	-	-	4.5	5.1	-	-	-	-	-	-	-	-	0.1	-
Total $m.	133	434	3,225	6,555	115	1,004	137	433	116	976	665	1,733	70	244

Note: that these figures do not agree with country estimates or OECD stock data. They have been used because they represent the largest comparable set of data available, but they must be used with great caution.

Source: United Nations Centre on Transnational Corporations, Salient Features and Trends in Foreign Direct Investment, (United Nations, New York, 1983), Table 25, pp.67-8.

for import-substituting industries by export incentives, they could not open investment to transnationals. Complex regulatory and administrative regimes made entry by transnationals difficult, and export zones had to be created. It was fortunate that both countries had well developed entrepreneurial and skill resources, because direct investment was limited. The South East Asian countries were at this stage inward-oriented with the bulk of manufacturing being import-substituting. Foreign firms were dispossessed in Indonesia in the 1960s, and the bulk of large-scale agriculture, mining, manufacturing and banking moved to the public sector.

When Singapore broke with Malaysia in 1965 the limitations of its domestic market forced it to follow Hong Kong and become export-oriented. It turned to manufacturing relatively sophisticated products and tncs quickly found it a highly suitable base for export industries. Business externalities also helped this trend. The imposition of quantitative restrictions on Hong Kong's and Taiwan's clothing, textile and footwear exports brought new East Asian tncs to Singapore(3). By 1970, Singapore was the fourth largest developing country exporter of manufactures, and had a labour shortage that had to be met by 'Gastarbeiter' immigration from Malaysia and other countries in the region. DFI was the critical tool in this transformation.

Malaysia and Thailand followed the example of Korea and Taiwan in the 1970s, offsetting their relatively low and limited protection to stimulate exports of manufactures. They also followed Singapore in seeking to expand and diversify foreign investment. However, because they did not dismantle their protective regimes, foreign investment continued to be regulated as government officials tried to apply model II to import-substituting activities and model I to exports in a classic model III situation. The Philippines did not follow the outward-oriented lead until the 1970s, and its changes were largely cosmetic. Indonesia also remained an outsider whose 1970s growth was largely petroleum-fed. Its mining and forestry development limped despite foreign investment. It has had little industrial development because of highly restrictive domestic policies. Domestic entrepreneurs were at first not eligible for investment incentives, and, even now, domestic Chinese entrepreneurs have to remit funds abroad and then use them as 'foreign' funds to be eligible for investment benefits. Among the East Asian countries Indonesia has the strongest ideological commitment to a Prebisch view of the world, a distrust of markets, and hence a belief in the efficacy of the model II approach to DFI. Indonesia and the Philippines remain outside the East Asian mainstream in that most of their foreign investment is in import-substituting rather than export-oriented activities.

Table 3.3. Major dates of changes in policies relating to DFI

Country	Restriction on foreign ownership		Tax incentives		Export covenants required		Special import protection	
	Imposed	Relaxed	Granted	Withdrawn	Imposed	Relaxed	Granted	Eased
Hong Kong	(With no controls on international financial movements, foreign ownership or output of enterprises[a], Hong Kong's foreign investment policies differ from those in almost all other developing countries.)							
Indonesia	1974[b]	-	1974	1984	-	-	1968	-
Korea	1960	1984[a]	1960	-	1973	1984	1960[c]	...
Malaysia	1975	1984	1967	-	1967	-	1963	...
Philippines	1968	-	1970	-	1967	-	1946	-
Singapore	-	-	1967	-	1967	-	1963	1967
Taiwan	1954	...[c]	1954	-	1954	-	1954	...
Thailand	1960	-	1962	-	1962	-	1960	-

Caution: This tabulation is derived from a wide variety of sources (UN and IMF documents, national legislation, US Government reports, academic reviews, newspaper reports, and interviews with government officials). Some of the dates recorded for the imposition, granting, relaxation, or withdrawal of the individual programmes are highly judgmental choices as the dates of the most important in a series of changes. Hence, the observations here should be used with caution.

- Indicates that there was no adoption of a particular programme or no important change in one.

... Indicates that it is almost impossible to identify a date of change.

a There are environmental and health, etc, controls on investment.

b Foreign-owned petroleum companies are subject to a regime different from that applying to all other companies (in general they receive more favourable treatment). This survey applies only to non-petroleum companies.

c There were a few relaxations in 1983, but they were very limited. However, they indicate a possible move to a more relaxed regime.

DFI in services in East Asia, in banking, insurance, advertising, marketing, transportation and tourism grew with manufacturing, often in direct association. Service activities become increasingly important as an economy modernises. They are often technology-intensive, subject to very large economies of scale and important to a country's ability to manage its economy. Banking is the most important example. But service industries also have important social and political aspects. Newspapers, radio and television owners form public opinion; foreign investment in these industries has therefore been tightly controlled in most countries. Foreign investment in services in East Asia has been opened up more slowly than in manufacturing, with a strong leaning to model II. Hong Kong has been the exception, and Singapore again changed its policies almost overnight when it decided to become a financial centre. Foreign banks play an important role in Thailand and Indonesia; Table 3.2 is simply wrong in this respect.

East Asian foreign investment legislation is broad enough to have allowed shifts in emphasis through changes in administrative postures. A review of changes in legislation (Table 3.3) thus does not convey the shifts from model II to model III. One of the favourable aspects of DFI in East Asia is its geographic diversity, as shown in Table 3.4 although the table must be used with great caution.

Costs and Benefits

The foreign investment debate owes much of its vigour to the difficulties of isolating the effects of such investment from other trends in the economy. It is also difficult to disentangle the factors that determine the behaviour of transnational firms from the firms' inherent behaviour. However, the principal issues of concern can be identified and analysed in the light of accumulated evidence as it applies to this region.

Servicing DFI. DFI has to be paid for. In principle, its costs are no different from other capital service costs. However, whereas the interest on loans from financial markets has to be met (even if the amortisation can be postponed) whether the ventures for which the loans are used are profitable or not, dividends on equity only have to be paid if a venture is profitable. A tnc that makes a bad investment is much more likely to receive no profit and even lose its capital. This is certainly the case in an open economy such as Hong Kong's and for export-oriented industries. Private direct investment is therefore self-correcting.

The balance-of-payments effects of DFI, unlike most other

Table 3.4. Percentage of total value of stock of direct investment in East Asia by country of origin

Country of Origin	Country of Destination													
	Hong Kong		Indonesia		Korea		Malaysia		Philippines		Singapore		Thailand	
	1971	1978	1972	1978	1971	1978	1971	1977	1972	1977	1972	1978	1972	1978
North America	53.5	46.7	20.3	6.2	38.7	19.3	16.9	19.4	60.0	36.3	33.0	32.9	13.8	13.9
Western Europe	16.2	20.0	13.7	8.9	8.6	12.6	23.4	17.8	6.3	8.6	38.7	31.6	11.5	14.2
Japan	22.4	18.6	22.9	35.8	43.3	58.1	11.5	23.4	1.3	23.5	6.0	15.3	37.5	36.9
Oceania	4.1	4.1	3.8	2.7	-	-	2.0	2.7	-	4.1	-	-	-	-
India	-	-	0.4	0.2			0.4	1.0	0.3	0.4	-	-	1.0	1.5
Hong Kong	-	-	9.0	11.4	0.2	0.9	9.1	10.4	-	1.4	5.7	5.6	1.4	5.1
Indonesia	-	-			-	-	0.2	0.1			-	-	1.0	1.5
Korea	-	-	2.3	1.0			28.6	22.1	-	3.0	-	-	-	-
Malaysia	-	-	1.2	0.5	-	-			-	-	3.5	3.5	3.6	2.6
Philippines	0.3	0.5	8.4	4.1	-	-	-	0.1			-	-	-	-
Singapore	1.1	2.9	2.8	1.4	-	-	28.6	22.1	-	0.2			-	1.3
Thailand	0.3	2.7	0.2	0.2	-	-	0.1	0.1		0.1	-	-		
Other	1.3	1.2	0.5	1.6	0.2	0.1	0.8	0.3	6.6	6.4	-	-	15.7	12.8
Total $m.	133	434	3,225	6,555	115	1,004	137	433	116	976	665	1,773	123	188

Source: UNCTC, Salient Features, Table 24, p.65.

forms of financing, also tend to be cyclically compensatory rather than cyclically stable. Moreover, there is limited pressure on the balance of payments until investments are well established. In the 1970s when commercial rates were lower, profit remittances by transnational firms in Korea amounted to approximately 6% of the total amounts invested (including previously reinvested earnings); in the same period, the average interest paid on foreign commercial credits was slightly over 8%(4).

In contrast to bank loans (particularly of short duration), equity investment usually does not lead to sudden withdrawals of foreign funds because direct investment funds are tied up in buildings and materials and so are highly illiquid. The exceptions are 'footloose' industries that move from country to country to take advantage of 'give-away' incentives.

One qualification often made to the argument about balance-of-payment effects is that some, at least, of the returns on foreign investment are 'hidden' via transfer pricing. In East Asian countries, however, transfer pricing has never been the issue that it has been in other developing countries, and concern appears to have died down. The principal exception has occurred in the Philippines where the overvaluation of the exchange rate led to capital flight. Moreover, even there, domestic firms seem to have been more involved in transfer pricing than transnationals.

As an economy matures, it should not only be a 'host' for foreign investment, but also a 'home'. As countries develop, comparative advantage shifts from factoral endowments to management capability. Such trends have already become evident in East Asia. The initiatives taken by overseas Chinese (and to a lesser degree Indian) communities to form regional businesses are well known, but national indigenous firms are also moving in this direction, for example in construction, financial services and technical consulting. The balance of payments is thus beginning to reflect inflows as well as outflows of capital and technology service payments.

Ownership, Control and Sovereignty. Much of the concern with tncs arises from fears of the loss of sovereignty. It is argued that the foreign ownership of enterprises leads to the undermining or distortion of national economic, political and social objectives. Several East Asian countries have recognised that many of the characteristics of emerging industrial societies often associated with tncs do not result from their activities as such, but from the incentives which face both foreign and domestic producers. For example, Taiwan and Korea decided that, in the early stages of development, transportation was more efficiently provided by buses, trains and bicycles than by motor cars. There was considerable investment in public transport and the international firms that dominate motor car production were adamantly refused protection. This was in marked contrast to Indonesia, Malaysia, the Philippines and Thailand where protection was given on a scale that encouraged excessive entry into the industry. Private motor cars have accordingly turned Manila, Jakarta, Bangkok and Kuala Lumpur into traffic nightmares, at high cost to the community, to justify the entry of foreign firms. If national policies are focused on the production of low-cost mass consumption goods for the domestic market and on exports, particularly in the early stages of development, national values are not affected negatively(5).

In technology-intensive industries, and those where economies of scale are important, transnational firms often exhibit a competitive advantage in East Asian countries. Defensive investment at an early stage to prevent competitors gaining a share of sales has occurred where the host countries have provided protection. In addition to motor vehicles this has happened in durable consumer goods in the Philippines, Malaysia and Thailand, and is about to occur in Indonesia. In each case high protection was granted to such firms on employment grounds; the losses of employment in exports resulting from such protection were not counted. Protection was particularly easy to attain when joint ventures allied foreign firms with local entrepreneurs who had political access to government officials.

The argument for limiting the share of foreign ownership to less than 50% in enterprises (unless they are wholly or predominantly engaged in export) has been argued strongly in all countries except Hong Kong. The usual arguments were put forward: by acquiring a share in ownership, domestic investors would attain entrepreneurship and experience in, and access to, new technology and management in foreign markets; domestic control or at least influence would be obtained over business decisions; more of the profits of the enterprise would accrue domestically than if the firm were to be a wholly-owned foreign subsidiary. An additional reason in Malaysia and Indonesia was to engage the indigenous population in business and thus to 'catch up' with the Chinese community. Many European and Japanese tncs, moreover, like the political protection of joint ventures. Some joint ventures achieved their objectives. But there were also many problems. There were many 'Ali Baba' firms in which the local partners did not carry their weight. Some efficient foreign firms were discouraged. Domestic entrepreneurs were given an easy option instead of being forced into competition with foreign firms and thus into the creation of potential new transnationals. The political combination of a strong tnc with powerful local entrepreneurs in resource-rich industries, or in a protectionist environment, turned some of the joint ventures into the most rapacious exploiters of monopolistic rents in the community. Wholly-owned subsidiaries of foreign firms were usually much easier to control than joint ventures.

It is thus not merely for market-oriented reasons, but from a sophisticated understanding of ownership and control issues, that Hong Kong from the outset, and Singapore since 1965, adopted very open policies towards foreign ownership. They relied on competitive forces to ensure that the transnationals' behaviour would be in the national interest; government intervention has rarely been necessary. Such an approach is essential for countries wishing to become international financial centres or even to have important financial markets. Both Taiwan and Korea are accordingly now opening investment to 100% foreign ownership, in order to stay in the forefront of economic growth.

Best Practice, Appropriate Technology and Capital Utilisation. East Asian experience suggests that foreign firms are often excessively oriented toward best practice and capital-intensive technology, neglecting the creation of employment. But they can follow such practices only if high protection makes them possible, and cannot do so in unprotected domestically-oriented or export industries. The high costs of capital-intensive techniques are often exacerbated by low capital utilisation that further limits employment and raises costs.

Where the East Asian countries' policies have stressed competitiveness, labour-intensive production techniques have been followed. Total factors of production are better utilised, though in specific industries, because of greater labour intensity, capital utilisation may be lower than in countries that have poorer choices of technique. For example, Malaysian manufacturing is less capital-intensive than Philippine manufacturing, and has somewhat lower capital utilisation as a result. Protected industries tend to be more capital-intensive than competitive ones in countries such as Thailand and Malaysia. However, domestic and foreign-owned firms behave similarly in these respects(6). 'Economic' and 'engineering' men select products and technologies in domestic as in foreign firms, and must be given appropriate policy signals to ensure social as well as private profitability.

Training Local Staff. The transfer of technology is only possible with an ample supply of technically trained and experienced people, and the training of local staff at all levels is accordingly an important aspect of DFI for host governments. However, attempts to monitor the training of domestic staff, and to limit the number of foreign staff that may be employed, have not been successful. Foreign firms have often been accused of 'dumping' incompetent staff in East Asian countries; the firms have claimed in return that training takes time and undue speed in replacing expatriates reduces efficiency and adaptive capacity.

This is a poorly researched and accordingly muddy area. Quantitative assessments are not possible, and qualitative evaluations are of limited use. Transnational corporations sometimes pass on 'technology' effectively and sometimes do not. However, there are some general considerations. The cost of expatriates is high to a firm, and competitive conditions that require efficiency reduce the numbers of costly expatriate staff(7). The supply of domestic skill and hence national education policy is an extremely important determinant of training and the replacement of expatriates. They swamp the effects of training regulations and attempts to limit the number of expatriates.

A related fear is that foreign firms have crowded out domestic firms in obtaining scarce skills (and capital). They were said, in the 1950s and 1960s especially, to be able to bid for skilled workers, technicians and managers by offering them higher remuneration and better working conditions than domestic firms. These complaints have largely died out, as the shortages of skilled people were reduced. The improvement has been most notable in the countries with good education systems, and where emigration of skilled people has not been unduly high, as it has been in the Philippines.

'Unbundling' the DFI Package. Unbundling the DFI package has been particularly favoured in mining and other resource-intensive industries, contributing to the build-up of debt in Indonesia and the Philippines in the 1970s. These countries have turned to turnkey operations supported by technical, licensing, and management arrangements that provided continuing access to new technology in combination with bank loans. There are many variants on this theme, but they all tend to lead to management problems and high debt-service costs. 'Unbundling' has the longest history in Korea which has favoured such an approach in protected import-substituting industries to minimise monopolistic profits for foreign firms and to ensure control by local entrepreneurs. There have not been any detailed studies of the results. The evidence is largely anecdotal, but it suggests that 'unbundling' leads to new costs as well as new benefits. Korea has therefore decided to let the market be the most important determinant in the forms that foreign investment takes.

Cost and Benefits of DFI. To summarise, tncs are profit-maximising enterprises, and they will seek to earn the highest profits they can in developing as in industrial countries. Whether they earn 'normal' profits in competitive situations or the super profits and rents created by monopolistic conditions will depend on the government policies of the host country (and to some extent on the policies of their home country). If policies create monopoly conditions, then social and private returns will diverge, and DFI is likely to be costly. Where such conditions have been created in East Asia, countries such as Korea, Taiwan, Malaysia and Thailand have to varying degrees restricted foreign investment, retreating to the restrictive aspects of model II. However, as economic policies are liberalised, there is a general trend to a more open approach to foreign investment.

Economic Policies and DFI

All studies of DFI conclude that social and political stability combined with rapid and equitable economic growth is necessary for DFI to thrive and provide high returns to the host country. DFI has brought greater returns to the East Asian than to other developing countries principally because conditions in most of the countries of that region have more closely approximated to these favourable general development conditions than in other developing countries.

Financial Policies. Monetary stability is one key factor; East Asian countries have generally kept domestic inflation below world inflation. Financial policies are not only key to this monetary stability (and also to sustained growth) but directly affect the volume and characteristics of the DFI a country can attract. A combination of conservative monetary policies that discourage inflationary trends combined with market-oriented financial policies such as those of Hong Kong, Singapore and Malaysia, and to a more limited degree those of Taiwan and Thailand, make day-to-day business operations attractive. Financial repression, in contrast, not only discourages overall growth(8), but specifically impedes DFI because the depression of interest rates below their market level necessitates non-interest rationing of financial institutions' credit. This can have several effects on foreign investment.

Financial institutions may be prohibited from lending to foreign-owned or controlled enterprises, so that foreign enterprises are denied access to short-term credit which they would normally expect to be able to use in any economy where their cash receipts and payments are not synchronous. They must rely instead on home-country credits to cover cash discrepancies in host countries. Short-run exchange-rate movements are likely to be more volatile and less related to basic cost differentials than longer-run movements. The denial of access to domestic credits to cover short-run cash discrepancies will increase uncertainty and discourage investment. Corporations choosing an investment venue among several alternative countries will tend to move to countries where there is no credit discrimination against them.

At the other extreme, a foreign borrower may be regarded as a superior credit risk by bankers. As a tnc's obligations are considered to be guaranteed by an international company, its credit status will be higher than that of almost any national company, so that 'crowding out' will occur. Further, with local borrowing at relatively low interest rates, foreign enterprises will attempt to maximise their local borrowings as they are likely to be cheaper than borrowings in their home country. Hence, financial repression may lead to a diversion of host-country financing to foreign enterprises. 'Crowding out' then does take place, but it does not result from foreign investment but from inappropriate domestic financial policies. In East Asia, 'crowding out' has taken place in Indonesia and the Philippines where liberal policies toward DFI have been combined with financial repression. In Taiwan in the 1950s, in Indonesia till recently and in Korea to date, financial repression necessitated tight controls on DFI to avoid the 'crowding out' of local firms. Taiwan liberalised its financial policies in the 1960s, but Korea and Indonesia have taken much longer, and in some respects are still in the process of liberalising.

With a short-run outlook, foreign enterprises may be attracted by the monopolistic gains accruing to them in a repressed financial system. Yet, with a limited supply of credit resulting from financial repression and a channelling of a large part of it to foreign enterprises, the rest of the economy is deprived of organised credit and must resort to high-cost unorganised markets. Consequently, what foreign enterprises may gain on the roundabouts of preferred borrowing opportunities is likely to be offset on the swings of the consequent high costs of domestic supplies. A combination of financial repression and monetary accommodation leads to additional inefficiencies in domestic production. This becomes a critical problem for exporters.

In choosing among countries, foreign investors search for those that are economically efficient and have a capacity for sustained growth. After the experiences of the early 1980s when many developing countries became severely depressed, these searches are likely to become more rigorous. A country in which 'the overall' conditions are 'right' will be preferred to one with suspiciously low interest rates.

<u>Fiscal Policies</u>. Transnational corporations are both users of and contributors to the fiscal system: in a well organised economy their contribution, while no greater than it would be in other countries in terms of their income, should be greater than the cost of providing the infrastructure they use. It is important too, for both equity and revenue reasons that foreign firms are not the only ones taxed.

Low uniform income tax rates rising from 12.5% in the 1950s to 17.5% in recent times, with no tax on foreign activities, and low property taxes provide the bulk of revenue for Hong Kong. It has been able to maintain its tax policy because it has no backward hinterland, is growing rapidly, has been highly efficient in providing infrastructural facilities including housing, has relied on private services where they can be efficient, and has not had parliamentary, foreign service and similar expenditures. The other East Asian countries have more conventional tax structures embracing complex arrays of income and production and sales taxes. All have double taxation agreements with the principal countries providing DFI and these vary considerably. At one extreme Japan tends to be very generous in allowing tax offsets. At the other extreme, US corporations do not benefit if host-country taxes are lower than US tax levels. In general, however, tncs take a rather broad view of taxation conditions when they decide to invest or reinvest in a country, provided that tax rates are within limits generally imposed in industrial countries, and provided taxes are collected fairly and efficiently.

When choosing among possible host countries foreign investors compare both the cost of taxation and the infrastructure available. 'Infrastructure' in this context has to be defined very broadly. It includes not only roads, railways, water supplies, power, sewerage, and so on, but broader facilities such as an equitable and predictable legal system that determines disputes expeditiously, an educational system that is designed to meet the needs of production as well as of more basic cultural values, and an administrative structure that makes decisions with regard to foreign investment promptly and predictably.

The high quality and low cost of infrastructural facilities have been attractive to foreign investors in the three North East Asian countries, Singapore and Malaysia. In the three North East Asian countries and in Singapore, emphasis was placed on effective, cost-efficient education from primary to tertiary levels. In Hong Kong and Singapore for example, school buildings were used for two shifts during the day, with a third evening shift often running for adult classes. Basic health services and housing have been provided by private (Korea, Taiwan and Malaysia) or public (Hong Kong and Singapore) investment. In Hong Kong and Singapore in particular, foreign investors need have little contact with government officials and both have effective 'one stop shops' that make such contact quick and easy. Communications, transportation, power and ports also work efficiently. These reasons have made Hong Kong and Singapore very attractive to foreign investors, overcoming Hong Kong's problems of political insecurity and lack of natural resources and home markets, and the high relative wages of both countries.

Trade Policies. Trade policies are central to determining both the attractiveness of a country for DFI and the relationship of the host country's social gains to the social costs of DFI and the private gains accruing to investing transnational corporations. Protectionist policies raise costs of production and hence prices, and usually also create monopoly profits for investing firms. If attempts are made to offset monopoly conditions by encouraging internal competition, they may fragment production, raising costs even further above international levels. Protectionist countries may attract foreign firms for a time, until the first generation of import-substituting possibilities are exhausted, but countries with high protection cannot attract foreign investment for export industries.

The speed and success with which Korea and Taiwan switched from import substitution to export-led growth has created some policy illusions. Thus it is often argued on the basis of these countries' experience that import substitution is a necessary first stage for industrial development in countries with a 'hinterland'. There is no evidence of this in East Asia. Some manufacturers began to export in the 1950s in Korea and Taiwan, but their efforts were undermined by protectionist policies; food-processing and textile exports are examples. It is also argued that protection for the domestic market can be offset relatively simply by providing incentives for exporters. This is not so. Even though Korea and Taiwan turned to exports before protection became either pervasive or high, and although both had relatively well educated and experienced administrators able to devise an effective export incentive system, the introduction of export incentives was fraught with difficulties, the costs were high, and attracting foreign investors was difficult despite the advantages of low labour and other costs.

Industrial Policy. Most developing countries have considerable regulatory mechanisms that seek to stimulate 'essential', 'pioneer', or otherwise desirable industries while discouraging other less desirable ones by controls over entry. In marked contrast to the other East Asian countries,

Hong Kong has avoided such a regulatory approach, simply laying down environmental and health standards that all enterprises must obey; it has provided public assistance only to very small enterprises, and that on a small scale in the early years of acute building shortages. In Singapore complex entry regulations were simplified after 1965. All the other countries have had very considerable bureaucracies, however, and where protection and offsetting export incentives existed, the regulatory system grew, in part to avoid monopoly rents. It not only failed to achieve this but usually contributed to creating a high-cost and inefficient manufacturing and modern service sector. Despite attempts to use evaluation methods based on 'points' systems and later on more sophisticated cost-benefit methodologies to 'pick the winners', examinations of foreign firms' production plans with actual outcomes show wide discrepancies.

Cost-benefit evaluation of industrial investment plans has only been worthwhile where major private investments necessitated large public infrastructural expenditures, generally in relation to resource exploitation, or where large economies of scale were an issue, limiting entry to one producer. In such cases high-level bargaining was necessary between the host government and foreign investors. Where the former was well prepared (as the investors usually were), negotiations led to success; where this has not been the case, the social returns to the host country have not always been adequate.

Manpower Policy. Developing countries wish to improve living standards as quickly as possible by increasing employment opportunities and raising wages. Some have done so remarkably successfully. Except in the Philippines, real wages and family incomes have risen dramatically in East Asia, more than in other developing countries(9). In Indonesia, oil revenues played an important role, but in the other countries wage rises followed an initial focus on low-wage and labour-intensive industries. Their policies were widely regarded as exploitative at the time. They did not meet the International Labour Organisation's standards (designed for industrial countries). But where wages and fringe benefits were kept at labour productivity levels, so that labour costs were competitive in international terms, and combined with capital and technology in a competitive environment, employment grew rapidly as already indicated. In Singapore, real wages were lowered in the mid-1960s to increase employment, particularly of young inexperienced workers. Employment, skills, fringe benefits and family incomes rose. The informal sector was encouraged to provide subcontracting for larger firms, to extend low-quality but very low-cost manufacturing to rural areas, and to provide services throughout the economy, leading to another source of family income growth. As wages rose so did skills and capital intensity so that productivity growth enabled private and social profitability to be maintained.

The Role of Incentives

In the early 1950s, when transnational corporations considered most developing countries too risky for investment, the International Chamber of Commerce suggested that countries wishing to attract DFI should provide two types of special incentives: guarantees against political or 'sovereign' risk and measures that would increase profitability, particularly in the early years. To make the incentive systems equitable (and to avoid capital flight and re-entry), domestic investors had to be granted the same privileges. Out of these simple ideas, immensely complex bureaucratic systems of incentives have evolved in almost all developing countries. Guarantees of good intent are necessary, though not sufficient, to attract foreign investment. It has, however, been known for some time that give-away incentives such as tax holidays are not effective in attracting DFI and yet are costly, particularly when developing countries compete against each other(10). East Asian experience has underlined these conclusions.

Political Guarantees. After independence, many developing countries nationalised natural monopolies and resource-related foreign investment, particularly where foreign investors had appropriated high rents during colonial times. Balance-of-payments difficulties in the 1950s led to difficulties in repatriating profits and capital. Many countries rushed to attract DFI on favourable terms, and foreign investment codes that guaranteed against nationalisation without compensation and repatriation of profits and capital on reasonable terms began to flourish. Many countries went further and guaranteed foreign firms the same treatment as local investors. Such guarantees have become a standard indication that a country welcomes foreign investment.

Tax Holidays. The Chamber of Commerce suggested that foreign investors be offered tax holidays for periods of 5 to 7 years, sometimes extended to 10 years, with losses usually carried forward for such periods. To make such concessions worthwhile, accelerated depreciation often accompanied tax holidays. Most tax holidays were tied to the amounts of capital invested, thus adding to the encouragement of capital intensity rather than appropriate technology, already endemic in repressed financial systems and protection regimes. Malaysia broke away from this practice by tying the length of tax holidays to employment in the early 1970s, but it remained unique.

Tax holidays, in any case, did little to encourage foreign investment. Where good reasons for investment existed in the form of natural resources, protected markets, or a competitive basis for exports, transnational firms invested, and took the tax holiday if their home government permitted them to do so as an extra bonus. The US Government in any case did not allow such 'tax sparing' since the Treasury considers tax holidays to be against the interests of developing countries because they lead to 'beggar my neighbour' competition. The other principal home countries - Japan, the European countries and Australia - practise 'tax sparing' to encourage their firms to invest abroad.

It was well established by the end of the 1960s that as more and more countries introduced tax holidays, they became of less and less value. Where profits were large in the early years of a firm's activity, tax holidays were unnecessary, and where there were no profits, they were worthless. Singapore cut back on tax holidays after a few years' experience, confining them largely to export-oriented activities.

<u>Industrial and Free Trade Zones</u>. British industrial estates concepts were replicated in Hong Kong, Malaysia and Singapore in the 1950s by the colonial administrations. Free trade zones, on the other hand, took US experience in Panama as the model, but the zones also received stimulus from Japanese firms' desire for a clearly structured environment. In the early 1960s, the ability to provide such zones with Japanese-speaking staff were important in Taiwan and Korea, but by the early 1970s, when a free trade zone was organised near Penang in Malaysia to attract electronic assembly firms, Japanese language facilities were no longer required.

Free trade zones have not spread widely in East Asian countries. Hong Kong and Singapore of course did not need special customs facilities, and ample serviced land was made available for foreign as well as for local investors in close proximity to housing areas to reduce the private and social costs of workers' transportation. In some instances space for light industries was provided within housing complexes. Deepening and widening of the transnationals' production and service activities was encouraged. Each city was essentially an efficient free trade zone. Free trade zones are useful in countries with complex protectionist regimes that cannot be overcome through administrative channels. Such conditions were important in Korea and Taiwan in the mid-1960s, and they are now relevant for the Philippines and Indonesia. But 'zones' are a poor 'second best' to a competitive environment for they are not as effective as open locations for the integration of foreign firms' production into the local economy.

Outlook for the Future

Despite the debt problems of some developing countries in the early 1980s the net flow of private capital to rapidly growing countries can be expected to continue to rise, with an increase in welfare not only for the developing countries but for the world as a whole. The robustness of international capital markets, in the face of the difficulties of the early 1980s, suggests that the institutional mechanisms are adequate for a continuation of flows of private capital from countries where it is relatively plentiful, so that its private and social marginal products are relatively low, to countries where capital is relatively scarce, so that both private and social marginal products are relatively high. However, the excessive borrowing by some countries in the mid-1970s and their subsequent difficulties in the early 1980s, are likely to make some developing country borrowers and banks cautious into the 1990s and total private flows to developing countries are likely to be less buoyant in the 1980s than they were in the 1970s. Nevertheless, soundly structured and rapidly growing developing countries in East Asia are likely to be able to continue to borrow as much as they consider prudent, as they have in the past.

DFI is not a pre-requisite to development (Japan's industrialisation utilised little), but East Asian experience suggests that for countries seeking to compress industrialisation and the accompanying transformation of poor and predominantly agricultural economies into wealthy modern states in a mere generation, DFI can complement and stimulate domestic investment. DFI may be expected to grow somewhat faster than it did in the 1970s for several reasons. Relatively high real interest rates are expected to persist for some time, making direct investment relatively attractive. Acquiring advanced technology will become even more important to the NICs than it has been in the past, and the near-NICs will not be far behind. The competition among transnationals from industrial countries is growing, with new firms becoming interested in international activities. The developing country transnationals themselves are growing. The advantage of servicing direct rather than indirect capital flows is understood in East Asia. Finally, the role of foreign investment in Hong Kong's and Singapore's development is encouraging countries that did not previously have liberal attitudes to open their doors to DFI more widely than they have done in the past, relying on their overall economic policies to ensure that it contributes to high rates of growth and equitable development.

NOTES AND REFERENCES

1. Defined here as Hong Kong, the Republic of Korea, Taiwan and the five original members of the Association of South East Asian Nations (ASEAN), namely Indonesia, Malaysia, Philippines, Singapore and Thailand. Hong Kong, Korea, Singapore and Taiwan are often referred to as 'semi-industrial' or 'newly industrialising countries' (NICs), while the other ASEAN countries are viewed as 'second generation' or near-NICs.

2. World Bank, World Debt Tables 1984 (Washington DC, 1984).

3. Paul Luey, 'Hong Kong Investment', in Helen Hughes and You Poh Seng, Foreign Investment in Singapore (Australian National University Press, Canberra 1969). See also G. Shantakumar, 'Human Resource Development in Singapore' in You Poh Seng and Lim Chong Yah, Singapore: Twenty-five Years of Development (Nan Yang Xing Zhov Lianhe Zaobao, Singapore 1984), pp.166ff.

4. Bohn-Young Koo, Role of Foreign Direct Investment in Recent Korean Economic Growth (Korean Development Institute, Working Paper 8104, 1982). (Revised in 1984.) Bohn-Young Koo includes two measures of the cost of foreign investment. The one quoted here excludes royalties, etc., paid by foreign companies. If royalties are included, the payments by foreign companies rise to slightly more than 9%. However, it is assumed that, if the same technology had been used by Korean owned companies, the same royalties would have been paid and hence only the profit remittances are appropriate for this comparison. In a country like Korea, where income and similar company taxes are lower than in such countries as Japan and the United States (the major sources of foreign investment in Korea), there is little incentive to inflate royalty and similar payments so that domestic taxes may be reduced and home country taxes increased.

5. Among the considerable attention paid to the national characteristics of tncs, Kioshi Kojima has analysed Japanese firms (in Direct Foreign Investment, A Japanese Model of Multinational Business Operations, Croom Helm, London, 1978) and Raymond Vernon has written extensively on US firms (notably in Sovereignty at Bay: The Multinational Spread of U.S. Enterprises, Basic Books, New York, 1971). However, Isaiah Frank's study of 90 tncs from 11 industrial countries found no systematic behavioural differences among them. (See Isaiah Frank, Foreign Enterprise in Developing Countries, Johns Hopkins University Press, Baltimore and London, 1980).

6. See R.M. Bautista, H. Hughes, D. Lim, D. Morawetz and F.L. Thoumi, Capital Utilization in Developing Countries: A Case Study of Colombia, Israel, Malaysia, and Philippines (Oxford University Press, Oxford, 1982).

7. Price Waterhouse, 'Expatriate Survey', Jakarta, Indonesia, December 1983, surveyed 154 firms. The average cost of a senior manager was $91,000 in addition to salary and allowances but it is not clear to what extent housing, car allowances etc. were matched for domestic executives.

8. See R.I. McKinnon, Money and Capital in Economic Development (Brookings, Washington DC, 1973).

9. For example in Taiwan real wages in manufacturing rose by nearly 11% per year from 1969 to 1978 (S.W.Y. Kuo, G. Ranis and J.C.H. Fei, The Taiwan Success Story, Rapid Growth with Improved Income Distribution in the Republic of China, 1952-79, Westview Press, Boulder, Colorado, 1981, p.20); in Korea real average annual wages in manufacturing rose by 12% per year from 1967 to 1973 (Wontack Hong, 'Export Promotion and Employment Growth in South Korea', in A.D. Krueger, H.B. Lavy, T. Monson and N. Akrasanee, Trade and Employment in Developing Countries, University of Chicago Press, Chicago, 1981).

10. United Nations, Foreign Investment in Developing Countries, (New York, 1968), p.21 concluded in 1968, that is more than 15 years ago, that 'such empirical enquiries as have been made to elucidate the actual inducement effect and overall operation of various schemes confirm the expectation that, while prohibitive and discriminatory taxes may effectively impede otherwise worthwhile investments, temporary exemptions from normal tax burdens are unlikely by themselves to constitute a determining factor in many investment decisions'.

Chapter Four

DIRECT FOREIGN INVESTMENT AND MANUFACTURING FOR EXPORT IN DEVELOPING COUNTRIES: A REVIEW OF THE ISSUES

G.K. Helleiner*

The precarious condition of the global financial system has generated a wide range of suggestions for reform, and continuing advocacy of 'adjustment' for the developing countries. Among the most consistent instruments suggested for achieving the twin objectives of more stable development finance and structural adjustment in production is a quite traditional one: direct foreign investment (DFI). Too much reliance was placed upon debt finance in the 1970s, particularly short-term debt, the argument runs, a form that has proved highly unpredictable both in its servicing obligations and in its gross flow to the developing countries; its future is now very much in doubt, except for those few creditworthy countries who 'underborrowed' in the past (e.g. India, Malaysia), as commercial banks attempt to restructure their portfolios in response to the adverse experience of the post-1981 period. At the same time, the urgently needed key inputs of management and marketing skills, technology, and know-how in 'non-traditional' tradeable goods and services sectors - into which the balance-of-payments pressures of recent years are driving the developing countries - seem most readily available in the familiar and traditional 'packaged' form of direct foreign investment, however desirable it might be to 'shop around' for individual components in less desperate times. Efficiency considerations have led most analysts to place greater emphasis upon 'non-traditional' exporting - notably from the manufacturing sector - than upon new areas of import substitution.

To the longstanding advice to improve incentives for export-oriented manufacturing have now been added widespread calls for the relaxation of screening procedures, and the provision of fresh incentives for foreign investors in developing countries. The more internationalist of recent commentators recommend strengthened efforts to complete the UN's code of conduct for transnational corporations to ensure a more stable and balanced policy regime within which investors and governments can confidently encourage increased investment flows. According to the latest UN survey of transnationals and world development there has already been some relaxation in host country policies on DFI (1).

Questions must nevertheless be asked about the efficacy of the suggested new reliance upon DFI. By now there has been enough experience with this form of international economic interaction for it to be possible to anticipate some of the problems that will arise if there is to be a significant policy shift back to it. Particularly relevant, when every developing country is at the same time being urged to expand its exports, is the experience with export-oriented direct foreign investment.

A major initial constraint upon the use of DFI, analogous to that for other commercial sources of finance, is the geographic concentration that has always characterised it. Eleven NICs received more than half the total OECD direct investment flows to developing countries in recent years. Low-income countries (as defined by the OECD) received only 4% of the 1981 flow of OECD direct investment to developing countries and accounted for 7% of the end-1981 stock. (Foreign investment may nevertheless account for a significant share of a small or poor country's total external resource inflow.)

What is clear is that investment and trade policies must be considered together as 'co-determinants of the location of production and pattern of trade'.(2) Where there are scale economies, learning effects, other countries' trade barriers, investment incentives and trade-related performance requirements, and where oligopolistic transnational firms are key decision-makers, it would be foolhardy for a developing country to proceed with policy on the basis of traditional models of pure competition, perfect markets, and comparative advantage. On the other hand, the state of the policy art in these real world circumstances is still distressingly weak.

Alternative Approaches to Analysis of DFI Policies

Much of the new international emphasis upon DFI flows from disaffection with and gloomy forecasts of commercial bank lending as a source of external capital for developing countries. DFI is thus seen primarily, although usually not exclusively, in terms of its role as a source of international capital. But is this new foreign investment to provide additional capital? It could be extremely helpful if some of the current debt obligations could be converted to equity. The discussion is usually focused, however, upon the prospect of new inflows of capital and it is not always clear how the expansion of transnational corporate investments that is so widely recommended is to be financed.

Some may be financed from the firms' own earnings, although significant expansion would seem to be predicated upon substantially increased earnings (above previous 'normal', non-recession, rates) which do not at present seem to be in prospect. The bulk of any expansion would presumably have to be financed through new issues of equity or debt. An OECD-sponsored survey of 68 projects in which new capital was raised by direct foreign investors in the pre-banking-boom period found that almost half of the new capital was made up of debt rather than equity issues. Over half of the debt capital (54%) and 40% of the equity was raised in the developing countries themselves (3). By no means all of any expansion in DFI would therefore constitute net additions to local savings. Some governments inhibit and others encourage resort to local finance on the part of foreign enterprises; local equity is usually favoured relative to local debt.

Transnational corporations have nevertheless traditionally played an important intermediation role in international capital markets. As far as debt issues are concerned, such intermediation should be seen primarily as a device to keep commercial bank lending to developing countries a little higher and perhaps a little cheaper than it would otherwise be by assigning more of the risks in particular sectors and cases to direct investors and less to banks. There might be a somewhat wider spread of borrowing countries, a somewhat narrower range of activities and, conceivably, sometimes longer terms, notably when bond finance is involved, than was the norm for commercial bank finance in the developing countries in the 1970s. But otherwise little would be changed by redirecting bank flows through transnational corporate intermediaries. A relevant norm for comparison, if short- to medium-term debt finance is seen as a major source of expanded DFI in developing countries, is the cost, country-mix, sector-mix, and maturity of the financial flows that would follow from expanded World Bank or other official intermediation or co-financing activity instead.

New equity and bond issues, to the extent they are taken up in developed countries, rather than in the developing host countries, are a highly desirable means of acquiring expanded external flows to developing countries. Such flows seem to be what most financial commentators who speak of the need for expanded DFI in developing countries in the 1980s and 1990s actually have in mind (4). But how great are the prospects of significantly expanded flows? Are they responsive to governmental policies towards foreign investment in the developing countries? Are DFI and commercial bank borrowing substitutes for one another? What other means may be found for mobilising development capital and/or sharing risks in more acceptable ways than in current commercial bank lending arrangements? What about, for instance, developing the proposals for insuring bank lending to developing countries? (5) What are the relative merits of co-financing of various kinds and direct foreign investment? What can be done to ensure that any new gross inflows of foreign equity or bond finance will not be offset, as so much bank credit to Latin America was in the 1970s, by private speculative outflows?

A quite different strand of the literature relates not to the alternative forms or means of acquiring external finance but, rather, to alternative forms of economic organisation. In this approach, DFI represents an internalised or hierarchical form of trade in goods and services, a form with certain advantages and disadvantages relative to the market alternative (6).

Although the data are imperfect there seems to have been an overall shift away from traditional majority-owned foreign investment towards 'new forms' of investment in developing countries, notably joint ventures and licensing agreements, during the 1960s and 1970s. Most dramatic in the petroleum and metals industries, it was also found in manufacturing, and particularly in manufacturing for host-country markets (import-substituting activities) and in those with mature technologies, although there was considerable inter-country variation in manufacturing sector experience (7). There is also evidence of similar organisational restructuring in export-oriented agriculture (8).

This trend has been less noticeable in manufacturing for export. That direct investment is by no means necessary for successful export-oriented manufacturing is illustrated by the Korean case where the bulk of the exporting has been done by local firms (9). The UNCTC has noted that transnational corporate involvement has been unnecessary and relatively limited in the export of standardised labour-intensive goods; it has been much more important in the export of differentiated products and inputs for them, and, in the Japanese case, in capital-intensive raw material processing (10). In large part the changes towards non-equity forms of foreign investment or involvement were a response to governmental policies in the host countries. To the extent that government policies generated the alternative forms, their 'liberalisation' could be expected to induce some return to the original direct investment mode. To some degree, however, the new forms involved an independent evolution of investment and international business practices relating to risk-sharing, management and financing, and the appearance of smaller internationally-oriented firms, the product of business evolution and decision-making rather than government policies.

A careful consideration of the benefits and costs of alternative forms of interaction with foreign firms, including DFI of the traditional kind, is desirable, whatever the prospects for expanded finance of one kind or another. Some of the advocates of expanded DFI (particularly those in chambers of commerce and business) clearly feel that the DFI form is a superior one, whether for their own self-interested purposes or in the broader interests of social efficiency. More particularly, what they frequently mean to advocate is less governmental restriction of the range of business choice. They imply that easing policies toward DFI - an improved 'investment climate' - will, in fact, increase the flow of external capital. But this link is by no means self-evident. Only when previous prohibitions are removed can there be a reasonable presumption of increased foreign investment, and even that may not involve flows from abroad. Prohibitions have not typically been found in manufacturing activities likely to be competitive in world markets; indeed, in general, restrictions on foreign investors have typically been at their least in manufacturing for export.

The Supply of DFI

The most fundamental issue concerning the proposed new policy orientation towards DFI is its supply elasticity. How much expansion can one sensibly anticipate in response to altered policies, either at the national or at the global level?

The supply schedule for DFI can be expected to look different from industry to industry. One recent study hypothesises that the 'market' for DFI in manufacturing oriented to worldwide export markets is separable from 'markets' for DFI geared to national or regional product markets (11). Equally, individual country characteristics vary greatly with the result that 'price' variations are likely to influence the supply of foreign investment differently from country to country as well. No less important is the stage at which the foreign investor is in his relations with the host country. Responsiveness can be much greater at the point when an investor is still contemplating putting resources into a 'green-field' investment than after he has already made a commitment and is, in some respects, 'trapped' in his elected environment. (In some instances, however, the build-up of local political allies can increase firms' resistance to governmental pressures as time goes on (12)). Thus the supply elasticity of DFI is most usefully considered in terms of the specifics of a particular industry in a particular country at a particular point in time.

Generally, investment incentives have been considered to play a minimal role in foreign investment decision-making. A recent survey of 52 major international corporations based in 12 countries confirmed that the dominant influences on their foreign investment decisions were, overwhelmingly, the need to gain access to local or regional markets and to avoid trade barriers. This was as true of investment in developing countries as elsewhere although 'in the case of LDCs, higher risk and lower-than-expected growth rates were beginning to offset the desire to gain access to new markets' (13).

Most striking in this survey, from the standpoint of current concerns (and the concerns of this chapter), were its findings with respect to a) government policies and b) export prospects. Not a single respondent listed tax advantages in the top three influences upon investments in developing countries. As far as DFI for exporting was concerned, comparative labour costs were mentioned by relatively few firms in the survey (though twice as high a proportion with respect to investments in developing countries as elsewhere) - not at all by firms in high-technology industries, chemicals, food and drink, electrical or pharmaceutical industries, or even some labour-intensive industries - and 'the idea of using LDCs as exporting bases was not attractive to most companies' (p.32).

The survey did not include within its definition of DFI, however, any international subcontracting to independent companies or what the report calls 'direct investment without investment', in which frequently 'the local company has in effect been brought into existence and is kept in being by the international company' (p. 12), and 'the economic and balance-of-payments effects are almost identical to those of DFI' (p. 13). Growing resort to such non-DFI forms may seriously distort interpretations of foreign firms' interest in exporting that are based on questions relating purely to conventional ownership modalities.

One recent World Bank study (14) appears to argue quite differently, however - at least with respect to the industries and countries studied: automobiles, computers, food products and petrochemicals, in ten countries of which 7 were developing (Brazil, India, Indonesia, Kenya, Mexico, Philippines, and Singapore). In two-thirds of the 74 cases studied, host country incentives influenced the choice of country by investors. On close inspection, however, these results are seen to derive from including protectionist instruments - which are often harmful to the host country - within the overall incentives studied. The enormous variety of possible policy instruments (far beyond the tax issues that typically dominate debate) makes it extremely difficult to ascertain what exactly the overall net impact of any individual government's policy is; it also permits a high degree of 'product differentiation' on the part of governments seeking to attract investors.

In the competition for foreign investment, the effectiveness of any individual country's policies clearly depends upon other countries' reactions. These may themselves depend upon the direction of change; increases in incentives are more likely to be followed by competitors than are decreases. Competition among countries offering more or less the same incentives could explain why firms so frequently say that investment incentives do not influence their location decisions; yet if one country alone were to abandon its incentives there would indeed be effects upon the geographic pattern of investments. These results accord with the views of those who have predicted 'investment wars' for the future (15).

Evidence of competition tells one nothing about whether increased incentives will increase the aggregate flow of direct foreign investment to developing countries. It may still be true that 'with better general economic policies and a better entry system, the same amount of investment could be attracted at a lower cost'(16). There would also seem to be scope for joint, or at least co-ordinated, approaches to the provision of incentives. They need not require total uniformity of policies - probably an impossible attainment anyway - but they could provide explicitly for differential incentives, for instance, to offset the disadvantages of the poorest countries.

There must, in any case, continue to be doubt as to how much and what kind of incentive is necessary to induce the desired expansion in net foreign investment at the national level. It would certainly be wrong to consider that all of the investment that benefits from incentive programmes is additional to the investment that would otherwise have occurred. There is bound to be some 'redundancy' in incentive programmes, i.e. investors receive subsidies they do not require in order to invest; the selectivity and discrimination observed in actual programmes undoubtedly reflect governmental attempts to reduce such 'redundancy'. Even so, some of the additional foreign investment apparently successfully induced by selective incentives may simply displace investment by others, both foreign and local (17). There are also differential effects created by different kinds of incentives: product-oriented incentives, factor-oriented incentives, tax incentives of various types, etc. While such incentive arrangements may, in some sense, be aggregated in firms' calculations as to the desirability of alternative locations, they do not all generate the same structure of investments, the same product-mix, or the same technologies, in the incentive-granting country. These issues deserve more careful theoretical and empirical investigation.

Moreover, Radetzki has shown that one can be seriously misled about the response of foreign firms to changing investment regimes and Third World overall market shares if one relies purely upon traditional data sources (18). What at first blush looks like supply response and deteriorating market shares may in fact merely be altered forms of involvement. The great variety of institutional forms of foreign firms' involvement in developing countries' manufacturing for export has always made the interpretation of data on the degree of transnationals' involvement and the role of DFI in this activity very difficult (19).

Alternative Forms of Organisation

According to conventional industrial organisation theory, vertical integration (internalisation) is more efficient than market exchange when the relationship is ongoing, but complex and subject to frequent change. Foreign ownership thus carries certain potential advantages in entering world markets. Apart from foreign firms' ownership of particular technology and management not readily available to local firms, they can bring information about foreign markets, experience and expertise in the many complex facets of international marketing, and influence upon commercial policy-makers and customs authorities in home markets (20). They may also benefit from scale economies associated with their worldwide operations. (In some instances, foreign firms may restrict exports so as to protect the established markets of the parent firm or other subsidiaries; but this is unlikely to be important in cases where 'fresh' DFI is brought in specifically to expand exports.)

The advantages of foreign firms over local ones are obviously most marked in industries where technology is least standardised, scale economies are prevalent, and marketing is most difficult. In such industries, foreign firms have frequently been found to be relatively effective exporters (21), even if their export performance may not be decisively better overall.

DFI of the traditional type, by linking control over investment with a measure of control over international markets, provides some protection to the prospective exporting country against gross miscalculation. Where foreign firms are not directly involved in the profitability of new enterprises they may happily sell equipment or technology, especially if the sales are backed and insured by governments, to more competitors than can eventually be accommodated in world markets. The dispersed and unco-ordinated investment activities of a variety of national firms in developing countries, all competing with one another, may generate excess capacity, worsened terms of trade, and eventually some losers.(22)

Oman has pointed out (23) that 'the long-term global investment planning perspective which multinational firms are relinquishing may be assumed by multinational banks and international financial organisations, at least to the extent that host countries require foreign loans to undertake their investment projects'; but there are limits to their capacities in this regard. Besides, from the standpoint of individual national interest, the object of 'non-traditional' approaches ('new forms') is presumably to get loose from external control over domestic investment decisions, marketing policies, and the like. The substitution of external bankers for external producing firms, as controlling institutions, would seem to constitute rather limited progress toward the goal of greater independence.

The moves towards global industrial organisation and cartelisation outside the transnationals clearly involve major risks for the developing countries. At their worst they may lead to more MFAs, explicitly and unashamedly discriminating against 'low-cost' producers. Nevertheless, there is undoubtedly considerable room for further experimentation and development of non-DFI manufacturing for export. Some firms, notably some Japanese trading companies and recently others based in Hong Kong, already specialise in the assembly of efficient 'packages' of equipment, know-how, management and marketing skills from a variety of sources. As far as DFI is concerned, Third World transnationals may play an expanding role in manufacturing for export not only within the South but also to the North. Some Third World transnationals have developed considerable specialised knowledge of small-scale and labour-intensive production procedures in the manufacture of standardised products (24).

International trading and investment relationships may be formally constrained by international laws, codes and guidelines; but these do not begin to tell the complete story of how these relationships were built or the conventions by which they are maintained. A complex web of law, economics and custom operates to determine the details of particular relationships and contracts. Other things being equal, trust is probably maximised through internalised transactions, i.e. through relationships of ownership or family ties. In large and more Western-oriented firms, where family or traditional modes of interaction are of limited relevance, ownership ties are a prime means of reducing risk and uncertainty, lowering transactions costs, and frequently also deriving economies of scale in information, marketing, sourcing and production systems. As information and management systems become more sophisticated - and computerised - there is likely to be an even higher efficiency premium upon reliability. Tight control systems seeking to reduce the capital tied up inefficiently in inventories, while necessarily incorporating back-up procedures, build upon absolute reliability of delivery and quality. Modern management and information technology may therefore generate increased tendencies for more centralised control and, quite possibly, internalisation and direct investment.

In principle, the country that is host to a subsidiary engaged in exporting may gain both from the increased stability and from the increased income created by the foreign firm via such internalised organisational arrangements. But there is no guarantee that it will. Moreover, other exporting firms and countries may suffer from lower income and increased uncertainty and instability in consequence of one country's 'success' with such approaches.

It is striking that there has not been more independent study of the relative advantages of different forms of investment, different governmental policies and performance requirements, and different general relationships between host countries and foreign firms in particular industries, both for firms of varying characteristics and for various actors in different kinds of host countries. Business schools have addressed some of the issues in terms of firms' interests, but little research has been done on others' interests.

Government Policies

a) Developing (Host) Countries. If exports - and export-oriented investments - are to be expanded, government policies must be directed at the provision of the required incentives. There is a vast literature on incentive structures in developing countries, the bulk of which concludes that they have typically been characterised by an anti-export bias (and frequently also an anti-tradeables bias). Appropriate exchange rates and a fairly uniform tariff structure are the conventionally recommended recipe for maintaining efficiency and external balance, although due account is also to be taken of the possibility of terms of trade gains through targeted restrictions upon trade, learning effects and infant-industry encouragement, and irrational consumer preferences for imported goods and services, all of which are justifications for departures from unified exchange-rate systems (25). There remains some disagreement concerning the significance and the potential for 'learning', and therefore about the appropriate degree and character of infant industry policies (26). Analogous arguments can be deployed in support of the encouragement of infant national firms, presumably at the expense of foreign firms some of which may be investors or potential investors in the protecting country.

Another set of policy instruments that has been deployed in support of trade objectives is that of performance requirements, either with respect to raising exports or lowering imports. They may, of course, offset the effects of some of the investment incentives. US data suggest that whereas US affiliates overseas benefit from investment incentives with about the same frequency in developed and developing countries, they are subject to performance requirements (of various kinds, not all trade-related) four times as frequently in the latter countries as in the former (27). A GATT panel has recently ruled that requirements relating to domestic procurement and the consequent limitation of imports contravene the GATT, whereas those requiring a certain level of export performance do not. This legal distinction, whether or not it is eventually upheld in other cases, seems to have no justification in economics. Whether the 'free' market flows generated by imperfect markets are themselves socially efficient is a much larger question (that the GATT has never addressed). It can be argued that some performance requirements move the trading outcome back towards the equivalent of the competitive equilibrium solution that is theoretically optimal, serving to offset restrictive business practices and other real-world distortions that get in the way of efficient overall outcomes.

In some circumstances it may be possible to induce or require direct foreign investors who originally entered production in a developing country to meet local markets to shift to exporting, but this is typically more difficult than the encouragement of 'fresh' export-oriented investors since it requires alteration of the firms' global production and marketing strategies (28). It may also involve inefficiencies and large government subsidies to overcome them. The widespread existence of export restrictions - explicit or implicit - in technology contracts and subsidiary operations relating to import-substituting production is evidence that transnational corporate involvement can impede, as well as assist, the developing of exports. Project-specific performance requirements, in the form of 'buy-back' agreements, may also be deployed to ensure desired trade effects from new DFI. With the growth in counter-trade and state trading this non-market means of overcoming early marketing problems seems likely to increase in importance.

The deployment of trade-related performance requirements for foreign firms is a matter of growing international concern. If the developing countries that have been most active in their use are to take informed positions in their defence, and if others are to benefit from their experience, it is essential that there be careful assessments of the degree to which they have worked. There are many other possible objectives besides balance-of-payments improvements that might influence the nature of bargains struck with foreign investors, e.g. employment creation, training, local R and D, etc. If development is seen in terms of technical change, productivity improvement and learning-by-doing, these elements of performance are far more important than those relating to relatively short-term trade effects. There have been very few empirical analyses of 'learning', total factor productivity change and their correlates in export-oriented manufacturing as compared with other activities, foreign-owned firms compared with local firms, or combinations thereof (29).

If capital, management, marketing skills and the like are required in particular export industries, government policy must be directed at their acquisition. But there is no <u>necessary</u> connection between these two sets of objectives (exporting and the acquisition of scarce inputs) and therefore no necessity for linking them through the use of only one policy instrument. Some countries nevertheless seek particularly to steer foreign investment into export activities, notably via the so-called 'free trade zones' (FTZs), which typically provide strong incentives for export activity at the same time that they encourage the participation of foreign-owned firms. But despite considerable controversy over their role in development, there is still distressingly little careful empirical economic analysis of their overall costs and benefits.

b) <u>Developed (Home) Countries</u>. Governments of the home countries of direct foreign investors have been concerned to encourage their firms by promotional activities, favourable tax treatment and the provision of protection against otherwise uninsurable risks, particularly political ones. These insurance and related arrangements typically cover loans, suppliers' credits, service sales and even some earnings remissions, as well as equity.

But the importance of these policies can easily be exaggerated. The total share of DFI stock in developing countries that is covered by governmental insurance arrangements is only about 9 % (30). No doubt the percentage coverage of new flows is somewhat larger but most direct foreign investors do not seem to be heavily dependent upon such schemes; it is said that such insurance as is desired by direct investors is increasingly being obtained on private markets (31). Many elements of uncertainty concerning host country policies and circumstances are not readily covered by insurance contracts. Reinterpretation of the details of contractual arrangements, for example, are far more complex and difficult to protect oneself against in advance than such obvious measures as expropriation, exchange controls, or civil disturbances. There has consequently not been universal enthusiasm for the World Bank's new Multilateral Investment Guarantee Agency. But knowledge as to which types of firms seek which types of insurance in which industries and which countries is scarce.

Home governments providing insurance prefer to do so only for investments in countries with which they have intergovernmental agreements on foreign investment, and these are usually asymmetric in the obligations imposed upon the relevant parties. Foreign owners of capital benefit from 'national' treatment or most favoured nation provisions, assured convertibility of earnings and capital repatriation, fair and prompt compensation upon nationalisation, and the like; the only return to the host country is the increased likelihood that foreign investors will be insured by their home government against the very events (plus wars and insurrections) which the treaties ostensibly forbid. Vernon has described these treaties as 'patently unbalanced...too unbalanced to provide the basis for a durable regime' (32).

Home governments are also subject to other pressures regarding the nature of their promotional, insurance and overseas assistance programmes. The US Government, for instance, is mandated not to extend favourable export credit terms to projects that are likely to compete with American products in home markets, and has exerted pressure upon the World Bank similarly to constrain its lending. 'Industrial co-operation' agreements and programmes, such as those run by the EEC through the Lomé Convention, routinely incorporate protectionist biases in their advice, technical assistance and other supports.

The longstanding efforts to construct a code of conduct for transnational corporations under UN auspices continue. Less comprehensive codes and guidelines have been negotiated or are under discussion in the ILO, UNCTAD, and OECD; and there have long been proposals for a 'GATT for investment'. An overall legislative and regulatory framework that seeks to minimise conflict and encourage accommodation in the general global interest remains a worthy aspiration. But few expect any of the new codes significantly to affect the flow of new direct investment to developing countries (33).

The commercial policies of the industrialised countries to which most Third World manufactured exports at present are directed, are obviously of crucial importance, and as South-South trade in manufactures expands, the commercial policies of other developing countries will also become increasingly important. In the former case there is reason to believe that commercial policy may be responsive to domestic political pressures in such a way as relatively to favour imports from subsidiaries or affiliates of home firms; much of this relatively favoured trade is likely to be intra-firm. On the other hand, developing countries' governments can be expected to exert disproportionate bargaining effort on behalf of their own home firms, those that are <u>not</u> owned by foreign investors. Although econometric investigation of the US tariff is unable to confirm the hypothesis that imports from US-owned firms are particularly well-treated in international tariff bargaining (34), it seems roughly to accord with observed practice with respect to US non-tariff barriers. Even 'neutral' reductions in trade barriers may disproportionately benefit international firms relative to national ones, particularly in the short term, since they are better able quickly to serve established markets via known external sources and to capture the potential efficiency gains from liberalisation (35).

Selective barriers such as voluntary export restraints, apart from their direct effects upon current trade, can also influence the geographic pattern of further investments, as investors and buyers seek new 'uncontrolled' exporting bases and sources. These incentives for export-oriented DFI and sourcing in new locations are severely dampened, of course, when the trade managing authorities show signs of imposing restraints upon newcomers as soon as they begin to succeed.

A particularly significant commercial policy inducement for transnational and other firms to locate export-oriented production in developing countries is the value added tariff, offering customs duty relief on manufactured imports when inputs into the product in question originate in the country (or, in the case of the EEC, with a firm resident in the country) that imports the final product. A related policy is the special provision made for 'outward processed' textile products in the Multi-Fibre Arrangement. Outside the US, there has been very little information or research on the uses and effects of this important set of policies.

Also relevant is the Generalised System of Preferences, although it is subject to unilateral withdrawal without compensation, and such regional preferential arrangements as the Lomé Convention and the Caribbean Basin Initiative. In all of these programmes the rules of origin are crucially important to the determination of their value to the affected developing countries.

The direct effects of home government trade barriers have received quite a lot of research attention. So, in recent years, has their structure and its political determinants. Interactions between investment and trade flows have not, however, been fully explored. Nor have available data permitted a full investigation of the role of DFI in the determination of the structure of trade barriers. The distribution of the 'rent' from non-tariff trade barriers and preferential schemes is also relatively unexplored research territory.

Further Research Requirements

Despite the new conventional wisdom that export-oriented manufacturing and direct foreign investment deserve significant new encouragement in the developing countries, there is still distressingly little known about optimal policies relating to them. In a world of varied market imperfections and a myriad of governmental interventions, advice based on traditional models of pure competition is not persuasive. There is a need for simultaneous analysis of policies towards trade and policies towards investment since together they co-determine the location of global production and the pattern of future trade.

NOTES AND REFERENCES

* The author is grateful to Vincent Cable, Sidney Dell and Louis Wells for comments on an earlier draft. A version of this paper will also appear in a collection of essays in honour of Gamani Corea, edited by Sidney Dell.

1. UN Centre on Transnational Corporations (UNCTC), Transnational Corporations in World Development, Third Survey (New York, 1983), pp.9-11.

2. Rachel McCulloch and Robert F. Owen, 'Linking Negotiations on Trade and Foreign Direct Investment' in C.P. Kindleberger and D. Audretsch (eds.), The Multinational Corporation in the 1980s (MIT Press, Cambridge, Mass., 1983), p.353, See also G.K. Helleiner, 'International Trade Theory and Northern Protectionism Against Southern Manufactures' in G.K. Helleiner (ed.), For Good or Evil, Economic Theory and North-South Negotiations (University of Toronto Press, 1982).

3. Grant L. Reuber et al., Private Foreign Investment in Development (Clarendon Press, Oxford), for OECD, 1973, p. 67.

4. See, for instance, G.K. Helleiner, 'Direct Foreign Investment and Alternative Forms of External Non-Concessional Finance for Developing Countries', Seventh World Congress of the International Economic Association, Madrid, 1983 (mimeo).

5. An excellent summary of the issues surrounding such insurance schemes can be found in Henry C. Wallich, 'Insurance of Bank Lending to Developing Countries', Group of Thirty Occasional Paper No. 15 (New York, 1984).

6. See, for example, John H. Dunning, International Production and the Multinational Enterprise (George Allen and Unwin, London, 1981); Mark Casson, Alternatives to the Multinational Enterprise (Macmillan, London, 1979).

7. Charles Oman, New Forms of International Investment in Developing Countries (OECD Development Centre, Paris,

1983), pp. 201-4, 227-8; UNCTC, Transnational Corporations, pp. 40-46.

8. David Glover, 'Contract Farming and the Transnationals', Ph. D. dissertation, University of Toronto, 1983.

9. L.E. Westphal, Y.W. Rhee and G. Pursell, 'Foreign Influences on Korean Industrial Development', Oxford Bulletin of Economics and Statistics, Vol. 41, No. 4 (November 1979).

10. UNCTC, Transnational Corporations, pp. 182-3; see also Keesing, 'Linking up to Distant Markets: South to North Exports of Manufactured Consumer Goods', American Economic Review, Vol. 73, No. 2 (May 1983).

11. Stephen Guisinger, Investment Incentives and Performance Requirements (Praeger, New York, 1983).

12. Richard Newfarmer, 'Multinationals and Marketplace Magic in the 1980s' in Kindleberger and Audretsch, The Multinational Corporation.

13. Group of Thirty, Foreign Direct Investment 1973-87 (New York, 1984), p. 31.

14. Guisinger, Investment Incentives.

15. C. Fred Bergsten, 'Coming Investment Wars?', Foreign Affairs (October 1974).

16. OECD, Investing in Developing Countries (Paris, 1983), p. 14.

17. See Dan Usher, 'The Economics of Tax Incentives to Encourage Investment in Less Developed Countries', Journal of Development Economics, Vol. 4, No.2 (June 1977).

18. Marian Radeiski, 'Has Political Risk Scared Investment Away from the Deposits in Developing Countries?', World Development, Vol. 10, No. 1 (January 1982).

19. For example, see Deepak Nayyar, 'Transnational Corporations and Manufactured Exports from Poor Countries', Economic Journal, Vol. 88, No. 1 (March 1978).

20. J. de la Torre, 'Foreign Investment and Export Dependency', Economic Development and Cultural Change, Vol. 23, No. 1 (October 1974).

21. For example, see Sanjaya Lall and Sharif Mohammad, 'Foreign Ownership and Export Performance in the Large Corporate Sector of India', Journal of Development Studies, Vol. 20, No. 1, (October 1983); see also references in Newfarmer, 'Multinationals and Marketplace Magic'.

22. William R. Cline, 'Can the East Asian Model of Development be Generalized?', World Development, Vol. 10, No. 2 (February 1982).

23. Oman, New Forms of International Investment, p. 202.

24. L.T. Wells, Third World Multinationals (MIT Press, Cambridge, Mass., 1983); Sanjaya Lall, 'The New Multinationals' in Sanjaya Lall et al., The Spread of Third World Enterprises (John Wiley and Sons, Chichester, 1983).

25. Bela Belassa et al., Development Strategies in

Semi-Industrial Economies (John Hopkins University Press for the World Bank, Baltimore, 1982).

26. For example, L. Westphal, *Empirical Justification for Infant Industry Protection*, World Bank Staff Working Paper 445 (March 1981); Frances Stewart, 'Industrialization, Technical Change and the International Division of Labour' in Helleiner, *For Good or Evil*; Paul Streeten, 'Outward-looking Industrialisation and Trade Strategies', paper presented to the North-South Round Table, Fourth Session, Tokyo/Oiso, 1982.

27. McCulloch and Owen, 'Linking Negotiations on Trade and FDI, p. 342; A.E. Safarian, 'Trade-Related Investment Issues' in William R. Cline (ed.), *Trade Policy in the 1980s* (Institute for International Economics, Washington DC, 1983).

28. Douglas Bennett and Kenneth E. Sharpe, 'Transnational Corporations and the Political Economy of Export Promotion: The Case of the Mexican Automobile Industry', *International Organization*, Vol. 33, No. 2 (Spring 1979).

29. Some work has been undertaken by, among others, Leonard Dudley, 'Learning and Productivity Change in Metal Products', *American Economic Review*, Vol. 62, No. 4, (September 1972); Anne O. Krueger and Baran Tuncer, 'An Empirical Test of the Infant Industry Argument', *American Economic Review*, Vol. 72, No. 5 (December 1982).

30. OECD, *Investing in Developing Countries*, pp. 30-3.

31. *Ibid.*, pp. 117-18; UNCTC, *Transnational Corporations*, p. 96.

32. Raymond Vernon, 'Codes on Transnationals: Ingredients for an Effective International Regime', Harvard Business School, 1982 (mimeo), pp. 10-11.

33. More information on their contents may be found in OECD, *Investing in Developing Countries* and UNCTC, *Transnational Corporations*, pp. 95-6 and 107-21.

34. Real P. Lavergne and G.K. Helleiner, 'US Transnational Corporations and the Structure of US Trade Business: An Empirical Investigation' in UNCTC, *Transnational Corporations and International Trade, An Empirical Analysis*, forthcoming.

35. McCulloch and Owen, 'Linking Negotiations', p. 346.

Chapter Five

FOREIGN INVESTMENT AND THE STATE IN SINGAPORE

Pang Eng Fong

Role of the State

Singapore's rapid growth would not have been possible without a combination of private investment - domestic and foreign - and the active intervention of the state in the economy in a way which is peculiar to Singapore. The present government came to power in 1959 espousing the cause of democratic socialism. But its socialist rhetoric quickly gave way to hard realities: there was little industry to nationalise and the island's economy was too small for a policy of self-reliant development. From the outset, the political leadership emphasised the importance of private enterprise and foreign investment, especially by transnational corporations, to Singapore's industrialisation programme, and made no secret of its tolerance for profit-making and its aversion to production subsidies for firms. In the words of Prime Minister Lee Kuan Yew(1):

> (Singapore) never suffered from any inhibitions in borrowing capital, know-how, managers, engineers, and marketing capabilities. Far from limiting the entry of foreign managers, engineers, and bankers, we encouraged them to come.

In other words, Singapore's leaders perceive foreign investment, especially by tncs, as not just a method of meeting the gap in domestic capital, but as a quick way to gain access to foreign technology, expertise, and markets. Singapore's experience with foreign investments supports their belief. A study by Singapore's investment promotion agency, the Economic Development Board, reports that the bigger and more established the transnational corporation the higher the success rate, and the greater its contribution to output and employment(2). The study also concludes that the less experienced the foreign investor and the less advanced the technology it brings, the higher the failure rate. Wholly-owned subsidiaries from developed countries had a failure rate of 6% compared with 13% for firms from less developed countries like Hong Kong and Taiwan. When Singaporeans entered into joint ventures with firms from industrialised countries, the failure rate was 7% compared with 38% when they struck out on their own.

Unlike many developing countries, Singapore encourages but does not insist on joint ventures. It believes local ownership is not crucial to effective technology transfer, and that what counts is the quality and attitude of the foreign investor.

The government subscribes to a philosophy of economic liberalism, with selective but powerful state controls. In 1977 it removed all foreign exchange controls (which were never highly restrictive(3). It imposes few import tariffs, and these are intended to raise revenues or to curb consumption of 'luxury' goods. Protective tariffs on local industry even during the short import-substituting phase were never high, and now apply only to a few consumer products including clothing and non-essential foodstuffs. Import licenses are issued for only a few items (e.g. rice, refined sugar and chlorine), and for imports from a few socialist countries. No duties are levied on exports, and export licenses are required for only a few minor items including iron and steel scrap, raw feathers, and granite.

Apart from minor regulations imposed for health, social, or pollution reasons and industrial relations legislation, there are few controls on private investment or enterprise - no anti-monopoly laws, no approval or licensing process for foreign or local private investments, and no technology transfer controls or compulsory registration of contracts. Companies do not have to comply with any domestic content legislation or requirements. They are free to import capital, remit profits and repatriate capital. In short, the Singapore economy is very open, and characterised by an absence of regulation on the flow of capital and goods.

This does not mean, however, that Singapore, like Hong Kong, is a laissez-faire state. There are close to 500 government-owned companies and statutory boards involved in a wide range of manufacturing and service activities including iron and steel mills, textiles, electrical component manufacture, oil refining, hotels, shipbuilding and repairing, shipping, air transport, trading, financial services, and property development. The main reason for such government participation in the early years was to lead the way in large, high-risk projects - National Iron and Steel Mills is one example.

Government intervention is especially visible in the labour market. For example, prior to 1972, wage setting was decentralised and varied greatly by industry and firm. Thereafter the government strongly influences wage increases in both the private and public sectors through the tripartite National Wages Council. Up to 1979, moderate wage increases were recommended to preserve Singapore's competitive position in manufacturing exports and to maintain full employment.

From 1979-81, however, a wage correction policy was adopted to restore wages to market levels and to encourage firms to use labour efficiently. In 1986, with the consent of the unions, a wage freeze was instituted for as long as it takes the economy to recover.

Investment Climate

Over the years, the government has developed various institutions and investment incentives to attract foreign investment. The Economic Development Board is the main agency responsible (for industrial development as well as the promotion of foreign investment). Created in 1961, the EDB is a one-stop investment centre providing a comprehensive range of services and facilities to investors. Besides promoting investment, it administers fiscal incentives and manpower training programmes, and undertakes feasibility studies. Its efficiency greatly reduces the uncertainty, cost, and gestation period of investment by foreign companies.

Since 1960, the government has developed new investment incentives to attract direct foreign investment. The basic incentive was, and still is, pioneer status, which provides for exemption from the 40% company income tax for a period of five to ten years, depending on such factors as the level of investment, its employment of skilled labour, research and development spending, and so on. A second incentive, first introduced in 1967 and liberalised since then, encourages exports by taxing approved export profits at 4% rather than the usual rate of 40%. The normal incentive period is five years, but it can be as long as fifteen years for projects with fixed capital expenditure of over $150 million, provided Singapore citizens and/or permanent residents own over 50% of the paid-up capital.

Since 1979, to accelerate restructuring, the government has liberalised tax and investment incentives to encourage research and development activities, automation, mechanisation, and computerisation in manufacturing, trade, and services. In 1984, for example, the three-year accelerated depreciation allowance for plant and equipment previously granted to manufacturing firms was extended to cover all sectors, thus reflecting the government's recognition of the need to increase incentives for non-manufacturing industries, especially those engaged in the export of traded services. The tax incentive system is non-discriminatory: all incentives are available to both local and foreign firms. However, they have benefitted foreign firms more than local firms, mainly because foreign firms invest more per project and are more export-oriented than local firms.

The EDB uses not one but many criteria - technological sophistication, capital- and skill-intensity, export orientation, backward linkages - to determine the incentives for firms in 'priority' industries. Though it tailors tax incentives to suit particular investors, its incentive framework does not distort the production system because the primary objective is not to protect local firms but to promote the export of high value-added products.

The availability of investment incentives is clearly only one of many factors that determine a country's investment climate. Other important factors are its attitudes to foreign investment, and its social and physical infrastructure. Investment incentives, however, are likely to matter more to export-oriented industries - the kind Singapore is wooing - than to import-substituting or resource-processing industries which are location-specific. They are also only of value if the foreign investment is profitable. Moreover, their value depends on whether there is a double tax relief arrangement between the home and host countries. Singapore has such arrangements with some 20 countries, including Japan and most EEC countries, but not with the United States which allows only tax deferral. This has not deterred US investments in Singapore, however.

Foreign investors are attracted to Singapore by a combination of factors of which probably the two most important are political stability and the government's reputation for honesty and efficiency, and consistently positive attitudes to foreign investment. Other favourable factors include:

- no restrictions on capital flows and profit repatriation;
- no restrictions on ownership structure;
- a free trade policy that permits easy import and export of goods;
- tax incentives for approved investments;
- GSP benefits for approved products exported to the US, EEC and Japan;
- excellent infrastructure;
- adaptable, trainable, and increasingly English-speaking workforce;
- fast-growing supply of skilled and professional personnel;
- industrial peace and co-operative unions;
- competent and helpful government agencies;
- good living conditions for expatriates.

None of these factors by itself is sufficient to induce a foreign company to set up business in Singapore, but together they create a favourable climate that Business International, a leading consultancy firm, has rated as one of the best in the world.

Before economic restructuring began in earnest in 1979,

one key factor that attracted many labour-intensive firms to Singapore was the availability of relatively low-cost, disciplined, and trainable labour. But with growing labour shortages and rapidly rising wage costs since the late 1970s, Singapore has become less attractive to labour-intensive firms. Before 1979, the availability of tax incentives was not a significant attraction; other countries offered similar or better incentives. Also, most foreign investments were small and in labour-intensive industries where incentives such as accelerated depreciation for plant and equipment and investment credits were not of crucial importance. But for large, capital-intensive or high-technology firms, especially those operating in fast-changing fields, investment incentives and tax write-offs are increasingly important.

Interviews conducted in the late 1970s and early 1980s with a small sample - a dozen large and small firms from OECD countries - confirm the diverse motives of foreign investors. Some firms (e.g. Sanyo, a Japanese electronics firm) are willing to set up joint ventures while others insist on 100% equity ownership. Some firms e.g. Seagate, a US firm making disk drives, and Glaxochem, a British pharmaceutical firm, say tax holidays are important. A few, e.g. Tandon, another US disk drive firm, and Philips, the giant Dutch company, assign great importance to the availability of low-cost, dependable suppliers, but others - Demetron, a high-technology German company making film pastes for hybrid integrated circuits, and Seagate - are not deterred by the absence of a well-developed network of vendors. All the foreign investors attach importance to general business conditions rather than specific production factors and this suggests that a host country that wants to attract foreign investors must give priority to the development of a stable, predictable, hospitable investment climate.

The interviews also suggest that the higher the technological level of the investing firm, the stronger its preference for a wholly-owned subsidiary. This reflects not a reluctance to transfer technology to the host country but a need for efficient managerial control over key production decisions. It suggests that a host country must be flexible in its policy on ownership structure. To insist that foreign investors find local partners may be counter-productive, especially in the early stages of development when domestic technological capability is low, and the country needs to develop a clear image of welcoming foreign investment.

Finally, the interviews underline the importance of an efficient investment promotion agency that can facilitate the entry and operations of foreign firms particularly for technologically dynamic firms that need to start up operations quickly in order to maintain their competitive edge. Though they were aware of its attractions, many firms decided to establish themselves in Singapore only after they were actively courted by the EDB. Happy with their experience, they spread the word. Success in attracting foreign investment spurred growth and strengthened stability, reinforcing the island's reputation as a profitable, trouble-free investment location.

Singapore's investment priorities have changed with rapid development. While it once wooed employment-generating firms like Sanyo and Toshiba, it now welcomes skill- and capital-intensive firms like Glaxochem, Tandon and Seagate. The experience of Seagate is typical of the many disk drive manufacturers, including SyQuest, Maxtor, Computer Memories, and National Micronetics, that followed Tandon to Singapore in the early 1980s, and made it the leading producer of disk drives in Asia. Seagate went offshore to keep production costs down, and came to Singapore because it was the one place in Asia with little red tape, adequate infrastructure, and a government that could help foreign firms implement their investment decisions quickly; speed is essential in such a volatile market.

Singapore's success in attracting foreign firms, especially computer manufacturers, is as impressive as its previous success in attracting labour-intensive electronics firms. The key factor underlying this success is business confidence, a factor greatly influenced by government policies. The managing director of SGS-Ates, an Italian semiconductor company that decided to set up a wafer diffusion plant in Singapore far away from its main market in North East Asia, says Korea, Taiwan, and Hong Kong are important markets and places, but 'from the standpoint of peace of mind, this place (Singapore) is faring much better. That's the reason people are still coming in despite rising costs and labour shortages'(4).

Over the years, EDB's task has become more complicated and time-consuming because it is trying to attract small high-technology and support companies who are not very familiar with conditions in Singapore. According to its chairman, once the EDB has identified a company it wants to attract it follows up with corporate presentations and discussions before preparing an investment proposal; the whole process could take from two to ten years before a project materialises(5).

Foreign Equity Investment

The importance of foreign investment in Singapore's economy is clear from Tables 5.1 and 5.2. One-third of all firms are wholly or majority foreign-owned, and foreign funds amounted to two-fifths of all investments in 1981. At the end of 1983, these were estimated to be over S$20 bn, nine-tenths of which were in the form of direct investment and the remaining

Table 5.1. Singapore: Total equity investment, 1970-1981

	1970		1973		1976		1979		1981	
	S$m.	%	S$m.	%	S$m.	%	S$m.	%	S$m.	%
Total	4,725.3	100.0	10,591.2	100.0	17,687.3	100.0	25,516.6	100.0	45,727.6	100.0
Local	2,981.8	63.1	6,823.3	64.4	10,761.7	60.8	15,368.8	60.2	28,942.4	63.3
Foreign	1,743.5	36.9	3,767.9	35.6	6,925.6	39.2	10,147.8	39.8	16,785.2	36.7
Direct Investment	1,462.5	31.0	3,296.1	31.1	6,255.3	35.4	9,376.2	36.8	15,603.7	34.1
Portfolio Investment	281.0	5.9	471.8	4.5	670.3	3.8	771.6	3.0	1,181.5	2.6

Source: Ministry of Trade and Industry, Economic Survey of Singapore (First Quarter 1984), p.13.

Table 5.2. Companies by type of ownership, 1970-1981

	1970		1976		1981	
	No.	%	No.	%	No.	%
TOTAL	3,608	100.0	11,241	100.0	21,323	100.0
Wholly Singaporean	1,891	52.4	6,978	62.1	14,258	66.9
More than half Singaporean	750	20.8	1,895	16.9	2,762	12.9
Less than half Singaporean	296	8.2	732	6.5	1,336	6.3
Wholly foreign	671	18.6	1,636	14.5	2,967	13.9

Source: Ibid.

one-tenth in portfolio investment(6). The rapid influx of foreign investments since 1970 has now crowded out local investment which multiplied nearly ten times from S$2.9 bn in 1970 to S$28.9 bn in 1981.

Nearly half of the foreign funds flow into the manufacturing sector, the most important industries being petroleum (15.6% of all foreign funds invested), electronics (9.7%), and machinery (6.1%). Two other important sectors are finance and business services, primarily banks, investment holding companies, and property developers (with 29% of all foreign funds), and trade (16%). Since 1970, the share of foreign equity going into relatively low value-added industries like food, tobacco, textile and wood products has fallen; in 1981, these industries accounted for only 7% of all foreign equity compared with 14% in 1970.

In 1981, five countries - Britain, USA, Hong Kong, Malaysia and Japan - accounted for four-fifths of the foreign equity invested in Singapore. Britain was the largest investor with S$4.4 bn in 1981, over half of it in manufacturing, particularly petroleum refining. The United States is the second largest with S$3.3 bn mostly in manufacturing, not only in petroleum refining but also in a wide range of high value-added industries including electronics, computer peripherals, machine tools, and oilfield equipment. Unlike US funds, Hong Kong funds at S$2.2 bn flow largely into the non-manufacturing sector, including commercial banking, property development, wholesale trade and hotels. Malaysia, with S$1.8 bn, is mainly in financial and business services (49%), trade (25%) and manufacturing (22%). Japan, with S$1.7 bn, has half its equity investment in manufacturing, and most of the rest spread evenly among trade, transport, financial and business services, and construction where it has developed a strong competitive position with over 90% of all foreign funds in the sector.

On average, industrial country investors place more funds into every company they establish in Singapore than investors from developing countries. For example, the average equity invested in 1981 in a British-owned firm is S$8.7m. and in a US-owned company S$6.4m, compared with S$1.0m. for Malaysian-owned firms and S$0.5m. for Taiwanese-owned firms.

One reason why foreign investors have increased their equity stake in Singapore by ten times between 1970 and 1981 is high returns. Foreign investors earn an average return of 18%. US and British investors concentrated in high value-added manufacturing reap returns averaging 29% compared with 13% for Asian investors who are mostly in small trading firms and low value-added labour-intensive manufacturing. Of the S$3.2 bn foreign investors earned in Singapore, S$1.3 bn or 40% is retained either to finance business expansion or to upgrade production technology. The 60% of earnings flowing out is a significant amount but small compared to the S$16.8 bn that foreign investors brought into the country.

Foreign Investment in Manufacturing and Services

The EDB's figures show that the cumulative stock of foreign manufacturing investment amounted to S$11.1 bn in June 1983, an eleven-fold increase since 1970, 35% from Europe because of its large investment in petroleum refineries, 30% from America and nearly 30% from the Far East, mainly Japan.

Nearly 60% was in two capital-intensive and high-technology industries - petroleum refining and electricals and electronics. Other industries with fairly sizeable investment were transport equipment, metal and engineering, and chemicals. Investments in terms of gross fixed assets in the older labour-intensive industries like food and beverages, textiles and garments, wood, and paper products are declining in relative terms.

Net foreign investment commitments reached an all-time high of S$1.34 bn in 1984. At 1972 prices, total net investment commitments of nearly S$1.8 bn (including S$519m. by local investors) were almost S$100m. less than in the peak year, 1981. About half was in new and diversification projects, new projects being mainly in the computer field. In 1985, foreign commitments fell to S$1.14 bn, with the largest amount (S$432m.) from US firms, followed by Japan (S$244m.) its highest amount to date, and Europe (S$ 212m.).

The quality of foreign investments in terms of skill and capital intensity has improved in recent years. New investment projects, including those of disk manufacturers which require large numbers of female workers, are creating many more skilled jobs than the labour-intensive consumer electronics firms of the early 1970s. In 1984, the expected fixed assets per worker of new investment commitments at 1972 prices was S$53,200, four times that in 1976, and more than twice that in 1979. This increase accounts for the sharp rise in the expected value-added per worker in 1972 prices from around S$24,000 to S$49,000 between 1979 and 1984. But in 1985 fixed assets and value-added per worker were expected to be lower, an indication that Singapore's rapidly rising operating costs in the 1980s have diminished its attractiveness as a profitable offshore manufacturing site.

Official policy is to welcome investment in the services and trading sectors (except retail trade in which there is abundant local expertise), especially technical and professional services that expand the island's role as a regional business centre. It is recognised that investment in services often leads to direct investment in manufacturing, as, for example, in the conversion of sales subsidiaries to manufacturing facilities. Although it does not insist, the government prefers to see joint ventures in large retail ventures, and also in investments in property and hotels. In 1981, out of nearly S$4 bn of paid-up capital in the trade sector (including wholesale and retail trade, and restaurants and hotels), 30% belonged to foreigners(7). In contrast to manufacturing, most of this came from Malaysia and Hong Kong.

Foreign Investment in Manufacturing and its Impact

Since 1960, the manufacturing sector has expanded at a real growth rate of 12% a year. Foreign investments play a major role in its growth. The growing importance of foreign enterprises, and their large size relative to local enterprises, is evident from Table 5.3. Wholly and majority foreign-owned enterprises accounted for only less than a quarter of all manufacturing establishments in 1984, but they produced 71% of the output, contributed 82% of direct exports, and employed 53% of workers. Wholly-owned foreign enterprises have the largest average output, employment and capital expenditure, and highest value-added per worker. Wholly-owned local enterprises, most of them catering to the domestic market or supplying parts to foreign enterprises, rank lowest in these terms.

No single nationality dominates foreign investment in the manufacturing sector, largely because of official encouragement for investments from all countries. Table 5.4 shows that Singapore-owned firms account for 79% of manufacturing establishments and 48% of the employment, but only 26% of the direct exports and 38% of the value-added in manufacturing. Their average output per establishment in 1984 was only half that of the sector as a whole, and less than 10% of US-owned enterprises. Firms from Japan, the EEC and the US employ on average more workers, produce more output, and are more export-oriented than firms from Hong Kong, Taiwan and Malaysia, which are concentrated in labour-intensive industries like garments and textiles.

Singapore's development policy emphasises economic efficiency and growth, rather than national ownership of the industrial sector. In consequence, most foreign enterprises, especially those from developed countries, are wholly-owned subsidiaries, and they dominate high-technology and export-oriented industries. Joint ventures are common only in labour-intensive, low-technology industries and they usually involve partners from other developing countries.

Most investor countries have increased their preference for wholly-owned and majority-owned companies since the 1960s. Firms from the United States are most likely to be wholly-owned subsidiaries; Asian investors are more willing to share ownership. Japanese firms show the greatest shift in ownership structure; in the 1970s, only 39% of Japanese firms were joint ventures, compared with 90% in the 1960s.

Table 5.3. Singapore: principal statistics of manufacturing by capital structure, 1975, 1984

	Number of establish- ments (est)		Number of workers		Output		Direct exports		Capital expenditure		Output per est.	Capital expendi- ture per est.	Share of output exported
	Number	%	Number	%	$m.	%	$m.	%	$m.	%	$'000	$'000	%
1975													
Total	2,385	100.0	191,528	100.0	12,610.1	100.0	7,200.7	100.0	622.6	100.0	5,287.3	261.0	57.1
Wholly Local	1,595	66.9	62,903	32.8	2,276.5	18.0	641.8	8.9	129.0	20.7	1,427.2	80.9	28.2
Majority Local	265	11.1	29,038	15.2	1,346.2	10.7	500.6	7.0	91.3	14.7	5,080.1	344.4	37.2
Minority Local	228	9.6	39,211	20.5	1,901.5	15.1	1,295.6	18.0	108.7	17.5	8,339.8	476.6	68.1
Wholly Foreign	297	12.5	60,376	31.5	7,086.0	56.2	4,762.7	66.1	293.1	47.2	23,858.6	989.0	67.2
1984													
Total	3,648	100.0	274,391	100.0	41,077.9	100.0	25,057.8	100.0	2,168.1	100.0	11,260.4	594.3	61.0
Wholly Local	2,483	68.1	90,341	32.9	7,881.2	19.2	2,700.1	10.8	549.9	25.4	3,174.1	221.5	34.3
Majority Local	400	10.9	39,070	14.2	4,087.5	10.0	1,816.8	7.3	278.3	12.8	10,218.8	695.8	44.4
Minority Local	248	6.8	30,845	11.3	6,297.5	15.3	3,871.4	15.4	200.4	9.2	25,393.1	808.1	61.5
Wholly Foreign	517	14.2	114,135	41.6	22,811.7	55.5	16,669.5	66.5	1,139.5	52.6	44,123.2	2,204.1	73.1

Source: Singapore, Department of Statistics, Report on the Census of Industrial Production, 1975, 1980, 1984.

Table 5.4. Singapore: principal statistics of manufacturing by major source of capital, 1984

Major source of capital	Number of establishments (est)		Number of workers		Output		Direct exports		Capital expenditure		Output per est.	Workers per est.	Capital expenditure per est.	Share of output exported
	Number	%	Number	%	$m.	%	$m.	%	$m.	%	$'000	Number	$'000	%
Total	3,648	100.0	274,391	100.0	41,077.9	100.0	25,057.8	100.0	2,168.1	100.0	11,260.4	75	594.3	61.0
Singapore	2,893	79.3	130,673	47.6	15,019.0	36.6	6,549.0	26.1	838.8	38.7	5,191.5	45	289.9	43.6
Australia	38	1.0	2,358	0.9	292.6	0.7	96.9	0.4	24.0	1.1	7,700.2	62	631.8	33.1
Hong Kong	81	2.2	11,543	4.2	1,143.0	2.8	701.2	3.6	63.1	2.9	14,111.0	143	779.3	78.8
Japan	193	5.3	42,709	15.6	4,670.5	11.4	2,876.7	11.5	318.1	14.7	24,199.5	221	1,648.3	61.6
Malaysia	75	2.1	3,085	11	287.4	0.7	86.4	0.4	14.3	0.6	3,832.7	41	190.4	30.1
Switzerland	23	0.6	6,890	2.5	1,312.6	3.2	1,164.1	4.7	55.8	2.6	57,070.1	300	2,426.0	88.7
Taiwan	15	0.4	1,294	0.5	119.1	0.3	51.2	0.2	4.3	0.2	7,939.9	86	288.3	43.0
United Kingdom	73	2.0	5,687	2.1	631.8	1.5	384.1	1.5	44.9	2.1	8,654.3	78	615.6	60.8
United States	129	3.5	46,975	17.1	8,170.4	19.9	5,947.4	23.7	541.3	25.0	63,336.4	364	4,196.2	72.8
West Germany	35	1.0	5,911	2.1	435.4	1.1	349.6	1.4	24.9	1.1	12,440.3	169	710.7	80.3
Other European Countries	54	1.5	13,731	5.0	8,233.3	20.0	6,067.6	24.2	188.0	8.7	152,467.7	254	3,480.5	73.7
Others	39	1.1	3,535	1.3	762.8	1.8	583.6	2.3	50.6	2.3	19,558.9	91	1,296.4	76.5

Source: Singapore, Department of Statistics, Report on the Census of Industrial Production (1984), p.6.

European firms, many of them fairly small and going offshore for the first time, are moving in the opposite direction; in 1977-78, 11% of European firms set up in Singapore were minority-owned joint ventures, compared with only 3% in the 1960s.

Other 'new' forms of investment - licensing, management contracts, turnkey projects, for example - are not common, given the government's willingness to allow foreign firms to form wholly-owned subsidiaries. Firms with little or no foreign equity but having licensing or other arrangements with foreign technology suppliers account for less than 10% of recently established firms(8).

The manufacturing sector, as we have seen, is highly export-oriented. However, because of the island's limited resources and small size, manufacturing depends greatly on imports, and its contribution to foreign-exchange earnings is much less than the value of its exports. In 1978, for example, the latest year for which foreign-exchange earnings data is available, manufacturing exports amounted to S$ 16.6 bn, but net foreign-exchange earnings to only S$ 4.6 bn. In other words, a dollar's worth of exports produces S$ 0.27 of net foreign exchange. As foreign companies account for the bulk of manufacturing exports and remit only 60% of their earnings, they make an important contribution to the balance-of-payments position.

Net foreign-exchange earnings vary according to the import content and export value of the industry. Petroleum refining, for example, netted only S$770m. in foreign exchange out of S$8.7 bn worth of exports. After petroleum refining, the largest foreign-exchange earner is 'other communication equipment', an industry dominated by foreign capital, which netted S$586m. on exports of S$1.6 bn. Other export items earning net foreign exchange of close to or over S$100m. in 1978 are 'other outer garments' (S$164.3m.), plywood and veneer (S$ 99.0m.), pharmaceutical products (S$117.1m.), industrial machinery (S$123.5m.), radio and TV sets (S$166.8m.) and ships and boats (S$487.7m.). Of these industries, only ships and boats are dependent on Singapore's locational advantage, and have a significant proportion of local equity ownership.

Of the industries earning over S$100m. worth of foreign exchange in 1978, only three - medicinal and pharmaceutical products, industrial machinery and equipment, and ships and boats - have net foreign earnings to export ratios greater than 50%. The key foreign-exchange earners have much lower foreign exchange-export ratios. Nevertheless, manufacturing's foreign earnings are still substantial - in fact larger by S$233m. than those from services in 1978.

Export manufacturing led by foreign firms has been spectacularly successful in creating employment. Between 1957 and 1970, manufacturing employment doubled to 143,000 with most of the increase coming in the late 1970s mainly from electrical machinery, electronics, textiles and garments, and transport equipment. In the 1970s, it doubled again, helping to bring about full employment in the early 1970s.

Unlike larger developing countries, the indirect manufacturing employment impact of export manufacturing is fairly small, because of the high dependence on imported goods and the low degree of interdependence within manufacturing itself. One study estimates, however, that the expansion of the electronics industry, which created some 60,000 new jobs or one-third of all new manufacturing employment between 1968 and 1980, generated some 12,000 new jobs in supporting firms(9).

Not many linkages have been developed with locally-owned supporting firms(10). Transnational firms buy a significant proportion of their local inputs from other foreign subsidiaries or from local traders and agents who import them. Inputs produced in Singapore by locally-owned supporting firms are often not competitive in price, range, quality and delivery. However, their competitiveness is improving with financial support and encouragement from government agencies, and as they gain industrial experience.

Conclusions

Both internal and external factors have contributed to Singapore's economic success since 1965. The external factors, e.g. the state of the world economy and regional stability, are not within Singapore's control. As for the internal factors, some reflect the island's unique history and geography, while others are the result of government policies.

At self-government, Singapore had a mixed colonial legacy. Its advantages included an efficient port, a people exposed to foreign ideas and used to living by their wits, and only a small agricultural sector. On the debit side, it had no natural resources, a small domestic market, and no tradition of industrial entrepreneurship. The initial advantages would have been lost had the government pursued inward-looking policies. From the beginning, it steered a pragmatic course, emphasising institutional efficiency and the creation of an attractive business environment for foreign investment. Some of its measures to foster a congenial investment climate are uncontroversial, such as the use of tax holidays and export incentives, the development of infrastructure, manpower development, provision of industrial estates, and improving institutional efficiency. Other developing countries have done the same. But other government policies are more contentious, such as curbs on trade unions, extensive labour market interventions, and the suppression of domestic political opposition. They are not policies other developing countries can easily adopt. Nevertheless, there are lessons to be learned from Singapore's experience.

First, the government did not introduce price distortions. Even during its brief phase of import-substitution, it made little use of direct measures such as licensing, quotas, and price controls to influence production decisions in the private sector. As a result, price signals reflected world prices, and did not distort resource allocation. Moreover, powerful interest groups did not develop, as they have in countries that have followed an import-substitution strategy for an extended period.

Second, the government consistently made known its positive attitude towards direct foreign investment. Unlike other developing countries, it did not regard dependence on direct foreign investment as diminishing its political sovereignty. Rather it views foreign firms as crucial to its stability and prosperity, indeed to its political survival. But it made it abundantly clear to foreign investors that they were not free to pursue actions contrary to its national interests or to involve themselves in domestic politics.

Third, the Singapore experience highlights the importance of an orderly business environment. This was achieved, as we have seen, by both conventional incentives and services, and also by controversial measures, such as limiting union power and personal choices in family planning. Fourth, the need to take a long-term view of the benefits of direct foreign investment, especially by transnational corporations, is suggested. When electronics firms first established themselves in Singapore, they transferred little technology and forged few domestic linkages. Over time as they gained experience in the island, and as the pool of skilled manpower grew, they have transferred more higher value-added products and processes.

Fifthly, and a lesson that Singapore itself is learning, is the fact that a country's attractiveness to foreign investors can change quickly. In 1985, foreign investment inflows fell sharply, in large part because rapidly rising costs since the early 1980s have made the island a less profitable investment location. The government has initiated measures to cut labour and other costs to restore the attractive 'total business environment' in which OECD firms can earn higher rates of return than in their home countries(11). It is too early to tell whether these measures will enable Singapore to compete successfully for the kind of investments that not only other newly-industrialised countries but also OECD countries are seeking to attract. But one thing is certain: Singapore's maturing economy needs more, not less, foreign investments.

NOTES AND REFERENCES

1. Lee Kuan Yew, 'Extrapolating from the Singapore Experience', Special Lecture delivered at the 26th World Congress of the International Chamber of Commerce, Orlando, Florida, USA. Reprinted in Singapore, Ministry of Culture, Speeches, November 1978, pp. 5-30.

2. Quoted in Lee's lecture.

3. Singapore historically operated a Currency Board system under which every dollar was backed by an equivalent amount in gold and foreign exchange. The system ensured the external stability of the dollar and was retained after the Monetary Authority of Singapore (MAS) was established in 1970 to perform all the functions of a central bank, except currency issue. The Authority liberalised exchange controls from the early 1970s, ending with the abolition of all controls in 1977. It switched in 1973 from sterling to the US dollar as the intervention currency, using exchange rate intervention as its main instrument of monetary control. For an analysis of Singapore's monetary system, see Lee Sheng-Yi, 'Money, Banking and Finance in Singapore', in You Poh Seng and Lim Chong Yah (eds.), Singapore: Twenty-five Years of Development, (Nan Yang Xing Zhou Lianhe Zaobao, Singapore, 1984), pp. 108-38.

4. Anthony Spaeth, 'Foreign Electronics Firms Bring High Technology to Singapore', Asian Wall Street Journal, 2-3 December 1983.

5. Chan Chin Bock, EDB chairman, in an interview reported in Straits Times, (Singapore), 14 October 1983.

6. These statistics (and others in this section) are from a survey of foreign investments by the Department of Statistics. See the report on the survey in Singapore, Ministry of Trade and Industry, Economic Survey, First Quarter 1984, pp. 12-17.

7. These figures are from bi-annual surveys of wholesale and retail trades, restaurants and hotels carried out by the Statistics Department.

8. Pang Eng Fong, 'Foreign Indirect Investment in Singapore', paper prepared for OECD Development Centre, June 1982. Later published in Charles Oman (ed.), New Forms of Investment (OECD Development Centre, Paris, 1984).

9. Pang Eng Fong and Augustine Tan, 'Employment in the Singapore Electronics Industry', paper prepared for the ILO Asian Regional Team for Employment Promotion (ARTEP), April 1981, pp. 15-16.

10. Pang Eng Fong and Linda Lim, The Electronics Industry in Singapore: Structure, Technology, and Linkages, ERC Research Monograph Series No. 7 (Chopmen Enterprises, Singapore, August 1977).

11. For details of these measures, see Report of the Economic Committee, The Singapore Economy: New Directions

Singapore

Ministry of Trade and Industry, (Singapore, February 1986), pp. 4-20.

Chapter Six

FOREIGN INVESTMENTS IN MALAYSIA

Mohammed Ariff and Chee Peng Lim

The Malaysian economy is one of the most open and dynamic in the Third World. It grew at a annual rate of 7.8% in the 1970s and exports equal nearly one-half of aggregate domestic expenditure. Since independence in 1957, the resource base has been substantially diversified; while still being the world's largest producer of natural rubber and tin, Malaysia has emerged as the largest producer of palm oil, a major producer of pepper and tropical hardwoods and more recently an important producer and exporter of crude petroleum. There has also been a programme of rapid industrialisation; the contribution of the manufacturing sector to GDP has increased from 13.4% in 1970 to 20.5% in 1980 and is projected to rise to 26.6% by 1990.

The private sector played a key role in the implementation of these programmes, and as part of its overall policy of promoting a greater private sector contribution, the government has encouraged foreign investment as an important means of promoting industrial growth through technology transfers, skill development and better access to foreign markets. To these ends, a variety of fiscal and other incentives are offered to both foreign and domestic investors. Foreign investment is by no means unrestricted, however. There are guidelines and regulations governing foreign investment in conformity with the country's development priorities and overall socio-economic objectives.

Private foreign investment in Malaysia consists of both direct and portfolio components. As there is very little information on foreign portfolio investment flows in the country, this chapter concentrates entirely on the more important private direct foreign investment (DFI). The bulk of DFI is in joint ventures, although there are a few wholly foreign-owned enterprises. Turnkey projects are also very few. Licensing and franchising arrangements and management contracts - the new forms of foreign investment - are growing in importance.

Even as early as the second quarter of this century, there was a substantial stake of British capital in the Malay(si)an economy (more than 70% of the total) with a heavy concentration (over 90%) in the plantation and mining sectors.

It is also of interest to note that Britain accounted for more than 70% of all foreign capital in the country(1). British investment in the country increased from £33m. in 1913 to £108m. by 1980(2). After independence in 1957, the structure of foreign capital in Malay(si)a changed significantly in terms of both sectoral allocation and source of capital.

By 1970, foreign equity accounted for more than 60% of the total share capital in Malaysia, being predominant in agriculture, trade, mining and manufacturing. Since then in the wake of the New Economic Policy (NEP), which among other things aims to limit the foreign share to 30% by 1990, the ownership pattern has changed considerably. The foreign share of the corporate sector capital fell from 62% in 1971 to 24% in 1983 (see Table 6.1), notwithstanding its increase in absolute terms from M$4.1 bn to M$16.7 bn(3).

Over the period 1971-9 Singapore, Japan and Britain have been the most important investors, jointly accounting for about 62% of the total foreign investment in manufacturing in 1979 and about 66% of foreign investment stock by the end of 1983 (see Table 6.2).

The electrical and electronic and textile industries figured prominently in the late 1970s as recipients of foreign investment (35% in 1979), but by the end of 1983, this had dropped to 22% or 29% of foreign fixed assets in Malaysia.

Table 6.1. Malaysia: Ownership of share capital in the corporate sector, 1971-83 (%)

	1971	1975	1980	1983
Foreign	61.7	53.3	42.9	33.6
Share in Malaysian companies	32.9	31.3	24.0	18.2
Net assets of local branches	28.8	22.0	18.9	15.4
Malaysian	38.3	46.7	57.1	66.4
Bumiputra individuals	2.6	3.6	5.8	7.6
Trust Agencies	1.7	5.6	6.7	11.1
Other Malaysian residents	34.0	37.5	44.6	47.7
Total ($m.)	6,564.1	1,5084.4	2,420.4	4,9708.2

Source: Fourth Malaysia Plan and Mid-Term Review of Fourth Malaysia Plan, 1981.

Other industries of importance to foreign investors include food manufacturing, non-metallic mineral products, chemicals and chemical products, beverages and tobacco and basic metal products which together account for 43% of total foreign capital investment and 43% of total foreign fixed assets in the country.

These investments comprise both paid-up capital and loans. It is of interest to note that the loan component forms less than one-fifth of total foreign capital investment on average; for example, nearly 30% of total foreign capital investment in hotel and tourist complexes, but a negligible proportion in the petroleum and coal sector. There are also inter-country variations; for instance, loans account for more than one-fourth of the total Japanese capital investment but only about one-tenth of the total British capital investment.

Table 6.3 gives comparative statistics relating to the four major sources of foreign investment by industry. The bulk of Singaporean capital has gone into food manufacturing, non-metallic mineral products, basic metals and hotel and tourist complexes which jointly have taken up nearly 59% of the total. The pattern is very different for British investment, nearly 70% of which is in food manufacturing, beverages and tobacco, chemical products and petroleum. US investment interests are somewhat similar in terms of industrial coverage, except for the strong American presence (16%) in the electrical and electronics industry. It appears that Singapore and UK investments have gone mainly into import substitution, US investment also seems to focus on catering for the Malaysian domestic market, with the notable exception of the electrical and electronics industry in the free trade zones which are completely export-oriented. Japanese investment has centred on textile and textile products and the electrical and electronics industry - the two most important export-oriented manufacturing activities which are also labour-intensive.

This appears to be in line with the well-known Kojima hypothesis(4) according to which Japanese investment tends to be 'trade creating' as it facilitates the relocation of labour-intensive industries in which the home country is losing its comparative advantage, whereas US investment is 'anti-trade creating' as it focuses on import-substituting, high-technology industries in the host countries. It should be noted, however, that not all investments in export-oriented activities (e.g. textiles) can be regarded as 'outward looking' since Japanese affiliates in Malaysia sell the bulk of their output in the local market while US affiliates export the bulk of their output (see Table 6.4). The difference in market orientation is sharp enough to cast serious doubts on the relevance of the Kojima hypothesis.

As regards developing country investment (excluding

Table 6.2. Malaysia: Foreign investment in companies in production by country as at 31 December 1983

	Paid-up capital	Loans	Total capital investment		Fixed assets	
	M$m.	M$m.	M$m.	%	M$m.	%
Singapore	1,052.2	284.4	1,336.6	32.9	884.2	23.1
Japan	524.5	179.2	703.7	17.3	704.0	18.4
United Kingdom	582.3	62.5	644.8	15.9	680.0	17.8
USA	180.7	46.6	227.3	5.6	306.0	8.0
Hong Kong	304.1	68.6	372.7	9.2	357.5	9.4
W. Germany	85.8	23.5	109.3	2.7	109.6	2.9
Australia	79.0	7.9	86.9	2.1	44.5	1.2
Netherlands	41.7	10.3	52.0	1.3	74.5	1.9
India	39.2	18.2	57.4	1.4	52.3	1.4
Others	387.6	82.4	470.0	11.6	606.8	15.9
Total	3,277.1	783.6	4,060.7	100.0	3,819.4	100.0

Source: Calculated from unpublished data provided by Malaysian Industrial Development Authority (MIDA).

Table 6.3. Malaysia: Foreign investment in companies in production by selected country and industry as at 31 December 1983

Industry	Singapore		Japan		UK		USA		Total foreign capital investment	
	M$m.	%	M$m.	%	M$m.	%	M$m.	%	M$m.	%
Food manufacturing	290.0	21.7	74.6	10.6	137.4	21.3	11.5	5.1	705.6	17.4
Beverages & tobacco	28.8	5.9	-	-	104.2	16.2	52.3	23.0	278.3	6.8
Textile & products	77.2	5.8	224.3	31.9	6.4	1.0	5.5	2.4	490.6	12.1
Leather & products	5.4	0.4	-	-	-	-	-	-	17.1	0.4
Wood & wood products	60.8	4.5	67.0	9.5	4.9	0.8	2.8	1.2	199.6	4.9
Furniture & fixtures	14.6	1.1	1.4	0.2	-	-	0.5	0.2	19.3	0.5
Paper, publishing etc	21.7	1.6	0.2	-	2.7	0.4	0.4	0.2	29.0	0.7
Chemicals & products	63.4	4.7	19.5	2.8	105.8	16.4	83.0	36.5	327.3	8.1
Petroleum & coal	-	-	-	-	100.5	15.6	-	-	124.5	3.1
Rubber & products	25.3	1.9	11.8	1.7	19.3	3.0	10.3	4.5	105.2	2.6
Plastics products	8.4	0.6	11.9	1.7	0.9	0.1	-	-	24.5	0.6
Non-metallic minerals	190.5	14.3	53.7	7.6	38.8	6.0	1.0	0.4	401.6	9.9
Basic metal products	150.5	11.4	48.7	6.9	16.8	2.6	-	-	252.2	6.2
Metal products	42.9	3.2	19.2	2.7	25.5	4.0	1.6	0.7	136.1	3.4
Machinery	9.0	0.7	19.9	2.8	16.7	2.6	6.9	3.0	63.7	1.6
Electrical/electronics	80.9	6.1	109.2	15.5	35.3	5.5	35.5	15.6	394.1	9.7
Transport equipment	61.4	4.6	22.6	3.2	25.2	3.9	5.1	2.2	194.2	4.7
Scientific equipment	-	-	2.0	0.3	-	-	4.0	1.8	43.1	1.1
Miscellaneous manaf.	1.4	0.1	11.3	1.6	3.8	0.6	6.6	2.9	42.5	1.0
Tourism	148.3	11.1	4.9	0.7	0.5	0.1	-	-	212.6	5.2
Total	1,336.6	100.0	703.7	100.0	644.8	100.0	227.3	100.0	4,060.7	100.0

Source: Ibid.

Singapore), Hong Kong investment (92% of total foreign investment) is concentrated (more than 60%) in textiles, electronics and hotel tourist complexes, with other investment in food manufacturing and wood products. Indian investment (1.4% of the total) centres (more than 85%) on food manufacture, textiles and transport equipment. Capital from Taiwan (0.3% of the total) has gone mostly (75%) into basic metal manufactures, electronics and non-metallic mineral products, with other investment in textiles, wood manufacture, chemicals and plastic products. Korean capital represents a negligible proportion of total foreign investment and is confined to rubber manufacture.

It is interesting to note that investment from some developing countries, especially the newly industrialising countries (NICs), at least in some industries, appears to be largely motivated by the need to circumvent barriers put up by developed countries. Hong Kong, Taiwanese and to some extent Indian investment in the Malaysian textile industry has been made mainly to make use of the unutilised GSP Malaysian quota in several developed country markets.

As regards the motivation of DFI, a survey of foreign firms operating in Malaysia has shown that investment for the local market was the most important motive(5). The second most important reason, particularly significant for Japan, was to secure, maintain and/or develop raw material supplies including processing. Low labour costs rank third, of particular significance for US and European firms. Malaysia was also ranked second only to Singapore in terms of favourable investment climate in the ASEAN region. For Australian firms, the expected growth of the local market was the most important reason(6), with lower unit costs, protecting the export market and making use of patents or expertise cited as other important motives.

Foreign Investment Policy

Malaysian government policy towards foreign investment has been fairly liberal. However, two important qualifications need to be made. First, there are checks and controls to which foreign investment is subjected. Second, the incentives system designed to attract foreign investment does not discriminate against domestic investment.

Government policy towards foreign investment has been geared to achieve the overall objective of diversification and modernisation of the economy. There are also specific objectives behind the foreign investment drive, ranging from geographical diffusion of industries to export orientation of the manufacturing sector. Accordingly, incentives schemes have been designed to encourage the production of 'priority products', location of industries in 'development areas', the use of domestic material inputs and exports of manufactures.

Table 6.4. Sales destination of Japanese and US affiliates in Malaysia (%)

Investing country	Year	Local market	(% of Sales) Export market		
			Total	Home country	Other countries
Japan	1973	87.3	12.6	7.8	4.8
USA	1977	23.8	76.2	45.6	30.6

Source: H. Hill and B. Johns, 'The Role of Direct Foreign Investment in Developing East Asian Countries', Canberra (unpublished), 1984.

The Investment Incentives Act of 1968 outlines the incentives, while the Industrial Co-ordination Act of 1975 (including subsequent amendments) sets out to regulate investment activities by imposing a licensing requirement to ensure the 30% Bumiputra equity participation in accordance with the NEP. All industrial investments come within the ambit of the Ministry of Trade and Industry. In 1976 a 'one-stop' agency was established within the Malaysian Industrial Development Authority (MIDA). All investment proposals and approvals for industrial projects, both foreign and domestic, are co-ordinated by MIDA, while investment projects in the natural resource sectors, except petroleum, are approved by the respective state governments. All rights in petroleum are vested in the federal government and foreign investment in this sector is permitted through production-sharing arrangements with the National Petroleum Corporation (PETRONAS).

Investment Incentives. There are seven major forms of tax incentives: (i) pioneer status, (ii) investment tax credit, (iii) labour utilisation relief, (iv) increased capital allowance, (v) locational incentives, (vi) export incentives, and (vii) hotel incentives.

Pioneer status and labour utilisation relief provide for tax exemptions ranging from two to five years, depending respectively on the level of capital investment and the number of full-time paid employees. Both schemes also offer a further year of tax relief to investment projects if other criteria (i.e., location, type of product produced and extent of local raw material content) are fulfilled. The investment tax credit scheme allows for a credit of at least 25% of the total capital expenditure incurred on the project, with 5% of expenditure on the same criteria to a maximum of 40%. The increased capital allowance, aimed at modernising factories and production techniques, provides for an allowance of 40% (in addition to the normal allowance of 20%) of the plant expenditure, thus permitting more than 90% of eligible capital expenditure to be written off in five years. The location incentive scheme, available for companies which locate industries in designated development areas, provides a maximum tax holiday of 10 years depending on the size of capital investment or employment. Tax incentives for export promotion consist of an export allowance, an accelerated depreciation allowance and double deduction of overseas promotional expenses, while hotel incentives include an industrial building allowance, an accelerated depreciation allowance and an annual abatement of income tax on 15 to 30% of chargeable income (depending on location) for a period of 12 years.

In addition to these tax reliefs, Malaysia offers other forms of fiscal incentives including tariff protection, anti-dumping measures, import duty exemption for machinery and industrial raw materials. There are also export credit facilities at preferential interest rates designed to stimulate manufactured exports.

Investment Regulations. Foreign investment is highly regulated in Malaysia; however, except for a few industries that relate mainly to activities reserved to member states of the Federation, no industry is closed to private foreign investment. Guarantees against nationalisation of foreign assets without compensation are provided by the Constitution, and investment guarantee agreements have been concluded with several countries. In addition, legal disputes connected with foreign investment may be settled at the International Centre for the Settlement of Investment Disputes (in Washington, D.C.) of which Malaysia has been a member since 1966. Free transfer of currency for international transactions is also permitted in accordance with IMF rules. The system of exchange control practised is liberal and non-discriminatory. Transfer of profits and dividends, interest, royalties and fees and capital repatriation are freely allowed, although they are subject to nominal permission from the Bank Negara (the central bank). Double taxation agreements have also been concluded with several countries.

Malaysia

To ensure increased Malaysian (especially Bumiputra) participation in manufacturing in accordance with the NEP(7), the government encourages industrial projects on a joint-venture basis. However, it has made it clear that the 70:30 Malaysian/foreign equity ownership ratio represents a national target and is not meant to be implemented on an individual company basis.

Policy guidelines applied to new investment projects (after 1 January 1972) and to subsequent expansion of investment in existing projects which do not conform to the NEP equity target, require: majority Malaysian ownership for projects substantially dependent on the domestic market, and at least 70% Malaysian equity (including a minimum 30% Bumiputra) for projects involving the extraction and primary processing of non-renewable domestic natural resources. Majority and even total foreign ownership is permitted for projects manufacturing mainly for the export market. Factors which have a bearing on the foreign share of the equity structure include among others the following: the size of the investment, technology involved, location, degree of export orientation, linkages with existing industries and benefits to the country through spin-off effects.(8)

The government offers tax incentives (excluding companies already enjoying tax exemptions) to companies which undertake equity restructuring in accordance with the NEP. It has also resorted to selective participation in order to promote such restructuring through government agencies such as PERNAS (National Corporation), MARA (Council of Trust for Bumiputras), UDA (Urban Development Authority) and SEDCs (State Economic Development Corporations) which have acquired equity in a number of companies on behalf of the Bumiputra community (original inhabitants). In addition, the National Equity Corporation was established in 1980 to buy up shares which are to be divested eventually to the Bumiputras.

All foreign companies are required to comply with the guidelines relating to the employment of Malaysians at all levels, though they are applied more flexibly with respect to priority industries such as manufacturing industries which are wholly export-oriented. On technology transfers the written approval of the Ministry of Trade and Industry must be obtained by all manufacturers before entering into any agreement involving foreign partners and their technology to ensure the payment of fees and royalties commensurate with the level of technology transferred. Licensing agreements are generally approved for a period of 5 years and the guidelines require that the know-how transferred should include information on improvements made during the period of the agreement, and that the licensors should bear the cost of training local personnel whenever necessary. It is noteworthy that the Ministry approves licensing agreements only on condition that the licensor does not restrict the marketing territory of the licensee.

'New' forms of foreign investment which enable greater unpackaging of foreign capital and technology, and permit minority equity holdings by foreign firms in joint ventures(9) are beginning to appear. The proportion of DFI in total private capital flows seems to be declining, although the share of private capital flows in total foreign resource flows has been increasing, as shown in Table 6.5. Second, the share of DFI in gross domestic investment also seems to be declining. Third, foreign equity share in the Malaysian corporate sector has been falling steadily, as noted earlier. Fourth, the number of technology licensing agreements has been on the rise; technical assistance and know-how agreements account for about 54% of the total number of agreements signed during the period 1970-83 and Japan, the United Kingdom and the United States jointly account for about 55% of these.

The shift away from the 'traditional' foreign investment package is largely attributable to NEP guidelines governing equity, which render the traditional package unsuitable for Malaysia. This does not necessarily mean, however, that there is no more room for the traditional form of foreign investment; the 30% foreign equity share target is only a national average and is not inconsistent with majority or even 100% foreign ownership for individual companies. Moreover, other national goals broaden the scope for foreign investment which brings in expertise on technology and marketing, besides contributing much needed capital. Malaysia is probably not ready to unbundle the investment package completely, as its absorptive capacity for technology sourced through licensing appears to be limited. Thus it may continue to welcome traditional foreign investment packages in some fields. It is perfectly possible for foreign investment to grow absolutely, while its relative share in total investment in the country declines, provided domestic investment can grow at a much faster rate.

Be this as it may, the investment incentive schemes do not seem to have produced the intended results. Pioneer status and investment tax credit are the two most important schemes. Locational incentives do not seem to be popular, presumably because the cost of locating in a development area outweighs the gains conferred by the scheme. Labour utilisation relief has failed to elicit the desired response, because it is geared to the absolute number of workers rather than to the labour intensity of the investment projects. Moreover, the investment schemes are not entirely consistent with the objectives. Thus, the capital bias is in conflict with the employment objective, and the labour cheapening effect of labour utilisation relief may be offset by the capital cheapening effect of tax holidays.

The large number of project approvals (more than 50%) without tax incentives is striking. This does not necessarily

Table 6.5. Total net resources flows to Malaysia, 1969-81

Period	Average annual net flows US$ m.	Share of official flows in total (%)	Share of private flows in total (%)	Share of direct investment in total (%)	Share of direct foreign investment in gross domestic investment (%)
1969-71	80.4	71.3	28.7	31.3	3.4[a]
1972-76	245.5	49.7	50.3	36.7	4.5
1977-81	569.3	36.6	63.4	24.8	2.5

a 1971 only.

Source: *Ibid*, Tables 1 and 2.

imply that investment incentives are redundant.Those with tax incentive are far more important in terms of called-up capital (Table 6.6). The implication is that large-scale investments do require incentives.

Unlike some other developing countries, local investors in Malaysia are not discriminated against by the incentive regime. In fact, there is some bias against foreign investors in the sense that local counterparts are not subject to the same degree of government regulation. Even in the allocation of incentives, domestic investment is clearly favoured over foreign investment. This is brought out in Table 6.7.

Company Perceptions

Sample Survey of tncs. A sample survey of 35 manufacturing tncs was conducted in Kuala Lumpur and Petaling Jaya in July/August 1984, to determine their perceptions relating to the key elements in their motivation, both positive and negative, with regard to their foreign investments. The survey also tried to determine the extent to which more nega-

Table 6.6. Approved investment projects with and without tax incentives

Year	Number of approvals	Total called-up capital (M$ m.)	Number of approvals	Total called-up capital (M$ m.)
1971	190	505.4	115	61.0
1972	185	242.5	170	59.0
1973	236	440.4	237	97.1
1974	221	570.6	304	189.5
1975	172	386.4	289	179.1
1976	203	341.6	223	116.9
1977	182	257.4	218	100.5
1978	203	369.4	225	110.8
1979	183	332.2	301	922.5
1980	184	458.2	276	294.7
1981	216	1,149.6	397	559.5
1982	177	1,637.1	304	284.4
1983	179	788.9	319	491.4

Source: MIDA.

Table 6.7. Foreign investments (called-up capital) in projects granted approval by tax incentive (M$ m.)

Year	P S	I T C	L U R	L I	Other tax incentives	Without tax incentives	Total
1975	52.5	43.3	2.2	21.1	2.0	32.3	153.4
	(36.6)	(36.1)	(26.6)	(20.5)	(16.4)	(18.1)	(27.1)
1976	68.2	19.7	0.7	0.7	2.8	22.0	114.1
	(30.0)	(24.4)	(24.7)	(3.8)	(21.7)	(18.8)	(24.9)
1977	35.4	14.8	4.5	31.4	0	21.7	107.9
	(34.4)	(32.5)	(19.7)	(40.5)	(0)	(21.6)	(30.1)
1978	101.6	33.5	-	18.2	0	24.5	177.8
	(49.7)	(27.0)	(1.1)	(51.6)	(0)	(22.1)	(37.0)
1979	100.0	25.8	2.6	18.3	0	348.7	495.6
	(52.1)	(30.1)	(73.3)	(36.2)	(0)	(37.8)	(39.5)
1980	140.2	41.2	0.4	2.1	0	64.3	284.3
	(43.7)	(32.4)	(14.0)	(25.0)	(0)	(21.8)	(37.8)
1981	120.3	133.8	2.0	53.9	2.7	132.6	495.3
	(36.7)	(29.2)	(100.0)	(30.6)	(5.1)	(23.6)	(29.0)
1982	185.1	109.6	0.4	180.1	0	52.5	527.6
	(37.1)	(26.5)	(7.6)	25.9)	(0)	(18.4)	(27.5)
1983	122.6	47.1	0.3	115.6	33.0	115.6	329.1
	(35.7)	(23.6)	(100.0)	(23.5)	(18.1)	(23.5)	(25.7)

Figures in brackets express foreign share as percentage of total called-up capital (foreign plus domestic)

PS = pioneer status, ITC = investment tax credit, LUR = labour utilisation relief, LI = location incentives.

Source: Calculated from unpublished material provided by MIDA.

tive perceptions could be altered in the short run (e.g. changes in foreign investment regulations, incentive systems, etc.) and in the medium term through improvements in infrastructure. Another objective was to determine the extent to which the Malaysian Government's foreign investment policy was geared to meeting the negative perceptions; in short, to determine the advantages and disadvantages for foreign investors in Malaysia.

Most of the sample tncs were large firms (more than 100 employees) established in the last 20 years or so, especially since independence. All were either subsidiaries or affiliates of foreign companies, mainly in the UK, Japan and Singapore. Local shareholders generally owned less than 50% of the tncs' total equity. The majority of the sample were engaged in producing chemical products, electrical machinery and food products.

Motives of Foreign Investors in Malaysia. The most important reasons derived from the sample were the potential of the local market; the favourable government incentives; the good physical infrastructural facilities and the availability of relatively cheap labour. We will now discuss each of these factors in turn.

(i) Unexploited Local Market. This factor agrees with the findings of Lewis Mann and Deepak Nayyar(10) that, because of stiff tariff barriers established by many Third World countries, foreign investors often feel that the best way to capture the local market is to produce in the host country. Edwards in his study of tariff protection and industrialisation policies in Malaysia(11) revealed that import-substitution industries regard tariff protection as a more important incentive than tax holidays. In any case the data presented earlier in this Chapter show that most tncs invested in import-substitution industries.

(ii) Government Incentives. As noted earlier, Malaysia offers tax relief for investors in various forms and this and other exemptions make it easier for tncs to establish a firm footing in the country. In addition, the government welcomes foreign investment, unlike some other developing countries which appear rather hostile. The government provides many other incentives to foreign investors, especially those who produce manufactured goods predominantly for export. For instance, if a foreign investor invests more than M$1m. in an underdeveloped region he is eligible for a 45% tax exemption for 10 years.

(iii) Good Infrastructural Facilities. Malaysia has some of the finest infrastructural facilities in the Third World. All year round roads connect all the major towns. There is adequate water and electricity and the rates are reasonable. Some investors also referred to the free trade zones which were a great inducement.

(iv) Low Labour Costs. According to Mann and Nayyar, it is advantageous for tncs to produce abroad because labour is much cheaper in Third World countries. A more important factor, however, is the difficulty many transnationals find in recruiting labour to perform tedious jobs at poverty wages in their home countries. For example, according to one of the electronics firms in the sample, the wage rates in Malaysia are about 10 times lower than in the US and 4 times lower than in Japan. However, according to a number of other investors, Malaysia no longer has a surplus supply of labour. In fact, countries like Thailand, Indonesia, India, Burma and Sri Lanka have cheaper labour and Malaysia's wage rates are only marginally lower than Singapore's. Nevertheless, the quality of labour in Malaysia is still relatively high.

Other factors which attract tncs are the stability of the Malaysian Government as well as the stability of its currency and economy; Malaysia's strategic location in South East Asia; the relatively high level of technology in the country; and the rapid economic growth rate. Many of the factors cited by the sample respondents are essential in helping tncs secure a high rate of return on their investments. In fact, a recent study points out that Malaysia is one of the most profitable countries for tnc investment(12).

Disadvantages. The firms surveyed were also asked to list the various disadvantages or handicaps they had to face when they undertook to invest in Malaysia. That cited by the largest number of respondents was government regulations. Many firms are unhappy with government regulations which they feel are too numerous and restrictive. The regulations cited most often were the Industrial Co-ordination Act and the guidelines for Acquisitions, Mergers and Takeovers. Briefly, most respondents complain that these regulations impose too many restrictions on their activities and are generally cumbersome and bureaucratic.

Other disadvantages related to the intensive competition in a limited domestic market, bureaucracy, shortage of skilled workers and a relatively high tax burden. These will now be discussed in greater detail.

Malaysia has so small a population that tncs find the local market quickly saturated. In addition, there are numerous firms, so that few of them are able to operate at full capacity. Bureaucracy is another source of complaint. Transnationals attribute this partly to the maze of government regulations and the government's desire to control every aspect of business operations. In addition, approval for licenses or permits often takes a long time. All this adds to production costs. Skilled workers are difficult to find and government training programmes are inadequate and ineffective. Consequently tncs complain that they have to steal workers from each other, resulting in high labour turnover rates. Another major problem is the high tax burden, both in personal and corporate tax. In addition, various duties are imposed on locally manufactured products from the point of raw materials to the finished product. The numerous customs procedures, rules and regulations impede efficiency and waste man-hours as well as increasing the cost of manufacturers' operations.

Despite these many problems, half the tncs surveyed indicated that they would still have invested in Malaysia, even if they had anticipated the problems encountered. 51.7% of the firms indicated that they felt the problems faced in their operations could be solved in the future. They also expected the investment climate to change. The most significant expectations were: a revision of government policies and regulations; the introduction of high and advanced technology; an improvement in infrastructure facilities and stability.

The sample were also asked to suggest ways of improving the investment climate in Malaysia. The most common suggestions related to a reduction in government regulations and red tape, improved training in institutions, improved attitudes and work ethic on the part of manpower, and revision of taxes and fiscal incentives.

Most respondents felt that the economy should be deregulated and restrictive legislation like the Industrial Co-ordination Act amended. At the same time, they suggested that the government should continue the process of up-dating techniques and information systems to allow quicker response aimed at enhancing manpower productivity and also to improve the information flow.

On training, they urged the government to upgrade and build more training facilities to improve the supply of skilled labour. In addition, they suggested that fiscal incentives be given to firms to train workers. They approved the government's attempts to improve the attitudes and work ethic of workers but felt that more should be done in this direction. They were more vocal in suggesting fiscal changes. Many felt that the Excess Profits Tax should be repealed on the grounds that, apart from being arbitrary, it penalises efficiency, discriminates against companies which pay higher dividends and reduces retained earnings. It is especially painful for companies with sharp fluctuations in year to year earnings.

Some respondents tried to relate fiscal incentives to the need to increase productivity and to upgrade the quality of the work force. They felt that the Director-General of Income Tax was interpreting the word 'bonus' in very wide terms. It is taken to include a variety of payments including productivity and other payments, many of which are made under contractual arrangements between employer and employee or form part of a negotiated Union Agreement. Therefore, they strongly recommended that all contractual payments, including bonuses, should be fully tax deductible. Their philosophy is that, while the general level of wages should not be allowed to get out of hand, merit should be rewarded.

Other respondents were eloquent on the need to include Group Relief - in other words, to allow the tax losses of one company in the group to be offset against the profits of another company in the group. This is not permitted in Malaysia and has adversely affected companies which have diversified into joint ventures by introducing local participation and the creation of subsidiary companies whose business was previously carried out by a division of the company. Losses in these newly-created subsidiary companies cannot be offset against profits of the parent company, whereas losses incurred in divisions of the same company are permitted to be offset against profits in other divisions of that company.

Conclusion

Available data give a clear indication of the importance of foreign investment in Malaysia, especially in the industrial sector. They also reveal the heavy concentration of the sources of foreign investment as well as of its allocation in a few industries. There have been shifts in the sectoral allocation pattern in recent years in accordance with the shift in industrial policy in favour of exports. Although there are signs that new forms of foreign investment are emerging, direct foreign investment still represents by far the most important form of foreign investment.

Malaysia has been actively seeking foreign investment for a number of reasons and through a variety of incentive schemes. Modernisation of the economy, diversification of the production structure, employment creation, technology transfers, industrial dispersion, and export orientation of the manufacturing sector have been some of the important policy objectives. Investment incentive schemes have been designed to achieve these various policy goals. The contributions of foreign investment in these areas, however, have been somewhat limited, presumably due to built-in bias in favour of large-scale, capital-intensive projects and policy conflicts. Notwithstanding the active encouragement given to foreign investment, the New Economic Policy has imposed limits on the role of foreign investment in the country. On the one hand, the NEP calls for reduced foreign equity participation while, on the other, the NEP strategy requires a substantial injection of foreign capital and technical and managerial know-how. This conflict is partly being resolved by resorting to new forms of foreign investment - i.e., by unbundling the investment package through licensing and franchising agreements, management contracts and the like.

Much as Malaysia might like to reduce the ownership or equity component of foreign investment, current trends in the balance of payments may render such a policy extremely undesirable. Malaysia has been running into huge and persistent current-account deficits during the early 1980s. A large part of the deficit has been 'financed' by foreign capital flows. In other words, the balance-of-payments deficit problem would have been even more serious in the absence of foreign capital flows into the country.

Moreover, the new accent placed on 'heavy industrialisation'also introduces a new dimension. Such a policy tends significantly to increase the country's dependence on foreign investment at least in the short and medium terms. Thus, it is extremely difficult to reconcile the NEP equity objective with other national aspirations.

It is not easy to ascertain whether or not the various tax incentives given are really necessary. In any case, it is dangerous to make generalisations in this regard as conditions differ greatly between industrial projects and locations. That there are enormous social costs involved in these tax concessions and exemptions is readily obvious. Although tax incentives are seldom cited by investors as the main reason for investing in the country, it does appear that they are sometimes viewed as compensation for the costs or inconvenience associated with politically-engineered regulations. Thus, one might argue that less regulation or deregulation would make a lot more economic sense than increased tax incentives.

The present analysis also calls for a major review of the investment incentive schemes. In particular, the bias in favour of large-scale enterprises and capital-intensive production methods should be corrected. In the same vein, discrimination against small-scale, labour-intensive industries should be dismantled. The incentive schemes should be so designed as to make the most intensive use of the abundant factors and resources - so that the adverse effect of policy distortions on resource allocation is minimised - and to involve as large a cross-section of the community of entrepreneurs as possible.

It has been reported that most if not all countries seeking investment abroad are shying away from underdeveloped countries, a likely reason being the real and imaginary uncertainties and unpredictabilities of the developing economies along with the growing tightness of international capital markets and market limitations. This perhaps explains the comparatively sluggish inflow of foreign investment to Malaysia until quite recently. Investments did flow but they were mainly directed to mining and ore prospecting, and to raw materials.

There are, however, certain factors which may help attract the much needed foreign capital and technology. The availability of relatively abundant supplies of skills and technical knowledge along with a relatively high per capita income plus a low level of industrial activity clearly establishes a prima facie case for faster industrial growth in Malaysia. Faced with the scarcity and increasing cost of manpower at home, many developed countries are starting to establish labour-intensive industries overseas in countries like Malaysia.

Some manufacturers may also consider diverting some of their industries to less developed areas to avoid the pressures of anti-pollution legislation at home. Malaysia should of course be cautious about this type of investment, and formulate anti-pollution legislation to avoid the emergence of such problems in the future.

Another factor that may lead to an increasing flow of investment is of course the streamlining of Malaysia's administrative machinery, and the active promotional work that is now being undertaken in the developed countries. In this connection, it may be more profitable to attract medium-sized companies in the developed countries which are struggling to expand their operations rather than the giant tncs.

Assuming that, as a result of all the above factors, developed nations see the potential of investing in Malaysia, a very important link here would be to make the local investment climate as attractive as possible. In this connection, Malaysia compares very favourably with other developing countries. Apart from maintaining its relatively high political stability, no one can deny that the government has done much to create as attractive a climate as possible. In addition to the package of fiscal incentives provided under the Investment Incentives Act, the 21 industrial estates in various parts of the country, the nine free trade zones and the establishment of licensed manufacturing warehouses also do much to help attract foreign investment.

With the implementation of the Fourth Development Plan, Malaysia will be entering a more rapid phase of development, and the maintenance and intensification of this trend will require tremendous investment activities in the five years ahead. No one is more aware than the government of the paramount need to raise the level of productive investment in order to generate employment opportunities, raise the standard of living and secure future economic growth. The recent setting up of HICOM augurs well for the heavy industries strategy, especially in view of the local private investors' lack of interest in undertaking capital-intensive heavy industry projects probably because of the substantial financial requirements, long gestation periods and relatively unattractive returns of heavy industrial projects. With government acceptance in principle of state participation and intervention in industrial development, such a measure will not only bring about a greater pace of industrial development but also a better balance in ownership and control in the manufacturing sector.

As a final comment, it must be remembered that failure to win foreign investment should not mean pruning Malaysia's Plan programme. To quote the Prime Minister, 'We are not going to be held to ransom merely because we want to have a good investment climate.'

NOTES AND REFERENCES

1. H. G. Callies, Foreign Capital in South East Asia (Institute of Public Relations, New York, 1942).

2. Junid Saham, British Industrial Investment in Malaysia 1963-1971 (Oxford University Press, Kuala Lumpur, 1980).

3. Anuwar Ali and H. Osman-Rani, 'Malaysian Experience with the MNCs', (unpublished) Kuala Lumpur, 1984.

4. K. Kojima, Japan and a New World Economic Order (Charles E. Tuttle & Co, Tokyo, 1977).

5. T. W. Allen, The ASEAN Report, Vol. I: A Comparative Assessment of the ASEAN Countries; Vol. II: The Evaluation and Programs of ASEAN, Asian Wall Street Journal (Hong Kong, 1979).

6. Bureau of Industry Economies, Australian Direct Investment in the ASEAN Countries (Canberra, 1983).

7. The New Economic Policy as formulated within the framework of a long-term Outline Perspective Plan (1971-90) has two main objectives, to eradicate poverty and to restructure Malaysian society so as to achieve racial balance in the economy.

8. Malaysian Industrial Development Authority (MIDA), Annual Report 1979 (Kuala Lumpur, 1980).

9. C. Oman, New Forms of International Investment in Developing Countries (OECD, Paris, 1983).

10. Lewis Mann, 'Some Effects of Foreign Investment: The Case of Malaysia', Kuala Lumpur, undated (mimeo); Deepak Nayyar, 'Transnational Corporations and Manufactured Exports

from Poor Countries', The Economic Journal, Vol. 38 (March 1977).

11. C. B. Edwards, 'Protection, Profits and Policy - An Analysis of Industrialisation in Malaysia', Ph.D. dissertation, University of East Anglia, 1975 (unpublished).

12. E. L. Wainwright, 'Development Financing Through MNCs', paper presented at an International Seminar on Financing for Development, Kuala Lumpur, 1984.

13. The current-account deficit amounted to M$6.7 bn in 1983 and was projected at M$5.4 bn for 1984.

Chapter Seven

PRIVATE FOREIGN INVESTMENT IN BARBADOS

Delisle Worrell, Harold Codrington, Zorina Khan and Lawson Nurse

Over the past thirty years or so Barbados has moved from among the world's poorest countries to occupy a tenuous position in the ranks of middle-income less developed countries. That development came with the emergence of light manufacturing and tourism, which eclipsed the sugar industry, the centre of economic activity in the island for three hundred years. During this period of transition, light manufacturing expanded to become the main source of employment outside of government service. Its contribution to GDP in 1985 was greater than for any sector apart from domestic services (distribution, personal services, etc), government and tourism.

Economic development was stimulated by technological change in the industrial world, particularly the introduction of jet transport, and both tourism and manufacturing expanded in the wake of this revolution in transport. Barbados was among tropical destinations to benefit from the boom in holiday travel that jets made possible. Falling air transport costs and growing wage costs in North America created an incentive for US firms to locate assembly and light manufacturing plants in developing areas with lower labour costs, a development which was to Barbados's advantage. In addition, Barbados offered to potential investors the attractions of a literate population, a stable political system, long-standing ties with North America, good internal and international communications and a well developed infrastructure of roads, ports and utilities.

The signing in 1973 of the treaty creating the Caribbean Economic Community (Caricom), with provision for internal free trade and a common external tariff, created a regional market of sufficient size to attract some modest-scale manufacturing. Government welcomed foreign investment with an incentive package, starting with the Pioneer Industries Act of 1958 and encompassing tax holidays, import rebates, promotional activity, provision of factory shells and other inducements.

Trends and Characteristics of Foreign Investment

Foreign capital of all kinds has played a vital role in capital formation and balance-of-payments financing in Barbados throughout the post World War II period. In the late 1940s and the 1950s identified capital inflows were mainly for the public sector, the largest single transaction being a sterling bond issued in London to finance construction of a deep water port at Bridgetown, the island's capital. Foreign capital for the private sector rose to significance in the 1960s, and made substantial contributions for the remainder of the period. The public sector continued to borrow abroad during these years, especially after 1976.

In the past twenty years there have been two periods when total capital inflows grew rapidly, 1969-71 and 1977-80; the first was due mainly to private sector activity, while the second owed more to government projects. Private long-term capital inflows were quite large throughout the post-1960 period, but their relative importance was greater in the second half of the 1960s and the early years of the 1970s. More recently government borrowing and short-term financing have reached larger proportions.

Foreign capital inflows (private and public) have been the equivalent of about one-quarter of total capital formation for the years when we have detailed information, from 1965 onwards. However, the contribution of foreign capital is noticeably lower in the last few years; between 1965 and 1973 it ranged from 23% to 39%, compared with a range of minus 9% to 32% for the period 1974-84. Private capital inflows per year between 1974 and 1984 were 42% lower than for 1965-73. The contribution of foreign capital to capital formation, other than stocks, does not rise above 20% for the years following 1974, when our series on stock-holding begins (Table 7.1).

Apart from loan finance for public utilities and companies engaged in oil production and distribution, two-thirds of foreign investment in the private sector has been equity participation. The remaining one-third was, for the most part, loans from head offices and overseas affiliates of firms which were owned, wholly or in partnership, by foreigners. In a study of a cross-section of industrial activity Codrington(1) found that the extent of foreign ownership of the firm was the only significant factor influencing foreign portfolio investment.

In the 1960s foreign investment was directed mainly towards tourism and manufacturing; both sectors recorded episodes of rapid expansion (see Table 7.2). However, we do not have a detailed sectoral breakdown until 1977. Public utilities contracted substantial foreign loans in the years from 1980 to 1984, especially for financing the purchase and installation of equipment such as electricity generators,

Table 7.1. Investment ($m.)

	Gross capital formation (I)	Stocks (S)	Foreign capital (Net of Outflows)					Ratios		
					Private sector					
			Total (K)	Public sector (G)	Total (P)	Direct equity (PD)	Portfolio loan (PP) [a]	K/I	P/I	P/(I-S)
1965	34.6	-	9.9	7.2	2.8	3.0	-0.2	0.286	0.080	-
1966	41.7	-	16.4	0.7	16.4	12.8	3.6	0.393	0.393	-
1967	43.6	-	10.3	-3.9	14.3	12.2	2.1	0.326	0.327	-
1968	63.3	-	15.0	-0.5	15.1	15.8	-0.7	0.236	0.238	-
1969	75.6	-	17.7	0.5	17.2	14.3	2.8	0.234	0.227	-
1970	98.5	-	24.5	0.6	23.9	16.9	7.0	0.248	0.242	-
1971	95.6	-	32.4	0.5	32.4	29.2	3.2	0.338	0.238	-
1972	101.3	-	37.9	4.9	32.9	33.4	-0.4	0.374	0.324	-
1973	119.4	-	44.6	41.0	5.6	5.1	0.5	0.372	0.046	-
1974	169.2	14.5	21.5	-7.1	28.6	12.4	16.2	0.127	0.169	0.216
1975	156.2	4.7	50.7	-0.5	51.3	44.7	6.6	0.324	0.328	0.407
1976	235.9	4.5	44.3	5.4	38.8	12.3	26.5	0.187	0.164	0.197
1977	194.1	3.2	38.9	11.1	27.8	9.3	18.5	0.200	0.143	0.141
1978	254.5	2.2	44.2	31.9	12.2	18.8	-6.6	0.173	0.047	0.058
1979	317.2	18.3	-15.9	8.9	-24.8	10.1	-34.9	0.050	0.078	-0.083
1980	424.3	29.0	44.2	53.7	-9.5	1.8	-11.3	0.104	0.022	-0.024
1981	525.0	7.1	155.0	98.7	56.3	14.3	42.0	0.295	0.107	0.109
1982	450.5	-3.9	29.9	35.2	-5.3	8.8	14.1	0.066	0.012	-0.012
1983	421.2	6.2	44.4	57.5	-13.1	4.6	-17.7	0.105	-0.031	-0.032
1984	400.7	-5.7	-35.6	11.7	-47.3	-17.7	-44.6	-0.089	-0.118	-0.117

a This is mainly interfirm lending. There is no foreign investment in equity form which is not 'direct' investment.

Table 7.2. Total private foreign investment ($'000)

	1977	1978	1979	1980	1981	1982	1983	1984	Total 1977-84
Public utilities	2,050.9	1,921.3	1,810.3	9,989.8	61,272.2	26,143.4	53,589.9	26,710.9	183,479.7
Distribution	47.6	884.2	2,806.6	1,290.0	434.4	820.8	423.2	-559.3	6,147.5
Oil companies	1,140.7	-332.6	4,908.8	35,668.2	31,608.0	2,978.4	-554.0	-	75,417.5
Manufacturing	6,361.0	1,478.8	9,876.3	5,794.4	12,353.3	8,648.4	3,309.8	3,760.2	51,582.2
of which food, beverages	514.8	347.0	274.6	723.5	-75.7	297.8	-1,078.3	524.9	1,528.5
textiles	-293.7	-	4,493.1	-	1,306.4	1,165.8	1,609.6	2,191.3	10,472.3
chemicals	4,569.6	165.3	1,103.5	20.0	900.6	1,573.6	1,583.4	165.0	1,080.9
wood, furniture, etc.	180.0	-55.4	-46.6	-	25.0	-	-	-	103.1
non-metallic mineral products	38.9	-	-	-	-	-8.5	-	-	30.4
basic metal products	6.0	-	-	-	-	-	-	-	6.0
metal products & assembly products	1,225.4	-	4,964.1	5,050.9	9,657.0	5,079.7	655.1	750.1	27,382.4
miscellaneous products	120.0	1,021.9	-912.4	-	540.0	540.0	540.0	128.9	1,978.4
Hotels	489.4	769.1	585.7	1,789.9	3,433.3	1,530.0	-	2,162.6	10,760.3
Real estate	82.9	97.8	83.6	-	-	-15.0	-	-	249.3
Sugar	-	-	-	-	-	-	1,500.0	-	15,000.0
Insurance	6,248.4	7,980.8	8,412.5	-2,717.6	8,946.7	25,527.9	26,464.9	33,255.0	114,118.6
Total	16,420.9	12,799.4	28,483.8	51,814.7	118,047.9	65,634.2	98,223.8	65,320.4	456,755.1
Outflows(-)	-11,396.1	578.4	53,257.8	61,072.7	61,708.9	70,920.2	111,367.8	112,632.4	
Net Total	27,817.0	12,221.0	-24,774.0	-9,258.0	56,339.0	-5,826.0	-13,134.0	-47,312.0	

Source: Central Bank, Balance of Payments Survey

telephone switching gear and transmission facilities. Most of their foreign funding was by borrowing. Both the telephone and the electric supply companies are part-owned by foreign companies, which were used as the source for some of the borrowing. Funds were also obtained from foreign governments and international institutions. Firms engaged in oil exploration, refining and distribution - all foreign-owned up to 1982 - borrowed from overseas affiliates. Apart from oil companies, a very large part of direct foreign investment in the 1977-84 period went into manufacturing, with only small amounts for tourism (Table 7.3).

Service charges (67%) on long-term private foreign investment substantially exceeded those on government borrowing (45%) for the years 1973-84 (the limit of available data) even though the foreign finance accumulated by the two sectors over the decade was of comparable magnitude (see Table 7.4). The private sector's payments were fairly evenly split between dividends and interest, despite the preponderance of private equity. The ratio of interest payments to outstanding government debt ranged from 6.9% to 14.5% (except for 1973, which registered 4.5%). A similar ratio for private investment cannot be directly calculated because estimates of the stock of private foreign debt and equity are subject to a wide margin of error. However, dividends, profits and interest paid to foreign investors by the private sector exceeded government service payments by 31%, although the capital inflows for the private sector between 1973 and 1984 were only 35% of the capital inflow for government. Moreover, the overall returns to foreign holders of private obligations appear to have been much higher than for the holders of Barbados government obligations.

There is also some support for the proposition advanced by Girvan(2) in a Jamaican context, and others more widely, that large inflows of direct private capital investment tend to lead to outflows eventually. Our own study has found that, in the case of Barbados, between 1973 and 1984 the payment of dividends and interest by the private sector constituted $247.7m. or twice the new private sector long-term investment. A net inflow of private sector foreign capital is achieved only by ever-increasing inflows of new capital.

Between 1975 and 1984, our data permit us to examine whether foreign investors sought out activities that were export-oriented, capital-intensive and growing rapidly, and whether they benefitted more than others from government incentive programmes. We also investigate any important differences in the operations of wholly-owned subsidiaries and joint ventures.

As regards the sector distribution, the data on foreign investment in manufacturing between 1977 and 1983 suggest

Table 7.3. Total private foreign investment ($'000)

	1977	1978	1979	1980	1981	1982	1983	1984	Total 1977-84
Public utilities	-8.0	-	-	538.4	-	-	3,393.2	-1,250.0	2,619.6
Distribution	44.6	841.9	448.8	569.0	16.9	747.1	109.0	-1,182.8	1,594.5
Oil companies	1,140.7	-332.6	-618.9	-616.2	4,863.1	2,978.4	-554.0	-	6,860.5
Manufacturing	4,079.9	1,358.7	3,564.0	255.4	12,519.7	5,315.5	1,560.0	692.3	29,345.5
Hotels	-	-	-	728.0	584.9	-	-	-	1,312.9
Real estate	-	-	-	-	-	-	-	-	-
Sugar	-	-	-	-	-	-	-	-	-
Insurance	1,970.3	1,504.6	3,386.7	-1,424.7	915.8	1,686.7	1,805.3	2,104.3	11,949.0
Total	7,227.5	3,372.6	6,780.6	49.9	18,900.4	10,727.7	6,259.5	363.8	53,682.0

Source: Ibid.

Table 7.4. Foreign debt and service payments ($m.)

	National debt (foreign) (1)	Public sector long-term capital inflow (2)	Government interest payments (foreign) (3)	Private sector long-term capital inflow (4)	Private Sector		Ratio of government interest payments to national debt (6)
					branch profits & dividends (5)	Interest	
1973	55.4	41.0	2.5	5.6	10.4	6.7	4.5
1974	42.8	-7.1	4.6	28.6	4.5	8.0	10.7
1975	44.1	-0.6	4.5	51.3	8.4	8.7	10.2
1976	50.2	5.5	3.7	38.8	6.2	3.3	7.4
1977	55.2	11.1	3.8	27.8	6.6	9.3	6.9
1978	89.2	32.0	5.7	12.2	7.3	5.5	6.4
1979	112.1	9.0	16.3	-24.8	9.9	10.6	14.5
1980	163.9	53.7	15.6	-9.5	9.2	10.3	9.5
1981	259.4	98.8	21.9	56.3	19.7	14.0	8.4
1982	287.0	35.2	35.2	-5.3	14.8	8.0	12.3
1983	347.3	57.5	36.2	-13.1	11.3	15.5	10.4
1984	365.3	11.7	39.7	-47.3	13.6	25.9	10.9
Total		347.8	189.7	120.6	121.9	125.8	

Source: Col. 1 Central Bank of Barbados, Annual Statistical Digest 1984
Col. 2, 4 Central Bank Barbados, Balance of Payments, Table 3
Col. 3, 5, 6 Central Bank of Barbados, Balance of Payments 1983, Table 8

that it was attracted to relatively export-oriented activities. The assembly of electrical components and the manufacture of metal products attracted 53% of all foreign investment in manufacturing between 1977 and 1984; 88% of firms involved in the manufacture of electrical goods and components in 1983 were foreign-owned. These activities tend to be highly export-oriented, indicated by a value of 1.89 for the ratio of export sales to domestic value-added (a ratio surpassed only by tourism). They are also relatively fast growing, increasing their local value-added by over one and a half times during the six-year period. They are by no means the most capital-intensive segment of manufacturing: they show an incremental capital/output ratio (ICOR) significantly lower than for food processing, and somewhat below that for furniture and chemicals. Their average wage levels are somewhat above the average for all manufacturing (Tables 7.5 and 7.6).

Rather less important are chemicals and clothing manufacture. Chemicals accounted for 20% of foreign investment, with 41% of firms engaged in their production having foreign participation. Chemicals were destined mainly for the local and Caricom markets, and grew rather slowly. Clothing manufacture, which is a low-wage, labour-intensive activity, was much more export-oriented.

Foreign investors showed little interest in activities geared for local markets: food processing, furniture and plastics. In general, they seem particularly important in supplying extra-regional export markets. Of all wholly foreign-owned firms, 38% produced for extra-Caricom markets, compared with 5% of all locally-owned firms, mainly in assembly activities.

It is often argued that foreign investors use inappropriate capital-intensive technologies, but the assembly operators in Barbados are not especially capital-intensive and their wage levels not particularly high. Codrington(3) finds an inverse relationship between capital intensity of production and the proportion of foreign investment in any sub-sector.

A survey of industrial establishments was undertaken to identify differences between wholly-owned subsidiaries and joint ventures, and to pinpoint additional characteristics such as the proportion of skills in the work force, technology transfer arrangements and the sources of capital for expansion. As only one-third of the thirty questionnaires sent out were completed, all our inferences are open to question, though the responses covered most of the larger companies operating in Barbados. (A similar survey for hotels failed to elicit a useable number of responses.)

Three firms which sold their total production outside the Caricom market were wholly-owned subsidiaries and they all

Table 7.5. Foreign investment, exports and capital intensity

	% of total foreign investment 1977-84	Ratio of exports to value-added 1984	ICOR	Cost per new job ($000)	Relative wage 1982	Ratio of output in 1984 to 1978
Public Utilities	40.2	-			170	1.44
Hotels	0.4	2.56			116	1.08[a]
Distribution	0.1	-			100	1.13
Manufacturing	11.3	1.05			139	0.99
Food, Beverages	(3.0)	0.35	1.52	77.43	160	0.82
Chemicals	(19.5)	0.78	1.09	26.65	217	0.96
Textiles	(20.3)	1.76	0.67	6.80	93	0.94
Furniture, wood products	(0.2)	1.00	12.90	74.00	n.a.	n.a.
Metal products & assembly	(53.1)	1.89	0.88	23.17	157	2.66[b]

[a] Tourism

[b] Electronics

Sources: ICOR (1971-77): Winston Cox, 'The Manufacturing Sector' in D. Worrell (ed.) The Economy of Barbados 1946-80 (Central Bank of Barbados, 1982), Table 8, p.59.
Cost per new job (1971-77): Cox, *ibid*, Table 10.
Ratio of exports to value-added (1977-80): Cox, *ibid*, Tables 7 and 17.
Percentage of foreign investment: Table 7.1: in brackets, percentage of total investment in manufacturing.

Table 7.6. Foreign ownership and export orientation

(Number of firms)

	Firms with foreign participation			Firms with no foreign participation			
	Export-oriented	Not export-oriented	Total	Export-oriented	Not export-oriented	Total	Total all firms
Food & Beverages	-	7	7	2	31	33	40
Clothing	7	6	13	4	33	37	50
Furniture	-	2	2	-	15	15	17
Paper & printing	-	3	3	-	22	22	25
Chemicals	1	8	9	-	13	13	22
Plastics	-	4	4	-	8	8	12
Electrical	12	3	15	1	1	2	17
Total	20	33	53	7	23	130	183
% of all firms	11	18		4	67		100

Source: Extracted from Barbados Industrial Development Corporation, List of Manufacturing Establishments 1983.

used intra-company transfers for their marketing, two exclusively. The other three wholly foreign-owned companies and all the joint ventures produced for the Caricom market only. Only one of the companies from whom returns were received used any local material inputs, and these accounted for no more than 15%. We could detect no systematic pattern in the sources from which the companies secured finance for expanding their operations. Those which reported expansion on their initial operations used retained earnings as well as new injections of overseas finance, sometimes in conjunction and, at other times and for other firms, one or the other. The joint ventures also received injections of local funds.

There is a very slight tendency for larger firms to employ a smaller proportion of skilled workers. Although this evidence must be considered very tentative because the nature and comparability of the skills in various activities were not explored in the questionnaire, it seems plausible that there would be economies of scale in the use of skilled personnel by assembly-type firms. Training expenses were much less than 0.5% of sales for companies reporting such spending, with two exceptions; one firm reported training expenses as high as 2.5% of sales. With one exception, all firms had some form of technical agreement with their foreign parent or partner. The most popular was simply the use of a trademark, followed by technical services agreements, use of patents, franchise arrangements and, in a small minority of firms, management contracts. Most firms combined several of these arrangements.

Government Incentives for Foreign Investment

Increasingly liberal incentive schemes have been developed over time to attract foreign investment in manufacturing, though, of course, in offering generous tax and other incentives, government opts to forego tax income. Measures included the Pioneer Industries Act (1958), the Industrial Incentives Act (1963) and the Industrial Development (Export) Industries Act (1969). In accordance with the scheme for harmonisation of fiscal incentives to which Caricom countries subscribe, they were all incorporated into the Fiscal Incentives Act (FIA) 1974. Under this Act an enterprise may be designated 'an approved enterprise' for the purpose of receiving incentives to produce 'approved products'. Approved enterprises qualify for tax benefits which reduce their operating cost, thus making the rate of return on the investment more attractive. The length of time a company is permitted to enjoy benefits is determined by the local value-added, which is weighted by local wage and salary payments(4). Incentive benefit periods vary from six to ten years; except for enclaves (which are essentially labour service contracts) and highly capital-intensive enterprises, the length of time is determined by the degree of local processing carried out.

The incentives are designed to attract companies meeting one of three criteria:

(i) Companies which pursue a 'deep' manufacturing process as measured by the percentage of local value-added - in contrast to simple assembly (screw-driver) or mixing operations.

(ii) Companies which require from an off-shore location only dependable, skilled or semi-skilled labour which is capable of high output. These enclave companies usually depend neither on local raw materials nor domestic markets.

(iii) Highly capital-intensive companies, investing more than BDS$50m. which provide a large contribution to capital formation in the island and the inflow of foreign capital.

In addition to the tax holiday, there is provision for carrying forward losses incurred during the tax holiday period against profits made in the following five years. Dividends paid during the tax holiday are also exempt from personal income tax, except in the case where the non-resident shareholder is liable to tax on such dividends in his country of residence; then a withholding tax at the lower rate of 45% (the Barbados corporate rate) and the applicable foreign tax are levied. At the end of the tax holiday, the company may be allowed to pay corporate tax at a reduced rate of 22.5%.

Export incentives are available to companies which do not receive benefits under the FIA. Depending on the percentage of extra-Caricom exports to total sales, a company can qualify for an increasingly higher percentage rebate on taxes, up to a maximum of 50%.

The state-owned Barbados Industrial Development Corporation (BIDC) provides factory space at subsidised rates in ten fully serviced industrial parks. An industrial training grant scheme reimburses an investor for up to half the wages paid to any employee recruited and trained during the first six months of operation and for subsequent upgrading of skills.

In the tourist sector capital expenditure for construction or improvement of a hotel may be off-set against profits in the year of expenditure and for nine years following. The conditions of eligibility (size, amenities) are biased in favour of foreign-owned hotels, which tend to be larger and are often operated by international chains. For example, hotels with less than 50 rooms and fewer than two dining rooms do not qualify.

Barbados

Since 1965 there has been an Exemption from Income Tax Act, aimed at attracting foreign companies which do not normally produce or trade in Barbados to set up offices in the island. Two additional recent pieces of legislation cover the regulation, taxation and administration of offshore banks, trust companies, insurance companies and management companies.

An International Business Company (IBC), defined as a company incorporated in Barbados which does not trade on the domestic or Caricom markets, and with local and/or Caricom ownership of less than 10%, is taxed at a concessionary rate of 2.5%. For an investment company dealing in securities tax is graduated in such a way that a rate of 2.5% is levied on gains or profits up to $10m. and the rate is reduced by 0.5% for every additional $10m. of profits thereafter to a minimum rate of 1%. Most of these companies are exempt from exchange-control regulations.

Several parastatal institutions such as the BIDC have been put in place to promote investment inflows. The other official institutions are mainly for the support of local enterprise, though they may be used by foreign firms in need of their services. The Barbados Development Bank provides medium-term financing; the Barbados Institute of Management and Productivity (BIMAP) provides training in organisation and management; there is also an Export Promotion Corporation (EPC) and the Barbados National Standards Institution (BNSI). A recently formed co-ordinating and consultative body, the Co-ordinating Committee on Industrial Development, has been established to ensure consistency of policy among these institutions.

In the Annex to the Caricom treaty 'member states recognize the need for continuing inflows of extra-regional capital', although the encouragement of national ownership is advocated. The Annex proposes that the Caricom countries should work towards a common policy on direct foreign investment, wherever possible. The harmonisation of fiscal incentives was the first step in this direction. However, there is no mechanism at present to monitor its implementation adequately. To the extent that the territories find themselves competing for direct foreign investment it becomes more critical to establish a set of rules to ensure that all adhere to the common policy.

<u>The Motives of Foreign Investors</u>

Possible objectives of foreign investors include maintenance of sales in the host country in the face of regional protective measures for products which previously were supplied from non-Caricom sources; exploiting protected regional markets, where they appear large enough to support new lines of production; and taking advantage of lower costs of transport, tax exemptions or lower labour costs in Barbados than in some alternative location.

We have no conclusive evidence for the importance of cost factors. Nor does the evidence we have, as presented by Ranis and associates(5) and Whitehall(6), suggest that official measures for protecting manufacturing have played a significant role. Electrical goods, the foreign investor's first choice, attract no official protection. In chemicals, the second ranking category for foreign investment, protection is low by Whitehall's measure, and negative for the single item reported by Ranis. For clothing Whitehall reports low levels of protection (less than 1% of value added); Ranis reports two items, one with a low level of protection, the second with a remarkably high level (almost 400%). Whitehall finds low to moderate protection levels for the sectors where local investment predominates - food and furniture. Ranis finds negative protection (a reduction in returns to local factors as a result of taxes, concessions, and official measures) for three food items - eggs, orange juice and biscuits - and high protection for local sales of rum and chicken.

Our analysis(7) is also inconclusive about the effects of incentives; the dummy variable Codrington uses to represent a bias in favour of selected activities in the incentive package suggests a significant preference for such activities by direct foreign investors. However, we cannot be sure that the dummy variable does not in fact pick up other peculiarities of these sectors which are not explicitly accounted for in Codrington's analysis - for example, their export bias or the cost of transporting the commodity or its raw material.

Our tentative assessment is that cost factors - transport costs in particular - may define the range of possibilities which a foreign investor is willing to consider seriously. Within this range the country's actual rate of foreign investment may depend on other factors.

In a 1984 survey carried out by the Research Department of the BIDC covering 22 of the 26 wholly-owned foreign manufacturing companies in Barbados(8), the country was considered 'stable' by 50% of the respondents and 'very stable' by the remainder. This was identified as the major factor influencing their decisions to invest in Barbados, with 80.7% identifying this factor among their top three reasons. This finding agrees with a July 1980 Study of Manufacturing Costs in Barbados and Europe by a consultancy group(9).

A survey published in June 1984 by the Economist Intelligence Unit, How to Make Off-Shore Manufacturing Pay(10), identifies 'the ease of establishing and of operation' as another incentive for location in Barbados. It measures such factors as simplicity of legal, bureaucratic and administrative facilities, procedures for establishing qualification for incentives, foreign-exchange controls, ease of making remittances, and customs clearance procedures. The survey, which covered twenty-five developing or semi-industrial countries, placed Barbados and three other countries in the top category characterised by 'exceptional ease, freedom and absence of red-tape'.

Natural and human resources were an important attraction particularly as regards tourism in the 1960s and manufacturing in the early 1970s. A literate labour force with good basic education, which could be quickly trained to competent levels of performance in assembly operations by firms which boasted good organisation(11), does not seem to have been the prime consideration for many firms, but it may have been the deciding factor when combined with others already mentioned. It may also have been more important to firms looking at alternative Caribbean locations than to those contemplating a wider range of geographical alternatives.

The establishment of the Caribbean common market seems to have been a greater stimulus to domestic than to foreign investors. However, a significant minority of foreign firms put up plants to cater to the Caricom market, mainly to produce cosmetics, personal care products, pesticides and other chemical-based products. There are several examples of domestic firms entering into licensing arrangements for local production of formerly imported items, in most cases with no foreign equity - particularly in food processing.

Other factors have played a very minor role. Some investment has come from Trinidad, Barbados's closest neighbour with higher per capita income. Some has resulted from personal ties with Barbadians and sometimes the foreigners involved choose to become resident; this is particularly the case with hotels, restaurants and ancillary tourism services.

<u>Foreign Investment Projections</u>

In Table 7.7 we present foreign investment projections for 1986-90, all conditional on specific expectations about Barbados's ability to exploit new export markets, government fiscal policies and the persistence of habits of spending and saving. The projections assume a target of 5% per year output growth. However, in the current circumstances there is little hope of attaining that target before 1989. Growth will necessarily be export-led, as it always has been in Barbados, and currently (in 1985-6) exports are hardly increasing at all. Incentives are geared to the introduction of new manufacturing and agricultural products, the development of techniques appropriate to the country's skills and comparative labour costs, and the exploitation of new untapped market segments, all designed to open the way for vigorous export expansion. During the period when these adjustments are taking place, relatively slow export growth must be anticipated. Real export growth is not expected to reach 5% until 1988.

As a result, output is expected to be sluggish from 1986 to 1988. We expect some expansion in government expenditure in 1986, which is an election year. However, the expansion will be tempered by the need to avoid foreign-exchange reserve depletion, and fiscal pressure should ease in 1987. By then the early entrants in export production may provide sufficient value-added to replace the fiscal stimulus, and this sector should provide the momentum for faster growth in subsequent years.

The projections do not allow for any erosion in the end-1985 foreign-exchange reserves position. We presume the authorities would consider lower reserve levels inadequate and that fiscal, monetary and trade policies will be instituted to safeguard reserves, if necessary at the expense of slower overall growth. The projections are conservative, allowing for quite a substantial outflow of short-term capital and unidentified balance-of-payments items. If the outflow turns out to be less damaging, faster output growth should be possible, given the expected growth in exports. No official borrowing for balance-of-payments finance is contemplated in the projections, while heavy government long-term borrowings are expected only in 1986. The country's overall debt-service ratio (payments of principal and interest in relation to exports of goods and services) is less than 15% for the projection period and beyond; we assume there is no desire to see it go much higher and that the level of borrowing will be cut back after 1986. A large jump in amortisation payments in 1990 will make for a sizeable net capital outflow in that year.

The table provides summaries of expenditure on GDP, government savings, the balance of payments and the financing of investment, showing a foreign private capital requirement consistent with expectations about exports, government expansion and the balance-of-payments constraint. The foreign private capital requirement averages $119m. per year (in 1985 dollars) between 1986 and 1990. The private investment demand depends directly on the level of government foreign borrowing. In 1986 when government is expected to borrow heavily private investment needs are only $40m.; the requirement is four times as high in 1990 because of the anticipated outflow on government account.

Table 7.7. Savings and investment projections ($m.)

	Current prices					1985 prices				
	1981	1982	1983	1984	1985[c]	1986	1987	1988	1989	1990
Expenditure on the GDP	1557	1592	1667	1840	1953	2018	2059	2120	2226	2338
Consumption	525	451	421	401	406	544	554	540	567	594
Gross capital formation	1148	1270	1490	1625	1598	1600	1623	1713	1799	1889
Exports	1315	1323	1466	1562	1488	1639	1672	1723	1809	1899
Imports	1915	1990	2113	2303	2474	2523	2573	2650	2873	2992
GDP at market prices										
Memo items (Trade adj.)[a]										
Export adj.	7	-12	59	-70	-2					
Import adj.	-43	-17	-19	-40	-2					
Government savings										
Revenue	447	486	546	567	622	631	643	663	696	731
Current expenditure	442	464	486	533	610	671	704	739	776	815
Current account balance	5	24	60	23	12	-40	-76	-80	-84	
Balance of payments										
Exports	1141	1282	1431	1695	1600	1600	1632	1713	1799	1889
Imports	1353	1340	1485	1592	1490	1639	1672	1723	1809	1899
Private foreign investment	56	-5	-13	-47	2	40	132	119	104	202
Gov't borrowing (Long-term)	99	35	57	12	86	100	20	20	40	-50
Other items (Net)	-17	47	24	-66	-105	-101	-112	-129	-134	-192
Official financing	34	47	29	9	-7	-	-	-	-	-
Reserves [b]	45	-66	-43	-11	-86	-	-	-	-	-
Financing of investment										
Foreign capital (gov't & private)	155	30	42	-35	88	140	152	139	144	152
Gov't savings	5	24	60	28	12	-40	-61	-76	-80	-84
Private savings & depreciation	365	397	319	408	306	454	463	477	501	526
Gross capital formation	525	451	421	401	406	544	554	540	567	594

Table 7.7. Savings and investment projections ($m.) (continued)

	Current prices					1985 prices				
	1981	1982	1983	1984	1985	1986	1987	1988	1989	1990
	Ratios to GDP (%)									
Consumption	81	80	79	80	79	80	80	80	80	80
Imports (BOP)	71	67	70	69	60	65	65	65	65	65
Gov't revenue	23	24	26	24	25	25	25	25	25	25
Savings	19	20	15	18	12	18	181	18	18	18
	Growth Rates									
Exports c		-11	12	18	-6	-	2	5	5	5
GDP (constant prices)	-2	-5	-	4	-	2	2	3	5	5
Gov't current expenditure		-	-	10	14	10	5	5	5	5

Notes:
a Negative sign for adjustment indicators BOP figure is higher than GDP figure.
b An increase is recorded with a negative sign.
c 1981-85, nominal; 1986-90, real.

Sources: 1981-5
Expenditure on the GDP
1981-4, Central Bank, ASD 1984
1985, Barbados Economic Report 1985
Government Savings
Central Bank, Economic Outlook, 26 March 1986
Balance of Payments
1981-84 Central Bank, BOP 1984
1985 Estimates based on Central Bank, Economic Outlook, 26 March 1986.

The projections depend on a domestic savings ratio of 18%, the average for 1981-4. However, if savings were to remain at the comparatively low 1985 ratio of 12%, the foreign investment requirement would be twice as large. The import ratio is projected at 65%, higher than the 60% of 1985, but somewhat below the 69% average of 1981-4. Were the import ratio to return to 69% the foreign investment requirement would once more be almost twice as large as current projections indicate. With government spending rising 5% a year except for 1986 (a 10% increase), government dissaves every year of the projection period. If it were to balance the current account, the foreign investment requirement could be reduced by about 50%. (The model does not discriminate between the impact of government and private investment on the country's ability to export.)

Because of the conditional nature of the forecast and the large element of judgement it involved, we must not hold too firmly to the actual dollar amount of foreign investment projected. A reasonable interpretation would be for requirements somewhat in excess of $100m. per year, in 1985 values, provided that exports revive and that the savings patterns of 1981-4 prove typical. The requirement could be much higher if savings were as weak as in 1985, or if imports attracted as large a proportion of GDP as they did in 1981-4. On the other hand, foreign investment needs could be much lower were government to return to surplus on its current account.

Conclusions

Foreign private investment may be expected to maintain its importance in future capital formation in Barbados, though there is no reason to expect it to make a greater contribution than it has to date. Extra-Caricom exports (goods and tourism) have provided the engine of growth for much of the post-war period and foreign investment has been involved especially because foreign firms have been more knowledgeable about export markets. Foreign investors have been in the forefront of the development of tourism and the manufacturing of clothing and electronic components to exploit extra-regional demand. This is a trend which the government will wish to see continue. Joint ventures and local firms have yet to follow the wholly-owned subsidiaries' lead into extra-Caricom markets, to any significant extent.

Long-standing political and economic stability seems to have been the major attraction for foreign investors, once we admit that the range of firms interested in Barbados is bound to be limited to those which can transport raw materials and finished products with relative ease. Overseas investors identified fiscal incentives only as a secondary consideration. However, incentives are widely available, and it would be unwise not to offer them and irrational of a company not to seek and accept them. Nevertheless, the decision to locate an overseas subsidiary is often based less on short-term maximisation of profits than on achieving a predictable minimum rate of return on investment. An enterprise which depends heavily on tax concessions to be viable is basically marginal. Conversely, for a company which is capable of showing a net profit at an acceptable level with the prevailing corporate tax rate, the lack of incentives would not constitute a disincentive.

This survey does not suggest the need for general changes in official policy. The system of incentives is admittedly biased in favour of import-substitutes - because they benefit from tariff protection which exporters cannot enjoy - but this bias has not been injurious to exporters. The kinds of activity which are directed towards the extra-regional market (tourism, the manufacture of electronic components) tend to be quite different from those aimed at the region (food products, personal care products). The foreign investor arrives already knowing what he plans to make and sell and what markets he is aiming for. He will take advantage of any incentive which enhances the return on his investment, but there is not much to be gained by reducing incentives for one kind of activity and increasing them elsewhere. The incentive system does not make a measurable difference to the costs of operation.

The government commands a panoply of specialised institutions designed to promote industrial and tourism development - an Industrial Development Corporation, an Export Promotion Corporation, a Board of Tourism, an Export Credit Insurance and Guarantees Facility, an Industrial Credit Fund (the latter two at the Central Bank) and a Development Bank. Between them they should be able to supply most of the support new firms need, whether they be local or foreign. The government's concern must be to see to their effectiveness.

NOTES AND REFERENCES

1. Harold Codrington, 'The Distribution of Private Foreign Capital in Barbados', Central Bank of Barbados,mimeo, April 1984.

2. Norman Girvan, Foreign Capital and Economic Under-Development in Jamaica (Institute of Social and Economic Research, University of the West Indies, 1971).

3. Codrington, 'Distribution of Private Foreign Capital', p.9.

4. The labour weighted value added is calculated by the formula

$$V_1 = \frac{(100 + W)}{100} V$$

where V = Local value-added as a percentage of total sales of the approved product.

W = Salaries and wages paid to local and/or Caricom nationals, as a percentage of total sales of the approved product.

5. Gustav Ranis and associates, 'Production and Export Incentives in the Caricom Region', Caribbean Community Secretariat, mimeo, (May 1982).

6. Peter Whitehall, 'Production in the Manufacturing Sector of Barbados, 1960-80', Central Bank of Barbados, Economic Review, (September 1984).

7. Codrington, 'Distribution of Private Foreign Capital', p.9.

8. The study is an unpublished document of BIDC. Joint ventures were not included. On average the companies had operated in Barbados for seven years; the longest established was twenty years old.

9. Study of Manufacturing Costs in Barbados and Europe, (P.E. Consulting Group, U.K., July 1980), p.11.

10. Anthony Edwards, How to Make Off-Shore Manufacturing Pay, Special Report No. 171, (Economist Intelligence Unit, London, June 1984).

11. In the survey by BIDC 100% of the respondents found the labour force to be easily adaptable and trainable. Some stated that this allowed them to reduce costs by shortening training programmes. In addition, 90% found the discipline and attitude to work either 'good' or 'very good'.

Chapter Eight

DIRECT PRIVATE OVERSEAS INVESTMENT IN EXPORT-ORIENTED VENTURES: RECENT DEVELOPMENTS IN SRI LANKA

R.C. Wanigatunga

Recent Change in Policy

Sri Lanka provides a good example of a country which has revised its approach to foreign investment as part of a far reaching programme of economic liberalisation. Like the vast majority of developing countries, independent Sri Lanka experienced declining terms of trade for the few primary crops (tea, rubber and coconut) on which it was for long almost entirely dependent for its export earnings. This led in turn to a preference for import-substitution policies and heavy state involvement in economic activities. There was large-scale nationalisation of the private sector - both domestic and foreign owned. Under this regime, there was an increasingly acute foreign-exchange shortage, low growth, rising unemployment, and for many, declining living standards. By electing the United National Party (UNP) Government in 1977, the country 'opted out' of this strategy, and the change brought about high economic growth, significant diversification in the economy and in export earnings, and the ending - for the time being at least - of the foreign-exchange constraint.

The new approach to policy had several components. A dual exchange-rate system under which exports of tea, rubber and most coconut products and imports of 'essential' food items were effected at a preferential rate was abolished in 1977 and the rupee devalued. Simultaneously, the extremely restrictive regime of controls for 'visible' and 'invisible' trade transactions, including imports of raw materials and capital goods, was lifted.

A major acceleration of the Mahaveli river basin development by means of multilateral and bilateral aid and increased Sri Lankan public sector investment substantially enlarged the capacity for hydro-electric generation and irrigation. The new government also undertook heavy investment in expanding and modernising the telecommunication network and improving cargo handling facilities in the port, with special emphasis on containerisation. The heavy public sector involvement was to be financed, at least in part, by substantial cut-backs in welfare expenditure, notably on food and petroleum subsidies.

Export-oriented industry, with an emphasis on the establishment of free trade zones (FTZs), was assigned a major role for the first time in generating foreign-exchange earnings, and employment; tourism too. The state also sought to attract new, but efficient, import-substitution manufacturing industry while at the same time exposing the heavily protected existing industry to competition from imports.

The UNP government had inherited an economic structure in which the state owned the bulk of the larger plantations, which had been nationalised by the previous government from foreign and Sri Lankan ownership. The state effectively monopolised the import trade and held a sizeable proportion of the export and internal trade. It had a monopoly over transport and insurance (since 1961), and by the mid-70s also owned most of the banking system. It had established the whole of the 'heavy' industry ranging from cement, steel rolling and petroleum refining to ceramic ware, and owned diverse businesses ranging from coconut refining to brick manufacture.

The new government did not embark on a massive denationalisation programme, but some of the smaller businesses were returned to the original owners and the state monopolies ended in the omnibus transport service and in most of the import and internal trade. The private sector was permitted, and encouraged, to play a much more active role as a result of the liberalisation process. There was also state support in the form of rapid infrastructural development - especially in relation to export-oriented industry - as well as more tax holidays, cheap credit and long-term finance. Direct foreign investment (DFI) was assigned a key role in the new development strategy, but it was to augment, rather than compete directly with, the domestic private sector.

Foreign Investment - Pre-1977

There are no reliable data available relating to the stock of DFI at any point in time. With respect to flows, information has been computed by the Central Bank from balance-of-payments data. Re-invested profits are excluded as are borrowings from domestic banks (but not from the offshore banking units established since 1978). While Sri Lanka attempts to follow IMF conventions on the treatment of DFI, in practice most investment/disinvestment in equity held by non-residents is simply registered as DFI flows. The data thus shed little light on ownership and control exercised in relation to DFI. Some foreign long-term borrowings of businesses are also included as DFI flows. There are also data in the post-1978 period that relate to foreign loans to finance the fixed assets of the private sector.

At independence in 1948 about half the land under tea and

Table 8.1. Balance of payments: net flows of private capital

(Rs.m.)

	Direct investment	Other private long-term	Investment income
1961	− 6	− 2	− 46
1962	− 2	0	− 47
1963	+ 5	0	− 47
1964	− 1	+ 2	− 26
1965	− 1	− 3	− 3
1966	− 14	− 2	− 23
1967	− 5	− 2	− 31
1968	− 12	+ 1	− 22
1969	− 11	+ 1	− 51
1970	− 2	0	− 42
1971	+ 2	0	− 29
1972	+ 2	− 1	− 22
1973	+ 3	− 2	− 18
1974	+ 9	− 1	− 13
1975	− 1	0	− 17
1976	0	+ 48	− 13
1977	− 9	+ 29	− 10
1978	+ 23	+ 8	− 66
1979	+ 732	+ 141	− 98
1980	+ 710	+ 667	− 237
1981	+ 946	+1,019	− 136
1982	+1,323	+4,046	− 211
1983	+ 887	+2,233	− 255
1984	+ 830	− 119	− 291
1985	+ 810p	+ 620p	− 278p

p denotes provisional.

Sources: Central Bank of Ceylon, Annual Report and Review of the Economy (various issues).

Table 8.2. Impact of direct foreign investment on balance of payme

(SDR m.)

	Direct investment			Suppliers' credits	Outward remittance of profits	Merchandise trade	
	Total	GCEC	FIAC			Exports	Imports
1975	0.5	n.a.	-	n.a.	2.0	464	632
1976	0.1	n.a.	-	36.6	1.3	484	557
1977	0.4	n.a.	-	13.0	1.1	651	622
1978	1.6	1.2	0.4	0.4	3.4	675	819
1979	38.2	27.3	10.9	30.3	4.9	759	1,121
1980	33.0	24.0	9.0	46.0	11.0	818	1,576
1981	44.0	31.0	13.0	41.3	6.0	903	1,596
1982	60.0	11.0	49.0	60.1	9.5	918	1,805
1983	35.4	16.8	18.6	36.9	10.1	993	1,794
1984	36.2	9.0[a]	27.0[a]	36.2	11.2	1,427	1,880
1985	30.3[p]	-	-	30.3	10.0[p]	1,284[p]	1,981[p]

- not available. n.a. denotes not applicable. a Figures rounded to nearest SDR million. p provisional.

Note:

The figures on direct investments prior to 1978 are based on balance-of-payments data and exclude re-invested profits but include most equity investment. Data on or after 1978 are those provided by the FIAC and the GCEC. Post-1978 data possibly include some long-term loans/suppliers' credits, including loans obtained by Air Lanka, the national carrier, retrospectively registered as a GCEC business in March 1982. The figures on suppliers' credits relate to gross disbursements of long term credit.

Source: Ibid.

rubber, most of the banking business, trade-related services, foreign trade and some of the distribution trade, notably of petroleum, was in the hands of foreign (largely UK) capital. After independence, there was a clearly discernible trend, albeit gradual, for the dominant position of foreign capital to be eroded and replaced by local private capital. But various measures in the 1960s and 70s, culminating in the nationalisation of the plantations, effectively dealt a death blow to DFI in its traditional role: by 1977, with the exception of a few restricted banks and a small number of major tea-exporting firms (notably Brooke Bond and Liptons) little was left.

In contrast, the establishment of import-substitution industries had been responsible for a new form of DFI involvement from a number of sources, though much of the capital invested (equity and long-term loans) was Sri Lankan. Lever Brothers (a subsidiary of Unilever), Indian Hume Pipe, Reckitt and Coleman, Pfizer Dumex, Usha Industries, ICI, Shell and Bata were among the firms participating. The figures in Table 8.1 show little net DFI inflow even in the heyday of import substitution. The small positive net flows in the early 1970s are largely explained by the stringent controls on capital outflows. With the decline in the stock of DFI, outflows of investment income gradually dwindled.

Foreign Investment - Post-1977

DFI flows picked up spectacularly with the liberalisation of the economy after 1977, which was also associated with a major increase in long-term commercial loans, especially suppliers' credits. Though outflows of investment income have also increased dramatically since the liberalisation they remain small relative to total inflows of DFI. The net effect of these flows on the overall balance of payments (Table 8.2) has been small.

The new UNP government needed DFI for several purposes, though its basic objective was to obtain additional resources (capital, technology, marketing) to augment those available domestically. DFI was allocated two major roles in the new economic strategy: to provide a major impetus for labour intensive export-oriented industry, tourism and offshore banking; and to promote economic development more widely through major construction work such as urban re-development, including housing, and in engineering projects (largely related to the Mahaveli Development Scheme) and highly capital/technology-intensive industrial and agricultural projects, often of an import-substitution variety. The government bodies responsible for soliciting, vetting and approving DFI in 1978, soon began an aggressive promotional campaign.

The government's two-pronged approach (described below), reflects to a large extent its desire to treat as much foreign owned and controlled investment as possible on an 'enclave' basis in FTZs. Despite the liberalisation measures in 1977/8, Sri Lanka was not (and indeed, was not intended to be) as 'open' as Hong Kong or Singapore. Rapid liberalisation would have exposed most of Sri Lanka's existing manufacturing capability to serious disruption. The government chose instead to liberalise partially the highly restrictive trade regime and expose the nascent industries to limited competition, while providing domestic capital with additional incentives to invest in export-oriented activity. Given the importance of rice production in the economy, and the instability of the international market, only limited liberalisation was contemplated in this area also. Overall, it was judged that liberalisation within too short a time would have induced domestic capital to switch from production to trading (importing) leading to adjustment problems; indeed there is evidence to suggest that even the partial liberalisation that took place did bring about such a (marginal) shift in the deployment of domestic capital. In the new export-oriented thrust in economic policy, the enclave nature of the FTZ, in which domestic capital could also participate, offered growth potential without the risks, or disadvantages, entailed in a complete, and rapid, liberalisation. While DFI was welcomed 'with open arms' into the FTZ, its access to the rest of the economy was more restricted - to those activities where it was deemed essential to augment domestic resources.

Investments effected under the aegis of the Greater Colombo Economic Commission (GCEC), which is responsible for the enclave-type investment, have to find their requirements of working and fixed capital from external sources. Where there is participation of Sri Lankan capital, local funding of factory buildings is permitted. At the same time, there is no restriction on foreign ownership of equity. GCEC businesses are permitted to import their requirements of capital goods and raw materials duty-free, and are obliged to export their output. They are exempt from exchange control and have their own contractual and income tax regime. The investments made under the GCEC aegis are largely related to manufacturing and, to a far lesser extent, to 'export-related' services.

The foreign investments approved by a revamped Foreign Investments Advisory Committee (FIAC), the body responsible for other forms of foreign investment, can find their capital from the domestic banking system which makes them eligible to benefit from credits extended in Sri Lanka on favourable terms. Majority local ownership of equity is the norm (75% for garments) and majority foreign ownership is only permitted in exceptional circumstances (e.g. for large

Table 8.3. Sources of investment for selected GCEC industries: Number of units in operation, February 1984

	Garments	Hosiery/ gloves	Rubber products	Jewellery lapidary	Rubber footwear	Rubber tyres	Electrical products	Other	Total
Hong Kong	3								
Hong Kong - Sri Lanka	6	1[a]	1					2	13
Korea - Sri Lanka	1	1			1				
India								1	3
India - Sri Lanka	2[b]				1				4
Thailand - Sri Lanka	1			1				1	3
West Germany	1						1	1	
West Germany - Sri Lanka	2[c]		1					1	7
Netherlands	1								1
Belgium	1								
Belgium - Sri Lanka						1			2
Luxembourg	1								1
Switzerland		1							1
Monaco				1					1
Lichtenstein	1								1
UK							1	1	
UK - Sri Lanka	2			1					5
US	1								
US - Sri Lanka	4[d]								5
Australia - Sri Lanka			1						1
Norway - Sri Lanka								3	3
Japan								1	
Japan - Sri Lanka							1		2
Other	1	1	1					3	6
Sri Lanka	1		1	2				2	6
	29	4	5	5	2	1	3	16	65

a Cotton gloves. b Includes a business making textile yarns. c Includes a business making leather garments. d Includes a business making terry towelling.

Source: Greater Colombo Economic Commission.

five-star hotels and selected engineering projects). Businesses are also subject to the (currently not very restrictive) import and exchange-control regimes which, inter alia, provide for import duty rebates on imported inputs for the export of finished products. When approval is granted in respect of export-oriented investments, the volume of sales to the domestic market is stipulated, though the practice has been for all garment manufacturing firms to be denied the local market. An agreement approved by the FIAC is subject to the general law of the land. FIAC investments can, and do, cover the entire range of economic activity ranging from large-scale 'non-traditional' agricultural ventures and large-scale manufacture for the local market, to horticulture and garment manufacture for export.

Though the tax incentives under the two schemes are rather different, for (most) DFI - as opposed to domestic investment - they have little impact since Sri Lanka has double taxation agreements with almost every significant capital-exporting country. A tax holiday therefore generally means a loss to the Sri Lankan exchequer and no real gain to the individual DFI. For Sri Lankan domestic capital, however, additional tax concessions which permit approved investments to be deducted from assessable income are important particularly for capital-intensive FIAC projects (e.g. big tourist projects and the cement plant). FIAC projects are also more attractive for Sri Lankan capital because of the restrictions on DFI participation under that regime and the variety and number of investment opportunities available.

The Greater Colombo Economic Commission

The GCEC was created by statute in 1978, to be, inter alia, responsible for the establishment and operation of export processing zones. In practice, the GCEC has had to provide developed factory land, infrastructure services within its (two) industrial estates, and water and sewerage. The GCEC is expected to break even in its financial operations.

The first six years of GCEC activity had resulted in the installation of 65 plants, while 12 more were being constructed. Altogether, 183 businesses had been approved, and 99 had signed agreements. A tapering off in the rate of establishment after a massive surge of interest at the outset was hardly surprising, given the preponderance of garment manufacturers in the GCEC projects. GCEC garment manufacturers were permitted 'access' only to about half the country's US garment quota (imposed from 1980 and virtually fully utilised from that time) and were from the outset formally barred from the country's Western European quotas.

Table 8.3 attempts to show the type of industry in operation under GCEC auspices. In terms of numbers (and employment generated), garment manufacturing was the most important (29 businesses), followed by rubber products manufacturing and the polishing of precious stones and jewellery (five businesses each), hosiery and electrical goods (four and three businesses respectively). Other businesses included a tea-packing and two light engineering firms, a fish net assembly plant, toy manufacturing, and tropical plant exporting firms.

Taking into account the volume of investment, most of it has been in 'services' (eg the national airline) followed by other manufactures and then by textiles and garments, while non-metallic minerals (largely lapidary and jewellery) and rubber products were also important. Several factors explain the origins of industries attracted by the GCEC. In respect of garments, many of the GCEC's manufacturers have strong connections with Far East-based garment businesses which had begun to face quota restrictions in major markets. Sri Lanka has relatively low wages, fairly stable political conditions, a healthy 'climate' for foreign investment, and efficient communication and transport facilities. In addition, its garment exports to the US market did not become subject to quotas until 1980. The country was therefore an attractive location in which to invest.

Although the GCEC has been insisting on a minimum of 40% value-added in rubber products, there were, in early 1984, five businesses manufacturing latex products, one manufacturing small industrial tyres and two manufacturing rubber footwear. Latex products are ideally suitable for Sri Lanka, on account of their high natural rubber content, the relative cheapness of latex (it is a product expensive to transport and Sri Lanka's export duty on natural rubber (NR) makes latex available at about half the price in NR-importing economies), and the labour-intensive nature of the manufacturing process. The last factor has also been largely responsible for the establishment of the other (vulcanised) rubber products firms; indeed the single GCEC (Belgian) industrial tyre manufacturer shifted its operations from the EEC to Sri Lanka. But the Korean-backed rubber footwear business appears to have been established largely because of the likelihood of the reimposition of US VERs against rubber footwear exports from Korea. The lapidary/jewellery firms have been attracted not only by the cheapness - and skills - of Sri Lankan labour, but also by the prohibition of the export from Sri Lanka of uncut/unpolished stones.

The sources of DFI have in fact been largely determined by the nature of the industries established. In terms of numbers Far Eastern sources (other than Japan) heavily predominate, followed by West Germany, and then the UK, the US and the rest of the EEC. Only about one-tenth of the investment is Sri Lankan. But much of the investment in respect of businesses in the process of being established is

Table 8.4. Basic statistics on GCEC projects by industry, February 1984

Industry	No. of[a] projects	Value of[b] investment (Rs mn)	As % of of total[b]	Investment by DFI[b] (Rs mn.)	(% of total)	Employment potential (Nos)	As % of total	Investment per employee (Rs)
1. Food, beverages etc	1	5	neg	2	40.0	56	neg	53,571
2. Textiles, clothing, leather	42	1,232	23.7	895	72.6	28,353	57.2	43,452
3. Wood and wood products	1	2	neg	1	50.0	250	0.5	8,000
4. Chemicals, petroleum, and plastic products	12	327	6.3	230	70.3	2,330	4.7	140,343
5. Non-metallic mineral products	13	594	11.4	498	83.8	4,882	9.8	121,671
6. Metal products	4	111	2.1	67	60.4	1,043	2.1	106,423
7. Other manufactures	23	1,316	25.3	880	66.9	10,711	21.6	122,864
8. Services	3	1,612	31.2	1,515	94.0	1,965	4.1	820,356
Total	99	5,199[c]	100.0	4,088	78.6	49,590	100.0	104,840

N.B. Data exclude Air Lanka

a 99 projects on which agreements have been signed (65 in operation, 20 at construction stage)
b Equity and long-term loans (approximately equal to value of fixed assets at cost)
c Actual investment in GCEC projects, excluding Air Lanka, as at end June 1983 was Rs 1,590m. (Rs 656m. in equity and the balance in long-term loans)

Source: Ibid.

Table 8.5. Exports of selected manufactured products 1975 - 85 (Rs m.)

	Total, excluding petroleum products			Textiles and garments			Rubber products			Engineering goods		
	Total	GCEC	FIAC	Total	GCEC	FIAC	Total	GCEC	FIAC	Total	GCEC[e]	FIAC
1975	119	nil	n.a.	25	nil	n.a.	1	nil	n.a.	7	nil	n.a.
1976	221	nil	n.a.	70	nil	n.a.	3	nil	n.a.	2	nil	n.a.
1977	298	nil	n.a.	143	nil	n.a.	3	nil	n.a.	4	nil	n.a.
1978	904	nil	n.a.	481	nil	n.a.	4	nil	n.a.	17	nil	n.a.
1979	1,772	152	n.a.	1,117	145	n.a.	6	1	n.a.	42	nil	n.a.
1980	2,534	524	n.a.	1,826	490	n.a.	28	13	n.a.	70	nil	n.a.
1981	3,922	1,163	n.a.	3,022	963	n.a.	56	45	n.a.	104	20[d]	n.a.
1982	4,991	1,653	n.a.	3,502	1,307[b]	n.a.	144	90	n.a.	157	34	n.a.
1983	6,139	2,249[f]	1,150[a] est	4,738	1,917[b]	660 est	137	109[c]	n.a.	196	93	n.a.
1984	9,303	3,338[f]	1,573	7,535	2,889	n.a.	267	136[c]	n.a.	182	86	n.a.
1985	10,103	3,608	2,134 est	7,899	3,053	n.a.	292	n.a.	n.a.	312	n.a.	n.a.

n.a. not available.
est estimate.
a FIAC exports for Jan-June 1983 comprised textiles and garments Rs 330m., other manufactures Rs 245m., specialised services (excluding tourism) Rs 39 million, and exports of plants and fish Rs 3m.
b garments and footwear.
c rubber and plastic products.
d electrical and electronic products only.
e may not include all relevant items in a given year.
f excludes services.

Source: Central Bank of Ceylon, Annual Reports and Reviews of the Economy, (various) and Bulletin, January 1986, FIAC, and W.S. Nanayakkara, 'Sri Lanka's Experience in Attracting Foreign Investment', in Papers and Proceedings of the Seminar on Foreign Investment Policies and Prospects: Asia and Pacific, (Commonwealth Secretariat, London, 1986).

from Western Europe and the US, with Japan playing a small role. The main interest is in light engineering, electrical products and metal fabrication industries. Harris, a US transnational in electronics, is the most noteworthy recent 'acquisition'.

Table 8.4 provides aggregated data on investment in GCEC projects. All figures relate to equity (direct and portfolio) investment and long-term loans, including long-term suppliers' credits. By far the larger proportion of the capital invested has been obtained from external sources, accounting for 94% of investment in the services sector, 84% in fabricated metal products and 73% in textiles and garments.

But investment in equity is only around one half of the total. A noteworthy feature of the foreign investment is the substantial role played by long-term loans (chiefly long-term suppliers' credits) in financing investment in fixed assets. The volume of loans reflects the relative attractiveness of the terms of suppliers' credits, especially for capital goods, at present. Working capital, which is very important for activities like garment manufacture, is largely obtained from the offshore banking system.

As observable from Table 8.5, with the exception of rubber products, GCEC enterprises do not yet export as much (non-petroleum) manufactured products as the rest of the country; though the investments are at a very early stage. Table 8.6 lists our estimates of the foreign-exchange expenditure and net foreign-exchange earnings in respect of GCEC projects. There is a clear net gain, of between 17 and 26%. Depreciation (largely on imported capital goods) has not been allowed for, however; it could be around 8% of sales value in most cases. There are, of course, wide inter-firm and inter-industry variations. It was not possible to obtain information on the foreign-exchange expenditure related to the establishment of infrastructure specific to the industrial processing zones, but much of this could reasonably be expected to be depreciated over a very long period.

There are no computations available on value added by GCEC businesses to the Sri Lankan economy though it is unlikely that the figure could be very high. The investment is largely from abroad (which makes much of depreciation, profits and interest accrue to external sources), so that what accrues to the country are the rental payments to the GCEC, payments for utilities and other services, and earnings of nationals. The World Bank has estimated value added (in garments) to be in the region of 12%, while another authoritative estimate for value added in GCEC projects is around 14%. GCEC data suggest a similar figure. The point to note, however, is that even a modest value added could make a significant contribution to economic development.

Table 8.6. GCEC: Exports and net foreign-exchange earnings (Rs. m.)

	Value of exports	Net foreign exchange earnings[a]	2 as % 1
	(1)	(2)	(3)
1979	152	30	19.8
1980	525	120	22.9
1981	1,163	291	25.0
1982	1,653	437	26.4
1983[b]	2,196	376	17.1

a Net of interest charges, royalty, technical fees and sales expenses; rubber used in production is valued at hypothetical f.o.b. values for computation of net foreign exchange earnings.

b January-November.

Source: GCEC.

Furthermore, once garments decline in relative importance, overall value added as a percentage of export values will rise. It is arguable moreover that Sri Lanka could increase garments value added through the auctioning of garment export quotas; foreign investors are, after all willing to pay higher wages in other developing country locations (e.g. almost three times those of Sri Lanka in the Maldives). Moreover, f.o.b. unit values of Sri Lanka's garment exports to the US suggest that f.o.b. export values are well below those of the established exporters in the Far East.

While in the longer term there is the prospect of greater backward linkages, the types of industry established up to now in GCEC projects do not lend themselves easily to such developments, at least in the short term. On the other hand, industries producing packaging materials (plastics and cardboard cartons) have received a major fillip from their supplies to the GCEC (and other export-oriented industries). In the longer term, impetus has been provided for the textile industry to become more efficient, especially with regard to finishing, to supply the export-processing activities. With regard to rubber products, stearic acid, a small but vital input, which is a by-product of vegetable oil refining, is likely to be produced in a factory close to the

Katunayake FTZ shortly. In Thailand and Malaysia, rubber product manufacture, some of it export-oriented, eventually led to the establishment of carbon black plants.

It is the employment generated by what are largely labour-intensive industries, particularly garment industries, that has been the GCEC's major success. The average income generated per worker - say Rs. 900 ($37) per month in early 1984 - may be low, but it represents a clear economic gain in a country where unemployment is high and the marginal productivity of underemployed unskilled female labour is near zero in alternative employment. In 1983, GCEC industry accounted for an estimated 6-8% of total employment in manufacturing.

With regard to the acquisition of new skills by the workforce and new technology (ranging from production to marketing fields) by the country as a whole, the GCEC establishments have had some positive, albeit rather limited and unquantifiable, impact. A GCEC business typically trains its own work force, though the latter have some basic skills when recruited. A garment machinist 'first-timer', quite apart from acquiring skill and speed at sewing, also benefits from the experience of factory discipline (though it can have its negative aspects). To take another example, the Korean-associated - but lately Sri Lankan-controlled - rubber footwear manufacturing concern is achieving technology transfer from Koreans on contracts of employment.

Foreign Investment Advisory Committee Projects

The FIAC is not a statutory body like the GCEC. It consists of representatives of key ministries on an *ex officio* basis. The FIAC thus centralises, facilitates and expedites decision making, but is not a 'one-stop' agency. It gives 'approval' for a comprehensive package (e.g. management and consultancy agreements, royalties and technical fees) involving a foreign investment, which will be enforced by the appropriate authorities. This approval is not, however, a contract between the foreign investor and any of the government agencies, including the FIAC.

As at end June 1985, of 476 projects approved, 276 were in operation and 47 under construction, 74 still under negotiation and 79 unimplemented. Some statistics are given in Table 8.7 with regard to projects in operation, showing that the sub-sectors with the largest number of projects were textiles and garments, tourism and specialised services, followed by chemicals, civil engineering and basic metals and engineering. The influence of export demand is clearly seen in the large number of garment ventures. Investments in hotels have been to service the envisaged increase in tourist traffic (though fiscal incentives have played a major part in the mobilisation of domestic capital). The demands arising

Table 8.7. Basic statistics on FIAC projects in operation and under construction/implementation by industry type - end June 1985

	No. of projects	Envisaged investment[a] (Rs. m.)	Committed investment[a] (Rs. m.)	: as % of total committed investment	Foreign component of committed investment and as % of total for industry (Rs. m.)		Employment potential (Nos)	Actual employment (Nos)	: as % of total employment	Investment per employee (Rs)[c]
Agriculture & fishing	27	4,264.2	1,497.9	13.6	923.8	61.7	6,303	4,915	12.0	304,761
Textiles and garments	52	770.8	944.2	8.6	248.5	26.3	14,993	19,367	47.4	48,753
Food and beverages	14	702.5	820.2	7.5	746.7	91.0	815	1,120	2.7	732,321
Wood and paper products	8	53.4	38.1	0.3	8.1	21.3	1,690	175	0.4	217,714
Chemicals, plastics and rubber products	35	566.7	539.9	4.9	92.3	17.1	3,228	2,586	6.3	208,778
Non-metallic minerals	14	529.1	667.8	6.1	356.2	53.3	1,274	2,329	5.7	286,732
Basic metals & engineering	26	763.7	105.9	1.0	38.1	36.0	2,571	753	1.8	140,638
Other manufactures	15	148.5	122.2	1.1	29.5	24.1	3,364	2,062	5.1	59,263
Construction and property	28	2,444.0	937.5	8.5	279.6	29.8	3,318	1,949	4.8	481,016
Tourism	58	5,914.5	4,454.4	40.5	2,106.6	47.3	7,218	4,487	11.0	992,735
Specialised services	46	469.3	871.8	7.9	234.2	26.9	1,139	1,086	2.7	802,762
	325	16,626.7	10,999.9	100.0	5,063.6	46.0	46,093	40,829	99.9[b]	269,414

a Loans plus equity. b Figures do not add up to 100 due to rounding. c Committed investment/actual employment.

Source: Nanayakkara, 'Sri Lanka's Experience in Attracting Foreign Investment'.

from the Mahaveli development and urban renewal programmes have stimulated investment in construction (and in some electrical goods industries). Many investments have been influenced, inter alia, by the dynamism in the economy following its liberalisation.

Detailed information on the source (i.e. exporting country) of capital is not available in respect of FIAC projects. The UK seems to have a relatively large number, and wide diversity, of investments (in contrast to its relatively low showing in GCEC projects). Indeed, the UK is particularly important for agriculture (two large sugar-related projects), construction and electrical goods (which may not be unrelated to the volume of UK grant aid for the Mahaveli project). Japan comes next, with a third of its investments in garments. There is a substantial number from other developing countries: Singapore (at least 14) India very significant in financial services); Hong Kong at (least 12). There are at least seven US investments, of which two are in chemicals. And West Germany has 10 investments, four of which are in tourist projects (it is a major tourist market for Sri Lanka), and three in garments.

According to Table 8.7, committed investments in 325 projects stood at around Rs.10 bn (approx. $400m.) as at the end of June 1985. Foreign capital in both equity and loans was below 46% of the total committed, and in most industries it was well below 50%. It was in excess of 35% only in food and beverages, agriculture and fishing, non-metallic minerals, tourist hotels and basic metals and engineering. In a number of capital-intensive projects greater stress has been laid on securing a management role, and on providing machinery and equipment on credit, than on acquiring a large equity stake. FIAC projects had produced over 40,000 jobs by end-June 1985, 69.5% in manufacturing (with textiles and garments alone providing 47.4%) 12.0% in agriculture and fishing, 11.0% in hotels and recreational facilities, 4.8% in civil engineering and 2.7% in specialised services. Investment per employee has been relatively low for manufactures, and high for hotels, specialised services, civil engineering and agriculture and fisheries (largely because of the large sugar project).

Data are not readily available on foreign-exchange earnings of FIAC projects. The FIAC obtains information in its annual surveys on the gross foreign-exchange earnings of some projects under its aegis. As in the case of the GCEC, but to a lesser extent, ready-made garments dominate (Table 8.5.). In the absence of full data on foreign-exchange earnings and expenditure, it is not possible to assess the balance-of-payments impact of FIAC activities. Nor are figures available on value-added, or about the linkage effects in the economy. Nevertheless the mix of activities suggests substantial beneficial effects through investment in

Table 8.8. FIAC and GCEC: Foreign contributions to investment

	FIAC projects - JUNE 1985			GCEC agreements - end 1985		
	No. of projects	Total committed (Rs m.)	:of which, investment (%)	No. of projects	Total investment (Rs m.)	:of which investment (%)
1. Agriculture & fishing	27	1,497.9	61.7	-	-	-
2. Textiles & garments	52	944.2	26.3	46	1,506	68.5
3. Food and beverages	14	820.2	91.0	2	28	57.1
4. Wood & paper products	8	38.1	21.3	3	35	80.0
5. Chemicals, plastics and rubber products	35	539.9	17.1	15	354	26.0
6. Non-metallic minerals	14	667.8	53.3	13	595	83.7
7. Metals and engineering	26	105.9	36.0	7	161	65.2
8. Other manufactures	15	122.2	24.1	27	1,652	69.1
9. Civil engineering	28	937.5	29.8	-	-	-
10. Tourism	58	4,454.4	47.3	-	-	-
11. Specialised services	40	871.8	26.9	5	1,215	70.0
TOTAL	325	10,999.9	46.0	118	5,546	67.9

Note: 'Investments' include long-term loans.

Source: Calculated from Nanayakkara, ibid.

services and urban re-development, etc., the attraction of foreign management and technology, and the catalytic effect of mobilising domestic savings for investment, especially in large projects.

Brief Comparison of the two Schemes

On the basis of the limited data available, a comparison of the two schemes relating to DFI reveals the following. In terms of the total volume of investment attracted (Table 8.8) the FIAC has obtained substantially more, reflecting its relative attraction for domestic public and private sector capital on account of the wider range of activities coming under its aegis, tax incentives and the provision of long-term loan capital on favourable terms. The DFI share of total investments is lower in FIAC projects (which is to be expected, given the greater role assigned to Sri Lankan investment under the FIAC regime). Moreover much of the DFI flows consists of foreign loans and suppliers' credits; these are relatively higher for the FIAC scheme than for the GCEC.

With respect to the types of industry attracted under the two schemes, garments account for 39% of GCEC investments (and would have accounted for more had there not been the external quota constraint), and 18% for FIAC. On the other hand, tourist projects, civil engineering, property development and specialised services activities, largely precluded under the GCEC regime, account for 39% of FIAC investments. Far Eastern and other developing country sources predominate for the GCEC, and the developed economies for the FIAC.

The evidence available with respect to foreign-exchange earnings suggests that FIAC projects earn less from exports than GCEC in gross terms. At the same time, FIAC projects have on average longer gestation periods, and tourist earnings are not included in the available data. With regard to employment, garments predominate for the GCEC and still account for well over half of the employment generated by the FIAC. Average investment per employee, is however three times higher in FIAC projects. But these projects probably contribute relatively more in technology transfer, including training.

Conclusion

In broad terms, DFI has had several major effects on the Sri Lankan economy within the space of a few years. Export-oriented DFI - defined to include both loans and equity and DFI flows for tourism - has accounted for around 60-65% of total DFI flows. This export-oriented DFI was at first concentrated in the labour-intensive garment industry, but soon faced a severe quota constraint, especially with regard to the US market, from 1980. There have also been investments in rubber products, jewellery and lapidary, and diamond polishing (under GCEC and FIAC auspices), and investments in the pipeline include shipbreaking, ship repair and electronics. Moreover, given the international recession since 1979, it is perhaps premature to expect substantial investments in technologically sophisticated but labour-intensive industries (e.g. optical instruments), in a relatively short space of time. DFI has also made an important contribution to major agricultural projects, and in the establishment of a number of sophisticated service industries, principally to serve the domestic market.

Foreign involvement has played a catalytic role in mobilising Sri Lankan private and even public capital (most notably in the hotels sector) for a number of investments catering for both export and domestic demand. Local investors have been induced to invest by the 'reputation' of foreign investors in respect of management (five-star hotels and sugar projects), technology/brand names (Distillers project) and marketing (five-star hotels). Favourable tax treatment helped, too. <u>In toto</u> however, for FIAC, unlike GCEC, domestic capital appears to have provided much the larger proportion of capital employed.

DFI has also helped to mobilise foreign borrowing, especially in the form of long-term suppliers' credits. Suppliers' credits, usually at subsidised rates of interest, form a very important element in financing fixed assets (viz. long-term capital). Many of the projects would not have got off the ground within the last few years had it not been for the availablity of long-term suppliers' credits and these suppliers' credits were far more easily mobilised when there was foreign involvement in the equity or management of the projects.

There is also evidence that foreign investors have been able to mobilise long-term loans from foreign banks, especially for some of the relatively capital-intensive GCEC projects and a few of the bigger FIAC ones. GCEC projects have mobilised foreign-exchange resources to finance their requirements of working capital, (indeed there is legal requirement that they do so).

The contribution of DFI flows to the balance of payments is not yet substantial but inflows in recent years have considerably exceeded remittances of profits. Moreover DFI has helped to generate foreign-exchange earnings, largely through increased exports of manufactures. A considerable proportion of the foreign exchange generated does not however, accrue to Sri Lanka, (as it is remitted to meet the cost of imported inputs, profits and interest, and short-term balances are retained outside Sri Lanka's banking system for GCEC projects). Net gains for GCEC projects are in the region of 15-20% of export earnings and for export-oriented

FIAC projects - where some interest is paid to Sri Lankan sources of capital and there is much larger equity ownership - the net gain is possibly much higher. Limited as they are, these gains help to relieve balance-of-payments constraints.

The contribution of DFI flows has been quite big in respect of employment generation. At the end of 1983, out of about 250,000 employed in manufacturing, about 23,000 were in GCEC enterprises and 20,000 in FIAC projects engaged in this sector. Most of these gains in employment were in garment industries, where the wages are low and the labour employed is largely female. Nevertheless, in a country where unemployment among the young is very high and the opportunity cost of such labour is near zero, this contribution is still significant.

There has been a rather limited DFI contribution in regard to the transfer of technology and skills to the work force, though the impact is greater in non-garment industries. Of note are rubber products manufacture and heavy industrial projects and, to a more limited extent, hotel management.

DFI may also involve certain costs. Thus it is arguable that, given the quotas on Sri Lankan garments in Europe and North America, DFI in garments 'crowded out' domestic involvement in the industry. However, GCEC projects have been restricted to about one half of the volume eligible to be shipped under US quotas and have no claim to Western European quotas: they account for 35-45% of Sri Lanka's total garment exports. FIAC projects, where at least 70% of ownership is Sri Lankan, account for another 25-30% of total exports, while 30-35% of garment exports are effected by purely Sri Lankan firms. Thus export-oriented DFI has largely augmented local resources in the short and medium term. Given the fact that Sri Lankans have been attempting to export since the late 1960s - albeit rather constrained by government policy until 1977 - the case against DFI in this regard is somewhat weak.

Foreign equity investment in capital-intensive import-substitution projects and five-star hotels has been relatively small, especially in the context of the actual foreign involvement in the project (supply of equipment under long-term suppliers' credits, management contracts) and indeed the size of the investments themselves. Government agencies have effectively owned most of the equity of two five-star hotels for nearly 14 years, and most of the equity in the vast majority of the recently established large hotels. Yet neither the government nor the private sector has chosen to manage even one of these hotels. Instead, management contracts have been negotiated with international hotel chains/managers who in most instances have chosen not to aquire an equity stake. In a number of instances where there has been low foreign investment in equity there has nevertheless been effective control exercised over the affairs of the enterprises by foreign management.

Government policies specifically aimed at DFI have involved major tax concessions, the provision of industrial estate facilities (GCEC projects) and some help with long-term and export finance (FIAC projects), and 'favoured' conditions for operation and access to the domestic market. For a foreign company however, a tax holiday does not affect the tax it pays in its country of residence, if there is a double taxation agreement, such as Sri Lanka now has with most capital-exporting countries and at the end of the tax holiday the company will be paying the same amount of tax. And where Sri Lankan capital has been mobilised to finance (often capital-intensive) projects, it has been attracted on very 'artificial' terms due to the massive concessions made available, so that a project giving a negative real rate of return becomes viable for the individual Sri Lankan investor. Thus in practice the incentive structure remains, still, in favour of domestic investment.

To conclude, the changes that took place in Sri Lanka soon after the 1977 General Elections had a major impact on private investment, and especially on DFI. The liberalisation of the economy (devaluation, freedom to import raw materials and capital goods) made export-oriented activities, including tourism, more profitable. New opportunities for DFI also arose in services, banking and in a large number of import-substitution activities, and through the acceleration of the Mahaveli Development Programme.

DFI flows responded swiftly to the new environment, and increased from miniscule to significant volumes. The recent decline in annual DFI flows, is at least partly explained by the "saturation" of long pent-up demand for DFI, and Sri Lanka's garment exports being constrained by foreign quotas. Of course, continued political stability is essential for Sri Lanka to continue to attract the DFI on a scale necessary for satisfactory economic development.

Chapter Nine

FOREIGN INVESTMENT IN INDIA

Bishakha Mukherjee*

Introduction

India has a long history of foreign firms participating in its economy; it once had one of the Third World's largest stocks of foreign investment. But there has been little new foreign investment in the last 15 years. India, indeed, has had a highly selective approach to foreign investment and this, combined with high rates of taxation and much regulation have led to a very small role for DFI. Since 1980, however, the general economic outlook and investment climate have improved. Foreign companies seeking markets for sales of capital goods, technical collaborations, and, to a lesser extent, equity investment, are taking a fresh look at the country's prospects. More recently, in early 1985, the government announced a wide-ranging relaxation of industrial controls.

The increasing attraction of India to foreign companies arises from a relatively good economic performance and prospects at a time when the world economy is not doing very well. The overall growth over the Sixth Plan Period, 1980-85, was 5.2% which is a significant improvement over earlier plan periods. India also has a high reputation as a cautious and reliable borrower in international financial markets. And it has also a good record of political stability.

Although there have been moves to liberalise the Indian economy, and to strengthen the private sector, India is still very far from having an open-door policy towards foreign investment. Indian statutes governing foreign investment remain restrictive and selective. The basic policy is that foreign investment is welcomed only if it is accompanied by technology transfer or if production is primarily for export. Additional goals are savings of foreign exchange through import substitution and import of energy-saving technologies. In general, private overseas capital is not given much emphasis as a source of financial flow to augment national savings. And in particular foreign investment is not regarded as a major factor in overall economic growth, though it is now recognised as important in certain sectors - notably electronics and vehicles - and for certain specific purposes: acquisition of technology and increasing exports.

As a consequence of its past policies, India has been given a low rating by foreign investors; a Business Environment Rating Index in the early 1980s placed it bottom of a list of 43 countries for foreign investment. But recent policy developments might well have changed the picture substantially. In this chapter we examine the emerging trends particularly as they relate to foreign investment in high technology areas and in export-oriented investment.

Profile of Private Foreign Investment in India

The OECD estimates that the stock of foreign investment in India is currently around $2.5 bn (Rs 25 bn)(1). This represents around 15% of GNP and 8% of the stock of India's external debt, and on both counts is very low by comparison with most developing countries. And most of the stock relates to investments made long ago. Data collected by the India Investment Centre show that in 1969-82 new foreign investments of Rs770m. ($77m.) were approved. Of this, a substantial proportion never materialised (around 60%). On the basis of a figure of under $40m. of investments being undertaken for the 14 years to 1982, this results in an average of under $3.0m. per annum (and this is a gross figure, not including repatriation). This compares with net direct investment inflows of around $18 bn to Brazil and $11 bn to Mexico.

Other sources which give a useful indication of what has been happening over time, are the Surveys of the Reserve Bank of India of assets and liabilities of 'corporate, industrial and commercial undertakings' (Table 9.1). The total (Rs10.6 bn in 1980) is very much less than that quoted above, reflecting different coverage and methods of estimation. What is significant, however, is the way in which overseas branches of foreign companies have largely disappeared; the decline of majority-owned subsidiaries since the mid-1970s (when the current legislation covering foreign investment was passed) and the rising relative importance of foreign investments in the form of minority shareholdings. Portfolio investment - at least until 1980 - is minor.

One major change which has taken place is the decline in the importance of foreign investment from the UK. In 1948, 84.8% of the foreign investment in India was of companies from the UK. This share came down to 53.9% in 1980 - still, however, a large percentage. The US share which was only 4.3% in 1948, had increased to 21% by 1980. During this period West Germany, which had no investment in 1948, had increased its share to 7% and Switzerland's share went up from 2% to 5.9%.

Table 9.1. Stock of Investment in India (Rs m.)

	Direct Investment				Portfolio	Total
	Branches (100% owned)	Subsidiary (50-100% owned)	Others (50% owned)	Total		
Mid 1948	14.6	4.5	4.0	23.1	5.7	28.8
End 1955	24.3	11.9	2.4	38.6	3.9	42.5
End 1961	27.0	20.7	5.0	52.7	4.3	57.0
End March 1965	26.2	26.8	8.2	61.1	5.5	66.6
End March 1970	22.3	37.3	13.9	73.5	9.4	82.9
End March 1975	22.7	51.7	22.9	97.3	10.8	108.1
End March 1980	6.0	45.5	41.8	93.3	12.2	105.5

Source: Reserve Bank of India

The latest Reserve Bank study(2) of the finances of 313 foreign-controlled companies shows that 71% of them in 1980-81 belonged to the group called 'processing and manufacturing - metals, chemicals and products'. Lall has calculated(3) indirectly the importance of foreign-owned firms in different industries (among large publicly-quoted companies). Among 28 industries, the highest foreign shares are held in 'other chemicals' (50.5%), 'other food' (47.7%), pharmaceuticals (43.4%), rubber (42.5%), tobacco (38.3%) and chemical fertilisers (34.5%). The lowest are in textiles of various kinds, paper, printing and publishing. Two have no foreign investment. And the average ownership in the large corporate sector by this measure is around 20%.

The major change which has influenced the level and type of foreign investment in India has been the 1973 Foreign Exchange Regulation Act (FERA), which was designed as a mandatory measure to achieve the 'Indianisation' of wholly foreign-owned companies. Enterprises with over 40% of foreign ownership were classified as FERA firms and were required, if they were to continue in operation, to dilute their equity. The only exceptions allowed (under which they could retain 51-74% shareholding) were for companies meeting stiff requirements in respect of 'high technology' or being 'export-oriented'. This Act was followed by a long and, in some cases, painful divestiture. Since the imposition of

FERA in 1974, of a total of 800 odd affiliates in the country, 61 left India, 112 were asked to dilute foreign shares to 51-74%, 231 to dilute to 40% or less, 72 diluted on their own, and the rest were already under the 40% limit. The number of branches of foreign companies fell from 123 in 1975-6 to 8 in 1980-1. Several sectors of industry were closed to foreign firms altogether. In many others, official entry conditions were so difficult, cumbersome and restrictive that new foreign capital inflows were effectively excluded.

Foreign equity investment is now allowed only if it is part of a foreign technology acquisition proposal, except in the special free trade zones and 100% export-oriented units. Even this has been a rarely used route to foreign investment, since outright purchase of technology through lump-sum payments or limited duration royalty arrangements or both are preferred to equity participation. Further, where there is foreign equity, the share capital has to be by way of cash without being linked to tied imports of machinery and equipment or to payments for know-how, trade-marks, brand names, etc. And all investments involving foreign equity participation require the endorsement of the Foreign Investment Board, the central agency for screening foreign participation proposals.

While direct foreign investment now constitutes a small proportion of India's foreign capital flows, minority joint ventures and non-equity collaborations have been arranged. The number of foreign collaborations has risen significantly in recent years. Proposals for foreign collaboration agreements approved in 1985 numbered 1,024, compared with 752 in 1984, 673 in 1983, 590 in 1982, 389 in 1981 and 526 in 1980. Since 1957 more than 7,000 foreign companies have entered into collaboration arrangements. A quarter of the approvals in 1985 were for joint ventures in which foreign companies took equity; the rest were technology-licensing agreements. The main sources of collaborative arrangements continue to be the US, followed by West Germany and the UK (Table 9.2). There is increasing French interest too, while Japanese collaborations increased substantially over the last three years in the automotive sector.

Some Recent Changes in Foreign Investment Policy

Until the last few years it could reasonably be surmised that the role of foreign investment in India was marginal, highly circumscribed and subject to controls. While the fundamentals remain unchanged (including FERA legislation), there have been two significant changes. One is the relaxation of controls in relation to particular categories of investors: those from OPEC countries (1980) and non-resident Indians (NRIs) in 1982. Investments from OPEC

Table 9.2. Foreign Collaborations 1957-82

Countries	Approvals				Foreign investment involved 1969 to end 1981	
	1957 - 30.6.82		1969 - 30.6.82			
	No.	%	No.	%	Rs.m.	%
UK	1,604	23.0	810	20.2	91.02	11.8
USA	1,356	19.5	830	20.7	304.61	39.6
West Germany	1,232	17.7	795	19.9	72.41	9.4
Japan	579	8.3	329	8.2	45.38	5.9
France	327	4.7	214	5.3	40.68	5.3
Italy	244	3.5	162	4.0	44.74	5.8
Others	1,617	23.3	865	21.7	171.06	22.2
Total:	6,959	100.0	4,005	100.0	769.90	100.0

Source: India Investment Centre.

countries and NRIs need not be associated with the transfer of technology. The main channels of investment for NRIs are deposits (including government securities), portfolio investment in shares and debentures, corporate securities through stock exchanges and direct investment. The concessions given to NRIs relate to interest rates, exemption from taxes, etc. NRIs are considered to have great investment potential. Already total funds which have come to India through NRI sources increased from Rs10.9 bn in 1981 to Rs37.9 bn in 1985. An associated development is the launching (by Merrill Lynch and the International Finance Corporation) of an India Fund - a form of investment trust designed to channel portfolio investment by NRIs into the Indian stock exchange.

The second change has been a much more explicit welcome for foreign investment and other forms of technological collaboration in areas of high technology. For the last three decades the government's broad industrial and trade strategy has attempted to control the technology entering the country, assist adaptation and to promote and protect indigenously developed technologies. Although this policy has been successful in regulating certain quantitative aspects of technology imports (payments, duration, etc.), its success in promoting technology development activities within Indian industry has been limited. A large and diversified technological base with relatively small inputs of foreign technology co-exists with large areas of technological underdevelopment and stagnation which have been officially acknowledged. This has created the recognition that a policy of allowing more liberal imports of technology and capital is a necessary condition for increasing the technological competence and efficiency of Indian industry.

A significant shift in policy direction is already evident in certain technology-intensive sectors. The electronics sector has been accorded high priority in the present planning period and production of electronic goods is targeted to grow by more than five times over the next five years. In the last two years, 1984 and 1985, following a policy of liberalisation, the number of collaborations in the electronics sector has increased substantially - a total number of 62, involving a foreign investment of Rs 248m. (including majority foreign investment in selected areas).

In the automobile industry manufacturers have been encouraged since 1981 to upgrade technology and production has been deregulated. There has been a substantial spurt in foreign collaborations - from 39 in 1983 to 63 in 1984 and 115 in 1985. Japanese companies accounted for a substantial portion of these collaborations. Some involve foreign equity (but only up to 40% in this sector).

In the oil sector too there is growing interest in foreign technical collaborations in areas including those relating to supply of equipment and services for oil and gas exploration. Eleven foreign collaborations involving foreign investment of Rs203.6m. were approved in 1985, 9 with foreign equity of up to 40% and 1 with above 40%.

Apart from the above sectors, there has generally been a liberalisation of industrial policy. The measures adopted include delicensing of industries; easing of the anti-monopolies legislation; and the opening up to private enterprise areas previously reserved to the public sector; the import and export policy has been liberalised so as to strengthen the base for export production, facilitate technological upgrading and generally streamline procedures. These measures have been supported by tax cuts for business and salary earners and the creation of a stable, long-term fiscal policy.

Foreign Investment and the Balance of Payments

A major reason for the past lack of interest in foreign

investment in general was the belief that it would lead to a drain on foreign exchange, since remitted dividends, plus a relatively high reliance on foreign inputs, would almost certainly exceed the value of capital inflows except in the very short term. Implicit in such a relatively pessimistic cost-benefit assessment was the assumption that foreign investment would be in projects oriented towards the domestic market. Now, on the other hand, where foreign investment could pay for itself by means of exports, it is more welcome. The other area in which foreign investment is welcomed is in high technology activities where there are foreign-exchange outlays in any event, whether the technology acquisition occurs under a licensing agreement or via direct investment.

Analysis of the current stock of foreign collaboration agreements (which include, but are not exclusively composed of, direct investment) suggests a generally unfavourable balance-of-payments impact. From a recent survey by the Reserve Bank (Table 9.3), it appears that while exports as a proportion of total production hardly changed over the period studied (1977-8 and 1980-81), there was a substantial increase both in the absolute amount and in the relative proportion of imports between the two years. The foreign-exchange balance for private sector companies with foreign collaboration agreements turned from a small positive figure to a negative figure between the two years (Table 9.3). Government companies had a worse performance (Table 9.4). Further, restrictive clauses in the agreements surveyed numbered 716, more than 80% of which related to exports, and the tendency to impose export restrictions increased over time.

The longstanding concern to ensure that foreign investment should be selectively controlled to maximise foreign-exchange earnings and minimise leakages has been given a new twist by current economic priorities. The success of the Seventh Plan (1985-90) hinges on achieving a rate of export growth which is exceptionally high by the standards of the recent past (6.8% in real terms) both to permit continued import liberalisation and to keep debt-servicing ratios sustainable. A series of new policies is being put in place: tariff and licensing concessions for exporters; removal of export taxes; rationalisation of subsidies; and special incentives for firms exporting all or most of their output. None of these policies are exclusively or even primarily concerned with foreign investment but they have created a more clearly defined role for export-oriented foreign investment. We examine below what the results are, so far.

Table 9.3. Total Production and Value-Added, Production and Value-Added Under Collaboration Agreements, Exports of Indian Private Sector Companies with Foreign Collaboration Agreements (FCAs) IN 1977-78 and 1980-81 (Rs.m. except when otherwise stated)

	Item	1977-78	1980-81
1	Value of total production	53,312.0	87,395.0
2	Aggregate value-added	18,290.0	27,797.0
3	Percentage of row (2) to (1)	34.3	31.8
4	Value of production under FCA[a]	12,112.0	18,665.0
5	Aggregate value-added under FCA[a]	3,790.0	5,437.0
6	Percentage of (5) to (4)	31.3	29.1
7	Exports of companies with FCA	3,094.0	5,130.0
8	Percentage of (7) to (1)	5.8	5.9
9	Imports of companies with FCA	2,848.0	6,249.0
10	Percentage of (9) to (1)	5.3	7.2

Note: a) Whereas the other figures in this Table relate to 594 private sector companies covered by the survey, rows (4) and (5) relate to a smaller group of companies with FCA.

Source: Reserve Bank of India.

Table 9.4. Indian Government Companies with FCA - Value of Production, Value-Added, Exports and Imports, 1977-81 (Rs.m.)

	Item	1977-8	1978-9	1979-80	1980-81
1	Value of total production	11,827	12,386	15,155	19,052
2	Value-added	2,737	2,845	2,926	3,304
3	Percentage of (2) to (1)	23.1	23.0	19.3	17.3
4	Exports	435	504	562	329
5	Imports	2,770	3,967	5,668	6,193

Source: Reserve Bank of India

Export-Oriented Foreign Investment in Free Trade Zones

India has two free trade zones (FTZs) at Kandla and Santa Cruz, and four others are under construction. The Kandla zone, established in 1965, is the oldest in Asia, and the Santa Cruz zone was set up in 1974. The two existing zones contributed only Rs3.3 bn in 1985-6, 1% of India's exports. Moreover, the import content of production is high - over 75%. Of the two zones, Kandla is the more substantial - it exported Rs 2.5 bn in 1985-6 - and varied - its firms produce garments, light engineering goods, pharmaceuticals, cosmetics and stainless steel products. The Santa Cruz zone (SEEPZ) is confined to electronic goods, of which it accounts for 60% of India's (extremely small) exports.

The two FTZs have been, by any reasonable standard of assessment, a failure. Despite the long history of endeavour and the attractions of India's low wage rates, the zones have failed to stimulate private investor interest and, specifically, foreign investor interest. Why is this?

As far as foreign capital is concerned, its status is somewhat ambiguous. In general terms, foreign investment in exporting firms is welcomed but in practice each proposal is considered on its merits, and not unconditionally. Blanket permission is, however, given for non-resident Indians. Only 9% of the firms in Kandla have foreign tie-ups and these mostly with a foreign partner that was related to the unit management. In SEEPZ, the record was better - 40% of the firms have foreign participation and in 15% the foreign collaborator had a controlling share. Nearly all these investments were made by non-resident Indians, with members of the family managing both the foreign and Indian sides of the business. Only two firms have 100% foreign equity.

The almost negligible foreign presence in Kandla might be due to the following factors: the lack of access to the domestic market; the existence of trade union activity in the zone; underdeveloped infrastructural facilities; the lack of direct overseas shipping services from Kandla port; perceptions of foreign firms about government policies and bureaucratic constraints; and the lack of certainty about long-term policies. In SEEPZ, the infrastructural conditions are relatively far better than in Kandla. This is due to its location in Bombay. However, the space allotted to the zone is posing a severe constraint and the telex and telephone systems are inadequate. A special problem of the zone arises from the requirements of some software units for links to computers in Western client countries. Moreover, there is doubt about the economic value of the units with foreign collaboration in Kandla, in particular. This is because foreign firms have been using the zone for channelling exports to the Soviet Union and its allies under an Indo-Soviet rupee agreement.

The Kandla zone's exports are mainly to the Soviet Union;

from a 3% share in 1978-9, the Soviet market now accounts for 90% of Kandla's exports. This rapidly growing and almost complete dependence has raised some concern as to the net benefit from the zone, as India is using imports paid for in hard currency to earn roubles. It is the case however that India buys with the rouble earnings essential commodities from the Soviet Union - oil, fertilisers, chemicals (accounting for more than 70% of Indian commodity imports currently) and defence equipment, which would otherwise have had to be paid for in hard currency. There is however a high dependence on the Soviet market where sales are very much conditioned by politico-economic factors over which the firms have little control. For example a recent decline in the value of imports from the USSR, primarily as a result of the drop in oil prices and a slowdown in defence equipment purchases, resulted in more than 20 firms closing down or producing only at a fraction of their capacity.

Overall, firms in the zones have had a precarious and not very profitable existence. The average life of firms at Kandla is 3.2 years and at SEEPZ 4.1 years; and 80% of firms established have since closed. One cause for this high mortality rate appears to be the breakdown of buy-back arrangements with foreign collaborators. Domestically-owned firms, especially the smaller ones, are completely dependent on these tie-ups for their exports and have proved to have neither the capacity nor the willingness to diversify their markets. A related cause of high mortality is regulation, for example, the slightest alteration in product specifications or design has required a fresh application for a licence to manufacture a new product. The mortality and instability rates in India are significantly higher than for zones in Malaysia or Korea(4). The main lesson seems to be that small Indian-owned firms operating on the basis of 'arms-length' collaborative arrangements with foreign importers are highly vulnerable; foreign investors with an equity stake in their Indian factories would ensure much better performance but so far the overall operating environment and incentives have not been sufficient to attract them.

Incentives and Constraints to Export-Oriented Investment

The package of incentives for the Indian zones appears to compare quite favourably with those offered by other Asian zones, but it has evolved in a piecemeal and sporadic fashion. This tinkering with incentives, however, prevented the zone management from using the package effectively for attracting investment. The predictability of policies that investors prefer cannot be assured given the ad hoc manner in which incentives to the zones have been handled. In evaluating the incentives available we have to take account both of the competitive nature of incentive programmes adopted elsewhere and of the cumulative incidence of costs in the incentive-giving location, which determines the pre-tax profit(5).

a) Tax Incentives. There is some ambiguity about the importance attached by investors to tax concessions. An ILO study(6) found that mounting rivalry had made lengthy tax holidays an almost indispensable feature of the incentive structure. Even if these incentives are not a major factor influencing an investor's decision, once tax incentives have been freely given by neighbouring countries it may be difficult to withhold them. In the light of these considerations, India has revised its regulations to include such an incentive but whereas a government Committee recommended a 10-year tax holiday, specifically to attract foreign companies, the government announced in 1982 a 5-year tax holiday for new firms. This is less generous than other FTZs in the region and has not been extended to firms which have been established for more than 5 years (this discrimination against the older units may penalise firms which have already demonstrated their ability to compete in adverse circumstances).

One weakness of the tax-holiday incentive is that it takes effect from the date of production and not from the emergence of profits. This effectively reduces the benefit period and tends to attract firms which have very short gestation periods which may, therefore, be simple assembly operations or even footloose industries with low capital and some one-off export contracts. In any event, the recent incentive package has failed to attract any significant additional interest from foreign companies.

b) Access to the Domestic Market. A central problem in any policy designed to attract export-oriented investment to a large developing country such as India (and for that matter China or Indonesia) is that a principal objective of most foreign investors is to secure access to the domestic market rather than to export. Motives include the relatively high risks of exporting; the potentially large long-term profits in selling to India's protected home market; and the relative unattractiveness of exporting from India in relation to other Asian locations. In order to meet investors' aspirations in this respect, a good deal of consideration has been given regarding the optimum level of access to the home market in order to provide an incentive to investors without losing all the benefits of export orientation. A government Committee recommended unrestricted sales of up to 25% of the total output of the zones (and other export-oriented units) on payment of normal customs duty as levied on similar imports. However, the government has allowed 25% of sales only against valid import licences. This 'concession' is of doubtful significance as most of the products fall under 'banned items' - i.e. consumer goods - and so there remains a significant disincentive in this area.

c) <u>Administrative Infrastructure</u>. In India, one of the primary incentives offered to potential investors in the zones is single-window clearance. In practice, this has not been achieved. Every application for establishing a new firm is still referred to the Ministry of Commerce and also to the Secretariat for Industrial Approvals in the Ministry of Industry. For every ambiguous case or situation where the 'law' is not clearly stipulated, several central Ministries have to be referred to.

To introduce effective single-window clearance, a government Committee had recommended that comprehensive legislation be enacted establishing an autonomous FTZ authority with full responsibility for the zones and defining clearly the powers of zone management. Such legislation still has to be passed. Again, unless this is done, the potential foreign investor who has some knowledge of the industrial control and regulation regime in India with its attandant delays and complexities - and also of freer regimes elsewhere - will not be encouraged to move to India as a base for export-oriented investment.

<u>100% Export Units</u>

The government also instituted in 1980 a system of 100% export-oriented units (EOUs) which enjoy the same facilities as the FTZs, but which can be located anywhere. There has been some interest in this scheme, as evidenced by the 609 applications which had been approved by 1985. However, only 94 firms were in production, indicating poor implementation, and annual exports are far below Rs1 bn. The main attraction of EOUs is that they can be used by firms which are not footloose or where industry-specific agglomerations occur. For these reasons, EOU-type incentives are being considered for tourist complexes and also for gold jewellery, a product for which India has great export potential but little to show.

Apart from the unrestricted choice of location, the main differences between the EOUs and FTZs are first, that the EOUs are not entitled to a 5-year tax holiday; second, EOUs are permitted to 'debond', and sell in domestic markets - after 10 years ordinarily and 5 years in the case of products having a high degree of technological change, while FTZ units are not; third, while the zones are expected to have 100% exports from the very start of production, an EOU is allowed to achieve this target in a phased manner over a period of 2 years; fourth, the minimum value-added for the EOUs is 20% of the value of exports against 30% in the zones.

Despite its superficially attractive features, the scheme has not taken off. Even among the firms operating, very few are generating new exports (as opposed to transferring existing production from the domestic tariff area); exceptions are exporters of hovercraft and xerographic equipment. Significantly, one public-sector firm accounts for the bulk of exports (an iron ore pellet exporter, established before the scheme came into effect). Foreign investors have shown negligible interest; only a quarter of the established firms have foreign collaborations in any form.

There are many reasons for the failure of the scheme to attract investors: the confusion caused by changing incentive schemes (a subsequent relaxation of import policy allowed all exporters to claim effectively the same facilities without the export obligation); the delays in obtaining licences; the delays in creating infrastructure facilities; the complicated bonding procedures; the ambiguities in the concessions (for example, freedom to sell some 'rejects' domestically); the delays in obtaining bank loans and the onerous requirements by lending agencies(7).

Conclusion

As the evaluation of special schemes shows, India has been almost wholly unsuccessful in creating 'enclaves' within which export-oriented investment - both domestic and foreign - can be attracted without changing the fundamental constraints exercised by trade and industry policy as a whole. For them to become more successful would require an internationally competitive package of incentives and infrastructural facilities, combined with greater freedom from bureaucratic rules and procedures and a single speedy decision-making authority.

More generally, there remain major impediments to significantly higher levels of foreign investment in India. Foreign companies would like to see a reduction in the high burdens of taxation to international levels; more liberal terms for the remittance of profits; higher royalties; longer periods for technical collaborations; stricter laws to protect patents and brand names; and simpler bureaucratic procedures. Moreover, foreign investment remains a highly politically sensitive area. Transnationals are viewed with deep popular suspicion, especially after the Bhopal disaster. The main liberalisation and expansion in foreign investment is occurring in minority foreign-owned enterprises (up to 40% foreign equity) usually linked with technical collaborations. And the main route through which foreign equity financing is likely to be encouraged is by non-resident

Indian investors, whose operations are regarded as more acceptable and whose perceptions are more favourable. In short, the opening up of India to foreign investment is, and is likely to remain, a slow and hesitant process.

NOTES AND REFERENCES

* The author is grateful to Mr. Sharad Kelkar, Ministry of Finance, Government of India, for his invaluable help and comments. The section on Profile of Foreign Investment draws heavily on a paper by Mr Kelkar which is reproduced in full in Commonwealth Secretariat, Papers and Proceedings of the Seminar on Foreign Investment Policies and Prospects: Asia and Pacific, (1986).

1. OECD, Investing in Developing Countries, (Paris, 1983).
2. Reserve Bank, Foreign Collaboration in Indian Industry: Fourth Survey Report, 1985.
3. Sanjaya Lall, 'India' in J.H Dunning (ed.), Multinational Enterprises and Industrial Competitiveness, forthcoming.
4. R. Kumar, Export Processing Zones in India: An Evaluation, (Indian Council for Research on International Economic Relations, New Delhi, 1985).
5. H.F. Samuelsson, Transnational Corporations in the Export-Processing Zones of Developing Countries, (UNCTC, New York, 1982).
6. R. Maex, Employment and Multinationals in Asian Export-Processing Zones, (ILO, Geneva, 1983).
7. M. Gupta, 100 per cent Export Oriented Units: Problems and Prospects, (Economic and Scientific Research Foundation, New Delhi, 1983).

Chapter Ten

LESSONS FROM NEGOTIATING WITH TRANSNATIONAL CORPORATIONS: TWO CASE STUDIES FROM AFRICA

THE VOLTA ALUMINIUM COMPANY AGREEMENTS IN GHANA

Rod Sims

In 1962, agreements were signed establishing the Volta River project in Ghana. The government-owned Volta River Authority (VRA) was to supply hydro-electric power to the Volta Aluminium Company Limited (Valco), 90% owned by Kaiser Aluminium and Chemical Corporation and 10% by Reynolds Metals, two of the six companies that still dominate the world aluminium industry. Twenty years later, in 1982, the Government of Ghana renegotiated these agreements.

Valco is extremely important for the economy of Ghana. Its dollar revenues (US$250m. in a 'normal' year) are of a similar level to the country's cocoa exports, by far the main export commodity (almost 30% of the total). Being a tolling company, Valco's revenues do not count as exports in the statistics but the net foreign-exchange benefit of the project to the economy averaged approximately US$70m. in 1980-2, admittedly the only years when the company has paid tax. In terms of net foreign-exchange contribution, Valco probably then ranked second only to the cocoa industry.

The agreements signed in 1962 were to run from the start of operations, which turned out to be 1967. But problems soon began to emerge. First, over the power rate which, though renegotiated by the VRA in 1972 and 1975, was cited by the early 1980s as one of the lowest in the world, and certainly the lowest applying between two arms-length operations. By 1982 the VRA's other customers were paying much higher rates.

Secondly, a power ceiling was agreed which, when Valco's fifth potline was installed, left less than 40% of power available for VRA's non-Valco customers by the early 1980s even after a second hydro-electric facility was opened at Kpong. By 1982, however, a power link was just about to be constructed to the Ivory Coast and there was talk of one to Nigeria. Such links provided the opportunity for the VRA to sell power for US dollars at very high rates. In addition to the ability to export power at very high prices, there was also some concern that, when the Ghana economy recovered, there would be insufficient power for local industry. In 1982, the economy was felt to be running at less than 50% capacity.

Thirdly, it was agreed in 1962 that Valco's revenue would come from a tolling fee. This fee was to be 56% of the lower of two metal prices, one quoted in £ sterling and the other in US dollars. The shareholders were obliged to provide Valco with alumina and to take the aluminium; Valco was therefore regarded as a service facility, which smelted the alumina into aluminium and received a fee for this function. Looked at another way, the shareholders retained 44% of the aluminium price for the services they provided, i.e. providing alumina, shipping metal, selling the metal, etc. The 56% fee was to increase to 60% if, after 10 years, Valco was not using alumina produced in Ghana. Since there were no attempts to refine Ghana bauxite into alumina, the tolling fee increased to 60% in 1976. By 1982, the Ghana Government regarded the 60% fee as too low; the 40% retained by the shareholders provided them with more compensation than they needed for the services provided. This was largely owing to the declining price of alumina relative to aluminium, due to the former's efficiency gains. The shareholders were also concerned about the fee. Both the prices listed were now producer list prices as distinct from realised prices; from 1980 to 1982 there was a large gap between the two.

The government also felt it was getting insufficient remuneration from the shareholders for the premium products produced at Valco. It was also unclear when Valco had to tender the metal to its shareholders; the holding of higher inventories in response to lower prices worked to the benefit of the shareholders and the detriment of the Ghana tax authorities.

The 1962 agreement put Valco's tax rate at 40%, and its taxable income was to be calculated according to the 1962 Income Tax Act and to be unaffected by subsequent amendments to that Act. No dividend withholding tax, interest withholding tax or export taxes were to be payable. Valco had a five-year tax holiday, plus the ability to carry forward depreciation allowances and claim them from year six onwards. The effect was to give Valco a ten-year period within which its profits were not taxed.

Included in the 1962 agreements was an innovative profit-sharing proposal, in many ways a forerunner to the additional profits tax regime applicable in many current petroleum and mining agreements. According to Kaiser's original letter of intent, Valco was to pay half its cumulative earnings into a Valco Fund. These earnings would be computed after Ghana taxes and after deducting, firstly, an allowance to provide a 6% return on the shareholders' equity capital and tolling charge pre-payments; secondly, an allowance to compensate the shareholders for their services in managing Valco, computed as 3.5% of the world price of aluminium ingot; and thirdly, the amount reinvested by Valco out of undistributed earnings in new capital facilities with the approval of the Government of Ghana. By the time this letter was formalised into a Trust Deed, however, the formula for calculating payments into the Fund had been varied. Under the terms of the Trust Deed not only taxes paid were to be a deduction, but also taxes 'relieved' by the government. In addition, all investments were to be a deduction provided that it came out of undistributed earnings. These amendments to the original intention meant lower payments to the Fund of roughly US$9m. by 1982. This sleight of hand, as it appeared to Ghana observers, caused considerable resentment.

By 1982 the current tax legislation in Ghana was in many ways different from that of 1962. It allowed for taxes at the rate of 55% and 50%, depending on the type of company, although it did provide certain tax concessions which may or may not have been applicable to Valco. The difference between the Valco tax rate of 40% and the standard US tax rate of 46% also meant that there was a continuing possibility of taxes being paid to the US tax authorities on Ghana-sourced income.

Other features of the 1962 agreements are worth mentioning. There was no reference to the backward integration of the industry. From statements made by President Nkrumah and others at the time, it is clear that Ghana expected one of its main benefits from the deal to be the exploitation of its bauxite reserves and the later construction of an alumina refinery. By 1982, however, there had been no move to exploit Ghana's bauxite; Valco studies had concluded that it was not profitable. Under the agreements Ghana did not have the right to impose any duty on imported alumina, even if locally produced alumina was available for Valco's use. The agreements also fixed for 30 years harbour and wharfage dues, water rates and other fees. By 1982 ordinary users of the port of Tema paid harbour and wharfage dues some 45 times as great as those paid by Valco. Consumers of water paid rates 20 times as high. Moreover, the governing law of the agreements was the law of Ghana frozen as at 1962, which meant that two systems of law were operating in the country.

Spread of Project Benefits: 1962-82

Valco's balance sheets since 1967 do not suggest a very high return to the shareholders. They invested over US$32m. in 1964 and 1965 and a further US$8m. in 1970-1, and received over US$27m. from 1973 to 1979 in repayment of tolling charge prepayments, along with a dividend of US$20m. paid in 1980. They also received interest-free credit extensions which, for the period they are outstanding, constitute positive cash flow. During the renegotiations they claimed that they had received little from the project - just over a 5% discounted cash flow return.

The government felt two other benefits should be taken into consideration. The shareholders supplied various services to Valco and received the benefit of a lower tolling fee. Using the renegotiated outcome as a guide (see below), throughout the early 1980s the fee should have been at least 65%. How much earlier in Valco's life this higher fee should have applied is uncertain. We have also noted, however, that Valco was poorly compensated for producing high purity metal and premium products, and that the metal price used to calculate the tolling fee favoured the shareholders. A second benefit to the shareholders came from the re-investment of Valco's substantial profits. The book value of the shareholders' equity (total assets less total liabilities) had increased from its initial US$12m. to over US$136m. by the end of 1982.

The government's return from the project is difficult to gauge. Until 1979 it received little revenue, but from 1980 to 1982 it received US$74m. in taxes and Valco Fund payments. The Ghana economy also gained because of its over-valued exchange rate: between 1978 and 1981 Valco on average had to bring into Ghana about US$20m. extra per annum.

The power rate paid by Valco to the VRA covered the direct generating costs. The major gain to the economy, therefore, was the extra power supplied from hydro power which would otherwise have had to come from thermal power, a saving of around US$50m. in 1982. To achieve these benefits the government had invested £35m. in the VRA for the construction of the hydro-electric facility from 1962-7. It also spent another £40-45m. over the same period on land resettlement (60,000 people had to be resettled from the area flooded for the dam), roads, housing and the harbour at Tema. The Ghana economy's discounted cash flow financial return from the project in 1982 was probably extremely low.

Renegotiation of the Agreements

Resentment within Ghana towards the Valco project built up over the 1970s. The three main gains to Ghana from the project - tax revenue, foreign-exchange inflow and cheap hydro-electric power - were relatively recent and felt to be insufficient. In late 1982 Valco's shareholders were invited to Accra to renegotiate the 1962 agreements; ten negotiating rounds were held from February 1983 to January 1985.

A number of events set the scene for the decisive third round. First, the second round had seen an acceptance by the shareholders of the government's principles on the main issue - the power rate; it was agreed to set the rate according to the average rate paid by aluminium smelters in the Western world, though the calculations had still to be agreed. Secondly, an understanding had been reached between the IMF and the Government of Ghana for a standby loan, which meant that the government did not have to be as careful in its attitude to the two US shareholders. Thirdly, the continuing drought in West Africa had left the water level in the lake at about 240 feet, compared to its minimum desirable level at that time of the year of 248 feet; there were therefore good technical reasons to stop supplying power to Valco to avoid the water level falling further. Fourth and most important, as part of its deal with the IMF, the government had devalued the currency from cedi 2.75:US$1 to cedi 30:US$1. This decimated the amount of US dollars Valco had to bring to Ghana to pay local costs, saving the shareholders US$27m. and thus undermining their argument that the exchange rate represented a 'tax' on their operations which prevented them from paying a 'reasonable' power rate. Nevertheless, the Kaiser negotiators overplayed their hand. They made an offer which could not be justified internationally, and so they had little defence against future government action. The power supply ceased and with it the negotiations, for two months.

The government's underlying principle throughout the renegotiation was that it wanted to achieve 'normalisation', i.e. it wished to normalise the Valco agreements as compared with similar deals in Ghana and overseas and to normalise the arrangements so that they reflected the original intentions of both parties. When applied to the power rate this meant that Valco should pay the average power rate paid by world aluminium smelters. In relation to power allocation, the government stated that the sharing of power should be the same as that originally envisaged from the Akosombo dam in 1962. For the tolling fee, the government's principle was that it should reflect a reduction from the metal value for the services the shareholders provided, valuing those services as if they were provided by an outside party at arms length. On taxation, it wanted Valco to operate under a fiscal regime similar to that for other companies operating in Ghana and overseas, particularly in the United States. It also argued that the Valco Fund Trust Deed should be amended to its original formulation in the Kaiser letter to President Nkrumah.

In defining these positions the government and its advisers had done a great deal of research on the aluminium industry and its cost structure, aluminium companies, and the power prices world aluminium smelters were paying. Its principles were difficult to refute from the standpoint both of an aluminium company and of international opinion. Indeed, most of the principles were eventually accepted by the company and formed the basis of the agreed amendments.

Table 10.1 summarises a broad comparison of the main issues agreed and their value to the government. On the price of power, a rate based on an average London Metal Exchange metal price of 73 cents a pound was agreed, with one-third to remain fixed while two-thirds were allowed to vary with average LME metal prices. The rate was also to be adjusted with lower power supply, which was an unusual feature. There was also to be a review every five years to determine whether the escalation had kept a reasonably close approximation to the average world power rate; if the two parties could not agree on what the average world power rate was, the matter was to be referred to an expert whose opinion was final.

A reduced power ceiling was ultimately agreed, which was worth a great deal to the VRA, since the extra power not supplied to Valco can be supplied to other users, at much higher prices. Agreement was also reached on allocations during power cuts due to drought.

On the tolling fee, the parties agreed, despite Valco's original preference for its own realised price, that from 1984 to the end of 1987 the fee would be 68% of the LME cash settlement price. The 1988 tolling fee was to be set <u>provisionally</u> at 62%, this figure being subject to later review and retrospective adjustment. There is growing acceptance within the aluminium industry of the LME price. The shareholders' main concern with the LME price was its potential for wide fluctuation; to meet this the parties agreed that the LME price used would be made up 50% of the average aluminium price for the latest available month and 50% by the price averaged over the previous six months. After an initial attempt by the shareholders to base the tolling fee on <u>their</u> cost of providing marketing, freight and alumina, etc. the parties agreed that it should be set as a residual amount after deducting the arms-length value of the services provided by the shareholders to Valco.

A major complication arose in determining the price of alumina. At the time of the negotiation prices were extremely low. The Valco shareholders wished, first, to use their own cost of alumina production from the high-cost Jamaica mines and refineries, and secondly the average price of alumina being paid by aluminium smelters at the time. This latter criterion would involve counting alumina under both new and old contracts; the government maintained that it was appropriate to look only at new contracts. The compromise reached was to value alumina at 11% in the tolling fee formula and thus arrive at a fee of 68% for the first four years, and then to use the figure of 14% which would set the fee at 62% for 1988 provisionally, to be adjusted, if appropriate, at the five-yearly review. The 68% tolling fee agreed probably is the same as a 66% tolling fee when using realised prices. By using the LME price instead of the lowest of the two prices measured in different currencies the government also improved its position. Valco was in a difficult position to negotiate for a fee below the 68% once it became clear that the government had done its homework and knew what the value of alumina, alumina freight, metal

Table 10.1. Comparison of provisions in Valco agreements and changes agreed

(Main Issues Only)

Issue	1962 Agreements	1982 Changes	Worth to Ghana in 'normal' year
A. Power Issues			
1. Base power rate	5.0 mills/Kwh	17 mills/Kwh But rate goes down if power supplied less than needed to run 4 potlines. Is floor price of 10 mills/Kwh however.	US$33m.
2. Escalation of power rate	On only less than 16% of rate	66.7% escalates up and down with the metal price	Depends on metal price
3. Review of power rate	None	Every 5 years	Depends on review
4. Power ceiling	Enough to run 5 pots	Enough to run 4 pots	US$10m.
5. Power allocation in force majeure	Valco and other VRA customers share cuts pro rata	Valco takes proportionately more cut	Depends on size of power cut
B. Tolling Issues			
6. Tolling Fee	60% of lower of two metal prices	68% of one metal price	US$6m.
7. Review	None	Every 5 years	Depends on review
8. Premiums	Little or no compensation for production of premium products	Reasonable compensation agreed	US$1.5m.

Issue	1962 Agreements	1982 Changes	Worth to Ghana in 'normal' year
C. Tax Issues			
9. Tax rate	40%	46%	US$1.5m.
10. Dividend Withholding Tax	0%	15%, but 5% on dividends declared from retained earnings	US$0.5m.
11. Valco Fund Minimum Payment	US$300,000 fixed	US$500,000 indexed	US$0.2m.
D. Other Issues			
12. Board Representation	Nil	2 members	n.a.
13. Integration of industry	Nil	If alumina of appropriate price and quality produced in Ghana, Government can impose duty on it	n.a.
E. Legal Issues			
14. Governing law	As at 1962	Law of Ghana and such rules of international law as may be applicable	n.a.
15. General review	Nil	Every 5 years	n.a.
16. Assurances	Strict limits over exercise of Ghana's legislative competence	Less politically offensive assurances given to Valco about protection of its investment	n.a.
Total Revenue Gain in Normal Year			US$52.7m.

freight, selling, marketing and technical services were.

Three other issues were decided which determine Valco's revenue. First, whereas the previous contract had valued the metal at the time of shipment, which could be open to manipulation, it was now agreed that it should be valued at the more objectively determined time of production. Secondly, whereas Valco had received no premium for producing metal in excess of 99.5% purity, it was now agreed that Valco would receive one-quarter of US 1 cent per pound for all metal produced as a proxy for whatever future mix of purity metal it produces. The figure is low, but the government accepted Valco's argument that to obtain premium for purity requires additional selling effort. Thirdly, the original contract provided that the premia for shapes and sizes (e.g. billets) would be agreed between the shareholders and Valco; the agreement now provides that for each premium produced the shareholders should pay 20% above the incremental cost of production. Valco are to supply the government with a list of premium products produced and their cost of production annually.

Discussions on taxation quickly focused on international comparability. The basic income tax rate was increased from 40% under the original agreement to 46%, dividend withholding tax was placed at 15% and interest withholding tax at 10%, both average international levels. Some allowance was made for the specific circumstances of the Valco project. The shareholders had retained earnings in excess of US$100m. in Valco and argued that these should continue to enjoy a zero rate of dividend withholding tax; a rate of 5% was ultimately agreed. The 10% interest withholding tax was not to apply to the loan under the existing Exim/Valco loan agreement, and Valco has the right to apply for future exemptions from this tax when raising loans.

A major amendment was to subject Valco to the currently applicable taxation legislation in Ghana. To obtain shareholder agreement a fiscal stabilisation clause was agreed, allowing for financial compensation when either party is significantly and adversely affected by changes to the tax law. There was also explicit provision for a loss carry forward of 10 years, and for the non-applicability of Ghana provisions which apply a minimum level of tax even if no profits are earned.

The government did not sustain its arguments about returning the Valco Fund formula to its original terms. These arguments did not sit well with the concept of normalisation, because most companies were not subject to a Valco Fund type of tax. An increase in the minimum payment was agreed, however, from US$300,000 per year to US$400,000 per year with a bonus of an extra US$100,000 whenever Valco operate three or more potlines. The new minimum payment was also to be indexed to the US wholesale price index, whereas the previous amount had been fixed in money terms.

The government did not press its argument that Valco should use alumina produced from Ghana bauxite. It was apparent from the alumina market that the construction of an alumina refinery in Ghana would not be profitable, and would therefore not be sensible for Ghana as a whole. Valco did agree, however, that if alumina of appropriate price and quality was produced in Ghana the government had the right to impose an import duty on alumina. Many other minor changes were also agreed. The government gained the right to appoint two members to the Valco Board, a move which would keep it much better informed. There is now to be a general review of the agreement every five years in addition to the particular reviews on the tolling fee and the power rate.

Spread of Benefits from the Renegotiations

What were the advantages and disadvantages of the agreed changes to the government and the shareholders? As Table 10.1 shows, when Valco is operating four potlines and the metal price is 73 cents/lb the Ghana economy will receive an extra US$52.7m. a year. The government also made other gains. By lowering the power ceiling and agreeing a more favourable power allocation system, it increased its flexibility of allocation. Secondly, the renegotiated agreement is a much better precedent to use in negotiations with other foreign investors. Thirdly, the government gained two Valco Board members. Fourthly, and very important, is its enhanced international stature. It showed an extremely capable handling of a potentially difficult set of problems. One prominent oil company has stated that the government's handling of the negotiations was a crucial factor in its deciding to invest in the country.

There are three areas, on the other hand, where it can be questioned whether the government gained enough. First, the power ceiling allows Valco to operate four potlines, yet potentially the VRA could still sell some of that power to other users at higher power rates. When assessing this issue, one must keep in mind that the VRA needs Valco as a customer. It would have been better to have kept Valco's power ceiling to three potlines. Secondly, some will question whether the government should have taken some equity or, indeed, should have taken control of the project. However, the Valco smelter does not necessarily represent a sufficiently attractive investment for the government, given its limited money; there is also the question of whether it could operate the smelter as efficiently. The option chosen of allowing foreign investors continued ownership and control yet improving its taxation and power payments seems to have been the most sensible approach in the circumstances. Finally, should the government have insisted that the Valco smelter use alumina produced from Ghana bauxite? While there is a lot of emotive appeal in such an arrangement, given currently low prices it is much cheaper to import alumina; without costly assurances and financial outlays, it would have been impossible for the government to force the Valco shareholders to agree to commit the necessary money to such a venture. The government now has the right to impose a duty on imported alumina when local alumina of comparable price and quality is available: this should provide sufficient power to attract an investor to utilise local Ghana bauxite if the market ever justifies it.

The main gain to the Valco shareholders is that they now have a more enduring agreement. Secondly, under the original 1962 agreement Valco's right to remit dividends was ultimately subject to Ghana's exchange-control law; exchange control had been in effect waived by legislative instrument for Valco but this could have been amended at any time. In return for making the many amendments to the agreements, the government gave Valco the right freely to declare dividends subject to a guarantee that it would always have enough funds to cover its local costs and charges. This was an extremely important gain to the shareholders; without it, the government could have prevented Valco ever remitting dividends. While this was an extremely large concession, it was one that eventually had to be made. Firstly, the government is currently trying to attract petroleum investment and will have to provide a similar guarantee to those investors to attract them to Ghana. Secondly, the shareholders would probably have stopped operating the smelter if they were prohibited from getting their money out of the country. While the government could have used such a move as an excuse for nationalisation, this would have met a hostile international reception. A third gain for the shareholders was the much more enforceable power allocation formula.

The main cost to the shareholders is the increase in the power rate. On the other hand, they have the future assurance that they will be subject to no more than the average price of power paid by other alumina smelters. This principle should provide them with a large amount of stability.

Conclusion

Why did no previous government take the bit between its teeth, equip itself with firmness of will and professional negotiating advice, and renegotiate the agreement? There were periods in the past when, if that political will had been summoned and organised, a substantial improvement in the terms of the agreement could have been accomplished. Of course, time had to elapse before the agreements became excessively imbalanced, but this had occurred well before

1982. Perhaps it was something to do with the nature of governments in previous regimes, perhaps also a little ambivalent feeling towards the smelter. The project was an enclave in terms of its legal status, financial arrangements, and fiscal regime, but it was also an enclave project in that there was a sort of high wall around it with its own route to the sea. When all else was in decline, Valco continued operating efficiently; indeed, its teams mended the drains and provided services in the Tema township. The timing of the renegotiation had much to do with the political preferences and will of various Ghana governments. The Valco experience demonstrates that governments can renegotiate inequitable agreements without damaging their international standing. Indeed, if handled well, such action can enhance it.

Some general lessons can be learned:

(a) Clarify the objectives. Government needs to decide, before negotiations begin, what its objectives are and how it will trade-off those objectives potentially in conflict. Companies usually come to negotiations with a clear objective and, if allowed, will make the running by offering things they consider of lesser importance.

(b) Obtain political backing. The negotiating team must be in regular contact with and have the support of the political leadership. Previous VRA attempts at renegotiation with Valco failed when Valco approached politicians who did not understand or sympathise with the positions being taken by the VRA.

(c) Understand the opposition. Government should understand the parent company's objectives, its current role in the industry and any peculiar circumstances that may affect its behaviour.

(d) Understand the industry. Government needs to know in particular the industry's cost structure and thus its capacity to pay. Will other companies in the industry come in if the company in the negotiations pulls out?

(e) Understand the precedents. What other deals has the company made? What deals have recently been made in the industry that have relevance to the current negotiation? Points (d) and (e) should enable government to understand the range of reasonable positions on each negotiable issue.

(f) Negotiate from principle. Government's bargaining positions are more difficult to counter when shown to be in accordance with prior stated general principles. The Ghana Government used the principle of 'normalisation' very well. Can a common thread to various government positions be generalised into an overriding principle of strong appeal?

(g) Detailed preparation. This is extremely important. Those involved in the government team must have sufficient time to devote to it. The Ghana Government relied partly on university academics and individuals from organisations who were freed from other work.

(h) Use available advice. Company negotiators usually specialise in this field. Without doing much extra work they understand the industry, the precedents and negotiating strategy. Government should obtain similar support. There are some international organisations willing to provide it. It is extremely important for government to have on its side someone thoroughly experienced in the negotiating process.

ATTRACTING OVERSEAS CAPITAL IN THE SEARCH FOR PETROLEUM: TANZANIA'S SUCCESS STORY TO DATE

Christopher Goss and Roger Nellist

Investment in exploration for petroleum in Tanzania has flourished over the last few years, at a time when circumstances for such investment would not appear to have been auspicious. This case study examines the extent to which the policies and strategies adopted by Tanzania have influenced both the rate of investment and the terms governing it.

Since petroleum exploration began in the 1950s, 23 deep test wells have been drilled and more than 30,000 line kilometres of seismic lines recorded. Although no oil has yet been discovered, one of the wells drilled in 1984 encountered an oil source rock, and surface oil seeps have been observed both in the coastal basin and in the western rift valley. Currently, 116,580 sq. km. of the country is under licence, representing about 55% of the total area covered by potential petroleum basins. 14 exploration and development licences are currently covering 5 different areas in which 8 companies, including the state oil corporation, Tanzania Petroleum Development Corporation (TPDC), have an interest.

Total expenditures on gas and oil exploration from 1969 to mid-1985 amounted to US$370m., 90% of which (US$335m.) has been financed from overseas sources, US$205m. of it by foreign companies under production-sharing arrangements with TPDC. This extensive use of foreign capital is particularly significant when viewed alongside Tanzania's declared policies of socialism and self-reliance. Even with the expansion of the mineral sector, which is now developing along similar lines to that of petroleum, there is no other sector of the economy which involves overseas private investment to this extent (one production-sharing agreement has recently been concluded with a foreign company for gold; an earlier agreement was concluded regarding uranium, but operations were later suspended following the collapse in the price of uranium).

Why is Tanzania giving foreign companies such a prominent role in developing its petroleum sector? First, the economic condition of the country since the late 1970s has prevented it from expanding its own very limited foreign-exchange resources. The 6% of total foreign-exchange expenditures financed by Tanzania in the mid-1970s in the government's initial efforts to prove the Songo Songo gas field were made during the boom in coffee prices. Thereafter the country's foreign-exchange reserves dwindled and the oil import bill (which now consumes about 60% of annual foreign-exchange earnings) became more crippling, at the same time intensifying the need to search for indigenous petroleum reserves. Second, it would be difficult to justify the continued use of foreign-exchange reserves in the high risk and fairly long-term search for petroleum, particularly as the need to use them to meet shorter-term basic requirements has intensified. Third, petroleum is a highly specialised, high-technology activity and it would have been almost impossible for Tanzania to acquire the technical and management know-how to initiate and sustain the comprehensive programme of petroleum exploration which is now under way.

Nevertheless, exploration to date by the international oil companies has been almost matched by direct and indirect operations on the part of TPDC, financed largely through grants and soft-term loans. It has concentrated on two activities: upgrading its geological knowledge by conducting initial seismic surveys in key prospective areas, and second, conducting exploration and development drilling in areas where there is no immediate prospect of international interest. Both activities have helped to attract foreign companies to Tanzania. The seismic information acquired, which has been sold to the companies, has increased their knowledge and reduced their risks, and has strengthened TPDC's hand in negotiating exploration programmes and economic terms with them. The second activity has been dogged with problems; it resulted, however, in the development of the country's only proven gas field at Songo Songo, which has helped to establish Tanzania as an area with petroleum potential.

Songo Songo gas field was discovered by Agip/Amoco's in 1974, but at that time the discovery appeared to be of no commercial interest to the companies and they relinquished the area to the government, as they were obliged to do under the agreement. This was the first real indication of hydrocarbons in Tanzania and the government and TPDC began exploration in the area with technical assistance from Norway, India and UNDP and ultimately US$70m. of soft-term loans from the World Bank (IDA), the OPEC Fund and the European Investment Bank. The resulting total of five wells drilled by TPDC proved the existence of a one trillion cubic feet gas field, half of which is now dedicated to supplying a world-scale export-oriented ammonia/urea fertiliser plant shortly to be constructed. Just over 25% of the equity investment in this plant is being put up by a joint venture of two overseas companies which will also have primary responsibility for managing the project. This is an encouraging example of appraisal work financed on concessionary terms from multilateral and bilateral sources which has led directly to further major overseas investment.

Songo Songo gas is very dry: that is, it contains a very small percentage of recoverable liquid hydrocarbons. TPDC's well 200 km to the north, at Kimbiji, and Agip/Amoco's last well, 100 km to the south at Mtwara, both encountered gas.

These wells have together given the southern coastal belt of Tanzania the reputation of being gas-prone, and it is reasonable to believe that a number of identified geological structures in this large area contain additional gas reserves. The prospect of discovering only an accumulation of separate gas reserves with no oil in a developing country that is very far from the main industrialised markets of the world is unlikely to attract foreign exploration risk capital. This is especially so if the local market (e.g. for direct use in industry as a fuel, or to generate electricity) is very small and dispersed (and therefore uneconomic), and even more so if the host country is unlikely to be able to bear the costs of full (or even partial) reimbursements in foreign exchange of the company's exploration expenditures in respect of any domestic gas consumption. Unless there is the prospect of gas reserves sufficient to justify producing liquified natural gas for export (upwards of 5 TCF of gas), the only alternative is for a joint-venture arrangement for the production of fertiliser (as with Songo Songo), methanol, etc. - something that is not of primary interest to a foreign oil company.

International attention has therefore focused until very recently on the inland sedimentary basin just west of the coastal belt, and in the western regions of Tanzania. There appears to be a strong interest by certain companies in obtaining access to exploration rights in Eastern Africa from Sudan down to Mozambique, which has potential as a new oil 'play'. These companies may wish to obtain exploration acreage in Tanzania in part to improve their picture of this play, and Tanzania prospects may therefore be enhanced by forming part of a much larger, regional prospect.

<u>Investment Terms</u>

Tanzania has established the ground rules for petroleum operations in a recent series of agreements modelled on the 1981 production-sharing agreement concluded with Shell. These, in turn, operate within the framework of the Petroleum (Exploration and Production) Act of 1980. The 1981 agreement with Shell was negotiated over a period of 2 years and, while in production-sharing form like the 1969 agreement with Agip, the terms were thoroughly revised and updated to complement the 1980 Act. These terms reflected the evolution of thinking and practice in the conduct of petroleum operations, which resulted, on the one hand, from the sharp increases in oil prices in the 1970s and the further establishment of the principle of national sovereignty over national resources, and, on the other, from the increasing search for oil in areas of high geological risk and uncertainty which require a greater degree of flexibility in negotiating terms. All these agreements include; rigorous work programmes to be carried out within clearly defined time periods; clear requirements covering the appraisal and development of an oil discovery (which have their basis in the Act); and economic terms which give the government a satisfactory share of profits and one which is responsive to changes in profitability. These ground rules provide potential investors with a clear and complete statement of how the government wishes them to operate. This, in turn, provides the government with a firm position in the negotiation of each individual agreement, but also allows sufficient flexibility on issues sensitive to investors.

Why should the investor think that the terms negotiated will be honoured by the government? The agreements contain terms for both exploration and production and can, in total, run for 30 years or more if petroleum is discovered and produced. The 1980 Act and the consistent approach taken by the government to all agreements since that of 1981 provide strong evidence that, on all the major terms, the government has thought through its position carefully and is unlikely to change it capriciously. Moreover, the economic terms are structured so as to cope with uncertainty over the profitability of petroleum production. This responsiveness to varying levels of profitability is achieved primarily from two elements in the economic package: the Additional Profit Tax (APT) and Joint Operations, both of which have featured in all agreements since 1981.

The agreements take the form of production-sharing contracts, whereby the contractor (which may comprise one or more companies) recovers its costs from a share of production (known as 'Cost Oil'), and the remaining production ('Profit Oil') is then shared between the government and the contractor, with the government's share increasing in accordance with the production rate. This arrangement by itself provides an imperfect link between shares and profits; high production rates are normally associated with large profits, but they may not be if costs are high, reservoir conditions difficult, or oil prices low. The contractor is then charged, however, on the profits it earns above a certain (negotiated) rate of return, and the rate of APT increases by a further step when a higher rate of return has been earned. The APT is aimed at collecting a share of the petroleum 'resource rent' for the government, and is only charged if the rate of return is high enough. If a petroleum field is only marginally profitable and does not earn any resource rent, no APT is paid; and because APT is included in the economic package, Tanzania's shares of profit oil at different production rates can be set low enough to leave the investor with sufficient profits on a marginal field. This 'swing payment' then varies the government share <u>automatically</u> as profits vary; no renegotiation of the agreement should be needed if profits turn out higher or lower than originally expected.

The TPDC also has an option to engage in so-called 'Joint Operations' with the contractor. This arrangement differs from standard equity participation in two main respects. First, TPDC does not contribute towards exploration but pays its share of development and operating costs once the development phase begins. Second, in return for its contribution to costs, TPDC does not take a share of the contractor's profit oil as it would as a participant in the contractor's consortium; instead, it takes an increased share of profit oil, but this percentage is <u>less</u> than its percentage contribution to development and operating costs. The arrangement is therefore generally less onerous to the investors than a state option to participate. This has two implications. First, the other economic terms can be correspondingly tightened. Second, it only becomes attractive for TPDC to participate if the petroleum field to be developed is likely to be profitable; this can generally be judged with some assurance at the time that the development decision is taken because the reservoir should, by then, have been thoroughly appraised. TPDC is more likely to participate, and Tanzania therefore takes a greater share of profits, when profits are high; this further reinforces the responsiveness of Tanzania's share to the level of profitability.

The APT and Joint Operations between them should thus enable the sharing of profits between the investors and Tanzania to vary automatically according to the economic circumstances of the project. The declared intention in negotiating the agreements has been that this automatic response should be sufficient to obviate any need to renegotiate terms at a later stage if the economics of production turn out to be different from those expected. This arrangement has resulted in agreements which should yield the government overall shares in profits comparable to those which are yielded by, for example, the UK and Norwegian financial regimes for the North Sea, which is an established oil province. But in contrast to those two regimes the Tanzanian agreements should not require continual adjustments to cater for variations in oil prices and production costs.

Establishing appropriate conditions for investment is not by itself sufficient, and both the Ministry of Water, Energy and Minerals and TPDC have energetically promoted exploration interest. They have encouraged companies to submit proposals and have negotiated in a brisk and businesslike way, and this has almost certainly helped to raise the level of company interest and competition. Tanzania has also demonstrated an exceptional capacity for drawing on competent outside advice and using it efficiently and productively. The UNDP and the Norwegian Government have provided resident geological advisers; the Technical Assistance Group (CFTC) of the

Commonwealth Secretariat assisted in drafting the 1980 Act and has actively participated in negotiating each of the subsequent agreements with the companies, as has the Petroleum Economics Adviser to the Ministry, who is also funded by CFTC.

Tanzania has obtained good terms from overseas companies exploring in the country, and this has been important in making acceptable the inevitably dominant role of overseas finance and expertise in investment in the petroleum sector. The government has also succeeded, however, in maintaining important principles relating to sovereign control over its resources, while presenting these in a form acceptable to investors. These principles relate to many aspects of the agreements, such as the obligation of the contractor to supply domestic petroleum needs, provision for training, involvement of nationals to the greatest possible extent, and the use of local firms and resources wherever possible. But, perhaps most important, under the production-sharing arrangements embodied in the agreements, the licence to search for and produce petroleum is granted not to the overseas company but to TPDC, which then contracts out the exploration and production work to the company. So, while finance and day-to-day management (with some important exceptions) rest with the company, the ultimate right to exploit Tanzania's resource rests with the national corporation. This separation of sovereignty from operational matters, while not new (modern production-sharing contracts for petroleum began in Indonesia in 1967), applies national policies on economic sovereignty to petroleum in a way which is acceptable to nearly all oil companies. A policy of majority holding from the outset by the state in a joint venture would have been unlikely to be acceptable, because it would have implied state control over management and technical decisions regarding the way petroleum operations were conducted. The government's understanding of this distinction between sovereignty and operational management and its willingness to reflect this in the agreements has removed what could have been a major impediment to investment.

While some of the strategies used should have more general application, the overall policy adopted towards investment in petroleum may be applicable to other (non-mineral) sectors only to a limited extent in Tanzania. The everyday visibility and socio-economic impact of overseas investment in other sectors would be greater; there would probably be more choice regarding the degree to which foreign investment was involved (in petroleum there is little alternative to using the oil companies for anything beyond initial prospecting); Tanzania's bargaining position in other sectors would be very much weaker, unless it could be established that it has a particular advantage regarding local resource endowments (tourism could be an example, were foreign investment to be required); and Tanzania has not given prominence to the role of foreign investment in its overall economic development. Tanzania's petroleum experience should, however, be of direct relevance to other countries with prospective natural resources, which share similar economic priorities and face comparable economic difficulties. In particular, the very enclave nature of petroleum seems to allow a country to attract foreign investment on terms acceptable to both parties, without creating conflict with its general development policies and without the circumstances prevailing in the remainder of the economy needing to add significantly to risks which the companies associate with investment.

Chapter Eleven

PAPUA NEW GUINEA - A CASE STUDY

Philip Daniel and Rod Sims

Papua New Guinea's small, open economy exports little other than primary mineral, agricultural and forest products; it imports almost all its fuel, capital goods and other inputs to production, together with the larger portion of its marketed food requirements. Only one-eighth of the economically active population in 1980 held formal wage employment. At the time of internal self-government in 1973, Australian grants met approximately half government expenditure.

Yet in the short period since internal self-government PNG has become a leading innovator in the design of relations between host countries and foreign investors in minerals industries. After successfully renegotiating the agreement governing the country's one large existing mine, Bougainville Copper Limited (BCL) in 1974, the government reached agreement with other foreign investors over the development of a copper and gold prospect at Ok Tedi in 1976, and approved development proposals in 1980. In May 1984, Ok Tedi began gold production, making PNG about fourth in the league of Western world gold producers, behind the USA but ahead of Brazil and Australia. When the copper stage of Ok Tedi is brought into production, PNG will rank just behind Peru and the Philippines, but ahead of South Africa in copper mine production capacity. Following the BCL and Ok Tedi agreements, and an agreement with Esso for petroleum by mid-1985 14 exploration petroleum prospecting licences had been negotiated with foreign companies, governed by full agreements along the lines of a standard model.

Despite its success in these areas, however, the government's foreign investment policies in relation to forestry, agriculture, fishing and manufacturing have been confused and sectoral performance has been poor. Among other problems these sectors have suffered from a relative neglect, compared to mining, at the higher political levels. At the same time, PNG has managed since Independence to dampen the severe fluctuations in economic activity levels characteristic of primary commodity exporters. Inflation has been contained at moderate rates, external payments have been kept in medium-term balance, and the local currency (the Kina) remains freely convertible for all current transactions.

Foreign Investment Stocks and Flows

Direct foreign investment in Papua New Guinea since independence is shown in Table 11.1. There is very little foreign portfolio investment, the most significant element being the 23% public shareholding in BCL. Valued at its historical cost, the stock of DFI financed by equity inflows probably reached around US$1 bn by the end of 1983, while associated loan-financed foreign investment had probably reached a similar figure. There is no satisfactory basis for estimating the sectoral distribution of this stock: it is probable that at least one-third of the combined total is accounted for by BCL, and a further one-third by Ok Tedi capital expenditure up to the end of 1983. Hence the accumulation of foreign investment outside the mining sector is probably fairly modest. The picture is complicated, however, by the fact that these figures are derived from the history of investment in PNG by non-residents; there is no reliable account of investment by resident non-citizens.

From the completion of the Bougainville mine in 1972 until the start of Ok Tedi construction in 1981, net direct investment inflows, discounting retained earnings, stayed at very modest levels. Retained earnings were a consistently important source of investment finance, but net private capital flows overall were negligible. From 1980, however, inflows increased rapidly, principally for Ok Tedi, but also for a number of agricultural and forestry projects. Both new equity investment and retained earnings were important as catalysts for inflows of foreign bank lending to private sector projects. By December 1983, the Bank of Papua New Guinea estimated private external debt outstanding at US$859.4m., of which US$650.3m. was owed by the mining sector, and US$120.5m. by new agriculture and forestry projects. The remainder was accounted for by the trading companies, commercial banks, and various smaller enterprises.

As might be expected, dividend flows to non-residents from companies other than BCL have been minor - usually less than K10m. per year. Interest payments in recent years have significantly exceeded dividend outflows. By way of comparison, remittances of savings by temporary residents (mainly expatriate contract employees) have run at, at least, five times the level of dividend remittances. The vast majority of dividends paid to residents, however, are still believed to be paid to resident foreigners; about half the dividends of PNG companies are paid to residents. Other forms of current commercial payments overseas (royalties, patent fees etc) are negligible.

Australia has continued to be the single most important source of investment flows during the 1970s and early 1980s: the foreign shareholding in BCL is Australian-based, and an Australian company holds 30% of Ok Tedi equity. In 1983, however, the total direct investment inflow from the USA was

Table 11.1. DFI inflows and outflows by source country (balance-of-payments data) 1976 - 83 (Km.)

Year	Total[a]		Australia		USA		UK		Japan		Hongkong		New Zealand		West Germany		Other[b]	
	In	Out	In	Out	In	Out	In	Out	In	Out	In	Out	In	Out	In	Out	In	Out
1976	4.5	3.0	2.5	2.7	-	0.3	0.5	-	1.0	-	0.4	-	-	-	-	-	-	-
1977	3.2	9.8	0.7	6.3	0.1	2.0	0.9	-	0.7	-	0.1	1.0	0.3	0.1	0.1	-	0.2	0.1
1978	5.4	6.4	2.3	5.3	0.7	-	1.6	-	0.9	-	-	0.7	-	-	-	0.1	-	0.2
1979	7.7	14.2	2.8	11.2	1.4	1.0	0.3	0.7	0.2	-	2.2	1.2	-	-	0.5	-	0.3	
1980	15.0	8.5	4.4	5.1	2.9	0.4	3.1	0.3	0.6	-	2.8	2.2	0.1	0.1	0.2	-	0.9	0.4
1981	17.7	5.5	8.0	3.3	5.2	0.9	0.1	0.1	-	-	0.8	0.4	0.1	0.1	2.5	0.6	1.0	0.2
1982	43.2	9.4	16.4	5.2	15.5	1.3	1.7	-	0.9	-	0.3	2.7	-	-	6.5	-	1.8	-
1983	90.0	4.3	29.6	3.5	36.7	0.1	2.3	0.1	0.4	-	-	0.1	0.1	-	18.6	-	2.2	0.5

\- means less than K50,000

a Equals flows of investment in/out of PNG by overseas residents, including Ok Tedi. Ok Tedi elements are estimated:

		Australia	USA	West Germany
1981	9.1	3.4	3.4	2.3
1982	25.2	9.5	9.5	6.3
1983	64.5	24.2	24.2	16.1

b Known to include Singapore, South Korea, The Netherlands and Belgium

General note: the Bank of Papua New Guinea treats mineral and petroleum exploration expenditure as a foreign investment inflow, whereas the National Statistics Office treats it as private final consumption expenditure for national accounts purposes, not as capital formation.

Source: data supplied by Bank of Papua New Guinea, May 1984.

greater; a similar US shareholding in Ok Tedi was supplemented by investment in minerals and petroleum exploration. The UK has tended to be an important source of agricultural investment (with the Commonwealth Development Corporation as the main element). There is no deliberate policy about country sourcing, flows by country vary according to the structure of foreign company participation in new projects. PNG has signed some form of investment promotion and protection agreement with the UK, West Germany, and the USA (via the Overseas Private Investment Corporation, OPIC), but there has been no initiative for one with Australia.

Foreign Investment Policy and Objectives

Since self-government in 1973 all political parties and nearly all PNG politicians and public servants have consistently held that foreign investment is to be excluded or restricted in areas where Papua New Guineans can in the short to medium term own and control an activity: in other areas foreign investment is to be welcomed wherever it is of clear advantage to the country. The interesting policy questions were therefore to define these areas. Essentially three schools of thought emerged on these questions. First, the 'nationalist' school, which takes an optimistic view of what areas or activities Papua New Guineans can seek to own and control in the near future. The second 'production-maximising' group is less concerned about the nationality of the investor and feels that increased production in the economy is on its own a good thing. The third 'benefit-maximising' school has always had its main following in the central Ministries of Finance and National Planning.

Each of the main groups had core support in one or more political parties. The Pangu Pati, formed by the country's first Prime Minister, Michael Somare (Prime Minister from 1975 until early 1980, and then again from mid-1982) contained many supporters of the 'benefits' school. The party of the country's second Prime Minister (Julius Chan, from 1980 until mid-1982), the Peoples Progress Party or PPP, largely supported the production-maximising approach. Finally, the Melanesian Alliance, made up of some people especially prominent in the Constitutional Planning Committee prior to Independence, largely supported the nationalist school.

Disagreement among followers of these approaches has adversely affected the climate in which to make sensible general or project-specific policy, and for government to make the best of its negotiating position by presenting a united front. These problems differed in intensity between sectors, however. In mining and petroleum projects very few problems arose. There never has been a serious school of thought pressing for a large national equity share or restriction of foreign investment in these sectors: they are generally felt to be too large, too technical and with too few linkages with the rest of the economy to justify such moves. The benefits to be gained from mining and petroleum were also clear: capital-intensive, with few linkages, and with the potential for large absolute amounts of profits, the essentially unchallenged criterion by which such projects stand or fall is their ability to generate government revenue. Moving to the other extreme, the manufacturing sector had few similar advantages. There has been continual dispute over the relative importance of revenue, employment, training and general economic linkage objectives, which has made policy formulation difficult.

A statement of policy on foreign investment is to be found in the National Development Strategy, put out in 1976 shortly after independence.(1)

> A number of large scale natural resource based (foreign) investments will be encouraged to raise revenue. With respect to investment in manufacturing and service sectors, the Government recognises the need for further growth and that further foreign investment will be required. Such investments will be encouraged if they: benefit consumers through lower prices; provide additional employment; provide additional government revenue; improve the balance of payments.
>
> On the other hand, investments that would result in considerably higher domestic prices (or require considerable subsidies) will not be admitted.

This statement illustrates the clarity of objectives for mining and petroleum projects in comparison with the other sectors.

PNG's Comparative Advantage

An understanding of PNG's comparative advantage is necessary to explain both the past and existing patterns of investment and the government's investment policies.

PNG has plentiful minerals, forests, fish, rainfall and sufficient arable land relative to its population. Exports reflect this, being dominated by copper, gold, coffee, cocoa, copra, logs, sawn timber, tuna and oil palm - which together comprised over 95% of exports in 1982. Domestically, the country's natural resources have meant that in most areas of the country people can obtain sufficient food, clothing and shelter for relatively little effort. PNG can also be considered fortunate in its location, near the rapidly expanding Asian and Pacific markets.

The negative side of the story is that PNG provides a small domestic market for local production. The average income is only around US$800 per head, and this is inflated by a transitory expatriate community, Australian aid and the country's mineral wealth. Around three quarters of the population are wholly or at least significantly still in the subsistence economy. Equally important, the population is spread throughout a wide geographical area that is poorly connected by road and often separated by high mountains or sea.

Urban wages in PNG are higher than those in comparable countries. Urban unemployment in unskilled and semi-skilled categories is high though this does not depress wages to internationally comparable levels. There exists a system of minimum wages which removes the ability to determine individual wages on the basis of demand and supply.

In terms of human resources PNG was one of the world's least developed countries at independence. Experience in the use of complex equipment and particularly in management is still limited. Skilled PNG labour therefore attracts a high scarcity premium and the shortage is filled by expensive expatriates. The skills are available, but the cost is very high.

Virtually all land (97%) is under customary ownership where title is determined by historical occupation and is not effectively registered, making commercial loan finance impossible. PNG is vastly over-regulated as a result of, first, inheriting its regulations from an over-regulated colonial ruler; secondly, the introduction of some paternalistic controls to protect the people; thirdly, a resort to regulations to make up for poor administrative capacity; and fourthly, regulations made complex by the limited administrative capacity of the public service. Dealings with government take considerable time, even to obtain simple approvals. A final point is that the country's imports equal approximately half of its GDP. Industries import more of their basic requirements than they would in other developing countries.

In summary, PNG has a comparative advantage in projects that extract and process its natural resources, projects that use them as an input to manufacturing, and projects that provide goods and especially services to its small market in industries that have 'natural' protection.

The General Regulatory Framework

NIDA. Since the early years of the first national government(2), PNG has followed the practice of explicitly defining activities in which beneficial foreign investment is encouraged, and those in which it is not. The practice was formalised in the National Investment and Development Act of 1974, which saw the birth of NIDA - the National Investment Development Authority.

All foreign businesses which began operations after 6 December, 1974 are required to register with NIDA prior to starting operations. NIDA's list of foreign investment priorities includes large-scale mining and petroleum exploration or production, forestry and integrated forest industries, ship building and repair and large-scale deep-sea fisheries. 'Open' activities in which DFI would be welcomed include most large-scale agriculture (though with a restriction to favour nucleus estates in the case of established export crops) and secondary industries, especially further processing of raw materials for export, and technical and professional services. 'Reserved' activities in which DFI is not allowed include alluvial gold mining, coffee growing (other than robusta, with arabica the main component of the country's production), coastal fisheries, all land transport, and virtually every type of activity potentially suited to small-scale local enterprise.

NIDA is supposed to do a lot more than simply register new foreign enterprises, however. Until very recently, its somewhat contradictory functions were to co-ordinate, promote, regulate, control and supervise DFI. It was initially hoped that NIDA would be a 'one-stop shop' for foreign investors. When it was established, however, the existing powers of other government departments and agencies were left intact. The NIDA conditions of registration have little substance in them, largely duplicating the requirements of various government departments. Perhaps the most important condition, the one requiring certain levels of equity to be held by PNG citizens within a period of time, has encouraged a non-productive class of 'front-men'.

We stated above that only foreign enterprises established after 1974 had to register. With the long delays and disincentive effect of NIDA this has created a 'ring fence' of protection around long established foreign enterprises in areas where citizens do not possess the necessary money and/or expertise.

<u>Other Regulations</u>. <u>Land</u> tenure presents problems especially in respect of 97% of the land where there is a customary title. A foreign investor coming to PNG will have some difficulty identifying available land, but this is not a major constraint. More important are the legal and administrative constraints on acquiring, improving, transferring and changing the use to which the land can be put. A huge backlog of applications for government approvals testifies to the difficulties.

PNG has a generally acknowledged severe shortage of <u>skilled</u> national <u>personnel</u>. In those categories where skilled manpower is short the employment of non-citizen workers is allowed but after long bureaucratic delays. In addition, the economy is generally held to be vastly over-regulated in everything from transport and building regulations to the variety of licences required by a Papua New Guinean to establish a business, and this has been acknowledged by government in recent years.

On the positive side all governments since independence have been committed to a strong and convertible currency and there are very few impediments to bringing money in or sending it out.

<u>Impact on Investment</u>. Two recent questionnaires have been sent to existing national and foreign investors in PNG, and several conclusions emerge. First, the high cost in terms of time and expensive professional advice to obtain the necessary approvals must frustrate and eventually deter some foreign investors - particularly the smaller ones. Many existing investors say they do not consider entering into new activities because this would bring their entire operations under NIDA scrutiny. Secondly, the combination of pervasive red-tape but poor enforcement causes a bias towards investors who are willing to flout the rules, or corrupt the rulers - a serious problem when a country is trying to maximise its benefit from DFI. Not only is there non-registered expatriate labour, but there is developing a non-productive class of PNG 'front' people to minimise detection under the NIDA Act. Finally, since the regulations have an obviously greater effect on new investors than existing ones they create a high barrier to entry, thereby limiting competition and creating oligopolistically controlled industries with presumably higher costs than otherwise. There has thus been a noticeable increase in the amount of investment in the hands of a few existing firms. Many firms leave, but relatively few are coming in as the existing firms expand by acquisition.

<u>Some Suggestions for the Future</u>. Several suggestions follow from the above. First, there is a need effectively to guide foreign investors through the government maze and co-ordinate government's approach to them. An independent arm of government could be established for this purpose.

Secondly, there is a need for a thorough review and simplification of the government's regulations in general. The idea of setting up a Government Regulation Advisory Committee (GRAC) in 1983 was a good one, but a continuing review is required. Specifically, in the case of NIDA, at minimum the Act could be amended to remove duplication of required approvals. Opportunities for significant gains also exist in de-regulating matters relating to land. And to speed up the establishment of new investment projects consideration could be given to allowing new investors to submit comprehensive training and localisation programmes after operations begin, when overseas investors are familiar with PNG conditions (say within one year). New investors could be restrained by laws which ban expatriates working in certain jobs and earning below a certain wage. Indeed, such constraints could generally substitute for specific Labour Department approval of each expatriate employee, while maintaining the general framework of approval of each firm's training and localisation programme. The Labour Department could then concentrate its scarce resources on approving and enforcing such programmes, and assisting industry with their implementation.

Evolution of General Fiscal Incentives

From a private investment policy viewpoint, the government at independence saw two areas as of high priority. First, considerable effort was put into policy for the mining and petroleum sectors which we shall review in more detail below. Secondly, it placed considerable emphasis on establishing a macro-economic policy framework that would ensure economic stability. Not only was this necessary anyway in a small, open economy, but it was possibly the main incentive that the government could provide to potential investors, since independence had generated a withdrawal of foreign investment from the country, mainly because of fears of impending economic and political instability.

By 1977 there were still essentially no fiscal incentives that applied across all sectors of the economy. The 'production' school, from the base of the Industrial Development Division of the Department of Labour and Industry, were continually putting forward comprehensive incentive packages, including tax holidays and the establishment of industrial estates. The 'nationalists' often supported such moves, looking for more incentives for national investors. Those adhering to the 'benefits' school successfully resisted. They argued that, given PNG's general cost structure, and its wages in particular, the country would only attract industries tied to a source of raw materials or the local market, whatever the tax incentives: the benefits would mainly go to industries that would come to PNG anyway. Incentives specifically tailored to the needs of the country were required.

Between 1977 and 1979, however, different incentive schemes began to emerge. The first were the Export Incentive Scheme (EIS), exempting 50% of export profits from tax, the Infant Industry Loan Scheme (IIL) and the Feasibilities Studies Contribution Scheme (FSC), whereby the government contributes up to 50% of the costs of feasibility studies. The Finance Minister's 1980 Budget Speech added three more incentives: accelerated depreciation; the provision of infrastructure for new projects in return for a negotiated user charge payable over the life of the project; and the allowance of a 200% deduction from assessable income for wages paid to apprentices registered with the Apprenticeship Board.

By 1980 the government had a range of incentives that had many advantages and few disadvantages. They could be manipulated to provide considerable assistance to a project: for example, the provision of infrastructure, accelerated depreciation and infant industry support could greatly improve the expected financial position for both shareholders and lenders. The incentives would not, however, subsidise profitable investors and ran little risk of having large sums of money outlaid or foregone for minimal benefit. Most importantly, they met the perceived needs of marginal projects in areas where PNG has a comparative advantage. Finally, they provided evidence of the government's commitment to investment and so help investor confidence.

The complaints against them are three-fold: first, their potential cost; secondly, that they did not go far enough; and thirdly, that they were biased towards promoting capital- rather than labour-intensive projects.

In 1984 new incentives were introduced. The first and most important was to allow for the first five years of production of a new manufacturing enterprise a tax rebate equal to a graduated (from 40%) percentage of the minimum wage per employee. This measure was politically popular given the increase in unemployment with the recession, and offset some bias in favour of capital over labour associated with the earlier incentive schemes. Only firms whose average rate of protection on their output is less than 15% higher than that on their inputs are eligible, so raising duties on inputs would now, in effect, cheapen labour. The second measure, taken directly from the mid-1970s fiscal package for mining and petroleum companies, allows new manufacturing enterprises to accelerate their depreciation to avoid paying tax until they have recovered their initial nominal investment. Thirdly, the export incentive scheme was further improved (it had earlier been made more generous) to allow 100% of profits from exports to be exempt from tax in the first 3 years of operation. In addition, in August 1983 the company tax rate was reduced to 35% (at the same time the dividend withholding tax rate was increased from 15% to 17%).

The package of incentives is wide, especially for manufacturing enterprises, by and large cost-effective and tailored to the country's needs and comparative advantage. It largely follows the thinking of the 'benefits' school, with some minor beneficial inroads from the 'production' school. The issue still separating these schools, however, especially in relation to manufacturing, is protection, the major outstanding issue of investment policy.

Mining and Petroleum

PNG's principal objective for the development of its mining and petroleum sector has been to maximise the long-term flow of government revenue from the sector, and thus help to meet its goals of fiscal self-reliance and provision of new infrastructure and services in rural areas. In the words of the Department of Finance(3):

> Papua New Guinea's minerals policy is premised on the view that large mines are useful not for any direct benefits that they bring, but for the financial support that they can provide for progress towards other national goals.

The government has been careful to distinguish the long-term revenue maximisation objective from the maximisation of the government revenue share in any individual project; it views the appropriate strategy as one which balances the need for incentives to project development (and efficient operation) with the immediate requirement for tax revenue.

From the time of the BCL renegotiation the government has demonstrated great reluctance to risk its own budgetary resources or borrowing capacity to promote mining projects. The general rule has been established that private investors assume exploration risk, that project sponsors will be responsible for provision of all necessary infrastructure, and that government equity obligations in mining will be limited to an option to purchase a minority share (maximum 30%, but usually much less) at par at the start of construction. In petroleum, the government's minority equity will usually be funded by means of a 'carried interest'. There have been two exceptions to this 'risk aversion': first, in wholly exceptional circumstances, such as those following the breakdown of negotiations with the Kennecott Copper Corporation on the Ok Tedi project in 1975, the government has taken strictly limited exploration risk; second, it has been willing to provide infrastructure (in exchange for equity or for a commercial return on the funds outlaid) where this would either reduce the investor's risk sufficiently to induce an otherwise excessively risky but potentially profitable investment, or would create significant external economies by establishing infrastructure that might reduce the cost of other major projects.

The government has sought long-term stability in its agreements with minerals investors. This is achieved not only by clearly setting out the rules of the game in advance, but also by designing the tax regime to adjust automatically to changes in profitability and the balance of negotiating advantage between the investor and the state during project life. PNG has also favoured a move towards a framework of general legislation and policy statements of wide applicability, rather than continuing case by case negotiation of fiscal terms. This approach is not, in theory, optimal since the supply price of investment can change over time and among minerals. It is favoured, however, on practical grounds: negotiating capacity is limited, and clearly stated terms are seen to function, in themselves, as an incentive to mineral exploration.

The concept central to PNG's current minerals and petroleum tax regime is that of resource rent. Following Garnaut and Clunies Ross,(4) this is defined as the value of the product of a mineral resource minus all the costs of production, including the minimum returns to capital that are necessary to induce investment. The government's aim is to tax away the highest possible proportion of resource rent, so defined, which is consistent with efficiency of resource use and the wider incentive to invest. Potential resource rent from an individual deposit will vary according to its relative cost competitiveness in the international league table of workable deposits of the minerals concerned; this position will be affected by a wide range of factors, including the richness of the ore, accessibility of the mine-site, cost of infrastructure and skills and so on. PNG has aimed at a tax system which creates a mutual interest in the efficiency of resource use, and thus of rent maximisation, but which also caters for both the marginal project and the highly profitable intra-marginal one. The emergence of these principles can be traced through the renegotiation of the Bougainville agreement, and the long negotiation process leading up to the commencement of construction at Ok Tedi.

The principles of petroleum taxation, and policy towards state participation, have evolved in close parallel to those for mining. Following a petroleum prospecting licence (PPL) agreement reached with Esso in 1976, a Statement of Intent on financial policies was issued in the same year, discussed with petroleum companies, and subsequently incorporated in general legislation. Negotiations continued, however, over two major issues that appeared to be of greater importance to oil companies than to mining companies: the degree of ministerial discretion over the rights of a company to progress from a PPL to a development licence in the event of a commercial discovery, and the rights of oil companies to hold foreign exchange offshore. Both issues were resolved in negotiations with different companies over the period 1978-80: the first by the application of suitable arbitration provisions and assurance of a right to proceed provided that all work had been carried out in accordance with good oilfield practice; the second by PNG's insistence that the convertibility of its currency would be maintained, and by the assurance that interest-free shareholder loans could count as normal loans (with certain restrictions) for foreign-exchange retention purposes.

There are four sets of criteria by which the success or failure of minerals policy might be judged: the share of cash flows obtained from existing producers, the extent of commitments to new productive capacity, the degree of exploration interest shown, and the amount of exploration work undertaken. On the first two counts, PNG's approach can be judged a broad success: BCL has continued to produce, and to invest, and has generated revenues for the government and its private shareholders in roughly the expected proportions. The Ok Tedi project has been launched, although it remains to be seen whether it will be interrupted by the depressed state of the copper market and whether its revenue contribution will match the expectations of 1979-81. On the third and fourth counts it is possible to form a judgement on the recent record of exploration activity in PNG; this has been fully researched for the first time by Charles Johnson and Allen Clark in respect of metal minerals.(5) As shown in Figure 11.1, expenditure in constant prices peaked in the early 1970s, fell sharply, and then began to rise again from about 1977. The boom in activity in the late 1960s coincides with the development of the Bougainville discovery; there was strong interest in PNG as a major new copper province in conditions of optimistic expectations about future copper demand and prices; during this phase a number of major deposits were identified, including Ok Tedi. The subsequent sharp decline resulted from the failure of the Kennecott negotiations, uncertainty surrounding the BCL renegotiation and PNG's transition to independence, and, just as important, from the sharp change in the prospects for copper prices and the fortunes of major mining companies. After the removal of political uncertainties and the establishment of PNG's clear fiscal framework, exploration outlays began to rise again, accelerating as PNG became recognised as a potential province of low-grade gold deposits. It is clear, from the recent volume of requests for permission to explore, that favourable market conditions for gold or copper will bring a substantial upsurge in exploration activity. All this confirms the broad acceptability of a fiscal package which yields the major share in revenues from profitable projects to the government.

The position in petroleum is similar. Because full petroleum agreements are normally concluded before a PPL is issued and exploration begins, a much smaller number of PPLs has been issued since the government's petroleum policies were formulated. At March 1984, 10 PPLs were valid, with a further six applications outstanding, involving 12 major and independent exploration companies or consortia. On the basis of commitments made by mid-1985 it is likely that 36 wells will have been drilled in PNG in the decade 1980-89, making

Figure 11.1 Trends in total exploration and grass-roots exploration expenditures

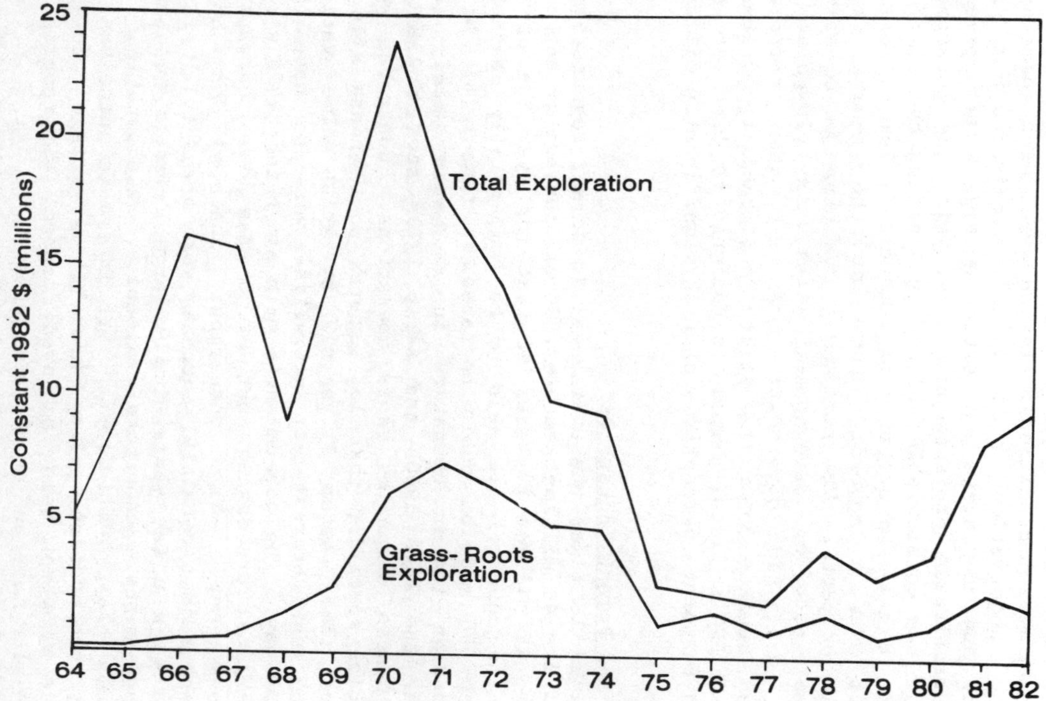

Source: C.J. Johnson and A.L. Clark, 'Mineral Exploration in Developing Countries: The Botswana and Papua New Guinea cases' unpublished paper, Resource Systems Institute, East - West Centre, Honolulu.

PNG, despite its size and the lack of a fully-proven commercial discovery, a highly sought after prospecting area in international terms.

PNG thus has the geological potential, legal framework and fiscal arrangements sufficient to offer considerable incentive to mineral exploration and investment, given satisfactory market conditions. In the event of a commercial discovery, negotiation over fiscal provisions is now minimised, and the state can expect a significant revenue flow if profitable projects are developed. The government has so far had considerable success in limiting the risks it is forced to take in securing an adequate inflow of foreign investment and a majority share of the rewards from profitable projects. The continuing challenge is to ensure an optimal pace of development (from the viewpoint of resource use and government revenues) when corporate objectives deviate from the strict profitability criteria with which PNG's fiscal regime is designed to deal, or when state and corporate perceptions of risk significantly differ.

Forestry and Forest Industries

PNG has over 13 times the average world forest resources per head. Of its 46 million hectares, 36 million are of enclosed forest and 15 million hectares of that (or over 30% of the area of the country) are held to be commercially operable, containing 500 million cubic hectares of timber.(6) While early foreign timber operators in PNG were mainly from Australia, the late 1960s and early 1970s saw at least 5 major Japanese companies begin operations. Contracts were signed which specified that log exports would cease after a period of time (often 5 years), by which time various processing and reforestation activities were to have been well under way. The government's main aim before 1978 was to encourage local processing, but in no case were contractual obligations met. The government insisted on quite extravagant terms: potential entrants were asked to stop all log exports in a few years, build large sawmills and other processing units, undertake extensive reforestation and provide all their own infrastructure in remote locations. Up to 1978, the forest policy had little effect and its objectives were not being achieved: indeed, the reverse was occurring with more and more log exports.

In 1977 detailed official surveys were conducted into the profitability of logging and sawmilling; these demonstrated that logging was very profitable, but that sawmilling was highly unprofitable. The Revised Policy announced in 1979 laid down clear packages: national, purely logging Forestry Development Companies (FDCs) would be allowed to harvest areas on the understanding that provision would be made for later alternative land use; limited log export in return for road construction (open to both foreign and national investors); and log export coupled with various specific forms of processing or reforestation. Foreign investors taking large forest resources would have to process at least 30% of the logs cut, would have incentives to process (no export tax is paid on sawn timber, a log export tax rebate is paid if processing obligations are met, and the general Export Incentive Scheme is applied on processed exports rather than the export of logs) and penalties if they did not (a proportionate cut in their log export entitlement): but the type of processing (sawn, veneer, woodchip) was largely left to them. In addition, the state would have a right of first refusal of up to 25% of log export entitlement, this right being capable of assignment to an international log trader, as a potential check on the correctness of prices. The new policy therefore took account of prevailing market circumstances: it stated reasonably clearly what was and was not wanted from foreign investment.

The government moved quickly to implement some aspects of the new policy. The log export tax was promptly doubled and the system of rebates for those meeting the processing requirements installed. The guidelines were presented to potential investors, and one agreement was soon signed along the lines of the new policy. In most respects, however, the policy has not been put into effect. First, the government has not yet appointed an agent to exercise the 25% right of first refusal, which now exists in a number of contracts. Secondly, no changes have been made to forestry legislation. Thirdly, no major reforestation projects have been started (the new policy assumed the Government would use its enhanced revenues for this purpose). Fourthly, there has been only limited evidence of the government being willing to enforce existing contracts. Fifthly, the government still shows a strong tendency to prefer inexperienced companies to develop its major forest areas. Finally, in its last major project negotiations at the time of writing, it appeared to have forgotten all the lessons that were behind the introduction of the 1979 policy.

For example, during the formulation of the 1979 revised policy, negotiations were held with Hyundai International for the Kapaluk resource in West New Britain. In contrast with the official policy, Hyundai had never undertaken a major forestry project before.(7) The agreement committed Hyundai to build and operate a chipmill and undertake reforestation, while they were allowed (in conformity with the new policy) to export logs throughout the life of the agreement. The chipmill was constructed on time, but at the time of writing it has never been operated. The company complains that there is no market for the chips, even though the parent company in Korea apparently provided a guarantee that it would take them. Reforestation did not take place, since profitability was adversely affected by not being able to use in the chipmill the trees that would be cut when the land was cleared; there have also been difficulties in acquiring the necessary land. While the government is apparently giving serious consideration to cutting the local company's log export quota, no action had been taken at the time of writing.

The FDCs are good in concept, but there now appears a danger that many will be started in areas that should not be simply logged, and where no reforestation or substitute long-term development will occur. The government is well advanced in establishing two further FDCs, on Manus and Bougainville islands respectively. It had been discussing the Manus resource with the United Africa Corporation (UAC), a subsidiary of Unilever, which has substantial experience in timber projects in the Third World. Agreement could not be reached, however, on the company's proposals, which involved a period of early log export to test the market.

Since the 1979 Revised Policy was released there have only been two major new forestry projects negotiated. Smaller operations have included direct dealings between landowners and foreign investors with the approval of the Minister for Forests, and some agreements allowing log export in return for road construction (including mainly foreign or national companies already operating in PNG). Direct dealings are increasing, and involve less onerous conditions for the foreign investor. The weakness of the forestry legislation in describing more than one mechanism for foreign investors to gain access to a timber resource, poses a serious threat to future forest policy and performance. For a country to gain the most out of the exploitation of a natural resource one central body must have effective control over it. The success of minerals policy illustrates this.

The Vanimo resource is generally agreed to be the nation's best. It is 2-4 times larger than most other PNG resources with an operable area of 225,000 hectares and an estimated volume of over 13 million cubic metres of sawn/veneer logs of greater than 50 cm width and a good species mix. In 1980 companies were invited to submit proposals to develop the resource. Many were interested, including the experienced international operators UAC, Inchcape, Weyerhauser and Bunning Bros., a very experienced Australian company, and a few others. After long negotiations an agreement was signed with Hetura Meja (a Philippine company) in April 1982, but was terminated in January 1983 since Hetura Meja failed to raise the necessary finance.

Four of the previously unsuccessful companies were then invited to submit proposals within three months according to comprehensive and stringent guidelines. When all four companies complained, the guidelines were substantially modified in October 1983: the proposed sawmill capacity was reduced by two-thirds, the other processing facilities were made optional although various studies were required, and the requirement to generate surplus power was removed. The companies were given just two months to submit proposals, however, and the two most experienced companies declined the invitation.

In January 1984 the National Executive Council began abortive negotiations with Hyundai, despite the fact that this was the company which by this time had failed to live up to its commitments at Kapaluk. Final agreement could not be reached and in September 1984 discussions began with Bunnings. One wonders what would have happened had the original 1980 guidelines been similar to the late 1984 agreement reached with Bunnings and had a reasonable period of time been allowed for proposals to be submitted. Not only would three years of wasted effort have been saved and PNG's reputation for dealing with foreign investors improved, but a much better deal might well have been secured.

Forestry has been a sector from which high growth was expected in processed timber output, employment, government revenue and general contribution to GDP. Performance has continually fallen well short, however. The problems have already been illustrated: pitching policy guidelines at unrealistic levels, choosing foreign companies inexperienced in major forest developments, and not enforcing contracts freely entered into. The problems are interrelated.

The Institute of National Affairs (INA), sponsors of much extremely useful research on general (including forestry) policy problems within PNG, obtained 'the opinions of some of the world's better known companies with experience in tropical timber ... to comment on their own absence from PNG activity'. They all blamed government policy and/or performance and many felt that those companies which are used to respecting contracts, or 'the serious investor, will be repelled'. The INA concluded that the results of its survey 'show quite clearly that the absence of the above companies from the PNG forest scene is certainly not due to ignorance of either the resource or the machinery of Government which prevails'. (8)

A major cause of the problems is the lack of clear objectives and widely accepted forest policy. PNG's mining policy, for example, was formulated amidst wide public discussion and political involvement at the highest levels: virtually the opposite is true of forest policy. Another cause of the problems is the inadequate resources devoted to forestry within government.

Agriculture

The efforts required to invest in any foreign country, compounded in PNG by the difficulties of acquiring land and

NIDA registration, suggest a minimum size of agricultural project suitable for foreign investment. Given the fragmented nature and small size of the PNG market, the traditional export crops (coffee, cocoa, copra) have usually been more attractive to foreign investors than producing to satisfy the local market. But with no access to redevelopment finance (commercial banks will not lend for long periods, the Development Bank cannot lend to non-citizens) the inherently uneconomic foreign-owned plantations have been hit hard by rising fuel and labour costs since the early 1970s. An amalgamation of properties by those with outside finance is required, but this has long been prevented by explicit government policy, particularly the abortive programme of land acquisition under the Plantation Redistribution Scheme launched in 1974 immediately prior to independence.

The most successful large agricultural export projects to be started using foreign equity have been in oil palm. They have a large smallholder component, and 50% government equity in each case: together with World Bank loans this has provided the necessary security of tenure. The other 50% equity was provided in each case by a single foreign partner who also manages the operation. The only large-scale foreign investment in import-substitution agriculture has been the foreign share of just over 40% in the Ramu sugar project.

Consecutive governments have voiced three objectives in relation to agriculture: first to increase PNG involvement, ranging from promoting smallholder production to a fervent nationalist call to remove all foreigners from possession of agricultural land; secondly, to increase agricultural production to benefit the general economy, with little reference to the fact that most existing production comes from foreign-owned plantations; thirdly, to produce local food items currently being imported. This mixture of objectives could have been pursued simultaneously with a well thought out policy which came to grips with the question of foreign investment. Unfortunately it was not.

Successive governments over-reacted to the initial demands of some traditional landowners for the return of their land and compounded this problem by then ignoring the question of duration of non-citizens' tenure over agricultural land. The failure to address this question led to problems with achieving the other two objectives. The oil palm nucleus estate projects cost the government heavily in terms of alternative expenditure priorities foregone. They were usually established with due regard for commercial principles, however, and can be regarded as successful. Politicians were frustrated by a lack of progress on import replacement. There arose a persistent danger that government would establish by decree a commercial project that was beyond its competence to manage or evaluate: the Ramu Sugar project was the result (a project majority-owned by the state which has needed domestic sugar prices at three times world levels - imports are banned - to avoid closure).

Was there an alternative approach to the question of foreign land tenure? Both in 1974 and since, a planned system of acquisition according to explicit criteria was and is required. The way may be to reissue leases to plantations that are not located in areas of land shortage and where there is a binding commitment to reinvest. The issue becomes one of simply informing foreign investors where they are, and are not, welcome. The government does not have the money or technical expertise to increase greatly agricultural production and employment. Foreign investment in some form is needed and can have many positive research and extension flow-on effects on smallholder production.

Fisheries

Foreign investors are involved in PNG's prawn and lobster industries which catch near their sustainable yield. By contrast, the tuna industry has enormous potential. The establishment of a tuna cannery remains the main component of PNG's development plans for the fishing sector. The government's poor handling of the project proposed by the US company Star-Kist in 1977 did not reflect underlying general antagonism to the idea, just the usual diverse opinions that must be reconciled if any major project is to proceed. Evidence for this came with the government's attempt to establish a tuna cannery in 1983, when a consortium of Italian companies offered management assistance to establish a cannery and fishing fleet. The project was well advanced in terms of political commitment and public awareness before previously unanswered questions on marketing, financing and overall viability brought it to a halt. These answers came when an expert assessment of the project was undertaken by an independent overseas company. Without this, the mistakes made in the implementation of the Ramu Sugar project, where no such objective assessment was made, might well have been repeated.

The government cannot undertake the cannery project without an experienced partner. The project needs a combination of experience, access to technology and overseas marketing connections. The Star-Kist proposal would have seen these elements provided by a company with a significant equity interest. Policy problems did not prevent it from proceeding, nor lack of finance. The problem was simply one of a lack of clear government objectives, planning and co-ordination.

Manufacturing
The main discussion in manufacturing policy has centred on protection, an area of considerable disagreement within the government. By the end of the 1970s the arguments for and against having a fully integrated and foreign-owned cement project using local limestone were an established part of the protection debate. Those in favour of the project argued that cement manufacture was a vital ingredient of a local manufacturing base. If the 'positive' attitude they hoped the government would show on this project were applied to others, then the industrial base of the country would expand, so would the demand for cement, and the project would eventually be viable. It was a matter of starting somewhere. In addition to the cost of the initial foreign-exchange loss, those opposing the project could see this experience being magnified many times over once the protection floodgate was open. The costs of such action (with associated infrastructure and subsidies) would seriously divert funds from development of the rural areas where most people lived. We have already stated that the 'benefits' school was largely in control of most aspects of economic policy during the 1970s and early 1980s. This, and the general appeal of policies that favour rural development in a society that places so much emphasis on the village, allowed the cement protection proposal to be resisted.

Stated government policy on protection since independence has usually been consistent and has not reflected disputes such as that surrounding the cement project. Successive governments have said that inefficient industries will not be protected or subsidised. The Ramu Sugar project, however, was a major deviation from stated policy. The government's resolve has generally held better with companies having higher levels of foreign ownership. In the late 1970s a steel rolling mill was established with 100% foreign equity. Officials were sceptical about its viability, given the small market and its reliance on imported raw materials, and immediately after start-up its owner asked for protection. The government wisely declined given the small local value added involved and the factory closed shortly after production commenced. It is a memorial to the perceived uncertainty of the government's protection policy.

Conclusions
The following general conclusions can be drawn:
(a) Control over natural resources should rest firmly with one central body (this is not currently the case with forest resources).
(b) Policy formulation needs high level political involvement, access to the best available technical advice, even if it must be hired overseas, and a campaign

of public awareness (the mining and petroleum sectors contrast with all other sectors).

(c) The smallest number of objectives must be formulated and stated for each sector, with trade-offs between multiple objectives clearly stated (the mining sector contrasts particularly with the agricultural sector).

(d) Sectoral policies must be targeted to real constraints (the time spent debating fiscal incentives for the manufacturing sector could have been better spent) and must be linked firmly and explicitly with the nation's overall development strategy (as was the case with mining).

(e) Foreign investors will be of most use to the country when they have a direct interest in project profitability (contrast the Ramu Sugar project with the national benefits gained from BCL).

(f) Government negotiating teams should have clear links with and the full support of senior politicians (forestry negotiating teams have often been undermined by political interventions outside stated government policy).

(g) Countries are in a relatively poor negotiating position without underlying macro-economic stability (PNG could not have negotiated the Ok Tedi project as successfully had it been in chronic balance-of-payments difficulties).

(h) Fair agreements should be enforced, but governments are in a good position to renegotiate those that are significantly out of line with world practice (PNG has benefited greatly from renegotiating the BCL contract).

(i) Once the effort has been made to formulate and implement policy in one sector, the lessons should, where appropriate, be enshrined in legislation and model agreements so that previous effort does not have to be duplicated. Leaving open one or two carefully chosen areas can cater for different project characteristics (in mining PNG has, within defined limits, left open the extent of its minority equity position and any contribution it may make to the provision of project infrastructure).

(j) Finally, investors should not be encouraged to feel that official policy can be avoided by one means or another; established policy and procedures will then be progressively undermined (in mining negotiations the PNG government ensured there could be no misunderstanding on this issue: investors interested in PNG's timber, however, may well feel tempted to explore unofficial channels).

NOTES AND REFERENCES

1. Central Planning Office, National Development

<u>Strategy</u> (Government White Paper, Waigani, 27 October 1976), pp. 13-14.

2. Overseas Development Group, <u>A Report on Development Strategies for Papua New Guinea</u>, prepared by the Overseas Development Group, University of East Anglia for IBRD/UNDP, (The Faber Report), Office of Programming and Co-ordination (Port Moresby, 1973), pp. 22-7, 85.

3. Department of Finance, <u>Financial Policies Relating to Mining Tax Legislation: Statement of Intent</u> (Waigani, October 1977), p. 2.

4. Ross Garnaut and Anthony Clunies Ross, 'Uncertainty, risk aversion and the taxing of natural resource projects', <u>Economic Journal</u>, Vol. 85, No. 38 (June 1975) and <u>Taxation of Mineral Rents</u> (Clarendon Press, Oxford, 1983).

5. This unpublished paper is cited by kind permission of Dr Allen Clark of the East-West Center, Honolulu, and of the PNG Department of Minerals and Energy. We are also indebted to Allen Clark and Charles Johnson for supplying additional tabulations not included in their paper.

6. Office of Forests, <u>Facts and Figures</u> (Hohola, 1983).

7. A.I. Fraser, <u>Issues in Papua New Guinea Forestry Policy</u>, Discussion Papers No. 7 (Institute of National Affairs 1981), p. 63.

8. <u>Ibid</u>., pp. xii-xiii.

Chapter Twelve

DIRECT FOREIGN INVESTMENT, THE TRANSNATIONAL CORPORATION AND THE PROSPECTS FOR LDC TRANSFORMATION IN TODAY'S WORLD: LESSONS FROM THE TRINIDAD-TOBAGO EXPERIENCE

Trevor M.A. Farrell

Trinidad-Tobago provides one of the most fascinating studies of the operations and effects of foreign capital in developing countries. There are five reasons for this assertion:-

(i) It is an important host for foreign capital and specifically for direct foreign investment (DFI). If the statistics are to be believed, its reported stock of DFI exceeds the absolute stock of DFI in 97 out of 116 developing countries around the world.

(ii) Like the rest of the Caribbean, it has had almost 500 years of experience with foreign capital; one might even go so far as to suggest that today's Caribbean was effectively <u>created</u> by foreign capital. Similarly, it has had long experience with the dominant form of DFI this century - the transnational corporation. (Shell entered Trinidad in 1913.)

(iii) Much of the DFI flowing into the Third World prior to the 1970s moved into the extractive sector - i.e. it was natural resource-based production. Part of the interest of the Trinidad-Tobago situation as a case study is how well it mirrored that pattern.

(iv) Trinidad-Tobago, as an oil exporter, was one of those countries that benefited from the boom in oil prices over the course of the 1970s. As its foreign-exchange reserves soared and it sought to implement ambitious new industrial ventures, it found itself involved in a whole range of relatively novel relationships with foreign capital.

(v) Lastly, part of the value to be derived from a careful study of the Trinidad-Tobago experience derives, paradoxically, from the fact that the country has been politically 'stable' over the years, and that it has had a government anxious to co-operate with foreign investors, cautious about offending them, and constantly concerned about safeguarding its good 'reputation' where foreign

Table 12.1. 'Deemed' capital flows related to direct investment in Trinidad-Tobago 1973-81[a] (TT$m[b])

Item	1973	1974	1975	1976	1977	1978	1979	1980	1981
Capital inflows									
Equity capital	n.a.	n.a.	n.a.	5.0	6.6	32.9	57.1	26.7	18.4
Loans received by DIE[c]	n.a.	n.a.	n.a.	-	18.2	19.6	279.3	211.7	170.9
Retained profits and allowances[d]	n.a.	n.a.	n.a.	383.0	449.2	364.0	747.8	654.2	550.5
Other capital inflows[e]	n.a.	n.a.	n.a.	358.6	365.3	256.6	356.9	289.5	402.3
Total inflows	195.0	691.2	866.5	746.6	839.3	673.1	1,441.1	1,182.1	1,142.1
Capital outflows									
Direct investment income									
Interest	0.9	7.3	6.8	5.8	3.8	4.9	12.0	38.4	32.9
Dividends	13.2	4.5	13.6	27.5	78.4	40.0	26.0	87.1	19.3
Profits	11.5	23.4	40.1	1.8	2.2	2.5	69.1	224.7	326.0
Retained profits	131.8	401.5	477.2	315.5	520.2	362.9	732.6	799.4	632.4
Sub-total	157.4	436.7	537.7	350.6	604.6	410.3	839.7	1149.6	1010.6
Other outflows reported[f]	66.6	474.5	364.7	485.5	503.1	368.4	1024.5	853.4	411.6
Total outflows	224.0	911.2	902.4	836.1	1,107.7	778.7	1,864.2	2,003.0	1,422.2

Table 12.1. 'Deemed' capital flows related to direct investment in Trinidad-Tobago 1973-81[a] (TT$m[b]) (Continued)

Item	1973	1974	1975	1976	1977	1978	1979	1980	1981
Inflows-Outflows	-29.0	-220.0	-35.9	-89.9	-268.4	-105.6	-423.1	-820.9	-280.1

Notes: (a) The flows recorded in this table are not necessarily actual physical flows of funds. For example, retained profits (i.e. profits not remitted abroad as dividends) are deemed to have gone out of the country as an outflow and then deemed to have been brought back in as a new inflow. This statistical 'fiction' is further compounded by the problem that the oil companies do not in fact bring the foreign-exchange proceeds for their sales revenue into the country.

(b) US$ = $2.40 from May 1976. Prior to this the TT$ was linked to the pound sterling and floated with this currency between 1973 and 1976.

(c) DIE = Direct Investment Enterprises.

(d) The figure for 'retained profits plus allowances' under capital inflows presumably differs from the figure for retained profits provided under Capital outflows 'Investment Income' by the amount for allowances. However, for 1977, 1980 and 1981, the official figures show retained profits (plus allowances) as smaller than just retained profits (as recorded under capital outflows). No reason can be found for this apparent discrepancy.

(e) 'Other Capital inflows' refers to such items as liquidation of real assets, provision for deferred taxation, decreases in current assets and increases in current liabilities.

(f) 'Other outflows' refers to various 'foreign uses of funds' - including increases in current assets, loan repayments etc.

Sources: Trinidad-Tobago, Central Statistical Office, The Balance of Payments of Trinidad and Tobago (various issues), Port-of-Spain, Trinidad.

capital is concerned.

There is no case on record of the government expropriating a foreign investor, or even engaging in compulsory nationalisation. There has been little or no regulation of foreign capital. In any event, the state's administrative capacities have been so weak, and maintaining consistent probity of all its officers has been so difficult, that effective regulation has never existed.

Stock of DFI and Capital Flows

No recent published data on the stock of DFI in the country exists. The United Nations Centre on Transnational Corporations quotes the figure of US$1.3bn for the stock of DFI in 1978(1). The petroleum sector accounts for by far the largest share of DFI in the country, with 3 main companies. Even allowing for other minor investments in the oil sector, and considering what is known to the author of the details of the foreign equity investment by other major industrial companies, the UNCTC figure seems rather high and to be regarded with considerable caution.

The reported data on inflows and outflows of foreign capital are somewhat better, and more up to date. Table 12.1 shows the figures for 'deemed' as well as 'actual' flows for the period 1973-81, i.e. all undistributed or retained profits are treated as remitted abroad as an outflow and then brought in again as an inflow.

Similarly, the financial effects of the normal day-to-day operations of direct investment enterprises are treated as outflows and simultaneous inflows or re-entries. Thus the absolute size of the figures indicated in the table considerably exceeds the actual flows.

Probably the most useful indication of the kind of actual inflows the country has been experiencing comes from the figures on equity capital and loans received by direct investment enterprises. These immediately raise the interesting question of the real role of DFI in terms of bringing capital into developing countries; whether foreign companies are important to developing countries because they can offer special access to banks and other credit-granting institutions, and whether the capital they bring in could in principle be obtained directly by developing country governments or domestic entrepreneurs, and the value of foreign capital lies rather in other areas (e.g. technology, market access etc.)

The data provided in Table 12.1 also show that there has been a consistent net outflow of capital as a result of the operations of direct investment enterprises. An older study by McIntyre and Watson, on the period 1956-67, also showed negative net capital flows in every year save one (1959)(2). At one level, this should not be surprising. Foreign

Table 12.2. Net direct investment capital flows by sector of activity 1974-81[a] (TT$m.)

Item	1974	1975	1976	1977	1978	1979	1980	1981
Petroleum industry	176.4	470.8	254.9	250.5	260.2	353.6	246.6	722.5
(Percentage of total)	(81.4)	(107.0)	(97.4)	(74.5)	(85.4)	(84.9)	(75.0)	(98.9)
Food processors and drink including tobacco	6.3	3.0	4.2	30.4	5.0	19.2	0.5	-5.6
Distribution	1.6	10.3	0.9	10.7	11.9	14.7	11.6	-1.2
Chemicals and non-metallic minerals	18.8	3.6	-39.0	6.9	3.2	12.2	26.4	3.6
Assembly tyre and related industries	6.0	0.3	4.5	18.6	8.9	0.5	19.4	5.3
All other sectors	7.6	-47.9	35.6	19.1	15.5	16.4	24.2	5.9
Total	216.7	440.1	261.1	336.2	304.7	416.6	328.7	730.4

Notes: a The data recorded here are derived from Flow of Funds data compiled by Trinidad-Tobago's Central Statistical Office in its Survey of Direct Investment enterprises.
The data is on a 'net basis', i.e. Capital Outflows (deemed and actual) minus Capital Inflows (deemed and actual).

Sources: T.T. C.S.O., Balance of Payments of Trinidad and Tobago 1980-81.

investors, like any others, invest their money in the hope and expectation that they will get out more than they put in. The conventional wisdom, however, on the advantages of, and even necessity for, DFI tends to suggest that during the years of a developing country's initial efforts at transformation, it would be a net absorber of foreign capital. Later on, the flow may be reversed, leading to the country in its turn becoming a capital exporter with its own domestic capital migrating in search of profitable opportunities abroad(3). The Trinidad-Tobago experience (like that of other developing countries) does not seem to bear this out, even though the strategy adopted had as its centrepiece the attraction of foreign capital for industrialisation(4).

As we have seen, foreign capital is consistently dominated by investment in the petroleum sector (see Table 12.2). There is no evidence from the data of increasing DFI involvement in manufacturing in the 1970s, as in some other developing countries. However, current developments in the country's petroleum sector are expected to lead to a diminution in DFI in this sector as the government finalises its purchase of the equity of Texaco Trinidad Ltd.

Portfolio Capital Flows. Portfolio capital flows are shown in Table 12.3. While the flows outlined in the first two rows of the table are disaggregated into 'private portfolio capital' and 'official borrowing abroad' following the presentation in the official statistics, this distinction is rather misleading. In fact, much of the 'private portfolio capital' flows recorded here really relate to borrowings abroad by state-owned companies, while some of the official borrowings also goes to state-owned commercial ventures.

The bulk of the portfolio capital flows is therefore related to the state and its activities, whether directly or through its agencies. There is little portfolio capital representing borrowings by local private enterprises or investment in local securities by foreign investors. Given the underdeveloped nature of the local financial markets, there is really little scope for this kind of capital flow. One of the interesting issues that arises therefore is whether it is possible at all, and, if so, under what conditions, to attract this kind of foreign capital into the economy of an underdeveloped country like Trinidad-Tobago by developing its financial markets.

One useful indicator of the relative significance of portfolio capital is to compare its net flows with those of direct investment capital. Whereas Table 12.1 shows that the latter were consistently negative over the 1973-81 period, line 7 on Table 12.3 which aggregates inflows of portfolio capital with outflows for interest payments and principal

Table 12.3. Portfolio capital flows (TT$m.)

Item	1973	1974	1975	1976	1977	1978	1979	1980	1981
(1) Private portfolio capital[a]	66.3	-56.8	-30.9	-20.9	8.1	128.3	444.1	49.6	260.6
(2) Official borrowing abroad	56.4	-14.4	-18.8	-85.4	364.2	256.8	132.2	147.5	35.7
(3) Sub-total (A)	-9.9	-71.2	-49.7	-106.3	372.3	385.1	576.3	197.1	296.3
(4) Interest paid on private portfolio capital	-10.1	-15.9	-22.0	-26.8	-11.4	-9.1	-37.8	-47.2	-139.0
(5) Interest paid by central government on external loans	-13.0	-24.3	-19.7	-15.1	-9.3	-44.5	-94.1	-83.1	-133.3
(6) Sub-total interest payments (B)	-23.1	-40.2	-41.7	-41.9	-20.7	-53.6	-131.9	-130.3	-272.3
(7) Net portfolio capital borrowings abroad (A&B)	-33.0	-111.2	-91.4	-148.2	351.6	331.5	444.4	66.8	24.0
(8) Official loans abroad	-	-110.7	-30.0	-180.0	-21.4	-	-	7.9	-264.9
(9) Portfolio capital flow	-33.0	-221.9	-121.4	-328.2	330.2	331.5	444.4	74.7	-240.9

Note:- (a) These figures are given on a 'net' basis - i.e. loan drawdowns minus any amortisation of principal, changes in the asset/liability position of firms other than direct investment enterprises, etc.

amortisation, shows a mixed picture; with a net outflow for the years 1973-6 and a positive net inflow thereafter. Portfolio capital therefore has apparently been of greater significance to the economy than direct investment, strictly from the point of view of net flows over the period.

It would also be very useful if we could measure the respective contribution of these flows to total investment in the economy (net capital formation). However, no data are available that permit us to do this with any degree of reliability.

A study of the data on portfolio capital flows over the 1973-81 period shows that, between 1973 and 1976, the country was using part of its petrodollar windfall to reduce its external indebtedness, with a fall of almost 50% in the debt between 1974 and 1976. Since 1977, however, external indebtedness has been steadily increasing as shown in Table 12.3. Between 1977 and 1983, the external debt more than tripled.

In the first half of this seven-year period, the increase in foreign borrowing was related to deliberate government borrowing to finance its investment programme, especially energy-based industries such as steel and fertiliser. These borrowings took place against a backdrop of steadily increasing foreign-exchange reserves (see Table 12.4), and reflected a conscious decision to take advantage of the country's fortunate economic position and its consequent creditworthiness. Apart from the presumed advantage of using other people's money rather than one's own, it was felt that this approach would build the country's reputation with foreign loan institutions.

The recent rapid increase in foreign borrowing is of a very different order. The economic situation post-1981 has been characterised by deteriorating foreign-exchange earnings and reserves, consequent on the decline in the country's oil production and the fall in oil prices. Increased borrowing seems to have been undertaken partly to ease the adjustment to lower levels of consumption and expenditure.

Up to now, however, the economic situation is not plagued by an onerous debt burden. We do not have separate figures for loan repayments over the 1973-81 period, but a comparison between the figures for annual interest payments on portfolio capital (line 6, Table 12.3) and the country's foreign-exchange earnings detailed in Table 12.4 shows that debt servicing does not constitute a serious problem at present. It can materialize in the future, however, if the pace of external borrowing is maintained, and the oil sector declines further and in a fashion not anticipated by the government.

A final noteworthy point is the significance of official capital exports in the 1974-7 period. Line 8, Table 12.3 represents the government's lending to its Caricom partners

Table 12.4. Foreign-exchange earnings on current account and foreign-exchange reserves 1973-8. (TT$m.)

Year	Value of exports of goods and services plus unrequited transfers	Foreign exchange reserves at year end
1973	$1089.7	$ 67.1
1974	2421.3	695.4
1975	2908.3	640.1
1976	3552.1	2125.1
1977	3921.4	3204.1
1978	4069.9	3,950.8
1979	5366.7	4,837.8
1980	8,217.1	6,336.7
1981	8,100.8	7,687.2
1982	7,352.6	7,160.1
1983	6,597.6	4,992.5

Sources: T.T. C.S.O., Balance of Payments of Trinidad-Tobago 1980/81; T.T. Central Bank, Annual Report 1983; T.T. Ministry of Finance, Review of the Economy 1983.

in the 1970s while it enjoyed a massive windfall from oil.

Other Capital Flows. In recent years, the involvement of foreign capital in Third World countries has taken new forms - licensing agreements, technology assistance, turnkey contracts, joint ventures, management contracts etc. Table 12.5 presents the official data on the outflow of capital to foreigners as payment for services rendered or for resources provided such as access to technology. Two points may be made here. The first is that these figures may well understate the actual capital outflows under this heading. Much of the recent involvements of foreign construction firms, for example, has hardly been documented. Also, the actual outflows of capital from the initial provision of resources may seriously understate the recorded flows (e.g. purchases of plant, equipment etc. from a firm's affiliates) because of the now well-known phenomenon of transfer pricing.

Secondly, it is interesting to observe that capital outflows under this rubric (i.e. payments for services) are one of the fastest growing categories in the balance of payments. This reflects (i) the growing significance of the new forms of foreign investment, (ii) the country's efforts to use its petroleum windfall to industrialise around heavy

Table 12.5. Capital outflows related to services recorded (TT$m.)

Item	1973	1974	1975	1976	1977	1978	1979	1980	1981
Management fees	-7.6	-7.2	-7.4	-13.9	-13.9	-14.8	-11.5	-20.3	-11.9
Professional and technical fees	-12.2	-24.0	-28.0	-46.5	-72.5	-122.9	-173.9	-176.3	-207.6
Commissions	-1.6	-2.3	-3.7	-4.8	-9.2	-12.0	-15.6	-15.8	-17.8
Royalties, patents and similar fees	-2.0	-2.7	-3.7	-4.9	-9.7	-8.1	-11.7	-13.3	-13.7
Total	-23.4	-36.2	-42.8	-70.1	-105.3	-157.8	-212.7	-225.7	-251.0

industry (such as steel) and energy-based industries such as fertiliser, and the use made of foreign contractors, consultants etc., (iii) the growing usefulness of this channel for exporting capital in situations of exchange control or political uncertainty.

Finally, in Table 12.6 we attempt to summarise the net effect on the economy in terms of capital flows from the operations of direct investment enterprises, plus net portfolio capital flows, plus payments abroad for the services of foreign factors of production. Interestingly enough, we arrive at a negative figure for each year of the 1973-81 period with the exception of 1978. If any credence can be placed in the statistics and consequently in the final figure, it suggests that Trinidad-Tobago is in the current period a net exporter of capital rather than a net importer as one might arguably expect given its stage of transformation.

Table 12.6. Net capital flows portfolio and direct investment plus payment for services (TT$m.)

Year	Amount
1973	- 85.4
1974	-478.1
1975	-138.3
1976	-487.8
1977	- 43.5
1978	68.1
1979	-191.4
1980	-971.9
1981	-771.8

The Petroleum Experience

The petroleum industry provides an important case study of the impact of DFI on the transformation path of a developing economy. Trinidad's oil production in global terms is small. At its all-time peak in 1978, crude production amounted to just about 230,000 b/d. Over the 1978-83 period, production has been declining. In 1983, it reached 160,000 b/d, the lowest figure since 1972. Trinidad is most important in the sense that it was developed by the petroleum transnationals as part of a chain of refineries set up throughout the Caribbean to produce residual fuel oil for the US East Coast market.

Currently, there are four major companies in the Trinidad-Tobago oil industry, two of them subsidiaries of transnationals. Texaco Trinidad is one of these. Up until recently, Texaco Trinidad was dominant in the refining sector. Trinidad was developed by Texaco as its refining centre in the Caribbean, and by the end of the 1960s, Texaco had built up its refinery in Pointe-a-Pierre into a facility capable of processing some 355,000 b/d of crude. Texaco thereby owned about four-fifths of the refining capacity on the island. The other main refinery, located at Pt. Fortin in the deep South of the island, was owned by Shell up until 1974, and had a design capacity of 85,000 b/d (though it was actually capable of running 100,000 b/d). In 1974, the Trinidad Government purchased the assets of Shell and created from these its first wholly-owned national oil company (Trintoc). Texaco's domestic crude production in Trinidad was much smaller than its refining capacity (less than one-third in the 1960s, and less than one-tenth in the 1970s). It brought in the major part of its crude for refining originally from its holdings in Venezuela (in the 1950s and early 1960s) and later on from the Middle East (Saudi Arabia, for example) and even Asia (Indonesia). Texaco did not refine domestically crude produced by any other of the companies in Trinidad.

The second wholly owned transnational subsidiary is Amoco, whose parent is the US company, Standard Oil of Indiana. Amoco entered Trinidad in the 1960s to search for cheap crude oil. Finding oil in 1968, it became the dominant producer by 1975, responsible for over half of all crude production. All of its production was, and is, exported to the US for refining there.

The third company of note is a joint venture, owned 50.1% by the Trinidad Government and 49.9% by a small US oil company, Tesoro of Texas. This company was formed in 1969, when BP pulled out of Trinidad, and the government, desperate to avoid the threatened unemployment of some 1500 workers, felt it needed the security of a joint-venture partner. This company currently accounts for about 13% of crude oil production.

Both Tesoro and Trintoc are relatively minor oil producers. Directly, they produce from their own holdings less than one-fifth of the country's oil. However, they are equal partners with Texaco in an offshore oil venture, Trinmar, which currently accounts for just over one-fifth of crude production.

<u>The Oil Industry, DFI and the National Economy</u>

Looking back over the last 30-35 years we find that oil accounted for 30% of GDP in the 1950s, 24% in the period 1962-73 and 40% in the 1970s and early 1980s. It has also made significant contributions to government revenues and to exports. Oil revenues accounted for some 37.5% of government revenues in the 1950s, approximately 25% in the period 1962-73 and a mammoth 60% between 1974 and 1983. However since 1981, its contribution has declined precipitously. In the decade 1964-73 (the period when Trinidad's role as a refining centre was at its height), oil accounted for nearly three-fifths of total exports (58.1%). In the decade or so since the oil boom, its share soared to over 80% (average 83.6% between 1974 and 1982). As a result of oil Trinidad-Tobago was (nominally) one of the most affluent developing countries by the early 1980s, with a per capita GDP in 1983 of approximately US$7,000, more than three times the 1973 figure.

It is no doubt tempting to ascribe the material benefits implied by these statistics to the beneficent operations of DFI. Without foreign capital and the transnationals, there would presumably have been no oil industry to provide these benefits. However, we must reflect on how much is due to the industry itself, and how much to foreign capital as the agents, and indeed the architects, of the industry's development. It would perhaps have been easier if there had been both local and foreign firms in the industry. But with the exception of Trintoc (which is in any event only ten years old), the industry has been dominated from its inception by foreign capital. What would have been possible without it is purely hypothetical.

Secondly, however, when we look at the role of the industry in true perspective it is clear that we need to separate out two distinct periods, pre-1973 and post-1973. The period of major material benefits is that of post-1973 and owes nothing to the activities of foreign capital. In fact, precisely the opposite. The post-1973 boom came about as a result of the successful exercise of countervailing power by OPEC <u>against</u> both the oil companies and the metropolitan consuming countries. Trinidad's affluence in the 1970s owed nothing to either the activities of the companies operating locally or to its own domestic exertions. All the government did was to take advantage of the dramatic changes in the international oil market and introduce a roughly similar tax regime in 1974 to what had become the standard around the world.

In the two decades prior to 1973, while Trinidad might arguably have been somewhat better off than many of its non-oil-producing Caribbean neighbours, economic conditions were most decidedly not good. In the 1960s, when its refining industry was growing apace, not only did the contribution of oil to GDP and government revenues deteriorate, but the economy itself slid steadily into crisis with unemployment soaring, growth slackening and foreign-exchange reserves diminishing(5). By 1970, in fact, the economic problems precipitated a full-blown social and political crisis with widespread strikes, industrial unrest, civil disorders and an army mutiny. Prior to 1973, the hosting of an oil industry organised and developed by DFI had done little to bring about either genuine structural transformation or real material affluence.

Capital Flows. The data on capital flows into the oil industry demonstrate, as we have seen, the premier role of this sector in foreign capital inflows into the country over time. Although the statistics are scanty and of questionable accuracy, they do also seem to indicate that investment in the petroleum sector has historically been a significant proportion of both gross and net capital formation in the economy. The most significant period was the late 1950s and the 1960s. The data available cover only 1956-65. In this decade, investment in the petroleum industry averaged 36.3% of gross capital formation in the economy as a whole(6). For the 1975-81 period, investment in the oil sector accounted for 25% or less of gross domestic investment, and the proportion tended to decline over the period.

The contribution of DFI to capital formation needs to be qualified by two considerations at least. First, the Trinidad-Tobago experience again demonstrates that, after the initial injection of capital, much of the subsequent investment was based on internationally generated funds - i.e. the ploughing back of profits, dividends etc, with occasional recourse to affiliates, the parent company or foreign loan sources. Secondly, even when it comes to the initial injection of capital, direct investment may provide little in the way of capital inflows, contrary to popular presumption. In fact, over the last decade or so, as we have seen, there has been a strong tendency for many transnational corporations to attempt to minimise their own equity capital in ventures in developing countries, and to rely instead on borrowing from international banking consortia, Export-Import banks and other sources of institutional finance(7). Over the last few years, the distinction between direct and portfolio capital was in practice considerably blurred. The setting up of the joint venture with Tesoro(8) illustrates this vividly; when the negotiations were completed, Tesoro had managed to acquire half of a company costing US$22m. for just US$50,000 investment.

Market Access. There are similar illusions about market access. DFI may provide this, or it may not (as the Tesoro experience also demonstrated). And sometimes the markets that foreign capital 'provides' are simply the necessary concomitants of its organisation of its operations to fulfil its own strategic imperatives. The refining industry in the Caribbean is a classic example. On one level the oil transnationals 'provided' access to fuel oil markets on the US East Coast, but this was the reason for their setting up the refining complex in the first place. In other words, this kind of market access is of a very different order from the way in which we have seen the Japanese, for example, make use at times of joint-venture arrangements in metropolitan countries.

Oil provides another important lesson. Over the last few years, the oil-producing countries have pushed the oil companies out of much of the oil market and are now selling a great deal of crude oil themselves(9). While displacement of the companies has clearly created certain problems for OPEC and the oil producers in terms of market stability, the fact is that the experience of the last decade clearly demonstrates how easy it is to exaggerate the notion that foreign capital, and the transnational in particular, are somehow indispensable from a marketing point of view. A more sensible conclusion would be that foreign capital sometimes has, and brings with it, 'genuine' market access - i.e. access to outlets for products that make good sense for a host country or organisation, and that, ideally, it has decided on itself. However, there is nothing automatic about this.

<u>Technology 'Transfers'</u>. Several years ago, the author undertook a detailed study of the impact of foreign capital and transnationals on the 'transfer' of technology and the development of a technological capability in the Trinidad oil industry(10). To summarise the findings: it was found that (i) after two generations of foreign control, the country's technological capabilities in the industry were unevenly developed; (ii) the areas developed locally were those that were important for the companies' local operations. Several critical functions (e.g. marine production, R and D, major projects and construction, petrochemicals etc.) were 'retracted' - i.e. undertaken outside the country in other locations; (iii) there was little impetus for foreign capital to seek to 'transfer' technology to the local economy.

<u>DFI in Oil and Exports - A Summary.</u> The data summarised above demonstrate quite clearly the significant role petroleum, and by extension DFI, has played in Trinidad's balance of payments over the years. In distilling lessons to be drawn from this experience, it is necessary, however, to enter certain caveats and qualifications.

(a) An industry's contribution to export earnings as measured either by statistics on absolute export values or percentage contribution to gross export values may not be the same thing as its foreign-exchange contribution to an economy.

Some of the foreign exchange generated by an activity may itself be used up to pay for imported raw materials and intermediate goods, to remit profits, dividends and depreciation allowances, or to amortise foreign loans for example. In the 1960s, for instance, while oil accounted for about 58% of Trinidad's exports, it only accounted for 25% of the foreign exchange used in the non-oil economy(11). It is therefore unwise to exaggerate the actual impact on foreign-exchange earnings that exports from an industry such as oil have on a developing economy, when the industry is operated under the aegis of DFI.

(b) It is also necessary to be clear on what should be as opposed to what is. In the case of the oil industry, the post-1973 experience demonstrated in spectacular fashion (i) how unequally the benefits had previously been distributed between producing countries and producing companies, and (ii) how much of the value produced had previously been appropriated as 'consumers' surplus', largely by metropolitan consumers, through the agency of the petroleum transnationals and their control over the industry.

In the late 1950s, Trinidad's significance came to lie mostly in its role as a refining centre; by the mid to late 1960s refinery capacity had been built up to some 455,000 b/d, more than triple domestic crude production. This activity contributed little to the domestic economy, however, save some employment (about 4000 jobs); the impact on foreign-exchange earnings and government revenues was negligible because of the companies' processing arrangements. For Trinidad-Tobago, the ideal situation would have been one which (a) maximised local value-added, through domestic refining of all or most of local crude production; (b) built up some of the variety of linkages to petrochemicals and downstream manufacturing activities; (c) maximised value-added from the refining process by a concentration on the 'light ends' and the distillates rather than low valued residual fuel oil.

Such a pattern of development would have ultimately maximised employment and would have enhanced export earnings and provided greater economic security through the creation of a much more diversified industrial and export sector. However, none of the foreign companies found it in their particular interests to pursue this pattern of development. It was more desirable to locate downstream linkages nearer to their markets in the main metropolitan consuming centres.

What can we conclude from all this? It is important to recognise that the interests of foreign capital and of a host economy can diverge. The issue simply is whose interests are to take precedence. Trinidad-Tobago is currently paying the price for its failure to ensure that it used its petroleum resources to build the kind of strong, diversified export sector based on the downstream linkages from oil (precisely what the Middle Eastern OPEC countries are now struggling to achieve). As a result of US energy policy decisions, and the changing strategic imperatives of the transnationals, we are now seeing the demise of the fuel-oil based refining industry in Trinidad and the rest of the Caribbean.

Foreign Investment and the Fertiliser Industry

The fertiliser industry in Trinidad provides another interesting case study of the nature and effects of DFI in developing countries. It begins with the setting up by W.R. Grace, a US-based conglomerate, of a wholly-owned subsidiary to manufacture nitrogenous fertilisers (ammonia, urea, and ammonium sulphate). Commercial production began in 1960 and was originally aimed at producing fertiliser for the regional market of the short-lived West Indian Federation (1958-62). With the demise of the Federation, the notion of a tariff-hopping, import-substitution type plant was abandoned by Grace, and the operations revamped and expanded into a world-scale, export-oriented facility.

In the 1970s as Trinidad-Tobago experienced its decade-long oil boom, the sudden availability of windfall foreign exchange coupled with the near-simultaneous discovery of large reserves of natural gas, led to decisions to go into the production of fertiliser on a massive scale. In 1977, a joint-venture operation (Tringen) between the Trinidad-Tobago Government (51%) and Grace (49%) was set up adjacent to Grace's original Fed Chem plant; it was really an extension of Fed Chem and was to be operated by Grace with Grace also handling the marketing operations.

In 1981, another large joint-venture ammonia plant (Fertrin) came on stream - this time a joint venture between the government and Amoco, and on the basis of a 51-49 split in favour of the state. By the end of 1981, Trinidad-Tobago had built up a capacity for producing over 1,200,000 tons of ammonia per year. This made it one of the world's largest exporters of ammonia. In 1984, yet another fertiliser plant was commissioned. This one, wholly owned by the Trinidad-Tobago Government, and designed to utilise some of the ammonia produced by the Fertrin plant, has a capacity of 246,000 tons of urea per year. It was to be operated by Fertrin under a management contract, with the marketing of the output being the responsibility of a large US chemicals company - Agrico Chemicals Company.

The Trinidad-Tobago fertiliser industry thus exhibits a variety of relationships between DFI through the medium of a transnational corporation and a host developing country. This variety is further enhanced by the impact of the engineering companies from the metropolitan countries, which were brought in to do the job of constructing and commissioning new plants. Thus Fluor, one of the large US engineering firms, undertook the construction of Tringen. Kellogg, another large US firm with worldwide operations, undertook the Fertrin project, and Snamprogetti, an Italian engineering contractor, built the urea plant.

The government's decision to stimulate fertiliser production domestically seemed at the time to be a sensible one. The production of ammonia (and downsteam of it, urea) draws on what is regarded in some quarters as the country's premier natural resource - its low-cost natural gas. Secondly, fertiliser is an important input into the production of much needed food - an activity which would seem to have an assured future. Modern fertiliser production is also relatively high technology, and the hosting of such activity seems at first glance to promise significant technological spin-offs. Finally, fertiliser production and export would also seem to confer the benefits accruing from expanded foreign-exchange earnings, government revenue, etc.

Modern fertiliser plants are highly capital-intensive, however, and in a small developing country with only a few plants, the industry was hardly likely to be a large employer of direct labour. The capital cost per person employed was also heavy. At the Tringen plant it worked out at TT$2.55m. per job place and at Fertrin roughly TT$3m. per job.

In terms of output generation, exports and foreign-exchange earnings, the Trinidad experience has to be divided into two periods - pre-1977 and post-1977. Pre-1977, because of the government's eagerness to attract Grace to Trinidad to begin fertiliser production in the late 1950s, very generous tax concessions were granted - e.g. a ten-year tax holiday, extended depreciation allowances, a ten-year waiver of customs duty, etc. As a result, the fertiliser industry contributed little or nothing to government revenues, and the local economy's share of value added produced was quite low. According to Parsan's estimates, between 1966 and 1973 the industry contributed about 1.9% of total GDP and a detailed analysis of data for the years 1966-70 shows that no more than 13% of value-added in the industry accrued to the local economy. 87-90% leaked abroad(12). In the post-1977 period the new joint-venture plants came on stream in and around the period of major world recession. As a result, to date the 'new' fertiliser industry has not made a significant contribution to foreign-exchange earnings or exports.

Since the net foreign-exchange contribution of a wholly foreign-owned industry (such as Trinidad's fertiliser industry was up to 1977) depends largely on tax obligations, wage payments and purchases of local inputs and services, it is quite clear that up to 1977, with relatively little employment, little use of local materials and supplies (other than cheap gas), and little contribution to government revenues, the fertiliser industry's contribution to foreign-exchange availability for the local economy was not large. What the future will bring is debatable.

The increase in state participation in the industry through the joint-venture route, and the injection of local capital, seems likely a priori to enhance the country's future returns in the form of foreign-exchange contributions. The significance of DFI in the industry in the future depends to a large extent on the role it can play in providing market access, its capital contribution, assistance in diversifying into new product lines, and, intimately related to this, its technological contribution.

So far the joint ventures have brought little sharing of control. As regards capital contribution, the actual equity contribution of the foreign investors was comparatively modest, given how highly leveraged the investments were. Access to loan funds was governed in the main by bankers' awareness of Trinidad-Tobago's petrodollar boom and its healthy reserves position. Foreign partners were not essential for raising the loan capital, as Trinidad's simultaneous experience with raising large amounts of loan capital for a wholly-owned steel plant shows. (Interestingly, Trinidad has no prior experience in steel production, a very different situation from fertiliser.)

This experience points up yet again a now well-established phenomenon of recent years. Partly because of the perception of political risk, there is an evident reluctance on the part of DFI and the transnationals to put very much of their own funds into overseas ventures in developing countries. It is regarded as much wiser to let these ventures raise the capital in the loan markets, preferably from international banking consortia.

This throws into question the notion that DFI is going to be available as a source of the capital needed to finance Third World development. It is little recognised that DFI has been linked in no small degree with the large-scale commercial bank lending to developing countries in the 1970s.

As regards market access, the presence of the transnationals provided no special facilities in the late 1970s and early 1980s. In fact, Grace has been steadily cutting back on its Trinidad production claiming difficulty in finding markets. At Fertrin locals are in fact doing most of the marketing and the hiring and disposition of freight despite the marketing contract with Amoco. Clearly unless nationals make a determined effort to get involved in the function and master it (as they seem to have done in this case), the foreign partner has no special interest in providing the country with the skills and the contacts, and there is no automatic mechanism that will make this happen.

The long-term viability of the Trinidad industry depends on its ability to adapt and move in new directions, but there has been no evidence of foreign investors playing a role in engendering these kinds of linkages and diversification. The two key transnationals involved are themselves very diversified companies, but their interest in Trinidad is quite narrowly circumscribed. Amoco sees it simply as an outlet for the large gas reserves it discovered in its search for oil, and for Grace it holds no attractions as a chemicals centre other than for fertiliser. The Trinidad-Tobago experience clearly demonstrates once again that DFI is unlikely to do for a country what it does not get up and do for itself.

The issue of technology is intimately interrelated with that of diversification and strategic movement. A small, developing country like Trinidad-Tobago is likely to derive little technological benefit (in terms of building technological capability) from the turnkey operations of large engineering contractors, or from joint-venture associations with foreign investors in industries like fertiliser. Neither the interaction with foreign engineering contractors, nor the association with transnational joint-venture partners has resulted in the development (even partially) of a technological capability in the country for the engineering of chemical plants, other than learning how to run them. If, on the other hand, Trinidad-Tobago could call on Amoco's technology in the area of plastics, through its association with it in a fertiliser venture, or if it could develop its capability in shipping operations through Grace's presence in the domestic fertiliser industry, there would be cross-fertilisation taking place from its relationships with the transnationals. A pre-condition of this would be a pretty precise definition of what technologies it wanted and what strategy of industrial development it was pursuing, and in the Trinidad-Tobago case unfortunately, not even this basic condition can be claimed to have been met.

Nevertheless by the mid-1970s a core of technicians and engineers, knowledgeable about and accustomed to fertiliser plant operations, has been produced. Fed Chem and Fertrin were thus the seed-bed for the generation of skills diffused subsequently throughout Trinidad's massive new industrial estate at Point Lisas. The significance of this becomes clear when this experience is contrasted with Trinidad's billion-dollar steel mill which has been plagued by losses, mismanagement and technical inefficiency from its inception. It is also claimed that the Fertrin joint venture has provided useful access to Amoco's technical assistance and R and D facilities in dealing with operational problems that crop up, e.g. in metallurgy.

The State and Foreign Investment

The official government position on foreign investment in Trinidad-Tobago exhibits elements of both constancy and change. In the mid and late 1950s great things were expected from bringing in foreign capital. It was presumed that DFI was attracted by low wages fortified by generous tax incentives, and would automatically bring in its train a cornucopia of benefits - employment, technology, management, access to markets, foreign-exchange earnings, contributions to government revenue, as well as the investment capital the country supposedly lacked. It was in this period that special legislation was written to induce Grace to invest in fertiliser, and that generous incentives were allowed to Texaco to stimulate the growth of the refining industry. The results of this initial 'Open Door Policy' quickly proved disappointing. By the mid-1960s, it was becoming steadily clearer that unemployment was rising not falling, that the complex of benefits that were supposed to materialise with foreign capital were not in fact being realised, and that the attraction to foreign capital in the Trinidad case lay less in low wages than in the opportunities provided by cheap natural resources such as oil (and to a lesser extent, gas).

As the economic conditions worsened and social discontent grew, so too did the intellectual challenges. While the open door policy with respect to foreign capital was not abandoned (one of the constancies mentioned above), increasing awareness of the potentially negative aspects of DFI led to adjustments aimed at avoiding some of these negative effects. Around the same time, economic strategy itself was undergoing something of an alteration, with import-substitution imported from Latin America coming to be officially espoused and emphasised as the appropriate developmental strategy.

Beginning in the late 1960s therefore nationalisation or localisation (majority shareholding by nationals) of key sectors of the economy began to be espoused. The government announced in a 1972 White Paper and in its third Five Year Plan (1969-73) that certain sectors (e.g. utilities) would henceforth be closed to wholly- or majority-owned foreign investment. The new approach had not run for many years, however, before the OPEC oil price hike of 1973-4 suddenly produced windfall oil wealth and with it the lure of 'instant industrialisation'. The perceived need for foreign capital to provide finance diminished; the state became the major investor in the economy and the prime agent in the setting up of a complex of heavy industry ventures in steel and fertiliser. The relationships with foreign companies tended to change. They were needed now as contractors or consultants or occasionally as joint-venture partners. Government participation in the economy, already quite significant in 1972, was massive by the end of the 1970s. The key change here was really psychological - the dawning recognition by the government that it could make its own independent decisions because it had the money to carry them through.

With the end of the oil windfall in 1983 has come a fourth phase - where the diminution in foreign-exchange earnings and reserves, combined with the fall in oil production, has begun to lead to a renewed interest in the role that DFI can play. The concern was aroused by what was perceived to be the need to 'monetise' the gas reserves which had materialised as the inadvertent 'by-product' of the search for oil. The proposals for change bid fair to permit a regression to the approaches used in the 1950s. Thus policy-makers are now advocating that the policy of not allowing wholly or majority-owned foreign investment in natural resources should be abandoned(13).

Nevertheless, certain constancies have been maintained. From very early on, the government has been wary of permitting the alienation of too much land to foreigners. It has also for a long time had a work permit policy, aimed at protecting employment opportunities for nationals and as a vehicle for influencing the 'transfer' of technology. Similarly, for more than a decade now, the policy on the localisation of the financial sector has been consistently maintained. The government has also consistently continued to believe that DFI is of value to the country, though it has always exhibited a certain caution and indeed a certain timidity in dealing with foreign capital, and has been concerned not to offend foreign investors(14). It has been very conscious of the supposed power of the transnationals and their home governments. It has never expropriated foreign investors, nor has it ever nationalised the operations of any major foreign investor who was unwilling to sell. Similarly it was never in the vanguard of progressive change where DFI was concerned. For example, Trinidad-Tobago twice refused invitations to join OPEC in the early 1960s. It has in fact taken positive pride in its 'model behaviour'.

By and large, there has been no attempt at detailed regulation of the activities of foreign investors, who, overall, have been left free to move into or out of areas as they desire. Similarly the government has been consistently weak in monitoring and controlling the operations of foreign capital. Bureaucratic inefficiencies have often permitted practices <u>de facto</u>, which are <u>de jure</u> not permitted.

We may thus summarise Trinidad's policy towards foreign capital in three points. (i) The government has consistently had a positive attitude towards foreign capital and sought to encourage it, even during the period when it emphasised majority national ownership in certain areas. (ii) The policy measures it has deployed have been pretty much the standard kit of incentives, work-permit controls, etc. Nothing out of the ordinary has been attempted. (iii) The overall policy has effectively been one of 'laissez-faire' with respect to control of foreign investors, not as much by philosophical decision, as by the inadequacies of the bureaucratic machinery.

NOTES AND REFERENCES

1. UNCTC, Salient Features and Trends in Foreign Direct Investment (New York, 1983), p.60.

2. Alister McIntyre and Beverly Watson, Studies in Foreign Investment in the Commonwealth Caribbean, No.1 Trinidad and Tobago (University of the West Indies, Mona, Jamaica, 1970), p.16.

3. Arthur Lewis, 'Economic Development with Unlimited Supplies of Labour' in A.N. Agarwala and S.P. Singh, The Economics of Underdevelopment (Oxford University Press, 1971), p.14.

4. See Eric Williams, 'Economic Problems of Trinidad-Tobago', People's Education Movement, Public Affairs Pamphlet No.1 (Port-of-Spain, July 1955) for an explicit articulation of the Trinidad Government's development strategy in the late 1950s and the 1960s.

5. See Trevor M.A. Farrell, The Economics of Discontent (Supaprint, San Fernando, 1975).

6. See Trevor M.A. Farrell, 'The Multinational Corporations, the Petroleum Industry and Economic Underdevelopment in Trinidad-Tobago', Ph.D dissertation, Cornell University, Ithaca NY, 1974 (unpublished) pp.258-62.

7. See Herbert Salzman, 'How to Reduce and Manage the Political Risks of Investment in Less Developed Countries' in George Ball (ed.) Global Companies (Prentice-Hall, Englewood Cliffs NJ, 1975).

8. See Trevor M.A. Farrell, 'In Whose Interest? Nationalisation and Bargaining with the Petroleum Transnationals: The Trinidad-Tobago Experience', University of the West Indies, St. Augustine, 1977 (mimeo).

9. See Brian Levy, 'The World Oil Market in Transition', International Organisation, Vol. 36, No.1 (Winter 1982).

10. Trevor M.A. Farrell, 'A Tale of Two Issues: Nationalisation, the Transfer of Technology and the Petroleum Multinationals in Trinidad and Tobago, Social and Economic Studies, Vol. 28, No,1 (March 1979).

11. See Farrell, 'The Multinational Corporations', pp.203-14.

12. See Elizabeth Parsan, 'An Evaluation of the Organisation and Development of the Fertilizer Industry in Trinidad and Tobago', MSc. thesis, University of the West Indies, St. Augustine, 1981 (unpublished), pp.144-51. The effective tax-free period for Grace extended far beyond the nominal ten-year period because of the provisions for loss and depreciation carry-forward which were written into the original agreement.

13. The main impetus for this is the notion that an LNG plant could rescue the economy from its current crisis by providing a new export staple. It is recognised that the

capital costs of LNG are enormous and the risks very great. It is therefore hoped that foreign investors might be found who will finance such a venture. The chances of this happening, however, can be rated as close to zero currently. A serious analysis of the current world energy market would also demonstrate that an LNG plant in Trinidad is likely to be a costly failure.

14. See Farrell, 'In Whose Interest?', for a detailed study of this.

Chapter Thirteen

HOST GOVERNMENT POLICY TOWARDS THE OIL INDUSTRY IN EAST ASIA

C.O. Khong

A Learning Process Within Changing Parameters

In the popular perception the policies of producer governments towards foreign oil companies have been transformed. From a position of inexperience in which the oil industry appeared as an enigma, with oil company operations remaining largely outside government purview, host governments appear to have moved to a new situation, in which effective control is exercised over foreign oil companies, based on a fairly comprehensive picture of how the industry works. In the move to this new position, governments have acquired the relevant expertise and technology, and are even beginning to be prepared to commit public capital for oil production ventures.

This perception of a profound transformation may be seen as only superficially accurate. It acknowledges that many host governments now possess formal means of control, but, at least in the East Asian oil industry, even those governments which have built up a fund of experience in dealing with companies over a period of time, have found it difficult to translate policy into effective practice. Two reasons may be advanced for this.

First, policy formulation is often characterised as a dynamic process, with governments increasingly able to apply the lessons assimilated from a continuous learning process. The problem with this view of increasingly knowledgeable governments turning the tables on their oil company opponents, is that the circumstances surrounding oil exploration and production do not remain fixed. Government officials may begin to fathom the intricate considerations governing particular oil extractive operations, but the operational parameters within which company decisions are taken change continually, as these parameters are shaped by a variety of influences which any local host government would find difficult to monitor. Such influences would include concerns extraneous to any individual extractive operation: the evolution of the company's relationships with other host governments, changes in prospective processing or marketing arrangements, and the state of the oil market.

Meanwhile, each extractive operation sets its own

particular criteria for profitability and long-term viability. Conditions acceptable for established production areas are unlikely to induce investment when companies begin to contemplate operations in less accessible terrain onshore or in deep-water areas offshore. Producer governments thus find themselves lagging behind the companies in tailoring their policies to present circumstances. Much in the manner of the Red Queen, they have to keep running just so as not to slide back. And in seeking change, they are not much helped by their limited flexibility to alter laws and regulations which are already set. Learning, it would seem, is a process which does not necessarily produce cumulative gains.

Secondly, what may loosely be described as political considerations are likely to hinder government control of its oil industry. It may be most effective for the host government to devise a set of policies which would maximise revenue, given the minimum price at which potential investment is forthcoming, and then to allocate the realised mineral rent towards the support of desired social and political objectives. But such a course of action may not be politic in the face of a range of social and nationalistic demands which can be and usually are articulated by various interest groups, demanding direct benefits from the extractive operation and desiring to see its functioning kept under close national control. Many Asian governments have been predisposed at least to appear to heed such injunctions, especially where they feel the need to reinforce their nationalist credentials and governmental legitimacy. The resulting policies are likely to dissipate oil revenues, however, as the resource is exploited in a manner which is economically inefficient. Revenues are also liable to be diverted to social groups or organisations other than the host government(1).

Inefficiency in the formulation of policies is often made worse in the course of their implementation. There seems to be a trade-off between revenue-raising capacity and ease of administration in the taxation of oil production(2). Those taxes which capture the larger part of the economic rent from an extractive operation, which possess the flexibility to adapt to realised profit (and so can be applied uniformly across a country's oil industry) and which avoid biasing investment decisions, tend to be more difficult to administer and to give later and more irregular flows of revenue. There may be little point in imposing a tax policy which in ideal form gains the maximum financial benefit for the host government, where a government has scarce administrative resources and limited experience in dealing with oil companies. Such a situation also leaves the government more open to the reality or the allegation of corruption.

In surveying various East Asian governments' oil policies

these qualifications need to be borne in mind. Yet it must also be recognised that the perception of change has still served to impel regional governments to seek to fashion new policies and to re-examine existing ones, in their negotiations with the oil companies. These negotiations centre around two basic issues: the division of the financial gains and control over the extractive operation.

The Problem of the Taxation Structure

The division of financial gains determines both the return on investment for the foreign company and the flow of government revenues. From this point of view, taxation is a technical problem for the host government, involving the application of rational systematic policies aimed at capturing as large a proportion as possible of the economic rent for itself, rent being defined as the surplus given by the difference between the commercial value of the oil extracted and the supply price of private capital. The policies should also be 'neutral' in not distorting investment decisions.

Taxation is also a political problem as the policies applied often come to be seen as an expression of the relative strength of government and foreign private interests. Taxation thus becomes a tool for the assertion of government power, and the form which policies take acquire an importance of their own quite separate from their revenue-gathering capabilities.

Given the complexity of the issues involved, it is not surprising that the types of possible tax arrangements seem myriad. We may divide contracts governing oil extraction into three basic categories: concessions, production-sharing contracts and service contracts. Even so, within each category, a number of different taxes may be imposed, each tax with its own fiscal and quasi-fiscal implications for the host government. It should be noted here that contracts may also be structured along joint-venture lines. This is not a separate form of contract, but rather a partnership arrangement applicable to any category of contract, by which the host government can participate with the company in the extractive operation.

Production sharing is the contractual form which has found wide acceptance in the East Asian region. The concept originated in Indonesia, and its apparent success there encouraged other governments to adopt modified versions of this type of contract. The idea of sharing the output of the extractive operation, in predetermined proportions, between foreign company and host government possesses a certain intuitive appeal on account of its simplicity. Stated thus, production sharing is no more than a royalty, a specific duty imposed on the amount or value of production, albeit at a very high rate.

In the Indonesian case, however, full deductions are allowed for all costs, including depreciation, after which 85% of production (or its monetary equivalent) is allotted to the government side. This 85:15 split of profits is arrived at by first dividing production (after deduction of costs) in the ratio 65.91:34.09 in favour of the government side. The foreign company share is then taxed at the normal corporate income tax rate of 45%, and a further 20% dividend tax is applied to the remaining balance. This gives the final 'profit' split of 85:15; and as the ratio is expressed in value terms, the foreign company is entitled to 15% of the market value of the 'profit' oil.

The fiscal effect is similar to that of an 85% rate of income tax. (And together with a requirement to market, Indonesian production sharing is equivalent to the application of a uniform 89% income tax). The system is hence no more than a tax on profits (as normally assessed for tax purposes) at a higher rate than usual.

An important reason behind the Indonesian development of the production-sharing concept was to simplify contract administration by reducing the need to monitor product prices and company profits. As applied, however, the system does not obviate the need for careful auditing of financial calculations. While these problems may be no more than those associated with conventional income tax arrangements, administrative difficulties can still be significant in countries like Indonesia, where the taxation system is rudimentary and supervisory resources limited. Indeed Pertamina (the Indonesian state oil company) accepts that the expense estimates of all its foreign contractors include a profit element(3).

Allowing full cost deductions under such conditions also poses another difficulty in weakening the company's incentive to economise. This problem is particularly acute given the smaller marginal offshore fields where exploration is currently taking place. Pertamina has had to be concerned that it obtain at least some return from the extractive operation after all costs have been deducted. This issue of 'commerciality' has led it to insist arbitrarily that 49% of all oil produced must go to the government side, before it can agree to allow an extractive operation to proceed. The application of this ruling has led to difficulties with oil companies concerned to recover their preproduction costs. It should be noted that full cost recovery had to be introduced as part of a restructuring of the production-sharing contract to enable US oil companies to credit their Indonesian tax payments against their US tax obligations.

Three further financial arrangements may be imposed on the basic Indonesian production-sharing framework. First, a series of bonus payments is generally required of the foreign company: a signature bonus when an exploration licence is issued, and various production bonuses when oil production reaches certain stipulated levels. Although companies competing for the same contract are invited to tender amounts which they are prepared to pay, the imposition of bonus payments is not a fully competitive process as the proffered sums are not a decisive consideration in awarding the contract. Bonus payments are a fixed charge, and when applied as an additional tax, provide a convenient way of raising additional government revenue from the marginal financial considerations of companies, given that rates of payment have already been standardised in the general contract. To the extent that company calculations of operational profitability are affected, bonus payments may reduce the level of oil company competition. The payments may also expend financial resources which could otherwise be used for immediate exploration.

Secondly, state participation in a contractual joint venture has been introduced in certain areas where the prospects are judged to be exceptionally favourable. The foreign company has to bear all expenses for the first three years, after which costs are shared with Pertamina. Oil production is divided between the two partners in the ratio of their respective interests, and the company's share is further divided according to standard production-sharing terms. As the government does not purchase an equity interest in the project, the arrangement gives the state a free carried interest; and as such its financial implications to the company are equivalent to an additional flat-rate tax imposed at a rate equal to the state's interest in the project.

Thirdly, companies having to implement secondary recovery of petroleum or facing initial high costs in developing a new oilfield, are given an investment credit of 20% of the capital investment cost. This is taken by subtracting petroleum equal in value to the appropriate amount from gross production, before the standard production-sharing division takes place. This expense deduction, equivalent to a tax reduction, is separate from and in addition to a further financial incentive whereby all companies may depreciate assets on a double declining balance basis over seven years. This latter incentive may no longer be allowed in new contracts, however, as the new Indonesian tax code requires depreciation to be effected over a longer period of up to 20 years.

Malaysia is perhaps the country most prominent in adapting the Indonesian production-sharing system to its own ends. The Malaysian system (until recently changed) limited cost recovery for company expenditure on exploration, development and production to 20% of total oil production. A royalty of 10% of gross production was charged, paid in equal shares to the federal government and to the appropriate state government. After deducting royalty and cost recovery payments, the 'profit' oil component was split in the ratio 70:30 in favour of Petronas (the Malaysian state oil company), with both foreign company and Petronas liable to pay income tax on their respective shares to the federal government. The 1967 Petroleum Income Tax Act, as amended in 1976, reduced oil company taxes to 45%, charged on the company's share of 'profit' oil. The tax payment therefore modified the 'profit' split in effect to 83.5:16.5. On top of this levy, the company was obliged to pay a 25% export duty on its portion of 'profit' oil, and a further 0.5% charge was imposed on the sale of its 'cost' and 'profit' oil, leaving the company's share of profits at about 12.2%. A series of fixed bonus payments was also charged, with a signature bonus payable on commencement of the contract, a discovery bonus for each commercially viable field discovered, and a production bonus.

It may legitimately be asked why the Malaysian Government found it necessary to impose such a complicated assemblage of charges. A system of production sharing in which cost recovery is limited to a relatively low level of output acts in large part as a fixed proportional charge on output, or in other words, as a royalty. Imposed as it was here, at a very high effective rate, it significantly raised unit costs of extraction, encouraging companies to reduce their rate of production and to concentrate on easily accessible high-value deposits. This system was probably unique in levying a further royalty charge on the main production-sharing tax, though this additional royalty was part of the settlement under which the various Malaysian states were required to surrender their oil extraction rights to the federal government which wished to regulate the petroleum industry at the national level. The export duty and other sales charge acted as additional flat-rate taxes (the export duty being introduced in 1980 to capture a larger share of profits following the 1979 oil price rises). And the bonus payments, being fixed in advance, did not even manage to equate the value of the resource at the margin with investor expectations.

The system on the whole had a set of taxes which were extremely inflexible in not responding to profitability (that is by not taxing more profitable projects at a higher rate than less profitable ones). Indeed, with the fixed charges on top of the unvarying proportional production-based tax, the system was not just severe but also regressive (in actually increasing the tax burden at lower rates of profit).

Production sharing is a fiscal system which is inherently unresponsive to profits. The Malaysian system did not manage to secure the increase in rent in a period when oil prices and hence company profitability rose (thus requiring the introduction of the export duty). Nor did it encourage the development of marginal fields, with high costs and limited reserves, which in fact comprise the larger part of Malaysia's new contract areas on offer to the companies. And in the current period of falling oil prices, the regressive nature of the system was sharpened, as the weight of taxes increased relative to output and costs.

In an effort to overcome these deficiencies, Malaysia revised its fiscal regime for new contracts in December 1985. The cost recovery component of production was raised to 50%, with the remaining 'profit' oil divided on a sliding scale based on average daily production. The first 10,000 barrels per day will be divided in the ratio 50:50, the next 10,000 in the ratio 60:40 in favour of Petronas, and all production above that in the ratio 70:30 in favour of Petronas. After the first 50 million barrels of cumulative production in each contract area, all daily production will be split 70:30 in favour of Petronas. All bonus payment charges have been scrapped, though the other taxes, including the royalty, remain. The contracts also require Petronas Carigali, the exploration and production arm of Petronas, to be given at least a 15% equity interest in each contract area, the exact figure to be decided by competitive bidding. To the extent that Carigali does not earn its interest in the contract by carrying a proportionate share of the work, this charge imposes an additional flat-rate tax, though designed to be applied at a rate which matches company expectations of profitability.

The changes modify the production-sharing system in a direction away from a royalty-type charge and towards a flat-rate tax (though a royalty element still remains). They are clearly aimed at reducing taxation on marginal fields, while retaining high rates of tax on areas with better prospects. Whether or not they can attract company interest in new contract areas remains to be seen, given the continued low price of oil. A fiscal regime based on production sharing, however modified, will remain relatively inflexible in responding to changes in profitability.

Production sharing has nevertheless been adopted in other countries as a method of taxing petroleum extraction. In the Philippines, its terms have been set at a generous level, reflecting the difficulty of sustaining oil exploration by foreign companies in an uncertain investment climate and with unproven reserves. In China, production sharing is incorporated in joint-venture arrangements with the China National Offshore Oil Corporation, which holds a 51% interest in each contract agreement. While development costs are shared, all exploration costs and risks have to be borne by the foreign company, thus providing state participation on a carried interest basis. The Chinese have conceded that initial high expectations of finding substantial offshore oil reserves have yet to materialise, and hope meanwhile to encourage the development of smaller fields. They have also had to amend their fiscal terms in their second round of contract negotiations, by easing various obligatory payments and royalties on smaller fields.

The service contract, to which we now turn, is also a contract-type arrangement; but formally, it differs from the production-sharing contract in that the oil company is paid in cash, not in crude oil (though it may allow the company to buy oil at international prices from established production, just as production sharing may also allow for payment in cash). In its basic form, the service contract is simply a contract of work whereby the contractor is paid a fixed fee for his services, whether for exploration or field development. Typically, however, the contract requires the contracting company to bear all exploration risks and investment costs. If no discovery is made, the contract ceases to exist. If commercial production is feasible, the company places the field on stream, after which production may either continue to be managed by the company or be managed by the host state. Capital is reimbursed with interest and a risk premium. Various East Asian governments have used the service contract label to cover a number of fiscal arrangements which are actually production-sharing agreements or concessions. The one government to have consistently attempted to implement service contracts in its petroleum industry is that of Vietnam.

The series of service contracts introduced by the Vietnamese in early 1978 departed from the basic 'fee for services rendered' form in a number of ways. A degree of production sharing had to be introduced by a government strapped for hard currency, with repayment of costs and a risk premium provided, at least in part, out of the oil produced. Under these contracts, all exploration risks were borne by the foreign company. Should commercially viable reserves be discovered, exploration costs were to be recoverable from any subsequent oil production. Further development costs were to be treated as an interest-bearing loan from company to government, and would be repaid in cash at market rates over a fixed period. As an incentive, the government undertook to pay a risk premium, allowing the company to purchase up to 50% of production at a preferential price ranging from 5 to 11% below the prevailing international price.

Vietnam later attempted to introduce a different form of service contract which came closer to being a contract for the supply of services for a fixed fee, with the company being given no share of the profits from the operation, nor on the other hand having to bear the risk of exploration. The Vietnamese side was to assume both operational responsibility and risk, the foreign company investing capital and providing equipment and services. Any subsequent oil production was to be used to cover the company's costs at international market prices and interest rates. If the venture was unsuccessful, repayment was to be made in cash. Negotiations on the Vietnamese proposal fell through, however, which was not altogether surprising given the difficulty for countries, other than established producers, of securing a contract agreement without offering any premium as an incentive.

Those companies which had earlier reached service contract agreements with Vietnam also eventually withdrew, after failing to obtain a more favourable renegotiation of their contracts. Despite some doubts over Russian abilities, Vietnam currently plans to begin offshore petroleum production with the assistance of the Soviet Union. It has, however, also recently begun to negotiate possible contracts with a number of Western firms(4). It may be observed that, in general, taxation is of lesser importance in service contracts, since the fee paid to the company should provide for company profitability.

Finally we turn to a consideration of concessions. These are usually granted through a petroleum or mining law, providing for the issue of licences or permits to explore for oil and of leases to exploit oil deposits. The fiscal elements of concession arrangements are generally provided by a royalty and an income tax which can be imposed in a number of ways.

The concession system in Brunei may be used to illustrate the terms of the traditional concession in its simplest form. The Petroleum Mining Enactment of 1963 (amended in 1969 and 1972) sets out long-term agreements under which a 50% tax on net profits is imposed. These profits are calculated from a jointly determined posted price. The government also charges a royalty which ranges from 8 to 12.5% of the value of output, though this royalty is credited against the 50% tax. Taxes had previously been levied on profits calculated from realised prices declared by the company; the change therefore made transfer pricing practices less easy for the company, though doubts continued to be expressed over the government's ability to ensure that it obtains its full half-share of profits(5). In any case, the tax imposed is a flat-rate charge at a not especially high level.

As for the royalty, being able to credit it in full against tax obligations (that is, counting it as a payment towards the profit tax) could significantly reduce, and possibly even remove altogether, any additional revenue to the government from the royalty charge. Normally, it will still be expected to assure the government of a minimum level of revenue regardless of project profitability. But the Bruneian petroleum agreement lays down various minimum expenditure obligations which the company has to fulfil in its work programme; and the company is allowed to set off its royalty payments against these. This allowance therefore nullifies the value of the royalty as an assurance to the government of some payment, whatever the level of company costs or petroleum prices.

Another country which operates a similar basic concession system, with a flat-rate tax and a royalty, is Thailand. In the Thai case, however, the royalty may not be credited against tax payments, though it may be treated as a deductible expense. The ultimate income allocation for a given royalty rate under this arrangement is more favourable to the government, while the royalty continues to serve as a floor on company payments.

Fiscal regimes for petroleum extraction in East Asian countries generally employ flat-rate taxes, regarded as easier to define and to apply, but less effective in gaining the maximum part of the economic rent for the government. Tax systems which capture a larger part of the rent, by adjusting their 'take' to company profitability, are rare. The new Malaysian production-sharing terms, which discriminate in favour of marginal fields, are a notable example of a form of production sharing approximating to a progressive profit tax, taxing more profitable fields at a higher rate than less profitable ones. There is no reason why such a tax should not be incorporated into concession agreements. It will then be necessary to establish suitable thresholds on profits, above which additional profits will be taxed at higher rates. These thresholds may be defined in terms of the ratio of the annual profit of the operation to the level of accumulated investment.

Flexibility in taxation may also be achieved by taxing the company's discounted cash flow rate of return, or, in other words, its declared profitability as conventionally measured for investment decision purposes. Such a tax, termed a resource-rent tax, is being introduced in a number of countries, and may be incorporated into a system of concessions for regulating petroleum operations. The government of Papua New Guinea has introduced such a tax.

Its concession system, laid down by the Petroleum Act of 1977, imposes three different taxes. A royalty, charged on the well-head value rather than volume of output, is deliberately kept low at 1.25%, its purpose being to secure the minimum revenue which the central government has to make available to the relevant provincial government, if petroleum from the extractive operation is exported. A standard flat-rate income tax of 50% is then imposed, with depreciation for capital assets allowed for over not more than ten years. An even more rapid depreciation is allowed in years of low cash flow for the operation. Flexibility is then introduced with an Additional Profits Tax which operates as a resource-rent tax, allowing the company a 27.5% rate of return on its discounted cash flow, before imposing an additional tax of 50% on cash flows net of the standard income tax (thus imposing a 75% rate of tax altogether)(6). It may be noted that, without the Additional Profits Tax, the tax rate imposed is reasonably generous. The Additional Profits Tax only comes into play at a fairly high threshold level and even then, results in a top tax rate which is not particularly onerous. The system, as adopted here, is particularly suited to attracting investment to a country without an established petroleum industry and under the conditions of the present weak oil market.

The government may, however, also negotiate participation rights for itself, which give it a carried interest equity for which it begins to pay at the point when the operation is judged commercially viable. It is then liable to pay for its share of all company expenditure up to that point at nominal value, and its share of all expenditure thereafter, less the same proportion of the operation's income from sales. The government receives no income from its part-ownership until all its expenditure obligations have been cleared; and meanwhile, interest is charged on the balance of its debit account at a rate above prime corporate borrowing rates. Government participation therefore amounts in part to an additional tier of resource-rent tax, as government income from this source depends on operational profitability. The operation is allowed a rate of return equal to the interest rate charged on the government's debit account, before the government levies the equivalent of a tax at a rate equal to its participation in the project. Fiscal flexibility is thus further increased.

The Problem of Effective Control

The purpose of control for the host government is to influence the behaviour of the foreign company so that it conforms to a greater degree to national, social and economic considerations. The interrelationship between the aims of financial gain and of control is complex. Control can imply the implementation of a supervisory process to ensure that the government secures that part of revenue allotted to it in the contract. Or if the government places greater weight on wider political and social goals than on profit maximisation, the financial potential of the project may not be fully realised; while tension with the company may result, the latter placing greater weight on the more efficient operation of the project. East Asian governments have tended to be rather cautious in seeking to keep a good deal of control over company activities through ownership of the extractive operation. As we have seen, state participation has fiscal implications for the foreign company, but the government may well be more interested in exerting direct control, and in learning as much as possible about the oil industry through active co-operation with the company.

In an effort to improve its supervision, the Government of Brunei embarked on a policy of steadily increasing its equity ownership of Brunei Shell Petroleum. It has ample funds to pursue such a policy and has now purchased 50% of the company, but it has not managed to translate this representation into effective control because of its shortage of technical and managerial expertise. Its determination to pursue the political objectives of control and learning has led it further to set up a so-called Petroleum Unit within the office of the Chief Minister in an attempt to establish a nucleus around which such skills could be developed, but this is likely to achieve results only in the very long term.

The Chinese insistence on their state oil company holding a 51% interest in each extractive operation may be attributed more to the government's ideological sensitivities over sovereignty than to its very real desire to exert control. In asserting its supervision, China has preferred to specify very stringent requirements for the foreign company to meet. The Chinese model contract specifies that exploration bases must be established in China, and that priority should be given to the use of Chinese service companies who have in effect the right of first refusal for any procurement contract. Requirements for companies to train Chinese nationals alongside expatriates have also been pressed. But such a policy, which is aimed at the country's long-term development objectives, has had mixed results, with foreign companies showing a marked reluctance to comply(7).

The government may go further in not only establishing part-ownership of the extractive operation, but in insisting on full ownership of the natural resource with the foreign company acting as a contractor to the host government or its state oil company. This is the formal legal basis of production sharing and service contracts. When Indonesia introduced its production-sharing contracts in the mid-1960s, it also included a provision giving its state oil company, Pertamina, sole responsibility for managing the extractive operation. This caused much difficulty with oil companies at the time, but company resistance abated when it was realised that conceding management rights on paper still meant that management remained on the side with the resources and abilities to make effective and informed decisions.

The Indonesian management clause has in fact served to allow companies to concentrate their attention on the economic and technical aspects of petroleum extraction, while shielding them from local political interests. It also provides a vehicle for involving Pertamina in all aspects of company operations, thus assisting in the transfer of managerial and technological expertise. It has to be accepted, however, that the possibility of more far-reaching change in the company-government relationship already exists, and may take practical effect if and when the Indonesian side manages to build up its own administrative and technical capability.

It is generally believed that the major disadvantage of the concession system is that it gives the government less direct involvement in the management of operations. The licensing system of concessions does, however, at least in theory, provide the government with the right to decide all essential aspects of the extractive operation. This control is to a certain degree indirect, with a web of government rules and provisions regulating the right of the company to organise its activities; but opportunities exist for the government to enter into operations directly to achieve such vital objectives as training of local personnel and obtaining knowledge of the petroleum industry, essential for government policy formulation. The concession may allow for government participation in a joint venture, and provisions may specify the setting up of training programmes and supervisory procedures.

In ensuring compliance with agreed terms, the basic problem of government administration and supervision is that it has largely to rely on information furnished by the subjects of its control. The more complex the content, the more difficult it is for the supervisory agency to vet the information given. Taken to the extreme, the policy of the controlling government agency may easily become based on premises assumed by its subjects.

Administrative problems of tax assessment and collection are minimised in the simpler forms of tax such as the fixed fee and the royalty, which, however, do not adapt to changing profitability and are inefficient in securing economic rent. Taxes based on profit, whether flat-rate or progressive, are more difficult to apply, posing the same problems of administration as an income tax system. Company returns have to be (but are not usually) thoroughly vetted to ensure that transfer pricing is not taking place. Such dangers are sometimes said to lead governments to favour the resource rent tax; but this, although apparently intrinsically simpler, is still based on declared profitability, and is probably even more difficult than a progressive profit tax, for a government to set appropriate rates of taxation and threshold rates of return.

The experience of the Malaysian Government is a sobering one, warning that without the necessary technical and managerial expertise, it is difficult to translate formal control into effective supervision. Detailed allegations in 1980 revealed that one of the major foreign oil companies in the country was producing more oil than it reported, that it did not follow government-approved work plans, and that the government was inefficient in claiming taxes and royalties due. These disclosures sufficiently embarrassed both sides to lead to the introduction of new, substantially expanded control procedures, though their effectiveness still remains open to question.

The problem of compliance could also arise from within the governmental organisation. The Indonesian Government's difficulty in the mid-1970s in controlling Pertamina highlighted the risk that the active use of a state oil company in a system of state participation could lead to decisions being effectively made by the state company, possibly under the influence of private companies, and passively endorsed by the government.

In conclusion, two main precepts may be drawn from the experience of East Asian governments in dealing with petroleum extraction. First, even though economic rationality may dictate the application of taxes which yield revenue flows closely related to realised profitability, governments should be sensible in matching the taxation system to their own supervisory capabilities. This may call for a degree of less efficient taxation, but the important point is that the taxation system should not be lumbered with a variety of taxes, some of which may be superfluous in having a similar function to others. The more complicated the system, no matter how severe its overall effect on paper, the more favourable it is likely to become for the companies, because of finite supervisory resources on the government side.

Secondly, it should not be assumed that what appear to be mistakes in oil policy are the result of lack of experience or knowledge. They could arise from bureaucratic practice, and more especially, from distinct political preferences. Companies have a greater flexibility here in responding to the requirements of a rapidly changing oil market and changes in the technology of petroleum extraction. In imposing new taxes to reflect changing conditions, governments usually find themselves in a position of having to catch up with the companies. The key to governments' controlling the industry and maximising desired revenue from oil operations still lies in improving their knowledge. Only then can they be sure of formulating policies which they can effectively impose.

NOTES AND REFERENCES

1. The issue of the dissipation and diversion of revenues is discussed in Ross Garnaut and Anthony Clunies Ross, Taxation of Mineral Rents (Clarendon Press, Oxford, 1983), pp. 188-96.

2. See survey of taxation system by Alexander G. Kemp and David Rose, 'Investment in Oil Exploration and Production: The Comparative Influence of Taxation',in David

W. Pearce, Horst Siebert and Ingo Walter (eds.), Risk and the Political Economy of Resource Development (Macmillan, London, 1984), pp. 169-95.

3. See Petromin Asia (Singapore), May 1982, p. 24.

4. Petroleum News (Hong Kong), No. 16 (October 1985), News Supplement.

5. See B.A. Hamzah, 'Oil and Independence in Brunei: A Perspective', in Institute of Southeast Asian Studies, Southeast Asian Affairs 1981 (Heinemann, Singapore), pp. 93-99.

6. The operation of the resource-rent tax is discussed by Charles P. McPherson and Keith Palmer, 'New Approaches to Profit Sharing in Developing Countries', Oil and Gas Journal (Tulsa), 25 June 1984: pp. 119-28.

7. Far Eastern Economic Review, Asia 1985 Yearbook (Hong Kong, 1985), p. 86.

Chapter Fourteen

FOREIGN INVESTMENT POLICY: KENYA'S EXPERIENCE

N.A. Rweyemamu

Foreign investment has been of considerable significance in financing development in Kenya, not only in manufacturing but in the primary and tertiary sectors also. Before Independence (December 1963), the bulk of it went into primary production and plantations. The few manufacturing industries established up to World War II were mainly for basic processing of agricultural exports and the processing of food for the local market. After the war, British manufacturing firms began to invest directly in manufacturing, in part because of the growing competition from non-British trading firms, which threatened Britain's share in the Kenyan market. Import substitution became official government policy, with the introduction of protective tariffs in 1958.

After the land settlement schemes between 1962 and 1964, the independent Kenya Government prevented foreign firms from purchasing land and, as a result, foreign ownership in agriculture was greatly reduced. In commerce and industry, by contrast, virtually all the expansion which took place (a 50% increase of output between 1964 and 1970 and a 100% increase in the annual level of investment) was foreign-owned. At first, much of this involved capital transferred out of agriculture, especially following the introduction of exchange control in 1965. But two years later, after an initial period of uncertainty as to the government's development strategy, a substantial inflow of foreign investment and its diversification from primary to secondary and tertiary activities occurred.

The expansion of foreign firms during this period was marked by the consolidation of existing enterprises and the entry of new firms from both British and non-British sources. Several British firms invested by means of taking over existing enterprises, prime examples of this being Lonrho, which, between 1966 and 1973, acquired approximately 50 subsidiaries in Kenya, the British American Tobacco Comp[illegible] (BAT) consolidated its monopoly over cigarette [illegible]uring and distribution by purchasing the Rothman's [illegible]y in 1966, and Brooke Bond, which bought out the [illegible]nificant European-owned tea estate in Kericho [illegible]n 1971, and also bought an interest in a local fruit and vegetable canning company in 1970. In addition, many firms that had traded with Kenya during the colonial period, mainly from the USA, Germany and Japan, began to set up manufacturing units within the country.

By the 1970s, however, the pattern began to change, as the joint venture or partnership became predominant. This involved a link-up between foreign industrial firms, international finance agencies and local state or private capital. Foreign investment at present represents a complex mixture of direct ownership and management and technology 'packages', and the relations between foreign firms and the host country have become increasingly subtle.

This chapter examines briefly the experience of Kenya in relation to foreign investment, looking explicitly at the manufacturing sector. While the main focus is on direct foreign investment, the country's experience with regard to the new forms of foreign investment (particularly joint ventures and management contracts) is also discussed, highlighting some of the constraints that have arisen, especially those relating to the distribution of risk and reward among the parties to projects. For the most part, the discussion will be on policy and the policy options which appear to be emerging, in the light of current economic conditions.

<u>Economic Development, 1964-83: An Overview</u>

In terms of growth performance, Kenya's first decade of independence (1964-73) was one of remarkable achievement, with an upsurge of domestic investment (from about 13% of GDP in 1964 to 20% by 1972) and an overall GDP growth rate of 6.8% per annum over the period 1964-72. Both agriculture and manufacturing, the key sectors of the economy, grew rapidly at 4.6% and 8% per annum respectively. The expansion of agriculture was stimulated by the redistribution of large estates to smallholders and the rapid growth of smallholders' output, from less than one-third of marketed agricultural output in 1963 to more than half by 1972. The rapid growth in manufacturing was made possible by, among other things, rising domestic incomes, in large measure reflecting rising agricultural incomes.

Growth slowed down after 1973. Two major turning points can be identified, the first around 1972-3, near the time of the first oil crisis, and the second around 1978-9, as a result of further major increases in oil prices, a precipitous decline in coffee prices, and the impact of the expansionary fiscal and monetary policies adopted during the coffee boom. The country experienced a sharp decline in its international terms of trade beginning in 1978. This was exacerbated by the 1980-82 world recession, which increased the cost of external capital and hampered Kenya's exports. As neighbouring countries experienced strong economic dislocations, their demand for Kenyan goods shrank. The difficulties were further compounded by drought during 1979-80, especially affecting coffee and maize production. The outlook was for continued deterioration in Kenya's external position and GDP growth slowed down again from 4.2% in 1978-9 to 3.3% in 1980. In 1982-3, however, the balance of payments improved significantly as imports declined, official transfers of foreign aid rose, and exports began to improve.

The manufacturing sector has been the most dynamic during the post-independence years. After having grown at an average rate of 10.7% in 1972-78, growth decelerated to 7.1% in 1979 and 5.7% in 1980, 5.0% in 1981 and only 2.6% in 1982. A rate of 4.5% after 1982 signalled a recovery by the sector, improvement in the availability of foreign exchange, and a reduction in import duties on certain essential raw materials being the main factors behind the modest increase in output.

Manufacturing industry developed very rapidly during the post-independence years, on the basis of the opportunities provided by the market of the East African Community (1); it was strongly protected against foreign competition by quantitative restrictions on imports and direct government financial assistance. But in recent years this growth has gradually weakened, as a result of the erosion of the foundations on which it rested. First, the abolition of the East African Community in 1978 and the collapse of the markets in neighbouring countries reduced the potential growth of domestic manufacturing. Second, the weak balance-of-payments position in recent years and the ensuing foreign-exchange shortages and related import restrictions threatened its ability to obtain foreign inputs. Third, the gradual elimination of formal government protection posed a threat to its domestic monopoly. Finally, domestic demand for manufactured goods slackened as a result of lower farm incomes; and bad weather, which entailed reductions in hydro-electric power and domestic agricultural inputs, hampered production.

The major thrust of current industrial policy is towards a transition from highly protected import substitution to a strategy which would result in greater use of domestic resources, a more rapid and diversified expansion of exports and greater employment generation. The main instruments for achieving this are: (a) a shift from quantitative restrictions to tariffs as the principal source of protection for industry, (b) a gradual rationalisation of the tariff structure to make it more uniform and moderate, and (c) increased institutional support and improved financial incentives for manufactured exports. Greater efforts are to be directed towards the production of intermediate capital goods, as opposed to consumer goods, with the closer regional markets as the main target areas. With the opening of the Tanzania border and the creation of the Preferential Trade Area for Eastern and Central Africa, Kenya's manufacturing sector is set to benefit from increased exports.

Scale and Allocation of Foreign Investment

Up-to-date data on stock, inflows and outflows of foreign investment in Kenya and its allocation between sectors are not available, but it is possible to sketch the overall trends. Uncertainty as to the government's development strategy led to a large capital outflow during 1961-2. In 1963-4, there were large inflows mainly into the electricity sector (which were later bought out). Retained earnings were more or less constant until 1967, when they rose by about 50%.

Since the early 1970s, there has been government pressure on foreign firms to reinvest a higher proportion of their profits in the country. From 1974, firms with a high repatriation rate have had their local borrowing rights restricted by the Central Bank. The government also attempted to cut down on the level of management remittances and technical fees by imposing a 14% withholding tax on them. These measures seem to have been successful and in recent years an increasing proportion of net foreign investment capital inflow has been accounted for by retained earnings. There is now a tendency for established foreign enterprises to finance expansions from retained earnings, sometimes supplemented by a loan, while new inflows of equity capital and a large proportion of new loans are associated with the setting up of new enterprises.

Table 14.1 gives some indication of the significance of private foreign capital inflows by comparing them with capital formation and current account balance-of-payment deficits (see Table 14.2). The percentages relating to capital formation also give an indication of the contribution made by private inflows to finance capital expenditure.

By 1972, just under half of the total equity of 1,000 sample firms was owned by citizens - either state or private shareholders. This change can be attributed to the increasing moves by the government to purchase shares in large foreign companies in some of the major sectors of the economy, notably oil-refining, power and lighting, meat processing and cement manufacture.

A remarkable feature of foreign investment in Kenya is the concentration of resources in a few enterprises. For instance, over 50% of new manufacturing investment in the period 1967-73 was directed to no more than 8 projects (see 1970-74 Kenya Development Plan, pp.274-84), though not all the capital was provided by the foreign investor. According to Langdon (2), in 1972-3, 20 out of the 55 largest manufacturing subsidiaries of transnational firms accounted

Table 14.1. Net inflows of private long-term capital and outflows of investment income 1957-68 (K£'000)

	Net inflow of capital	Net outflow of income	Retained earnings after tax, foreign investment	Total net inflow
1957	1,119	5,360	--	-4,241
1958	650	5,450	--	-4,800
1959	375	7,106	--	-6,641
1960	5,642	7,283	--	-1,821
1961	-5,133	5,341	--	-10,474
1962	-2,696	4,845	--	-7,451
1963	9,800	9,843	3,514	-43
1964	10,800	8,665	3,546	2,135
1965	8,800	8,731	3,019	69
1966	2,100	8,750	2,800	-6,650
1967	4,100	9,170	4,400	-5,070
1968	9,000	9,590	5,000	-590
--	--	--	--	--
--	--	--	--	--
1976	42,720	44,283	17,184	-1,563
1977	35,268	58,388	14,177	-23,120
1978	57,689	70,075	14,476	-12,386
1979	75,859	67,116	23,157	+8,743
1980	54,685	69,167	18,845	-14,932
1981	51,731	72,382	20,187	-20,651

Sources: 1957-68 data: EAC Statistics division (quoted from N. Swainson, The Development of Corporate Capitalism in Kenya (Heinemann, London, 1980)); 1976-81 data: Central Bureau of Statistics.

for 69% of the turnover and 86% of the capital employed. By the late 1970s, there was a significant shift of DFI resources away from food processing, beverages, chemicals and rubber to textiles, leather, paper and printing.

Government Policy in Relation to Foreign Investment

(a) Basic Policy and Objectives. Since Independence, the Kenyan Government has pursued a development policy that places strong emphasis on the role of private investment - particularly foreign investment - and has been anxious to create a generally attractive environment by providing a

Table 14.2. Kenya: net private long-term capital inflows 1972-82

	Net inflows (K£ m.)	% of current account deficits	% of total capital formation at current prices	% of capital formation by enterprices and non-profit institutions at current prices
1972	15.3	62.9	9.5	13.0
1973	31.3	66.8	17.8	24.3
1974	41.6	34.0	20.5	27.9
1975	15.6	18.8	6.3	8.4
1976	23.1	44.5	7.9	10.5
1977	48.0	421.0	12.3	15.8
1978	58.8	23.0	11.4	14.3
1979	77.5	41.5	14.3	19.0
1980	55.4	16.8	8.8	13.6
1981	72.9	22.3	10.6	15.4
1982	54.5	19.4	7.9	11.5

Source: Statistical Abstracts, 1972-84.

broad range of direct and indirect assistance. To foster the entrepreneurial society and to increase the role of indigenous citizens within it is, perhaps, the most concise way of expressing the government's basic development policy. This philosophy was incorporated in Sessional Paper No. 10 of 1965, African Socialism and its Application to Planning in Kenya, and has formed the basis of successive national development plans.

Since Independence the government has followed a cautious policy in nationalising industries or acquiring shares, and this has done much to reinforce investors' confidence. While some degree of state participation in new enterprises has become accepted and even desired by foreign investors, policies concerning investment protection, taxation and the provision of finance were designed to encourage both foreign and domestic private investment. African Socialism was seen as softening the impact of the market economy by bringing into play the 'mutual social responsibility' which operated in traditional African society. However, the government has never advocated a complete laissez-faire doctrine.

At Independence, faced with capital disinvestment on a large scale, the government's main preoccupation was to halt the outflow and restore confidence among foreign investors. It was in this context that the Foreign Investment Protection Act of 1964 was passed. This provided a system by which overseas investors could apply for a 'Certificate of Approved Enterprise' and once this was obtained there were no constraints.

In the 1970s, however, with the expansion of state capital into foreign-owned sectors and the advance of private domestic capital into industrial production, a number of state mechanisms were developed to regulate and control foreign investment. The most important bodies established in the 1970s were the Capital Issues Committee (CIC) and the New Projects Committee (NPC). The CIC was set up in 1971 to vet all issues of capital stock with a view to cutting down on capital outflow. The aim was to encourage foreign firms operating in Kenya to issue a proportion of their share capital on the Nairobi Stock Exchange, in order to promote a higher level of local ownership of large corporations. The NPC was set up in 1973 with the aim of regulating the flow of foreign capital into industry. The committee evaluates proposed industrial projects against a list of criteria in the 'national interest', such as employment creation, use of local raw materials, introduction of new skills and foreign-exchange savings. These are set against the type of protection - duty remissions and so on - demanded by the foreign investor.

(b) Investment Protection and Incentives. The major instrument of protection for the foreign investor in Kenya is the Foreign Investment Protection Act of 1964. Under the Act, the Minister of Finance issues, after evaluation and negotiation, a Certificate of Approved Enterprise to foreign nationals or institutions investing in foreign currency or reinvesting their profits in Kenya, if he is satisfied that the investment will be of economic benefit to the country. Generally, 'economic benefit to the country' has been interpreted to mean that a project will lead to an earning or saving of foreign exchange, a transfer of technical knowledge to the country, an increase in economic wealth and employment, utilisation of local resources, and the diversification of the economy(3). Before the certificate is issued, the investor must prove that the foreign investment assets have actually been brought into the country and that he has obtained the requisite approvals from the Exchange Control Department of the Central Bank. There are specific safeguards against granting of certificates for speculative investments and change of ownership of existing businesses or buildings (unless for expansion).

The certificate is granted for the nominal value of the equity or loan capital and provides liberal guarantees. It gives freedom to repatriate profits (in proportion to the foreign share of the equity), interest and repayments on foreign loan capital, and also 'the approved proportion of net proceeds of sale' if the enterprise should decide to withdraw part of its investment. If an enterprise does not possess a certificate, it is likely, upon liquidation or sale of a going concern, to find the value of its capital 'blocked' as far as repatriation is concerned. The only way in which 'blocked' sums can be remitted is through the purchase and eventual redemption at the date of maturity of 'approved securities', usually government stock.

For smaller projects, application for the certificate is generally made on the initiative of the firm itself. For larger projects, the government may take the initiative by preparing reports on particular production opportunities and arranging competitive bids from the transnational corporations. In such cases, consideration takes much longer, there is more overt bargaining with firms, and decisions are based on more detailed cost-benefit analysis of proposals. In these and other cases, the NPC operates as the bargaining forum on all aspects of a corporation's agreement to invest.

The Act was amended in 1976 in certain respects. Following the amendments, although loans may be designated and repayment guaranteed in foreign currency, equity investment must be denominated in Kenyan currency, which means that the original foreign-exchange value of the investment is guaranteed and the investor carries the exchange risk. Moreover, it is made clear that although the provision of foreign exchange for the repatriation of capital gains is not ruled out, the foreign-investment guarantee does not apply automatically to such transfers. The amendments were made retroactive to 1964, when the Act originally came into force. The government claimed that there had been no change either of policy or in the way the Act was administered but merely a removal of 'ambiguities that have up till now existed in the original wording of the law'.

The existence of the Foreign Investment Protection Act is an indication of the government's friendly attitude towards foreign investment. But the major general incentive, which is applied to all new investment in manufacturing and tourism, both local and foreign, is a tax allowance of 20% of the value of new fixed assets, including buildings. This is in addition to the normal depreciation allowance of 4% on industrial buildings, 12.5% on machinery and equipment and 25% on vehicles. The allowance can be carried forward if the enterprise makes a loss in its first few years.

In addition, there is a range of ad hoc trade protection concessions, often negotiated with individual investors. The range includes import tariffs of up to 100% ad valorem, specified tariffs on a per article basis, outright bans, foreign-exchange quotas, licensing arrangements and other forms of quantitative restrictions, import duty drawbacks and rebates, and even specific guarantees of duty-free imports of capital goods and materials.

A striking feature of this system is its highly variable and inconsistent character. For instance, the bans and import prohibitions might apply to certain specified articles within a range, e.g. certain sizes of pipe fittings but not other sizes. In addition to the NPC, the key institutions involved in administering the system include the Industrial Protection Committee (IPC), an inter-ministerial group for consideration of modifications in the existing structure of import tariffs, duty drawbacks and import licensing, and the Foreign Exchange Allocation Committee (FEAC), which administers foreign-exchange quotas. In instances of major investments, the process of negotiation regarding the various concessions a firm may receive begins at the political level. Even in cases where projects go through the normal channels, there is wide case-by-case discretion and it is difficult for the committees to acquire and properly analyse the information necessary for effective evaluation of the hundreds of requests received for various types of concessions.

Many potential investors visiting Kenya for the first time have expressed surprise at the lack of a tax holiday incentive. This is not offered because the authorities have traditionally felt that it would be ineffective. It is doubtful whether a five-year tax holiday, for example, as opposed to the 20% tax allowance, would prove a real inducement.

(c) Government Attitudes to Foreign Investment and Balance-of-Payments Constraints. With the increasingly difficult balance-of-payments position that Kenya has experienced, the government has in recent years been rethinking its policy in relation to foreign investment, with the objective of maximising its benefits. While no fundamental change is envisaged in the traditional liberal policy, there seem to be some differences of view in government on the direction the policy improvements should take. On the one hand, there are some who tend to believe that the traditionally liberal policy approach has been one of the central factors responsible for balance-of-payments problems and for what is considered to be a distorted pattern of industrialisation. On the other hand, there are those who believe that the policy improvements required should only involve simplification of existing administrative procedures, with greater emphasis on promotion rather than regulation and control. They see Zimbabwe as a major competitor in the Eastern Africa sub-region for the location of new foreign investment, and therefore advocate the creation of a more attractive environment for it in Kenya, including the introduction of a more liberal incentives regime. There is no easy way of assessing the strength of these viewpoints, since the question of foreign investment is intertwined with opinions about the role of the public and private sectors of the economy.

A process has recently started to review and rationalise the range of incentives available to prospective investors. The main responsibility for this exercise lies in the Investment Advisory and Promotion Centre (IAPC), an autonomous institution within the Treasury, established in November 1982. The IAPC is designed to ensure effective co-ordination of the functions of review, negotiation and approval of projects for which special concessions or government participation are being sought. The objective is to standardise the criteria for evaluation and approval and thereby minimise bureaucratic red tape. Prospective investors will be able to address their enquiries and requests to one central body, although in the case of industry, appraisal, evaluation and negotiation will continue to be undertaken by the Department of Industries and the NPC, with the IAPC establishing guidelines and approving decisions.

However, perhaps partly because of the difference of views on the basic policy approach to be adopted, the role of the IAPC is not yet clearly defined. Its management has been working out proposals for the Centre's legal framework in respect of its powers and responsibilities, on the model of similar institutions in operation in other developing countries, e.g. the Capital Investment Co-ordination Board in Indonesia, the Board of Investment in the Philippines and the National Investment and Development Authority in Papua New Guinea.

As part of this policy reform process, the government recently adopted policy guidelines with respect to new private investment (both foreign and local) in the manufacturing sector. Under these guidelines, priority was to be given to investment in resource-based export-oriented industries; export-oriented industries based on imported inputs, provided the net value-added is 25% or more; balancing, modernisation, and expansion of existing industries to improve their capacity utilisation; and 'producer-goods industries' needed to reduce the import requirements of existing industry (4).

The IAPC has also recently submitted proposals for a new investment incentives regime. While full evaluation of the IAPC package is beyond the scope of this paper, it should be noted that, in addition to a proposal concerning exemption from local income tax for resident expatriates, most of the proposals essentially represent a restructuring and simplification of existing incentives, in response to calls for a relaxation of screening procedures. The IAPC considers the simplification of the investment process an essential step towards improving the investment climate. Other measures under consideration include the licensing of industrialists to manufacture in bond at Nairobi, Mombasa and Kisumu on condition that the total output is exported, and the provision by the IAPC of serviced 500-acre industrial sites at Thika, Mombasa and Kisumu, thus cutting infrastructural and land costs for the prospective manufacturer.

Joint Ventures

Besides direct financial participation by the Treasury - an important feature in the expansion of the manufacturing sector - there are three main parastatal financial agencies serving the manufacturing sector: the Industrial and Commercial Development Corporation (ICDC), the Development Finance Company of Kenya (DFCK) and the Industrial Development Bank (IDB). The ICDC was formed in 1954. It succeeded the East African Industrial Management Board, which had been established in 1944 to supply certain essential products during the war. Its initial activities were largely directed towards trying to keep major expatriate concerns afloat during the years of the emergency. After Independence its focus shifted to include assisting African traders and industrialists to expand their operations and its main source of funds was the Kenya Government (61% in 1976).

The DFCK was established in 1963, a year before Independence, to stimulate and encourage large-scale investments. It was to specialise in larger projects (over £200,000) and the ICDC on smaller projects; in practice, however, the ICDC did not so limit itself. The Kenya Government owned 25% of the shares in the DFCK and the British Government via the Commonwealth Development Corporation (CDC), the German Government via DGWZ and the Dutch Government via the NFMO each held a quarter of the shares. The three foreign shareholders favour projects in which British, German or Dutch companies are involved, one of their objectives being to facilitate foreign investment by their respective national firms.

The IDB was set up in 1973 and, even more clearly than DFCK, was confined to new and in Kenyan terms large-scale projects and to manufacturing. Unlike the DFCK, the bank is fully owned by the government, with 49% of the capital held by the Treasury and 51% shared among other parastatals.

As with the range of official concessions to private firms, the criteria for government financial participation are ad hoc and highly discretionary. Government frequently participates in one firm in an industry, leaving other firms to fend for themselves. In some cases, these are competing firms within the same industry, with investment from different government and parastatal institutions; in other cases there are two or three such institutions involved in one firm and not in a competing firm. The most frequent reasons given for government financial participation include a firm's social contribution, employment generation, relationship to the development plan or inability to get established without government assistance.

A general characteristic of government-funded firms is that, with a very small number of exceptions, they are overwhelmingly oriented toward a protected domestic market. One reason for this is that a large number of the concessions potentially offered by government increase the profitability of import substitution rather than exporting. While it may be helpful for an exporter to have some kind of government financial involvement, it may be essential for the import-substitutor who does not want to compete with imports in the domestic market. It is estimated that only 12% of all government loans and equity investments go to firms with significant exports. Another problem with government financial participation in industrial enterprises is that when the government stands to lose money because of financial problems within its client firms, the pressure is strong to provide additional assistance or protection. The complete range of special concessions, licences, guarantees, and protective measures are far more accessible to the firm that has government financial participation.

In recent years, government has begun to rethink its role in financing the development of industry. This rethinking is most evident in the report of the Presidential Working Party on Government Expenditure issued in 1982, which concluded that government participation in industrial and commercial enterprises had been carried well beyond its original conception and had reached a point where it was inhibiting rather than promoting development. The report noted, inter alia, that (5):

> Government financial investment in commercial and industrial trial activities has absorbed an excessive proportion of the budget, and has frequently resulted in heavy losses. The Government has not attempted to dispose of its holdings in commercial enterprises to Kenyans, so that Kenyanisation has remained representational only through Government. Most of these enterprises are being operated inefficiently and unprofitably, partly because the Government has imposed public functions and excessive employment on them. Special measures have been taken to protect these enterprises from competition and to preclude effective competition from developing. Some inappropriate projects and technologies have been undertaken with Government participation. The result has been that revenues from the sale of shares have not materialised, dividends have been insignificant and subsidies and losses have escalated Government expenditure.

Some of the Working Party's specific recommendations, which have influenced government policy in redefining and rationalising its role in the industrial sector, include:

(i) enacting a 'State Corporations Act' for regulating the establishment of parastatals and providing a legal basis and set of principles by which performance of the sector can be measured;

(ii) studying the legal, financial and organisational characteristics of parastatals and determining
- those in which government involvement, direct or indirect, should be reduced or terminated;
- those whose functions can be absorbed by the parent Ministries or other parastatals;
- those which require legal, functional, financial and organisational re-adjustment or restructuring; and
- methods and strategies of implementing recommendations on the above items;

(iii) studying the existing capital markets and recommending effective strategies and appropriate mechanisms through which the government should dispose of its investments.

In keeping with this policy, the tempo of the investment activities of the main parastatal financial institutions - the IDB, the DFCK and the ICDC - has in recent years declined significantly, in terms of both the number of projects approved and the expenditures incurred.

The general thrust of current government policy is to encourage parastatal financial institutions to provide more assistance to local potential investors in order to enable them to enter joint-venture partnerships with foreign owners of capital and technology, rather than participating in all such joint ventures themselves. Greater emphasis is on the rehabilitation of existing projects and increased administrative control of those projects in which the government retains a financial interest (6).

<u>Management Contracts</u>

In recent years, the tendency in many companies has been for a greater degree of separation between the shareholders and the providers of management and technical services; and management contracts have become a prominent feature of newly formed joint ventures between local (usually government through various parastatal institutions) and foreign capital. In some cases, where a government institution acquires participation in an existing manufacturing company, the original shareholders decide to form a management company, which charges its services to the manufacturing company, thus enabling those shareholders to earn a higher return on their investment. A further refinement which is being increasingly adopted is for the original shareholder group to form a foreign-registered management company to provide managerial and technical services and to be remunerated in foreign currency.

The larger companies, involving sophisticated technology and being established on government initiative, e.g. sugar and textile mills, fertiliser plants and engineering works, usually include a minority foreign shareholder and technical partner to provide the required know-how. The technical partner plans the project, supervises equipment procurement, factory construction and commissioning, and may also supply continuing management and technical services under contract. Thus, the parties involved in these projects comprise (i) government in its regulatory and fiscal capacity; (ii) the shareholders, who include government (or a parastatal institution), a local private shareholder and a foreign shareholder; and (iii) the technical partner, who is usually associated with the foreign shareholder.

Management fees payable to a foreign company are subject to withholding tax of 20%, while such fees payable to a local company, whose profits are subject to Kenyan income tax, are not taxed. A foreign shareholder, who is also a managing agent, may be able to increase his total net remuneration if he receives a management fee (less 20% tax), rather than the same amount paid as a dividend out of profits, taxed at 45%. Thus, management contracts provide an opportunity for some foreign firms to increase their earnings from local companies by reducing their tax liability.

Where the payment for services under management contracts is in foreign exchange, the client has to seek the approval of the Central Bank. While the Central Bank is the controlling authority, major agreements are referred to the Capital Issues Committee (CIC), on which the Central Bank, the Treasury and the Ministry of Commerce and Industry are represented. (Management contracts in respect of large projects may also be referred to the Attorney General's Department.) There is a recurrent problem of ensuring adequate evaluation facilities within government bodies to deal with complex technological issues.

The rate and type of management fees differ from contract to contract between companies within the same industry. For example, fees have been based on (i) the amount of fixed capital; (ii) time, with a fixed fee per annum; (iii) sales; or (iv) 'gross profits'. The government normally requires each contract to specify the numbers of expatriate technical and managerial staff required to implement each stage of the project, with a view to phasing out most non-citizen posts. In the 1970s, the Kenyanisation Bureau of the Ministry of Labour became increasingly strict in demanding precise schedules from foreign firms for the replacement of expatriates by Kenyans and the provision of training for local staff. Hence, while negotiating management contracts, the Ministry is usually consulted on the question of training and personnel.

The government has in recent years been increasingly concerned that management contracts contribute to corporate efficiency and are not used as means of evading taxes and diverting foreign currency. The present policy is to enter into such contracts only when it is not possible to identify and recruit qualified non-citizen personnel directly. In cases where management contracts are considered necessary, the policy is to identify suitable contractors through competitive international bidding in every context in which it is feasible; to exercise greater care in the evaluation of bids, where necessary with the assistance of technical advisers; and to determine fees on the basis of profits and limit the durations to short periods, normally of three-five years each.

Perceptions of Foreign Firms in Kenya

Nearly all the foreign firms interviewed expressed concern about increasing state regulation and control over their operations and about the inconsistent and discretionary treatment of different firms in the exercise of such regulation. Responses from a small sample of foreign companies that were interviewed focused on five areas, which were considered to be more significant constraints: exchange regulations governing imports; restrictions on the repatriation of capital; restrictions on local borrowing; the limited market for sales; and, above all, price control.

(a) Exchange Regulations Governing Imports. Exchange control regulations require foreign-exchange allocation licences and pre-shipment inspection for almost all imports. All orders valued at KShs.20,000 or more are subject to pre-shipment inspection by the General Superintendence Company of Geneva. The Foreign Exchange Allocation Committee (FEAC) administers exchange quotas for imports for which a limited quota has been established in order to protect a local producer or group of producers. The quota is generally the difference between anticipated local production and market demand. The entire process of foreign-exchange allocation is highly discretionary and is almost entirely *ad hoc* and related to specific firms. Furthermore, exchange regulations governing imports have not been updated since 1975. The FEAC meets monthly and usually decides on some amendment to the regulations. The regulations are then superseded by specific circulars and FEAC minutes.

(b) Restrictions on the Repatriation of Capital. The rights of repatriation of capital provided for under the Foreign Investment Protection Act, 1964, were substantially modified under the 1976 Act which limited the amount eligible to the book value of the original investment plus reinvestment of after-tax profits. Foreign investors believe this amendment virtually undermines the original Act, because the book value reflects only a fraction of the true value of the owner's equity. Successful management, leading to high profits, will raise the market value of an ongoing concern, so that it can be sold at a price exceeding the book value of the assets. There is also the impact of inflation. It has been argued that because prices in Kenya are rising three to four times every ten years, allowing repatriation of only the book value amounts to expropriation of 75% of the market value of the foreign investment.

(c) Restriction on Local Borrowing. Under existing exchange-control regulations, non-resident-controlled firms are required to obtain approval for any local loan or overdraft in excess of 20% of the non-resident investment in the business, for any public offer of shares, for any purchase of shares in resident companies, for any foreign investment brought into new or existing enterprises and for any capitalisation of reserves. Resident-controlled firms with foreign shareholders are limited to 40% of their total investment in overdraft without special permission. In all cases, the CIC assesses applications, with representatives from the Central Bank, the Ministry of Commerce and Industries, and the Treasury. Only applications for over K£50,000 in overdrafts reach the committee, but this involves negotiations with some 100 firms each year. While the CIC does not do its own cost-benefit calculations on projects (often it relies primarily on the companies' own statistical analyses), its approval of requests is by no means automatic. Sometimes approval is tied to a condition that there be no dividend repatriation until the firm reduces its overdraft level to 20% of the approved total.

From the government's point of view, foreign firms find it advantageous to borrow in Kenya (despite the restrictions), because local interest rates are relatively low, compared to those prevailing in the international capital markets. Therefore, to the extent that foreign firms borrow locally for investment in Kenya, they conserve their own internal resources for investment elsewhere and, indirectly, the country's 'cheap money' is used to finance investment in other countries.

(d) Limited Market Sales. Many foreign firms came into Kenya because of potential sales in some six countries in Eastern Africa. As pointed out earlier, the collapse of the East African Community and the closure of the Tanzania border during 1978-83 (cutting off the markets of Zambia, Rwanda and Burundi, as well as that of Tanzania), the war and its aftermath in Uganda (which has become the third largest market for Kenyan exports), and poor relations with Somalia have hampered Kenyan exports in neighbouring countries and have led to increasing unutilised manufacturing capacity. Furthermore, a new competitor in these markets (and in the home market) has recently emerged in the form of independent Zimbabwe. In certain branches of manufacturing, the problem has been exacerbated by the duplication of plants making the same products. The most blatant example in recent years of duplication of projects in Kenya occurred in the vehicle assembly industry.

(e) Price Control. Price control is considered to be the most serious problem afflicting manufacturers in Kenya. Throughout manufacturing, there are complaints that price increases, which ought to be linked to inflation, are too little and too late; and that, as a result, profits are dented and expansion plans disrupted.

Summary and Conclusions

Despite the constraints, Kenya is among the African countries which can credibly boast of an attractive investment climate, with private companies operating alongside state institutions. By developing country standards, Kenya has good infrastructure in transportation, power, and communications, some good locations for industry, a well-equipped financial system and, above all, a stable government with a positive attitude towards foreign investment. These factors, coupled with a wide range of trade protection devices and other incentives, have helped to attract foreign investment into Kenya during the post-Independence period.

The post-Independence boom in manufacturing owed much to an import-substitution strategy, which allowed new investment to operate behind substantial government protection. By and large, the principal beneficiaries of this policy were foreign investors, although efforts were made to encourage domestic enterprise. The import-substitution strategy had some undesirable side effects. It resulted in a cost-permissive atmosphere and an 'anti-export' bias; the products were frequently overpriced and of indifferent quality. Since relatively high profits accrued to production for the domestic market, foreign investment tended to be unduly concentrated on import substitution.

With the severe balance-of-payments difficulties experienced after the 1976-7 coffee boom and the related foreign-exchange shortages, a strict import allocation system became essential. This was a formidable task and the country's first attempt to come to grips with the problem through import licensing schedules, introduced in late 1981, soon ran into trouble. By mid-1982, foreign-exchange reserves had fallen to less than KShs.2 bn, barely a month's import cover. By the end of 1982, many manufacturers were running out of essential items and there appeared to be no clear rationale behind the allocation of such foreign exchange as was available. Although the economy improved significantly in the course of 1983 and import licences became more readily available, it was acknowledged that the licensing system needed revision.

The overall effect was to underline the need for a review of industrialisation policy. The government recognised that the scope for further rapid growth in manufacturing through extending and increasing protection was limited and decided to switch to an export-oriented industrial strategy. This strategy has five key components: (a) new import licensing procedures, designed to make a more rational use of foreign exchange; (b) gradual replacement of quantitative import restrictions by tariffs, slowly reducing the level of protection that industry has enjoyed and forcing the sector to be more efficient; (c) an export drive with greater incentives, less red tape and a search for new markets; (d) a better investment climate to encourage new ventures and ensure that existing operations expand; and (e) maintenance of an appropriate exchange rate.

However, the implementation of these measures is likely to be difficult. For instance, measures for gradually eliminating quantitative restrictions on imports had been introduced in 1980 but came to a temporary halt during 1982-3 because of extreme foreign-exchange shortages; a revised import administration system became inoperative because the Central Bank was unable to authorise the release of foreign exchange for licences issued. Furthermore, the reduction of the anti-export bias in trade, increased industrial efficiency and the provision of more generous inducements to export-oriented investment, while essential to the mounting of a sustained export drive, may not induce substantial flows of 'fresh' foreign investment. With the increasing competition for export-oriented investment in developing countries, while it may be possible for Kenya to attract some 'fresh' investors from abroad, the country will, for a greater part, have to rely on encouraging existing foreign firms, which entered production in the country to meet the domestic market, to shift to exporting. This will not be easy, since it requires alteration of the firms' traditional production and marketing strategies. To facilitate this change from import-substitution to export-oriented production, a number of new measures, along with changes in existing schemes, should be considered; in particular, the present system of financial and institutional support will have to be strengthened. Such measures should include improvements in export compensation, increased access of exporters to foreign exchange and credit, and measures to give free trade treatment to imported inputs.

While recent statements by the government have left a confused picture of the official attitude to foreign investment, Kenya is still committed to a development policy that places a strong emphasis on the role of foreign investment. This commitment was reiterated by the Finance Minister in his June 1986 budget speech, when he called for the streamlining of investment procedures, greater access to local capital for foreign investors and a relaxation of price controls on all non-essential goods. In addition, Kenya's blueprint for economic development to the year 2000, approved by the cabinet at the end of February 1986 and endorsed by donors, stated that 'The mixed economy will continue to be Kenya's instrument for development, with increasing activity by the private sector which will be encouraged and regulated more by government-guided market forces than by direct intervention and controls'. The foreign business community in Kenya also feels there is still scope for increased foreign investment in the country. It is encouraged by the excellent trading possibilities with neighbouring countries, particularly Kenya's renewed co-operation with both Tanzania and Uganda.

NOTES AND REFERENCES

1. Up to 1978 Kenya was associated in a common market with Tanzania and Uganda, and its relatively early development of industry put it in a strong position with its common market partners. By the late 1950s, Kenya had become the manufacturing centre of the whole of East Africa, with about 20% of its manufacturing output sold to Tanganyika (now Tanzania) and Uganda. Its central position in the common market arrangements assisted the development of Nairobi into a natural location for the headquarters of the international firms entering the East African market.

2. Steven Langdon, Multinational Corporations in the Political Economy of Kenya (Macmillan, London 1980).

3. Kenya Government, Guidelines to Investors (1981).

4. Address by the Minister for Commerce and Industry at the annual meeting of the Kenya Association of Manufacturers, Nairobi, 18 April 1984.

5. Report of the Ndegwa Working Party (1982), p.12.

6. In 1986, the government introduced a series of policy changes mainly designed to encourage the localisation of ownership and control of industrial and commercial enterprises in the country. On 8 June 1986, the President

announced that foreigners who wanted to invest in Kenya must bring in Kenyan nationals as partners with controlling interest. He was quoted as saying that 'from now onwards, Kenyans must own 51% or more shares of any joint ventures with foreign investors..........Kenyans must take control of the country's economy'. It is not quite clear, however, how and when the 51% ruling will be applied since no clear guidelines have yet been issued. According to press reports, the government has also promised to accelerate the phasing out of the large expatriate workforce and to establish a task force to supervise the handing over of enterprises to African Kenyans.

7. Imports are divided into four restricted 'schedules' and those imported under 'Open General Licenses' for which there are no Central Bank restrictions. Schedule I is the list of goods for which specific licenses are required and which are 'being watched' but for which foreign exchange is generally available without delay. Schedule II specifies imports for which a limited quota has been established to protect local producers. Schedule III items are banned because local producers have convinced FEAC that they can supply the local market. Schedule IV is a list of quota-restricted items with balance-of-payments management rather than industrial protection being the explicit motivation.

Chapter Fifteen

ZIMBABWE'S EXPERIENCE OF FOREIGN INVESTMENT POLICY

Roger C. Riddell

Foreign investment has always played a major role in the economic history of Zimbabwe from the early period of colonialism down to the present day. For over 30 years, down to 1923, the country was administered by a foreign company, the British South African Company, while today conventional wisdom in both government and academic circles judges that some two-thirds of the capital stock in the country is foreign-owned. While the pace of inflow of foreign capital has varied during different periods over the past 90 years, new foreign companies have continued to invest in Zimbabwe during most of this century, the one recent exception being during the period of the Unilateral Declaration of Independence (UDI) from 1965 to Independence in 1980 when little new investment flowed in.

Following Independence the inflow of new foreign investment has continued again, although the present flows are not nearly as significant in quantitative terms as either during the early years of colonialisation or during the most expansive period from 1945 to 1963, the year of the break-up of the Federation of Rhodesia and Nyasaland.

The Stock of Foreign Investment Capital

No comprehensive analysis of the stock of foreign capital in Zimbabwe has been carried out; the figures that are used and have been used are based on estimates, and frequently guesses, and so the limitations of the data which are commonly quoted need to be recognised. The largest gap in estimating precise figures for foreign capital stock occurs not because of inadequacies in balance-of-payments data recording actual inflows and outflows; rather it lies in the lack of data which might record what has been happening to the profits of companies in the country with foreign links. For Zimbabwe, in particular, this type of problem is exacerbated because during the UDI period (and previously for some items) the vast majority of profits and dividends that under more normal circumstances would have been available for external remittance were prevented from being repatriated through Reserve (Central) Bank controls; while some of this money was placed in blocked funds - totalling between $400 and $500 million - some companies managed to avoid having their assets frozen in blocked accounts by placing part of the potentially blocked funds in investment and other specially created companies to finance expansion or to provide less controlled cash balances. Another complicating factor in assessing the stock of foreign capital has arisen because of emigration. Where nationals have left the country their assets have been frozen within the country, not infrequently changing 'local' capital into 'foreign' capital and hence building up the potential outflow of capital as well as altering the domestic/foreign ownership mix.

With these caveats we can now look at the data that are available, acknowledging that, as the sources indicate, these are crude measures and more indicative than strictly firm(1). Estimates, for 1978-9, suggest that of a total capital stock

Table 15.1: Estimates of total and foreign capital stock, 1982 ($m.)

	Total capital	Foreign	% Foreign
Agriculture	1,500	450	30
Mining	1,200	1,080	90
Manufacturing	2,400	1,680	70
'Local'	3,800	380	10
Other	2,500	1,250	50
Total	11,400	4,840	42.5
Total without 'Local'	7,600		58.7

Notes:

a) 'Local' embraces Electricity and Water Construction, Real Estate and Services. The 10% foreign, which may be an underestimate, would mainly be in the private construction sector. As 'Local' is mainly infrastructural 'non-productive' sectors, better comparability with earlier estimates is obtained by omitting it. The foreign share then rises to about 58%.

b) 'Other' is Financial and Insurance, Distribution, Hotels, Transport and Communications.

Source: Stoneman, personal communication, June 1984.

of $2,250-$2,750m., $750m. was domestic and between $1,500m. and $2,000m. was foreign capital stock. These figures suggest that foreign capital stock was between 66% and 72% of the total capital stock of the country(2). Work is in progress to analyse in more detail the influence of foreign capital on the Zimbabwean economy and its sectoral breakdown. While the figures are at present tentative, the following summary of work by Stoneman is included.

Stoneman's May 1984 estimate of total capital stock, including public sector capital, for 1982 is $11.4 bn, of which $4.84 bn, or 42.5%, is foreign. These estimates are based on output data for 1982, assuming a capital/output ratio of 2.5. Total figures and broad sectoral groups are reproduced in Table 15.1, indicating foreign capital dominance of the mining sector and, to a lesser extent, of the manufacturing sector.

Foreign Capital and the Balance of Payments

While one would expect that a substantial stock of foreign capital and a high proportion of foreign to domestic capital would lead to a sizeable outflow of profits and dividends, the potential outflow is decreased to the extent that after-tax profits are used for reinvestment purposes in the host country. There is no doubt that this phenomenon has been occurring in Zimbabwe.

In 1963, 68% of gross domestic capital formation originated from foreign companies. That this is still occurring is shown from more recent evidence. In the mining sector in 1980 and 1981, gross fixed capital formation of $216m. included at least $136m. of investment by foreign mining companies already operating in the country. Other evidence is revealed in a survey of current and future investment plans of manufacturing companies conducted in mid-1983 by the Confederation of Zimbabwe Industries(3). Investment intentions in the period 1983-5 at 1982 prices for the manufacturing sector as a whole were estimated at $282m. a year, over 70% from companies with substantial foreign participation. Out of 50 of such firms who responded to the survey only one mentioned new direct foreign investment as a source of capital for projected future investment. All the rest recorded internal sources as the method of financing expansion, with less than 20% recording banking or internal financial sources as a supplement to their own internal sources. The expansion of operations leads to an expansion of the capital base of these companies and hence to a growth in the future potential outflow of profits and dividends and thus to future and more substantial effects on the balance of payments.

After reinvestment of profits, income tax, branch profits and non-resident shareholder tax (as particular circumstances determine) have been deducted, one is left with a figure that theoretically could be considered the aggregate profit, interest and dividend outflow from companies that are either incorporated outside Zimbabwe or from external partners and/or shareholders of companies incorporated (usually as subsidiaries) inside Zimbabwe. Emphasis needs to be placed on the word 'theoretical' because all outflows of dividends and profits are subject to the approval of the Exchange Control authorities of the Reserve Bank of Zimbabwe, which at least since 1948 have exerted controls on external remittances. Indeed, during the UDI period (1965-80) the vast majority of declared potential profits and dividends were placed in frozen blocked accounts, and even since 1980 there has been a general restriction on the export of capital of those individuals who have left the country.

Actual Flows

We now consider the actual flows that have arisen in recent years. Inflows and outflows shown in the current account of the balance of payments are reproduced in Table 15.2. They reveal that the most important outflow results from company dividends and that the total net outflow on profits and dividends has been in excess of $90m. over the past two years. The migrant income remittances item is considered below the total line in the table because it does not arise from the commonly understood flows arising from foreign investment. An indication of the considerable difference between profits made from foreign investment and the actual outflow on the current account of the balance of payments under the heading of profits and dividends can be obtained by comparing these figures with the current net earnings of UK non-oil companies. In 1981, the net current earnings of UK non-oil companies in Zimbabwe amounted to $66m., the outflow of profits and dividends of all foreign investment was $79m. - and this latter figure would have included some backlog of blocked funds. In 1982, the figures were $56m. and $95m. respectively(4).

Finally, in considering the effects of foreign investment on the outflow of funds on current account, a word needs to be said about royalty payments. In 1980, royalty payments made by firms in the mining, manufacturing, construction and water and electricity sub-sectors of the economy came to $5.4m. However, royalty payments do not appear in balance-of-payments data as a separate item. This is because external outflows of royalties are judged by Ministry of Finance officials to be minimal; a maximum figure of $2m. a year is considered an approximate figure for current royalty outflows.

On the capital account of the balance of payments, the major items directly affected by foreign investment are the flows of equity capital and blocked funds. Table 15.3 gives

Table 15.2: Investment income on current account resultir
from foreign investment, 1981-3 ($m.)

	Credit			Debit			Net		
	1981	1982	1983	1981	1982	1983	1981	1982	1983
a) Direct income									
Profits:									
branches	-	-	-	4.4	7.0	9.4	-4.4	-7.0	-9.4
Dividends:									
companies	1.4	0.9	1.0	74.8	88.3	82.8	-73.4	-87.4	-81.8
Total	1.4	0.9	1.0	79.2	95.3	92.2	-77.8	-94.4	-91.2
b) Private									
Migrant income									
remittances	0.5	0.3	0.2	21.1	23.2	23.2	-20.6	-22.9	-20.4

Source: Government of Zimbabwe (unpublished).

the figures for these items over the last three years and compares them with both portfolio investment and official and parastatal long-term and short-term loans. The table shows that the total inflow of equity capital of $23m. between 1981 and 1983 is more than outweighed by an outflow of equity capital of $40m. However, this negative flow of equity capital is influenced substantially by an outflow of more than $25m. following government purchase from South African shareholders (taking 43% of the total capital) of the country's leading pharmaceutical company, CAPS. Excluding this transaction there would have been a positive inflow of equity capital over the period of $11m. The negative accumulated balance on portfolio investment of over $100m. between 1981 and 1983 is due to external bond and stock repayments and the lack of portfolio investment inflows.

The net outflow of equity and portfolio direct investment on capital account of $128m. between 1981 and 1983 needs to be contrasted with the net inflow of official and parastatal long-term capital of $700m. in the same period, and net outflow of official short-term capital of $26m. This substantial positive inflow, in the form largely of loans and to a lesser extent aid monies, was necessary not only to finance the net outflow of direct investment but to assist in financing the large overall current account deficit which amounted to a cumulative $1,529m. between 1981 and 1984. It

Table 15.3: Direct and portfolio investment, official and parastatal flows and blocked funds as recorded in the capital account of the balance of payments 1981-3 ($m.)

	Credit			Debit			Net		
	1981	1982	1983	1981	1982	1983	1981	1982	1983
1. Direct equity investment	7.0	11.3	4.7	21.5	11.5	7.1	-14.5	-0.2	-2.4
2. Blocked funds	-	-	-	4.5	0.8	0.4	-4.5	-0.8	-0.4
3. Portfolio investment	2.7	0.5	-	29.3	37.6	41.1	-26.6	-37.1	-41.1
4. Official long-term loan	61.7	97.7	261.7	17.0	6.3	45.3	44.7	91.4	216.4
5. Parastatal long-term	57.9	192.7	128.3	2.2	51.0	23.3	55.7	187.6	105.0
6. Official short-term	86.3	80.5	-	-	29.2	163.9	86.3	51.3	-163.9
7. Totals 1 & 2	7.0	11.3	4.7	26.0	12.3	7.5	-19.0	-1.0	-2.8
8. Totals 4 to 6	205.9	370.9	390.0	19.2	40.6	232.5	186.7	330.3	157.5

Source: Government of Zimbabwe (unpublished): 1983 figures are preliminary estimates.

has been to address the problem of the current account deficit, exacerbated by the need to repay substantial external loans over the coming few years - the debt service ratio is projected to remain over 25% until 1988 without further external borrowing - and the need to attempt to maintain import levels which dropped by over 25% in real terms between 1981 and 1984 and which have been increasingly under strain because of three years of drought, that action was taken in March 1984 to curb the outflow on invisibles.

Table 15.4 is the summary of the overall balance of payments over the past three years, revealing both the running down of national reserves and the increasing use made of standby credits.

Government Policy Objectives in Relation to DFI

Declared Policies and Objectives.

Since Independence in April 1980, Zimbabwe has been ruled by

Table 15.4: Balance of payments summary, 1981-4 ($m.)

	1981	1982	1983	1984
Net surplus/deficit on				
Capital account	133.6	342.6	285.9	232.6
Current account	-439.6	-532.9	-454.2	-101.9
Net errors and omissions	85.9	66.0	10.0	33.6
Balance on capital and current accounts	-220.1	-124.3	-158.3	164.3
Gold monetisation	15.2	2.2	41.5	29.0
Use of IMF resources	30.8	-	162.2	78.7
Extraordinary financing	218.3	110.3	-8.4	-223.0
Valuation factors	-28.0	25.2	-36.1	-21.7
Change in reserves	-16.2	-13.4	-0.9	-27.3

Note: Valuation factors relate to both gold and foreign assets; extraordinary financing represents borrowing related to reserves.

Source: Reserve Bank of Zimbabwe, Quarterly Economic and Statistical Review, December 1985, Table 6.3.

a party committed to socialism, indeed one that is committed to the principles of Marxist-Leninism. None the less, government policy is not only to recognise the reality of the private sector and of direct foreign investment in the country but to provide the conditions for an historically unprecedented expansion of the private productive sector, albeit in a changed form, and to welcome new foreign investment on conditions that have been spelt out in a number of key economic policy documents. The apparent tension between the thrust towards socialism and the nurturing of private enterprise, including the dominant foreign private sector, is well captured in the Prime Minister's foreword to the current transitional national development plan(5):

> The Plan... recognises the existing phenomenon of capitalism as an historical reality, which, because it cannot be avoided, has to be purposefully harnessed, regulated and transformed as a partner in the overall national endeavour to achieve set national plan goals. Accordingly, while the main thrust of the Plan is socialist and calls for a greater role by the State through the instrumentality of State enterprises, worker participation and socialist co-operation, ample room has been reserved for performance by private enterprise.

What is meant by ample room for private enterprise can be illustrated for foreign private capital in particular. Projections made in the Plan for private inflows on capital account give an average figure of $160m. a year between 1981-2 and 1984-5 compared with net new non-aid government borrowings of $180m. a year. The actual figures for 1981 to 1983 illustrate the vast difference between intention and reality.

All inquiries on foreign investment and applications by foreigners to invest in Zimbabwe are channelled through the recently established Foreign Investment Committee (FIC), a two-tiered body, consisting of a working party of senior officials and a group of senior Ministers headed by the Minister of Finance, Economic Planning and Development, whose function it is to vet and approve or reject applications. Given the high profile of foreign capital already present in the country, the committee's concerns include not only decisions relating to new equity capital but also decisions affecting foreign capital currently located in the country. All businesses in Zimbabwe, in which 15% or more of the issued share voting power is owned by non-residents, are defined as 'foreign'.

In addition to submission to the FIC, if a project is proposed for the manufacturing sector it has to have the approval of the government's Industrial Projects Committee (IPC). While this committee examines projects against criteria of employment generation, decentralisation and technological implication, the IPC uses specific criteria in regard to foreign exchange. While these have not been published, they have been spelt out recently by the Permanent Secretary in the Ministry of Industry. He stated(6):

> Capacity to earn foreign currency is .... an important criterion in assessment of projects - but I wish to emphasise two points here:-
>
> (a) All criteria are not applied in isolation and with a blind eye. There are therefore industries producing essential products for the local market, which utilise imported inputs and do not therefore generate foreign currency - e.g. food industries.
>
> (b) The financing for a project should be structured in such a way that the foreign currency outlaid must be recouped within a period of 12 months. This principle applies equally to projects that are geared to save foreign currency through import substitution.

In the sphere of taxation and incentives for foreign investors there is a fundamental principle of no discrimination between domestic and foreign investors, except in withholding taxes on dividends and branch profits taxes, and no discrimination whatever between new and potential foreign investors and those foreign investors already operating in the country. However, the Reserve Bank regulations for investments subsequent to September 1979 are now different from regulations applying to previous foreign investment inasmuch as the new investment is not subject to the recently-imposed freeze on profit and dividend expatriation.

For new equity capital, however, special provision is made. In summary, regulations provide for disinvestment of the original capital invested and free repatriation after two years and for the subsequent five years the remittability of capital at terms no less favourable than those in place when the original investment was made(7).

In the legal sphere, protection, for local and foreign investment alike, is contained in the country's Constitution within the section on the Declaration of Rights. As a result, government has resisted external pressure to institute additional legislation for foreign investors.

Government Policies in Practice.

In the short period since Independence and the even shorter period since the Foreign Investment Guidelines were published, a considerable amount of activity has taken place in the foreign investment sphere and hence in government's attitudes to particular proposals, even if the resulting flows in equity have not been great. Eight major initiatives have been made by government to participate in, or take control of, concerns owned by private foreign companies, while over 12 new foreign companies have come into Zimbabwe since Independence.

Direct action taken by government has involved initiatives to acquire foreign interests in key productive areas of the economy and to take over marketing of minerals and fuel oil. The eight major initiatives have been the following: the purchase of a 43% share in Zimbabwe Newspapers from South African interests with Nigerial capital; the purchase of a 61% share in (South African) Zimbank; the 47% share in the newly formed Bank of Credit and Commerce Zimbabwe; the purchase of the 42.6% international controlling interest in CAPS; the 40% equity share in Anglo-American's Wankie Colliery Company; the establishment of the Minerals Marketing Corporation; the establishment of the National Oil Company of Zimbabwe to procure fuel for the country from external sources; and the purchase of booksellers and stationers, Kingstons, by the Mass Media Trust.

Besides direct government action, the semi-parastatal Industrial Development Corporation has become more aggressive since Independence and government has stated its intention of acquiring the remaining 20% of private capital injected when it started operations in 1963 and ensuring that legal control will be directly under the government. Since Independence, the IDC has spent over $6m. in bailing out firms in financial trouble by forming equity partnerships. This policy has included foreign firms. For example, in October 1982, the IDC purchased the UK's John Brown's 52% stake in the engineering company F. Issel and Son for $1.6m., and in June announced its purchase of the British Steel Corporation's share in Lancashire Steel together with the iron and steel company ZISCO, itself 50% owned by the state; the IDC injected $2.5m. into Lancashire Steel which will continue to operate under independent management.

Responses to requests by foreign companies to invest put government in the passive role of accepting or rejecting proposals placed before it. Though there are many complaints that the criteria for new foreign investment are too vague, there have been no general complaints about consistency between the government's stated policy towards new investment and the decisions taken. There is one exception to this generalisation, and it refers to the proposed takeover by Turnall (UK) of the Zimbabwean-dominated company Mashonaland Holdings worth $39m. After approval had been given for the takeover in February 1981 this was withdrawn in early May, only 45 minutes before the extraordinary general meeting of Mashonaland Holdings called to approve the takeover. While this reversal of policy caused concern in business circles at the time, the final decision is consistent with the subsequently published Guidelines and did not lead to any long-term belief that policy and action would differ to the detriment of business interests. An indication of government policy in practice is revealed by the refusal of the FIC to approve an application by a US health products firm to expand its operations, because, even though competition would have thus been enhanced, expansion would have led to the creation of new capacity in a sector which already had excess capacity.

Perhaps of greater interest to the government's policy on foreign investment are the projects that have been agreed allowing new foreign investors to operate in Zimbabwe. Twenty-three instances of new agreements with foreign companies were made from Independence in April 1980 to mid-1984. While these agreements do not give a complete picture of the direction of the economy favoured by the government - because the most substantial investments have been made by foreign companies previously present in the country - they do highlight both gaps in the economy that can be filled by foreign companies and the areas that have received favourable treatment. Of those agreements that involve new investments (even if, as in the case of the Heinz deal, new foreign equity has not yet featured dramatically in balance-of-payments data), the most significant are those of

H.J. Heinz (USA) worth US$4m. in food processing and Dandy (Denmark) worth $3m. in establishing a new chewing gum factory. Eleven out of the 23 have been joint ventures, of which three have been joint ventures with the government or the parastatal Industrial Development Corporation. Seven out of the 23 have consisted of licensing or technological agreements, and 11 have explicit export potential.

Company Perceptions on Investing in Zimbabwe.
Potential foreign investors are influenced by an array of factors when formulating decisions on entering new markets: political, economic and financial assessments are made of the host country and of the potential investment risks, and these may be compared with alternative opportunities in other countries and with the option of staying at home. One critical factor in the Zimbabwe equation, given the dominant influence of foreign capital in most productive sectors of the economy and the presence of more than 300 foreign companies, is the perception of Zimbabwe as a host country by those foreign companies already in the country. It is the views of these companies that we shall examine first.

Perceptions of Companies Already in Zimbabwe. There are, at least in theory, three broad choices open to foreign companies with assets already in Zimbabwe: to withdraw from the country, to make the best use of the funds that are in the country and, thirdly, to bring in more external capital, while, of course, ensuring that the new capital is married with the old in the most beneficial way.

Although it can be argued that the first option is not an attractive proposition, given the poor return on government bonds (4%) and the fact that companies which invested prior to September 1979 will not be able to disinvest their capital assets until ten years after initial permission is given to disinvest, it is a possible scenario. Very few foreign companies have gone for this option. Government officials agree that there is more talk of disinvestment than there was two or three years ago, but few cases involving large sums of money (over $5m.) have been brought to the attention of the authorities. Views of officials in banking circles appear to confirm this view: those with assets in the country would prefer to use these to the best long-term advantage, building up the strength of current operations and enhancing their future profit and dividend position, rather than disinvest. And, finally, the views of head offices abroad tend to be consistent with this attitude; advice to Zimbabwean branches and subsidiaries is to improve cash balances and the medium- and long-term viability of their operations.

A general consensus rejecting the option to disinvest is

paralleled by a similar consensus rejecting the third of the three options, namely, to inject new funds into the country at the present time. Not only are next to no companies present in Zimbabwe injecting additional external capital into the country at this time, but none have been identified who expressed a strong desire to do so. Where foreign companies in Zimbabwe are looking for links with other external companies it is predominantly to achieve technological advantage rather than to expand equity, for example through joint ventures. Reasons for this decision are usually a reflection of a number of influences.

There is evidence to suggest that the international press coverage that Zimbabwe has received has negatively affected the perceptions of board members in their home countries to the extent that the boards of leading companies with investments in Zimbabwe are a significant negative influence on possible decisions to expand operations. These negative press influences embrace one or both of concerns about the future of foreign investment in the medium- to long-term in the country and concern about the security situation and hence about political stability. This point needs to be expanded. What is not being suggested here is that there necessarily <u>is</u> widespread political instability affecting investments or that there <u>is</u> a threat of nationalisation or the takeover of foreign assets. There is a perception that this is the reality; this perception is reinforced by press reports and it is on the basis of this perception that decisions are being made and future planning is being evaluated.

There is, however, another factor which does have an influence on the decision not to inject new capital and it relates to government policy on the inflow of plant and capital equipment. Although there is no doubt that the majority of large businesses need new equipment to replace old and obsolete plant that could not be replaced during the UDI period, and to facilitate the expansion of the operations of the company, there is no incentive for foreign companies to use their own external foreign-exchange resources, including new equity capital, to import such plant and equipment. If new capital is needed then companies, whether foreign-owned or domestic, apply to the authorities for foreign exchange to import this equipment which on purchase becomes a foreign-exchange loss to Zimbabwe and not to the company. Balance-of-payments data indicate that between 1981 and 1983 Zimbabwe experienced an outflow of over $159m. for new capital and replacement machinery including lines of credit, a substantial proportion of which will have been utilised by foreign companies. As foreign exchange so used enhances profit levels and so leads to a greater potential outflow of profits and dividends, there are clearly sound reasons for companies to use the country's foreign exchange and the recently expanded commodity import programmes to enhance their operations in Zimbabwe, using retained profits or internal commercial bank borrowing where necessary.

But to come back to the general issue of returns on present investment, there is evidence to show a declining trend in the most recent years. There is, of course, little surprise that returns on investment have declined in recent years because the fortunes of foreign companies in a foreign-dominated economy will tend to reflect trends in the overall economy, and as Table 15.5 shows the expansive period of the early years of Independence has been dramatically reversed in the more recent years.

It is the declining rate of return on current investments which, together with growing perceptions of uncertainty about the future, discussed above, is the main cause of the widespread rejection of the third option, namely, to inject additional equity capital into the Zimbabwe economy at the present time. Hence by a process of elimination, the option favoured by the vast majority of foreign companies already operating in Zimbabwe is the middle one - to attempt to make the best use of funds already invested so as to maximise future returns. What is of more interest in this particular study is not so much to record the evidence of a declining rate of return on investment but to discuss the perceptions of companies towards those aspects of policy which are affecting investment levels and which could be changed to enhance the expansion of investment, particularly 'domestic' investment by foreign companies operating at present in the country. It is a consideration of these factors to which we now turn.

For 'local' investors security issues and supposed threats of nationalisation play a small and, in the case of nationalisation threats, a decreasing part in influencing in-

Table 15.5: Real growth rates of the Zimbabwe economy

Year	Annual real growth rate
1980	11.0
1981	13.0
1982	0.0
1983 [a]	- 3.4
1984 [b]	1.3
1985 [a]	6.0
1986-1990	4.2

a) Preliminary estimate.
b) World Bank forecast.

Source: Central Statistical Office, Harare.

vestment decisions. The deterrents to higher levels of investment most commonly mentioned by companies are employment and wage legislation and regulations and price control regulations. The complaint is not so much the existence of regulations - all-embracing price control regulations have been on the statute books since 1954 - but the lack of agreed formulas and procedures for the determination of prices and wages which inhibit long-term planning. On the labour front, difficulties in obtaining permission to dismiss labour in time of recession, the unpredictability in the timing of legislated minimum wage increases and the continuation of the wage freeze for those on higher wages are all major deterrents to future investment planning. On the prices front, delays in receiving permission for increases and the fact that decisions on increases appear totally arbitrary are the main concerns, reinforced by the perception that increases are granted in relation to current profit levels rather than to considerations of a long-term return on investment.

There are other less widespread concerns, which are also affecting investment decisions. Decreasing levels of foreign-exchange allocations that affect turnover and profit levels and increase cash flow problems are a factor. High levels of personal income tax are also mentioned as a deterrent to increased investment, together with administrative delays in granting permission to employ expatriates and the low levels of income repatriation for expatriates that are usually granted by the authorities.

Perhaps embracing all these different factors is the growing feeling, particularly among larger companies with a portfolio of investments, of frustration on the part of senior management over the increasing inability to plan and to make decisions that would make economic and financial sense in the attempt to increase medium- and long-term rates of return on investment. As one senior manager of a foreign company put it: 'it is not the recession or the poor climate that is preventing me from investing more in the country, it is the controls that face one which are inhibiting all facets of management decision-making'. Or another managing director: 'I spend 40% of my working day on the telephone or waiting to see ministers and officials to obtain permission to do this and that and the other without which the day-to-day running of the company would be impossible'.

Two other significant deterrents to expanded domestic investment are also important; one concerns the use of blocked funds, the other uncertainty over the detailed future direction of the economy. As has already been mentioned, there are considerable sums of money (hundreds of millions of dollars) in blocked funds which, if not utilised within the economy, constitute a considerable potential foreign-exchange outflow. The predominant feeling especially among those companies with the largest blocked accounts, however, is that they would like to use these funds for reinvestment within the country. The question then is why more blocked funds are not used for investment. The answer, in part, lies in the often severe restrictions placed on the utilisation of these funds by the authorities. While it is clearly consistent for government to ensure that these funds are not used to buy up local capital interests and so increase the dominance and influence of foreign interests and frustrate even more the expansion of domestic capital interests, it is short-sighted not to positively encourage companies to utilise these readily available funds for productive investment, providing their use leads to capital expansion and, hopefully, employment generation and increased foreign-exchange earnings. Present policy, at best, can be interpreted as neutral on this issue and, at worst, as a disincentive. Those firms wishing to utilise blocked funds in the manner outlined have to apply to the Reserve Bank, and informed sources indicate a reluctance on the part of the exchange-control authorities to sanction a wider use of funds because of the (in the author's view unrealistic) belief that new equity capital will flow into the country in significant amounts. Clearly from a short-term balance-of-payments perspective it is better for new equity capital to flow in, but if this is not going to happen (and there are no applications before the FIC valued at over $100,000) there is a strong argument, which does have the support of senior officials, to encourage the productive use of blocked funds as 'new' investment rather than to create a climate that favours the long-term outflow of these funds.

The final deterrent to increasing investment results from uncertainty over the detailed direction of the economy. While the transitional development plan did make projections of growth and expansion both for the national economy and for the different sub-sectors, it remained vague on details - details of particular forms of expansion within different sub-sectors and details of precise forms of state participation in the productive sectors of the economy. For example, for the manufacturing sector the plan stated that 'a comprehensive industrial strategy will be formulated and articulated'(8), but three years later no details had emerged. It is contended that private investment will be substantially encouraged if such a strategy is devised and if the specific parameters of state involvement over a five or ten year period are articulated. Indeed there is validity in the argument that the thrust towards socialism and increased private investment could both be furthered with far more success once a detailed blueprint is produced, particularly if its production is the result of joint private and public sector planning. While plans are under discussion for this to occur, it is probable that future investment levels will be adversely affected until it occurs.

Perceptions of Foreign Companies Not Present in Zimbabwe. The perceptions of foreign companies not already involved in Zimbabwe of investment in the country will be influenced both by the government's attitude to such investment and the incentives it offers and also by the performance of those companies, foreign and local, in the country. In this section we need to take a broader sweep and consider additional factors which influence their decisions and perceptions.

To begin with, mention needs to be made yet again of the press coverage and media attention that Zimbabwe receives internationally. Zimbabwe suffers from being over-exposed but under-reported. Compared with other Third World countries, Zimbabwe has a very high profile in the European and North American media. As this is often the first point of contact potential investors have with the country, the image portrayed is both decisive and influential. In general the image today is frequently poor because negative factors - which for other countries would not merit international attention - are highlighted, while the context in which these negative factors are placed is frequently omitted. This generally poor image (there are exceptions, for example in the coverage and analysis given in the London Financial Times) is sometimes exacerbated by contradictions or what are perceived as contradictions emanating from different sources within the government. For example, Zimbabwe's voting record in the United Nations and particularly its record of voting against the USA (more often than Cuba according to a recent US newspaper report) places it in an adverse light for potential US investors.

There is clearly plenty of scope to correct these negative and contradictory influences which do have a significant effect on perceptions. One initiative could be to provide information on foreign companies that are operating in Zimbabwe and to highlight the little known fact that a considerable number of new companies have entered Zimbabwe since Independence. The importance of the media in forming opinions about investment is highlighted from a survey conducted for a 1983 report prepared for the US Government. Inter alia, the report states the following(9):

> Respondents were also asked how they obtained their information in making their risk assessments and investment decisions. By far, the main source of information on Africa for the business community is the mass media, primarily the press. Since the American press selectively focuses on trouble spots, impressions are more negative than positive. It is not unusual for executives considering investment decisions in Africa to be stopped dead in their tracks by a single unfavourable article. The chief executive officer of one American manufacturing company considering an investment in

Zimbabwe reported, for example, that he had decided after reading two recent pieces in the press that the threat of civil conflict and a socialist ideology dissuaded him from further consideration of his project. He made no attempt to corroborate or probe impressions gained in the press, either through contacting US government agencies or sending a company representative to Zimbabwe to verify the judgement.

Moving from the general to the particular, there are a list of factors commonly cited by potential foreign investors which they point to as inhibiting their involvement in Zimbabwe. Brief mention will be made of four areas of concern.

Delays in the Foreign Investment Committee. Practically every company interviewed reported delays in procedures within the FIC as a critical adverse factor affecting the decision to invest. Companies need quick decisions because the climate that produces the favourable decision to invest can change over a number of months. The track record of the FIC on decision-making has been extremely poor. Only in April/May 1984 did VMF-Stork of Holland's application receive approval, after an initial announcement of the joint venture with the local firm Cochrane in October 1982. And Dandy of Denmark only received FIC approval after two rejections of the project. In defence of the government it needs to be stressed that the consequences of these delays are now well recognised. However, recognition of the problem now needs to be accompanied by a speeding-up of the decision-making process, particularly approval at the political level. In addition, insufficient publicity has been given to the fact that under Zimbabwean law it is the Reserve Bank and not the FIC which has the power to give statutory approval to a foreign investor, as at least two companies have learnt to their cost and to considerable last-minute embarrassment.

Lack of an Investment Code. Whatever arguments the government might make about the constitution of the country providing all the guarantees necessary for potential investors, the reality is that potential investors do not read constitutions; it is agreements like those of the US Overseas Private Investment Corporation that provide the respectability that investors in the USA and elsewhere appear to need. That this issue is important is apparent from the recent visit of a senior OPIC official to Harare. He explained that the only countries in sub-Saharan Africa which have not signed a bilateral agreement with OPIC are South Africa, Angola, Mozambique and Zimbabwe, adding that Mozambique was expected to sign within the next few months.

Import Controls. Especially important in deterring Japanese investors in particular is the operation of the import quota system. Under the present system, when an investor starts an operation in the country and requires to import raw materials or intermediate products for manufacture he is given an import allocation. Thereafter the level of import allocation will vary in parallel with all other firms receiving allocations, global allocations depending upon balance-of-payments considerations. In a period of recession, the new investor will suffer cuts in allocations along with all other importers and will receive no special favourable treatment. As this plays havoc with production, and hence return on investment projections, it is considered a most serious impediment to new foreign investment. However, to bring about change would prejudice already established firms and there seems little likelihood that change will be made to accommodate this problem.

Taxation Levels and Incentives. Although corporate tax levels are high (51.75% at present) and incentives for investors are less attractive than those offered by other SADCC countries in the region, the high level of corporate tax, while it is a factor in investment decision-making, is not a dominant deterrent. However, as the Preferential Trade Area (PTA) for East and Central Africa becomes a greater reality and as tariff and non-tariff barriers between member states are reduced, so the need to provide a more unified tax and incentive structure will become more compelling. This would seem to be especially so for Zimbabwe vis a vis Botswana whither, in fact, a number of Zimbabwean firms have already relocated, especially within the clothing sub-sector, both because repatriation of profits and dividends are more favourable than in Zimbabwe and because Botswana is a member of the South Africa Customs' Union so that location in Botswana provides easier access for exports to the more lucrative South African market.

Finally we record the saga of the loss of a $9m. investment in the mining sector by a US company without previous experience in Zimbabwe, which highlights a number of the disincentives discussed in this section(10):

> After careful consideration, the company explored the possibility of a $9m. acquisition of a gold mine owned by white settlers who felt they could no longer keep up operations. 'We did not just barrel in; we were encouraged when we looked at the whole picture', commented the company representative who shepherded the application through channels. 'We realised it was somewhat dangerous, but we also recognised that the country has tremendous potential, especially in our sector. We were never active in the country before, but we had assessed that the situation had stabilised, that

the government was actively seeking foreign investment, and that the drift, if it materialises, toward a one-party state and the socialist rhetoric would not affect us'.

The firm formed a local company in Zimbabwe in the summer of 1981. It obtained an option to purchase and received official approval for the investment, even though more than half the equity capital would be foreign-owned. Approximately $200,000 was spent investigating the commercial viability of the mines. Through underground sampling techniques, it had been established that the mines were commercially viable. The investors were then rocked by a number of unexpected government decisions.

First, the government of Zimbabwe revoked the 100% capital redemption and depletion allowances which new businesses may recover as pre-investment costs before paying taxes. The new law allowed only 30% capitalisation of pre-investment costs to be recovered in the first year, with the rest to be deducted over the balance of the life of the mine. That meant that the firm was to pay a tax on 70% of its income, at a time when the gold price had begun to drop. After protests from the mining industry, the government recanted, agreeing to delay the implementation of the new law for one year for a select group of firms. Though many operating firms were not on the government list to qualify for this delay, this potential US investor was included.

A second problem arose when the government issued its new minimum wage law. The gold price was still dropping and the headquarters of the American mining corporation had laid off 4,000 people at home. The minimum wage was not considered unfair, but there were surplus labourers in the mining sector who could no longer be carried at that level. The mining industry plunged into a negative cash flow situation, forcing layoffs. The government then quickly enacted a law which prohibited any firm from dismissing, retrenching or laying off any worker without the written permission of the Minister of Labour.

Together with the freeze on managerial salaries, this had the effect of removing incentives for work. Since employees now were guaranteed their jobs and top management would not be financially compensated beyond a fixed ceiling, productivity dropped by as much as 50%.

A third problem arose when the government of Zimbabwe refused to sign the Overseas Private Investment Corporation (OPIC) agreement, which would have given the firm protection against non-convertibility of dividends and nationalisation. This delayed negotiations, forcing the firm to reconsider the security of its investment. By that time, the project had been lingering for two years, had cost the firm $300,000, and the option to purchase had expired (to be picked up by a South African company). Looking back, the American executive commented, 'we could have lived with less than 50% equity and with limited dividend repatriation. Effectively, we would have been allowed to take out only about 40% of our dividends, but we still thought it was an attractive proposition because we wanted to plough back money into development of the mine. We were hopeful that quite a bit of our investment could go in as loans. But we definitely needed an OPIC guarantee and we needed a lifting of the labour restrictions. If the South African firm does not succeed in its negotiations, we might still be interested, under these conditions. But our concern is that, by then, the owners may rip the guts out of the mine just to keep things going and our initial estimates would then be all wrong'.

NOTES AND REFERENCES

Where $ occurs in the text it refers to the Zimbabwe Dollar.

1. D.G. Clarke, Foreign Companies and International Investment in Zimbabwe (Catholic Institute for International Relations, London, 1980), pp. 31-3.

2. This is a figure derived from work by Stoneman. See especially C.F. Stoneman, 'Foreign Capital and The Prospects for Zimbabwe', World Development, Vol.4, No.1. (1976), pp. 25-58, and 'Foreign Capital in Zimbabwe' (UNCTAD, Geneva, 1979, mimeo).

3. R.C. Riddell and D. Nsiyaludzu, 'Investment in the Manufacturing Sector: Projections to 1985 and Foreign Exchange Requirements' (Confederation of Zimbabwe Industries, Harare, August 1983, mimeo).

4. British Business (London), 18 May 1984, p.39.

5. Republic of Zimbabwe, The Transitional National Development Plan: 1982-3 - 1984-5, Vol. 1 (Harare, November 1982).

6. Dr M. Hove, 'What Projects Appeal to Government', address given at Mashonaland Chamber of Industries Seminar: 'Industry's Role in Zimbabwe's Economic Recovery', Harare, 23 November 1983, (mimeo).

7. Government of the Republic of Zimbabwe, Foreign Investment Policy, Guidelines and Procedures (Harare, September 1982), pp. 2-3.

8. Transitional National Development Plan, p.27.

9. P.H. Baker, 'Obstacles to Private Sector Activities in Africa', Batelle Memorial Institute, prepared for The

Bureau of Intelligence and Research (Department of State, Washington DC, January 1983), p.50-1.

10. Ibid. p.27-8.

Chapter Sixteen

FOREIGN INVESTMENT IN THE FIJI ECONOMY: A BRIEF SURVEY

John Samy

In this chapter we shall analyse various factors that have influenced the nature and size of foreign investment in Fiji. Since Independence in 1970, considerable foreign investment has been undertaken and the government has played an important facilitating role through the provision of infrastructure and other support services including generous fiscal incentives and other concessions. It has also been directly involved through joint ventures to develop key sectors of the economy. Nevertheless, despite the generally stable political and economic climate, in recent years foreign investment has not been forthcoming to the extent desired by government. The chapter considers the reasons for this, and the particular problems of a small island state, with relatively high wages, seeking to attract foreign capital.

Foreign Investment in the Fiji Economy

Foreign capital, both public and private, plays an important role in the development process in Fiji. Table 16.1 shows the ratio of total capital inflows, and of the stock of private investment, to GDP in the period from Independence in 1970 to 1983. In general, it can be seen that foreign investment (stock), after declining as a proportion of GDP at Independence, has maintained a roughly constant share since 1972. There have been two periods of substantial private capital inflows, one up to 1973 (a tourist boom) and one after 1980, with stagnation in between.

A substantial part of direct foreign investment (DFI) is, however, in the form of re-invested earnings (undistributed income); $4m. in 1970. In 1979 it was $8.5m. In the succeeding years 1980 to 1983, while total direct investment has been estimated in the balance-of-payments statements at $10m., it is unlikely to have exceeded the 1979 levels because of the downturn in the economy. There has been a decline in total private foreign investment since 1981, as indicated by the figures on capital inflows.

It must be remembered, however, that capital inflows give rise to corresponding outflows: loans must eventually be

Table 16.1: Ratio of private foreign investment to GDP and net capital inflows 1970-83

Year	GDP	Total stock of private foreign investment	Ratio of FI to GDP	Total capital inflows			Ratio of total capital inflows to GDP
				Public	Private	Total	
	$Fm.	$Fm.	%	$Fm.	$Fm.	$Fm.	%
1972	239.5	52.7	22.9	9.7	22.0	22.7	9.8
1973	300.6	73.7	24.5	17.9	20.9	38.8	12.9
1974	410.5	82.6	20.1	5.7	31.9	37.6	9.2
1975	515.4	92.8	18.0	8.2	12.6	20.8	4.0
1976	570.6	122.9	21.5	12.3	5.0	17.3	3.0
1977	605.7	135.0	22.3	18.4	8.0	26.4	4.4
1978	642.9			-2.5	10.0	7.5	1.2
1979	779.4			18.5	19.4	37.9	4.9
1980	901.0			57.9	14.5	72.4	8.0
1981	954.7			63.3	53.8	117.1	12.3
1982	1,064.2			43.5	32.6	76.1	7.2
1983	1,100.8(p)	220.2	20.0	34.6	33.2	67.8	6.2

Source: 1) Current Economic Statistics and Balance of Payments Statements, Bureau of Statistics.
2) Development Plan Eight (1981-5), Table 1.15. Data for 1978 onwards not available. 1983 investment estimated at 20% of GDP.

Table 16.2: Foreign capital flows 1980-83 ($Fm.)

	1980	1981	1982	1983
Private				
Gross inflows	43.1	67.1	48.8	47.3
Gross outflows	38.5	23.3	26.2	47.2
Net balance	4.6	43.8	22.6	0.1
Official				
Gross inflows	65.1	71.0	52.0	49.6
Gross outflows	8.0	6.1	8.9	14.5
Net balance	57.1	64.9	43.8	35.1

repaid; interest must be paid on loans; and dividends and profits must be paid to overseas investors. Table 16.2 provides data on the net position of capital flows, and indicates a substantial outflow in respect of both the private and public sector after 1981. The net position of the private sector shows a decline from $43.8m. in 1981 to a paltry $0.1m. in 1983. This suggests stagnation in the economic activities of foreign companies (though the figures include other capital flows as well as direct investment). The net position of the public sector also shows a fall from $64.9m. in 1981 to $35.1m. in 1983, resulting from the completion of major infrastructural projects such as the Vaturu Dam and Monasavu Hydro Electricity Projects.

The Nature of Foreign Investment

Table 16.3: Distribution of foreign companies

Industry		Total	Proportion
1	Unable to be classified	74	11.2
2	Agriculture, forestry and fishing	7	1.0
3	Mining and quarrying	38	5.7
4	Manufacturing	61	9.2
5	Electricity, gas and water	5	0.7
6	Construction	44	6.6
7	Wholesale and retail and restaurant (includes hotels)	138	20.9
8	Transport, communication and storage	106	16.0
9	Banks, non-bank financial intermediaries, real estate and business services	179	27.1
10	Community, social, and personal services	8	1.2
	Total	660	100*

* error due to rounding

Source: ESCAP/UNCTC, Preliminary Survey of TNCs in Fiji, (July 1983).

Data up to January 1980 on the industrial distribution of companies with 50% foreign equity are shown in Table 16.3. Much of the tourism-related activities such as hotels, resorts, tour operations, rental cars etc are predominantly foreign-controlled. The major timber processors and exporters are also foreign-controlled. Other important areas of foreign involvement are mining and quarrying, manufacturing, and construction which together accounted for 21.5% of the total. The relatively small amount of manufacturing, which has grown rapidly in recent years, is concentrated in the area of import substitution.

Despite the withdrawal of the South Pacific Sugar Mills in the early 1970s, Australian investment has remained dominant. Wholesale and retail trade has traditionally been dominated by Australian-based companies. However, since Independence locally based firms have challenged them successfully and foreign companies are expected to become marginal in the future.

While local transport and communication is now mostly in Fijian hands, some foreign interest remains in the car rental business. This also applies to other tourism-related activities, such as tour operations. Foreign companies are also well represented in the international traffic business, although Fijian participation has been raised with the expansion of the national carrier Air Pacific. International telecommunications is monopolised by Fiji International Telecommunication Ltd (FINTEL), a joint venture between Cable and Wireless and the Fiji Goverment.

Of the six commercial banks, only the rather small National Bank of Fiji is locally owned. Foreign investment is also heavily represented in insurance and accounting.

Emperor Gold Mining Ltd of Australia has long had a dominant role in mining, although there has recently been a proliferation of overseas mining companies engaged in exploration for minerals and fuel. In 1980, it was estimated that 99.6% of turnover in this sector was controlled by foreign companies. In the industrial fisheries sector two Japanese transnational companies are dominant.

The Shift to Manufacturing and Foreign Investment

The Fiji economy has undergone considerable structural change since the 1960s. The manufacturing, processing and services sectors have expanded through considerable foreign involvement, and now contribute more than 60% of GDP.

In the years immediately following Independence government industrial policy concentrated on import substitution. More recently emphasis has shifted towards exporting, with greater attention being given to the need to rationalise the industrial sector to make it more efficient and competitive.

Fiji

Prior to Independence the manufacturing sector, primarily sugar processing, was predominantly controlled by foreign companies. For example, of the total value-added in manufacturing during 1963, 88% was generated by foreign-owned companies(1). In 1970 foreign companies accounted for 75% of total gross fixed capital formation in all industries.

Recent Developments in Foreign Investment Policy and Performance

Since Independence the Fiji Government has followed on 'open door' policy towards foreign capital. It has extended the same range of incentives and concessions to both local and foreign entrepreneurs. There are no major restraints on repatriation of profits or capital. However, for monetary policy and balance-of-payments reasons, the Reserve Bank of Fiji monitors capital inflows and outflows and imposes certain restrictions to ensure the maximisation of benefits to the economy.

In the post-1980 period, however, Development Plan Eight (1981-5) has emphasised the need to develop local expertise and control and greater self-reliance. The Plan emphasises the need for 'increasing local people's ownership of assets and total investment using appropriate fiscal policies and institutional arrangements; careful screening of foreign investment proposals as to their social and economic benefits, assessment of the appropriateness of technologies imported and used, and also development of greater local capacity to design and manufacture simple tools and implements' (Vol.1., p.19). The Plan further states that government 'will promote the development of local businessmen in preference to foreign investors in sectors where local expertise exists' (Vol 1. p.23).

These changes are in line with economic developments. While foreign companies accounted for 28.5% of GDP and 18.3% of total employment in 1980, these contributions are considerably lower than they were estimated to be in the early 1970s. In 1970 foreign companies accounted for about 80% of company turnover, but in 1980 this had come down to about 54%. Foreign companies still account for more than 50% of turnover in mining and quarrying, agriculture (basically fisheries and logging), distribution, hotels, and financial services; local companies are dominant, however, in such sectors as construction, manufacturing and transport - areas which were heavily dominated by foreign companies in 1970.

Given the emphasis of recent policy on manufacturing and the role of foreign investment in that sector, some salient features of foreign companies involved in Fiji's manufacturing sector are contained in Table 16.4. The figures show that foreign investors played an increasing role in absolute terms, but one declining relatively to locally-owned firms.

Foreign companies' gross output increased by 172% during 1973-81. However, their share in the total manufacturing sector dropped from 42% to 30% in the same period. Gross fixed capital formation of foreign companies rose from $2.9m. in 1973 to $4.5m. in 1981. But their share in the total manufacturing sector fell from 57% to 23%. The main characteristics of foreign companies as revealed by the figures is that their wage rates are relatively high per employee and per unit of output, but that export performance is relatively poor.

These statistical trends are borne out by qualitative analysis. A survey conducted in 1983 for the Fiji Employment and Development Mission(2) concluded that three pertinent trends were apparent for Australian-owned companies previously investing heavily in Fiji and the Pacific Islands: (i) a retreat 'back home'; (ii) a reorientation of overseas investment towards ASEAN, East Asia, Europe, and to some extent North America, and (iii) a dramatic disengagement and retreat from the Pacific Islands.

Burns Philp's recent sales of retail properties is evidence of this trend as is the rationalisation and restructuring of Inchcape's, Carpenter's and Burns Philp's engineering and ship repairing operations to create Industrial and Marine Engineering Ltd (IMEL) - with an incidential loss of at least 100 jobs. The Carpenter Group has also rationalised its retail and distribution operations. According to the 1983 survey:

> The disengagement of foreign capital can assume less spectacular but just as significant forms, especially through the sale of equity to local managers and the general process of 'naturalisation'. When this trend is viewed in terms of the power networks linking different types of business organisation, it is clear that foreign owned operations in Fiji are, in many cases, becoming increasingly peripheralised.

However, peripheralisation occurs not only through capital withdrawal but also through corporate takeover and merger outside Fiji. Thus, Emperor Goldmines at Vatukoula is peripheralised in a corporate sense following its takeover by Western Mining; the Australian company is now no more than a minor part of a major mining corporation.

The restructuring of Kiwi United in 1982 was also an interesting case. Having been established as a joint venture by Kiwi International, Bowater Scott and UEB, it was completely dismembered immediately before the merger which created the major Australian corporation Nicholas Kiwi in 1982. Before the merger three operations were conducted on one site outside Nausori; match production in a wholly-owned subsidiary (Pacific Manufacturers), container making, and

Table 16.4: Some selected performance indicators of foreign investment in the manufacturing sector 1973-81 ($Fm.)

Year	Gross output		Gross fixed capital formation		Book value of Capital stock		No. of persons employed		Compensation of employees		Exports		Value added gross output (%)	
	Total	Foreign companies	Total	Foreign companies	Total	Foreign companies	Total	Foreign companies (000)	Total	Foreign companies	Total	Foreign companies	Local companies	Foreign
1973	113.7	47.8	5.1	2.9	58.3	15.8	9.2	3.3	15.1	6.6	43.1	6.6		
1974	178.2	72.5	9.1	5.0	66.1	20.4	10.1	3.3	19.6	8.1	84.3	15.9		
1975	208.6	68.6	10.8	4.2	75.1	24.6	9.8	3.4	22.5	9.2	103.8	7.9		
1976	229.1	96.7	13.8	5.7	89.0	29.6	11.9	4.0	31.9	13.4	91.2	15.4		
1977	253.3	95.7	17.6	5.5	157.1	27.5	11.8	3.4	37.9	13.3	115.2	18.1		
1978	276.5	109.2	18.7	2.9	91.5	28.4	11.6	3.8	38.1	14.6	116.3	22.6		
1979	359.6	123.3	30.0	4.4	117.7	32.0	12.3	3.5	39.8	15.8	159.7	26.8	25.4	28.2
1980	423.8	127.1	32.6	4.0	140.0	28.0	13.2	3.5	47.5	18.2	197.1	26.9	24.3	24.4
1981	425.4	130.2	19.2	4.5	159.6	30.4	12.1	3.2	47.8	17.8	175.0	29.0	21.1	25.0

paper and plastic bag manufacture. With the growth of competition from locally-owned companies the end result was inevitable. The match production business was sold in 1982 to another foreign company, Wilkinson Sword (incorporating Bryant and May), the container division was sold to a locally-owned company, Golden Manufacturers Ltd, and the paper and plastic bag operations were sold to a privately-owned New Zealand company, Caxton Paper Co. Ltd.

According to Taylor, peripheralisation has important linkage consequences: first, export markets are made more fragile, since peripheralisation is associated with the adoption of narrow regional marketing strategies and exports to serve only other Pacific Islands. Thus, peripheralisation may jeopardise export-led growth. Second, exports may be lost altogether since the smaller firms to which some previously foreign-owned companies have been sold are characterised by localised intra-national transactions which can achieve no more than import-substitution benefits. In this regard it is perhaps pertinent to observe that, according to Table 16.4, the share of foreign companies in exports has remained constant at around 15% of total manufactured exports since 1973.

The reasons given by Taylor for the withdrawal of foreign capital included price controls, union pressures on wages, increasing overhead costs, fixed quotas on certain imports, restrictions on lending to foreign corporations, lower and falling commodity prices, the search for economies of scale, the management succession problem in small foreign-owned firms and the impact of independence. Three principal concerns revolved around what was seen as unfair competition from locally-owned organisations. The first was a perceived disadvantage in access to the local capital market. Although the foreign-owned companies recognised the need to bring in more expensive overseas capital, a number expressed the opinion that the Central Monetary Authority (now Reserve Bank of Fiji) frequently expected more capital to be raised overseas than government guidelines would have led them to expect.

The second concern involved what was considered to be 'unfair' wage competition between the large employers and many smaller firms. Wage rates in the larger firms whether locally-owned or foreign-owned are negotiated with the trade unions and policed by the government and are, therefore, 'visible' and open to scrutiny. Those in the newly established local and smaller firms are not determined in this manner since generally they are not unionised. According to Taylor's survey, hourly wages paid in small locally-owned firms are less than half and as little as only one-fifth of the wages paid in comparable larger organisations. What is more, there is a trend towards casual employment in these smaller firms so that the 44-hour norm is rarely achieved.

The third concern revolved around the poaching and general diffusion of technology bringing intensified competition. Thus, for example, scrapped moulds for concrete blocks are salvaged, repaired and used to start a new small business. Equally, the spread of technology has meant that whereas there was only one plastic bag manufacturer in 1964, there are now approximately 25. The problem of duplication of industries or overcapacity has been a matter of concern to government and the private sector for some time. The recommendations of a study commissioned in 1984 are now being studied.

Apart from withdrawing from Fiji, the foreign-owned business organisations appear to be adopting two strategies to cope with the new environment: i) avoidance of competition by investing in areas protected by major capital and technological barriers; and (ii) harnessing local enterprise through subcontractings. According to Taylor, the first strategy is coming up against the problem of lack of skilled technical and managerial personnel.

There is, however, definite evidence of the second strategy, principally in the furniture and clothing industries. The case of Courts Furnishers (Fiji) Ltd, set up in 1971, illustrates this process. The supply of furniture is controlled by subcontract and comes from 5 Indo-Fijian small firms; no formal subcontracts are involved in these transactions, making them flexible in the extreme. Taylor's survey suggests that Morris Hedstrom and H.P. Kasabia (a local builders merchant) are involved in similar informal subcontract relationships. Indeed, while the Yellow Pages of the Fiji Telephone Directory would suggest that no more than 35 furniture manufacturers are to be found in Fiji, a survey of Suva businesses alone suggests that at least a quarter of these business are tied into subcontract relationships with foreign-owned corporations. There would appear to be no reason why similar relationships could not develop in food processing, detergent and soap making, the supply of printing and packaging materials, and even vehicle repair and servicing.

Taylor concluded that there are a number of corollaries to the adoption of such a strategy by corporate business organisations. First, it involves a retreat from production into trading; what might even be called a return to basics. Second, it reduces the extent of foreign investment. Third, it in no way impairs the degree of control which a foreign corporation can exercise, in fact reducing risk and easing the burden of shepherding assets. Fourth, it introduces a downward pressure on wage rates by externalising the wage-fixing process to a large number of smaller firms not subject to government and union pressures. Fifth, it transfers the burden of raising capital to the smaller-firm segments of the economy - precisely those organisations which are receiving preferential treatment in Fiji at present. Finally, it places the onus of controlling trade credit on a large number of small firms, with an alarming growth in long-term debt.

Some Conclusions

The relatively favourable economic performance in the 1970s, due to the buoyant sugar and tourism sectors, constructive interventions on the past of the public sector, and favourable international conditions with a considerable inflow of private and public investment funds, enabled the country to maintain a relatively high standard of living. However, the situation is now threatened by sluggish economic growth, declining terms of trade, high unemployment levels, increasing disparity between rural and urban incomes, stagnant investment levels, a deteriorating financial position including increased debt servicing, and declining foreign reserves. Labour costs are relatively high and consequently limit the range of manufacturing/industrial activities the economy can pursue in a highly competitive and increasingly protective world economy. Consequently, Fiji cannot hope to attract transnational corporations which move across the world to engage in manufactures produced by cheap labour.

Further, during the expansionary phase of the 1970s there was a considerable increase in import-substitution manufacturing, with considerable government protection, concessions, etc. A considerable number of foreign-owned firms took advantage of the protective barriers and other fiscal incentives to move from retailing/distribution to manufacturing, but with low backward linkages, reflecting an increasing propensity to import inputs. Further, being a relatively inefficient and technologically weak sector, manufacturing is unlikely to grow significantly in the short to medium term, particularly in view of the high wages prevailing in the formal sector of the economy.

However, Fiji's industrial policy and strategy are shifting to an emphasis on export orientation, in which foreign capital can play a vital role in terms of its control of or access to markets, though it has yet to do so. Foreign technology and management can also be crucial. The Fiji Government is encouraging joint ventures and the number of joint-venture proposals submitted to the Business and Industrial Development Committee (BIDC) for approval has been increasing since the early 1980s. Agreements such as SPARTECA, New Zealand's Pacific Islands Industrial Development Scheme (PIIDS), the Australian joint-venture scheme, and the Lomé Convention also facilitate joint-venture enterprises.

As mentioned earlier, foreign investors have not played a dynamic role in exports, however, and as we noted from

Taylor's study the emphasis of foreign private capital is shifting towards management contracts and the provision of technical expertise and know-how. Products with international brand names carry marketing power and local firms are therefore getting into management and licensing agreements to manufacture products with such names under specified standards. It may be worth noting that between 1980 and 1982 Fiji companies paid a total of around $1.3m. on commissions, royalties, patents, brokerage and copyright charges. This pattern, rather than exporting by foreign investors, has become the norm.

Since Independence a major change in foreign private capital investment in Fiji has been its involvement with the public sector in crucial sectors of the economy, such as fisheries, agro-processing, and the proposed pine processing operations. For government, foreign investment is seen as necessary because of its management, technical and marketing skills. Given the nature and small size of the Fiji economy, the public sector plays an important facilitating and developmental role in most strategic sectors, such as sugar, pine, fisheries, rice, and civil aviation. Foreign capital also prefers joint-venture arrangements with the public sector in developing high-risk resource-based or agro-processing projects. While foreign private capital, especially its technological, management and marketing inputs, will continue to be important for the expansion and diversification of the economy, it is evident that it cannot be a substitute for both the public sector and local private capital which will have to assume greater and pivotal roles.

NOTES AND REFERENCES

1. S. Britton, 'Tourism in a Peripheral Capitalist Economy, The Case of Fiji', Ph.D. thesis, Australian National University, Canberra, 1979.

2. Michael Taylor, Business Organisation Segmentation and the Functioning of the Fiji Economy (July 1983).

INDEX